SURVIVING THE
KILLING FIELDS

SURVIVING THE KILLING FIELDS

THE CAMBODIAN ODYSSEY OF

HAING S. NGOR

WITH ROGER WARNER

CHATTO & WINDUS
LONDON

First published in 1988 by
Chatto & Windus
30 Bedford Square
London WC1B 3RP

Second impression

A CIP catalogue record for this book
is available from
the British Library
ISBN 0 7011 3187 X

Printed in Great Britain by
Redwood Burn Ltd
Trowbridge, Wiltshire

កូនសូមវិលីករវិញ្ញាណកូនូ លោកឪពុក ង៉ោ គា អ្នកម្តាយនាង លីម ង៉ោ ប្រពន្ធនាង ចាង ហួយ(ចាង មី ហួយ) ដែលបានចាកចារទៅយ៉ាង សែនទារុណកម្ម ព្រៃផ្សៃ និងអមនុស្សធម៌បំផុត ក្រោមរបបកុម្មុយនិស្តខ្មែរ ។ កូននិពន្ធសៀវភៅនេះទុកជាសក្ខីភាព និងជាប្រទីបមួយសម្រាប់បំភ្លឺពិភពលោកឲ្យស្គាល់ និងយល់ច្បាស់នូវរបបកុម្មុយនិស្ត និងប្រវត្តិខ្មែរគ្រប់របប ។๛

[I want to dedicate this book to the memories of my father, Ngor Kea, of my mother, Lim Ngor, of my wife, Chang Huoy (Chang My Huoy), who have died in the most miserable, uncivilized, and inhuman ways under the Khmer communist regime. I have written this book for the world to better understand communism and other regimes in Cambodia.]

CONTENTS

Introduction: The Prize, 1

1

Early Rebellions, 7

2

Education, 21

3

Romance and Coup, 32

4

Civil War, 46

5

The City of Bonjour, 59

6

The Fall, 70

7
The Wheel of History, 81

8
Exodus from Phnom Penh, 91

9
Wat Kien Svay Krao, 101

10
Medicine for Angka, 109

11
Return to the Village, 124

12
The Crocodile Loses Its Lake, 137

13
New Directions, 150

14
The Plow, 157

15
Sickness, 171

16
*The Parade of the Selfish and
Dying*, 180

17
Reorganization, 190

18
Bells, 203

19
Angka Leu, 215

20
The Wat, 228

21
The King of Death, 239

22
Candles, 251

23
The Rains, 260

24

Rice Farming, 268

25

The Dam, 274

26

The Cracks Begin to Show, 288

27

Drops of Water, 298

28

Happiness, 312

29

Crossing the Sea, 323

30

Grief, 334

31

Retreat, 340

32

Liberation, 352

33
Battambang, 360

34
The Danger Zone, 372

35
The Locket, 384

36
Saloth Sar, 395

37
Okay, Bye-bye, 409

38
To America, 423

39
Starting Over, 431

40
The Killing Fields, 441

41
Celebrity, 451

42
Kama, 459

Index, 467

SURVIVING THE KILLING FIELDS

INTRODUCTION:
THE PRIZE

I HAVE BEEN many things in life: A trader walking barefoot on paths through the jungles. A medical doctor, driving to his clinic in a shiny Mercedes. In the past few years, to the surprise of many people, and above all myself, I have been a Hollywood actor. But nothing has shaped my life as much as surviving the Pol Pot regime. I am a survivor of the Cambodian holocaust. That's who I am.

Between the years of 1975 and 1979, Pol Pot and his Khmer Rouge communists exchanged our traditional Cambodian way of life for a vast, brutal experiment in communism. Toward the end of those years I was living in the northwestern part of Cambodia in a tiny agricultural village. By then, the luxuries of life before the revolution were a half-forgotten dream. I went barefoot. My clothes were rags and my ribs were showing from hunger. To keep the Khmer Rouge soldiers from killing me, I had to pretend I was not a doctor. They had already killed most of my family. And my case was typical. By destroying our culture and by enslaving us, the Khmer Rouge changed millions of happy, normal human beings into something more like animals. They turned people like me into cunning, wild thieves.

I began stealing on a small scale. Slipping out of my hut after dark, blending into the shadows, pausing to look and listen for soldiers, hearing only the crickets and frogs in their loud nighttime chorus, I crept into the village garden. Reaching into the rows of ripening corn, pulling the husks carefully back, I twisted the corncobs from their stalks, pulled them out, and smoothed the empty husks to their original shape around the hollow space inside. In the daytime, to a casual observer, the corn would appear to be untouched.

At first I stole alone. But other people in the village were hungry too, and they needed a leader. My gang raided fields and gardens by night. Our favorite target was rice.

For Cambodians, rice is not a side dish. Rice is the center of our meals, a clean, neutral medium that sets off the flavors of other foods we add to it. Traditionally, until the Khmer Rouge took over, we had eaten rice every day. Under the Khmer Rouge, we hardly ever ate rice at all—not rice as it should be, with each grain separate and moist, and a clean, fragrant steam rising from the bowl.

Rice had become an obsession for my gang. I led them to rice paddies ready for harvest. Like madmen, we broke the stalks and branches of the rice plants with our hands, threshed the branches by rubbing them back and forth on the ground with our feet, and filled huge hemp bags with unhusked rice before hurrying away. Later, in hiding from the soldiers, we removed the husks with mortars and pestles, cooked the grains, and ate until our stomachs could hold no more.

We also raided vegetable gardens belonging to other villages nearby. I built up a large supply of stolen food and gave the extra food away. In all I fed more people in the village than anyone except the regime itself. But I wasn't content. It was time to strike back.

Under Khmer Rouge rule, all private property was outlawed. Cooking at home was outlawed. Everything from work to sex to family life was tightly controlled. Everyone in the village was supposed to eat together at a central mess hall, called the common kitchen.

One day at the common kitchen while taking a meal, the usual starvation ration of a bowl of watery broth with a few rice grains at the bottom, I glanced through the open doorway of a nearby storage shed. On the floor of the shed lay a small hand-powered rice mill.

As soon as I saw it, I knew that it was only a matter of time before the rice mill was mine.

Stealing the rice mill was not a rational idea. It was not like stealing food, where the benefits balanced the risks. Owning the rice mill wouldn't keep me from starvation. At most, it would allow me to remove the husks from stolen rice a little faster than with a mortar and pestle. And the risks were higher than stealing food. The shed was next to the common kitchen, and the kitchen was guarded by soldiers night and day.

To me, stealing the mill was a test: It was a test of my abilities as a thief, and a challenge to the miserable life I had been living. It was a way of finding out whether the gods wanted me to live or die.

Each time I went near the common kitchen I watched the shed without appearing to watch it. Very slyly. But there were always soldiers around.

Eventually I concluded that the only chance lay in trying to steal the mill when the area was full of people.

A few evenings a week the village leader held political indoctrination meetings that everyone had to attend. Like most Khmer Rouge, the leader had taken a new name to show that he had a new revolutionary identity. He called himself Mao, probably in imitation of China's Mao Tse-tung. He was an uneducated man who wore the standard black pajama uniform of the Khmer Rouge.

During the next meeting that Mao held near the common kitchen, I sat at the edge of the crowd with my back against the shed. The walls of the shed were made of a stiff, woven material, like rattan. The evening had turned to black, starry darkness. No moon yet.

Mao opened the meeting with the usual slogans. The rest of us got wearily to our feet and obediently shouted the slogans back to him, pounding our fists against our chests, and raising them in straight-arm salutes. "Long live the Cambodian revolution!" he shouted. "Long live the Cambodian revolution!" we yelled back, though we didn't mean it. He said it twice more and we repeated it for him, and then he started with the next set of slogans.

When he was done we sat down and he began telling us how lucky we were to be living under such a regime, where everyone was equal and where meals were served to us every day. How lucky we were to be struggling together to build a modern and powerful nation.

The truth was that under the communists the country was much worse off than it had ever been during my lifetime. We had no electricity. No clocks or automobiles. No modern medicines. No schools. No religious worship. Very little food. And we lived in constant fear of the soldiers.

He went on with his speech, reciting phrases he had learned like a parrot from his superiors. Every speech was almost exactly the same. The crowd sighed and settled down.

It was time.

"Lord Buddha," I prayed silently, "please forgive me. I do not steal to get rich. I share with others. Please protect my life once again."

I leaned forward, pulling the wall of the shed with me. The bottom of the wall overlapped the floor of the shed but was not fastened to it. I pulled myself backward and up into the narrow gap between the wall and the floor and into the even blacker darkness of the interior of the shed.

"Our workers, peasants and revolutionary soldiers," Mao was saying, "have launched an offensive to build up the economy! We are struggling with nature to become masters of our fate! All our cooperatives are waging an offensive, working with great revolutionary zeal for the sake of a spectacular great leap forward!"

Groping around on the floor I found a round, heavy object, heavier than expected. Fumbling, pulling at anything that stuck out, I broke the mill down into its parts, two heavy grindstones plus the casing and crank.

". . . they are now resolved to launch another relentless offensive . . ." Mao's voice droned on.

Pushing against the bottom of the wall, I managed to squeeze out the same way I had come in.

". . . and on to victory!" Mao bellowed.

In front of me, the silhouettes of heads and shoulders facing dutifully in Mao's direction. To the side, an irrigation ditch, part of a network of canals. With a grindstone under each arm and the crank in my waistband, I settled into the water. Go slowly, I told myself. Do not make a ripple. Do not make a sound. Going slow is much better than going fast.

The speech, interrupted by mandatory clapping, grew fainter. Only my nose and eyes were above water, like a crocodile; my feet pushed on the mud underneath. The stars shone in the sky and again in their reflections on the surface of the water. But a glow had appeared on the horizon. The moon was about to rise. Time to hurry. Time to speed up before it was too late.

Climbing out of the ditch, I walked as fast as I could to the fertilizer shed where I worked during the day and hid the mill under a manure pile. I ran to my hut, changed into dry clothes and ran back toward the kitchen, where once again slogans were being shouted and repeated loudly by the crowd. Then long applause. Too late—the speech was over.

In the moonlight, soldiers had come to inspect the spot where I had been sitting, beside the shed. Curious civilians peered around, some of them calling my name. When I ran up, out of breath, Mao called me to the front and demanded to know where I had been.

Walking toward him, I let my back and shoulders sag. My eyes lowered in deference and my mouth formed a silly apologetic smile.

"Sorry, comrade," I told him meekly, "my stomach was upset and I dirtied myself." I patted the seat of my trousers in case my meaning wasn't clear. "I just went home to change my clothes."

Raucous laughter came from the crowd, even the soldiers. Everyone knew what it was like to have intestinal problems. Everybody did, because of our unsanitary living conditions. Even Mao, a man of more than average cruelty, began to grin. He waved me off, like a parent who is amused by the wrongdoings of a child.

I walked back to the storage shed and sat with my back against it, as before.

I ground rice in the rice mill later that night.

And the next night I led my gang out to steal again.

On a very different night, six and a half years later, I was sitting in the Dorothy Chandler Pavilion in Los Angeles. I wore a tuxedo. On my feet were shiny patent leather shoes. On the stage a woman announcer read, Haing S. Ngor, pronouncing it *Heng S. Nor*, which is as close to the correct pronunciation as foreigners usually get.

Since leaving Cambodia, my life had changed as completely and as dramatically as it is possible to imagine. I had come to America as a refugee. With no experience in theater or film, I had been hired to play a fellow Cambodian named Dith Pran in a film called *The Killing Fields*. I was aware of mistakes in my performance, just as I was aware of making many mistakes in my real life. Yet I had been nominated, along with several other experienced professional actors, for an Academy Award.

But then, I thought, what is so special about acting in the movies? It is a matter of taking on a new identity and convincing others of it. Convincing others, perhaps, the way I had convinced Mao the Khmer Rouge village chief. Waiting for the envelope to be opened and the winner announced, I was excited, but my heart was at peace. Whatever happened, I could accept. Because I knew that my best performances were over before I left Cambodia. And the prize there was much greater.

1

EARLY REBELLIONS

MY EARLIEST MEMORY is standing at the back door of my parents' house and gazing at the rice fields. The fields fascinated me. Low earthen dikes divided them into a pattern like irregular checkerboards, with paddies instead of squares, and trees rising here and there where dikes met.

It was a sight that changed with the seasons. By January, partway through the dry season, the fields were covered in brown stubble. By about April or May when light rains fell, a few paddies were planted as seed beds, turning a delicate green. When the rainy season itself brought its heavy storms, teams of men and women transplanted the seedlings to the rest of the paddies. Over the rainy months, the rice plants grew thick and green and lush, and the dikes were hidden from sight until around August, when the rains stopped, and the plants gradually began to turn golden. The farmers went out and harvested, leaving only dry stubble behind. They threshed the stalks, milled the grains and sold the rice to families like mine.

We ate the rice gladly, and we always set some aside for the monks, who came to our house every morning with their alms bowls. The monks wore robes, yellow or orange or even brown if they had made the dyes themselves from tree bark. Their heads and eyebrows were shaved. They were calm and silent, speaking not a word as they walked from one house to the next in a single-file line.

Those are my first memories, the rice fields changing with the seasons and the monks coming to our house each morning. And that is how I would like to remember Cambodia, quiet and beautiful and at peace.

7

But in fact the first entire incident I remember was not so peaceful. I was about three years old. The year was probably 1950. My mother sent my older brother and me into the rice fields to get water from a pond. It was the dry season. Soldiers from the village garrison fished at the pond with their shirts and shoes off. We filled the pail. My older brother took one end of a pole on his shoulder and I took the other on mine and we put the pail between us. We were returning to the house, two little barefoot boys carrying a single pail, when we heard a sharp *bang!* behind us, near the pond. Then we heard another *bang!* and the soldiers shouting. My mother appeared at the door. I had never seen that expression on her face before.

"*Come here*, children! Put the pail down! Drop it right now! *Hurry!*" she said. We set the pail down and trotted obediently toward her. She ran out of the house anyway, grabbed us by the wrists and dragged us in. There was more shooting behind us, and our neighbors were yelling.

The next thing I knew, my brother and I were in the hole under the big low wooden table that served as my parents' bed. It was dark and cool in there, with sandbags on the sides—my parents had known there was going to be trouble. Some of my other brothers and sisters were already under there, and more came tumbling in, a half-dozen wiggling children. Then my mother came in and finally my father, who had run from the market and was breathing hard, his face wet with perspiration.

We heard a shot nearby, then more shots right outside our house. Something crashed, and glass broke on the tabletop above us, while my mother clutched us tighter and prayed and my father cursed. We children tried to make ourselves even smaller in our hole in the floor under the table.

Then after a while there wasn't any more shooting. We heard voices outside. Someone called my father by his name. He climbed out. A few minutes later the rest of us got out. There was broken glass on the floor and holes in the wall above the front door. Outside there was a big crowd, and more people running up to it on the street and everyone was talking at the same time:

"No, the rest got away. Nobody else killed . . ."

"The soldiers got back to the garrison and fired down from the watchtower . . ."

"He used this tree for cover. So many bullet holes in the trunk of the tree, huh? Even in the doorway of the Ngor house . . ."

I pushed my way through the legs of the crowd. I had to see for myself. By the tree in front of our house, in the center of the crowd, a man lay face down in blood. Next to him was a single-shot carbine. Other children had wormed their way in with me, some of them with younger brothers or sisters hoisted on their hips.

We looked on, wide-eyed.

The dead guerrilla was sturdily built, with a strong back and thick legs. His bare feet were wide and calloused, like a farmer's. His skin was dark brown. Tattoos covered his arms and shoulders. He wore a pair of torn short trousers. Around his waist were a *krama*—the Cambodian all-purpose scarf—and some strings hung with Buddha amulets and prayer beads. He had no shirt. He was not from the towns or cities. He was a man of the earth, from the countryside. From the very heart of peaceful Cambodia. And he had rebelled.

Now, many years later, grown up and living far away, I think: Yes, there was trouble even then. Maybe not revolution but a deep, hidden discontent.

To outsiders, and often even to ourselves, Cambodia looked peaceful enough. The farmers bound to their planting cycles. Fishermen living on their boats, and their naked brown children jumping in and out of the water. The robed monks, barefoot, walking with deliberate slowness on their morning rounds. Buddhist temples in every village, the graceful, multilayered roofs rising above the trees. The wide boulevards and the flowering trees of our national capital, Phnom Penh. All that beauty and serenity was visible to the eye. But inside, hidden from sight the entire time, was *kum*. *Kum* is a Cambodian word for a particularly Cambodian mentality of revenge—to be precise, a long-standing grudge leading to revenge much more damaging than the original injury. If I hit you with my fist and you wait five years and then shoot me in the back one dark night, that is *kum*. Or if a government official steals a peasant's chickens and the peasant uses it as an excuse to attack a government garrison, like the one in my village, that is *kum*. Cambodians know all about *kum*. It is the infection that grows on our national soul.

But the fighting had been so small-scale back then, before the other countries got involved, that the damage was limited. When those few ragged guerrillas attacked the garrison in my village, it was only news for those of us who lived there. Nobody else cared. The attack might have been reported in the Phnom Penh newspapers, but not outside the country. It was only a minor incident in an inconclusive, low-level civil war. Wars like this are always going on in different parts of the world. And those in the outside world know little about them.

Cambodia: It is just a name to most people. Someplace far away where something terrible happened, and few can remember exactly what. Mention Pol Pot or the Khmer Rouge and people start to remember. Or bombs dropping and genocide or even a film called *The Killing Fields*. But all that came later.

Cambodia is a part of Indochina, which in turn is part of the landmass of Southeast Asia. "Indo-china" because a couple of countries to the west lies India, which gave Cambodia its religion and alphabet; and a couple of countries to the north is China, which gave Cambodia its merchant class, including my father's side of the family. For many years the region was known as French Indochina, because France colonized Cambodia and the neighboring countries of Laos and Vietnam beginning in the mid-nineteenth century. The guerrillas who came to my village were trying to get rid of French rule. And in Vietnam at the same time as this shoot-out, Ho Chi Minh and his communists were also trying to force the French to leave, with a rebellion on a much larger scale.

Vietnam has usually overshadowed Cambodia in world news, because the wars there are larger, and because Western countries have gotten directly involved in the fighting. So more people know about Vietnam than Cambodia. But I have never liked having to explain that Cambodia is next to Vietnam, or even near India and China. To me, Cambodia means something very special. It was the name of the country around my village. And like all children, I believed my village was the center of the world.

The village was called Samrong Yong. It was a sleepy crossroads on the highway south of Phnom Penh, with houses one row deep and rice fields and forests beyond. After the shooting incident, my parents moved us children out of the village to a friend's house in the countryside, where they thought we would be safer. Every afternoon my parents came to the house and spent the night with us, and every morning they went back to the village to do business at their dry-goods store. Until one afternoon Papa didn't come back.

The guerrilla rebels kidnapped my father. My mother collected money for his release. After she paid them, they set my father free but took her prisoner instead, so then Papa had to raise ransom money for her. When they were both free, corrupt soldiers of the other side—Cambodian officers of the French-backed government—arrested my father and put him in jail. They accused him of working for the guerrillas. After all, he had been seen leaving Samrong Yong every afternoon to visit them. Of course, the soldiers were using this as an excuse for getting ransom money.

I was sent to stay in Phnom Penh. While I was there, the rebels and the military took turns kidnapping my father again. My father hated paying ransom, but there was nothing he could do. He had nobody to protect him. Like nearly all merchants, he was Chinese-looking, with pale-colored skin and narrow eyes. This made him an easy target. Most other Cambodians were of the Khmer race, with round eyes and dark brown skin, or else were of mixed racial descent.

When I finally came back to the village, the rice fields looked the same. The monks still made their rounds in the morning. But every afternoon, a new militia of young men and women marched around the village with machetes and wooden rifles. They were always out of step, and never looked like a real army, but they had the strong support of the people. The whole village was tired of the corrupt soldiers of the French-backed government, and tired of the corrupt guerrillas too. The man who had helped organize the militias, our young king, Norodom Sihanouk, felt the same. Sihanouk was trying to get the French to leave the country. He wanted the guerrillas to leave too, because some of them were communists allied with Ho Chi Minh. Sihanouk didn't want the country ruled either by a Western power like France or by communists. He wanted Cambodia to be independent and neutral. In the Buddhist tradition, he wanted the middle way.

Because of all the ransom payments my father was very poor. He sent me to a Chinese school with my older brother, Pheng Huor, but soon he took me out because he couldn't afford the tuition for both of us. I didn't mind. Pheng Huor was smarter than me. He could take an abacus, the Chinese calculator with rows of wooden beads, flick the beads around with the tip of his finger and get the answer to a problem in seconds, while I would still be trying to remember what each bead stood for. Pheng Huor had always helped my father after school. I had always helped my mother. My mother was darker in color, like me, partway between a Chinese and a dark rural Cambodian.

While my father rebuilt his business and my brother studied at school, my mother and I went off on daily bartering trips in the countryside to get the family's food. I carried a long piece of bamboo across my shoulders with a hook at each end. From one hook hung a basket with fresh pastries cooked by my hardworking father, and from the other hung another basket with peanuts, dried fish, salt, soy sauce, and anything else we thought we could trade. At sunrise we were off, on foot. The baskets bobbed up and down from my shoulderboard and I adjusted my stride to fit the rhythm. My mother wrapped her krama, or scarf, around her head and placed a basket on top, steadying it with one hand.

We walked away from National Route 2, the paved highway that passed through our village, onto oxcart trails and footpaths. Soon we were out of earshot of the automobile traffic and into an entirely different world of fields and forests. We walked through open rice fields to shady villages, where thatched-roof houses built on tall stilts stood among tamarind, mango, banana and palm trees. The villagers were ethnic Khmer, friendly, dark-skinned people who had mastered the art of living off the land without working very hard. Each house had its garden surrounded by a reed fence, with vegetables and tobacco growing inside. Chickens clucked and pecked at the dirt, and roosters crowed at all hours. Mostly we bartered for rice, because we could get it more cheaply from these villagers than we could in Samrong Yong.

We walked all day, and I became strong and healthy. On the way home, I foraged for lotus plants, whose roots and seeds are tasty in soups; for water convolvulus, which is something like spinach; and for *sdao* tree leaves, rather bitter-tasting, as many of the rural foods are. Whenever we passed through woods, my mother wrapped a few grains of rice in a leaf and placed it on the ground as a gift to the local spirits.

When I was about eight years old I was allowed to go out to barter on my own, without my mother. My favorite village was in a grove of sugar palm trees, which have tall, slender, curving trunks and fan-like fronds on top. Every morning the men scampered up the sugar palms to gather nectar from the flowers. They boiled the nectar in vats for many hours to make a crude brown sugar that tastes like molasses. They sold the palm sugar in the market, or traded it to me.

They also made an alcoholic drink that was slightly bubbly and tasted like beer. They made their best-quality beer right up in the palm trees. One morning when I walked into their village the men waved at me from the treetops. "Hey, boy! Hey! Ngor Haing!* Come up here! We've got something for you!" I climbed up the bamboo ladder. At the top, on a platform connecting several nearby trees, the men were sitting with loose, happy grins and glazed eyes. They were drinking fresh palm beer. I tried some. It was delicious. I drank more. The hours passed. We were laughing and joking up there in the tree until I realized that I had to get down and didn't have any control over my arms or legs. The ground looked far away and small, like the earth under an airplane. They had to carry me down. No more bartering for me that day. I was too busy weaving around on the footpaths and falling over. When I got home my mother scolded me and my father gave me a stern, angry look. He said I would never amount to anything if I spent time with the wrong people.

I disagreed with my father. The country people had always been nice to me. But I was very stubborn then; if my father said I was wrong about anything, automatically I felt I was right, without even considering what he said. That was my personality: If I hit my head against a wall accidentally, I would butt it again, to see if I could make the wall hurt.

Medically speaking, I was hyperactive as a child. I had a short attention span and far too much energy. I liked sports. I loved fighting. My gang, from the western side of the village, was always getting in fights with the gang from the eastern side of the village. If the eastern gang came at me when I was alone, I took my baskets off the hooks, waited calmly and got ready to swing my shoulderboard at their shins. I wasn't afraid. My fighting and playing displeased my father, who worked every day without a break and who expected me to stay home

---

*In Cambodia, as in most Asian countries, the family name goes first, followed by the individual's name. So I am Ngor Haing in Asia but Haing Ngor in the West.

and help his business. But the more he scolded me the more I stayed outside.

It became difficult to meet my father's gaze. My oldest or number-one brother, who was slow-minded, worked for my father all day long as an ordinary laborer, as faithful as a water buffalo. My number-two brother, Pheng Huor, the smart one, was already keeping my father's accounts. I was the number-three brother, with two more younger brothers behind me and three sisters too. I wanted to help the family, but I didn't want to work all the time. It was too much fun to play.

When I was about ten, matters came to a head. The government of Thailand, Cambodia's neighbor to the west, gave a large sculpture of Buddha to a monk in a town near my village, called Tonle Batí. The monk was very old and eminent, the equivalent of a bishop. The sculpture was to go inside a stone building made around A.D. 1200, in the period of an ancient Cambodian civilization known as Angkor. But before installing the statue, my father and the monk had to drive to Thailand to get it.

They set off together in Papa's old black and brown Ford truck, north from the village on National Route 2 to Phnom Penh and then in a northwesterly direction around the huge lake known as Tonle Sap and toward the Thai border town of Aranyaprathet. The roads were terrible. The truck kept breaking down. My father was irritated but he had to pretend to be calm, because of the monk. When they finally got the statue, it turned out to be unusually large and handsome. Once they re-entered Cambodia with it in the back of the truck they had to stop in every small town along the way to give a parade. The townspeople gave money, to make merit for themselves, to improve their chances of being reborn into a better life. The money paid for the truck repairs and for the gasoline. Papa, who was an impatient man, couldn't hurry things up.

In my father's absence my mother ran the store. I got in more fights than ever.

The morning before Papa returned, a box with a dozen packs of imported playing cards was missing from the locked cupboard above my parents' bed. The cards would have made a nice profit for the family if they had been sold. My mother came to me and asked whether I had taken them. I told her truthfully that I hadn't. But my mother was suspicious. Of all the children I was the only one who got in trouble regularly.

She got right to the point. "If you stole it and sold it, just say so," she said. "If I know you are telling me the truth, I won't tell your father, and he won't beat you."

There was nothing I could say to her. Papa beat us occasionally, as all Chinese fathers did. But he didn't hurt us much.

That day I kept close watch on my older brother Pheng Huor. When he saw I was looking in his direction he lifted his gaze and looked back at me blankly. Whoever had stolen the cards had been a member of the family. But even if my brother had stolen the cards, which seemed likely, I couldn't prove it.

The following day Papa drove up to the house in his Ford truck. He was tired and irritated from having to behave so well.

My mother told him about the theft. He came angrily toward me. Perhaps he felt that this was the sort of thing that went on when he was away and that he needed to restore his authority.

He led me out back of the house and tied me hand and foot to a big piece of lumber. Then he hit me on the shoulders with a wooden slat. He beat me for an hour. When he was tired he went into the house, and then after a while he came out again with the slat in his hand. My mother stood in the doorway with a pitying look in her face, but she didn't ask him to stop.

I don't know when he stopped beating me, because I lost consciousness. When I came to, my feet and hands were still tied to the lumber, but I had rolled over on my side. The sunlight was coming in at a low angle over the rice fields. It was late afternoon. My mother and my favorite sister, Chhay Thao, had come out of the house. They untied me, and they asked me what they could do.

I lay on the ground without moving. They stood over me. Gradually I collected my thoughts.

"You didn't trust me," I said slowly. "You treated me like an enemy of the family. So don't bother helping me."

My mother knelt next to me.

"Your will is still strong, eh?" she said gently.

They helped me upstairs and led me to my bed. I slept. But that evening I woke up puzzled and angry. What had I done to deserve a beating like that? I loved sports. I loved to get out of the house and play as often as I could. And yes, I got in fights with other boys. If that made me bad, if they were going to beat me for that, they could go ahead. That was their right. But I hadn't stolen anything. I didn't need any money. There was nothing I wanted enough to steal from my family. If they didn't trust me, how could I live with them under the same roof? How could I accept their authority?

Early the next morning I ran away.

My first stop was Samrong Yong's open-air market. It took up one corner of the village's only road intersection, across from the garrison of French-backed troops and their tall stone watchtower.

The market was the center of village commerce and gossip. Women thronged the aisles, bargaining, pinching the neat piles of fresh vegetables and fruits, peering critically at the basins of live, wiggling fish. Vendors sold grilled chicken and rice confections wrapped in banana leaves. At restaurant stalls, customers sat down to order bowls of soup prepared to their liking. I couldn't buy anything, though. No money. I talked with people I knew and kept an eye out for my family.

In the early afternoon, an old passenger bus rolled into the lot next to the market. The driver was a distant cousin, a man whose name was Kruy.

"Uncle, Uncle!" I called to him.*

"Well! Ngor Haing, eh? What happened to you?" Uncle Kruy said to me from the driver's window.

I came around to the door of his bus. "My father beat me last night for stealing playing cards from the store. But I didn't steal them."

"Well, come along, then. I'll give you a shirt to put over all those bruises." I got in, and off the bus went with a roar of its diesel engine as Kruy shifted through the gears.

Kruy and his wife lived south of my village, in central Takeo province. He was the sole owner and operator of the rickety passenger bus. Every day he made a trip from his village to Phnom Penh and back again along National Route 2, stopping in the marketplace of every village and town along the way.

At his house Kruy gave me a shirt and a straw hat. The next

*In Cambodia, if we feel close to older people we call them "Uncle" or "Aunt," whether or not they are actually related. If I felt close to a male my own age, I would call him "brother."

morning I began working for him, collecting fares. It was unbelievably noisy inside the bus: The pounding of the worn-out suspension on potholes had loosened all the bolts and rivets. Passengers squeezed in next to one another on the hard wooden benches until they were almost on each other's laps. Just when it seemed the bus could take no more, Kruy slowed and stopped for an old wrinkled monk standing beside the road with his parasol. The monk climbed up into the bus and headed for the seats in the back. The passengers shifted over to accommodate him and, amazingly, there was plenty of room. Everybody knew how important it was to treat monks with respect. It was particularly important that women not touch them, even accidentally, because monks had to be pure. And it would have been unthinkable to ask monks to pay fares. They rode free. Even I knew that, on my first day.

When he saw that I knew how to collect fares and count money, Kruy put me on top of the bus, in the luggage rack, and made me responsible for cargo. The luggage rack was piled higher than my head with packages and suitcases and bicycles and furniture. There were wicker baskets with live pigs grunting inside, baskets with chickens and ducks clucking and quacking, tightly woven baskets with live snakes and baskets with produce for the Phnom Penh market. At every stop, I lowered cargo from the roof to the outstretched arms of its owner on the ground, and reached down to pull the new cargo up.

I also helped with bribes. When Kruy came to government checkpoints, he downshifted, pulled over to the side of the road and stopped, while I scampered down the ladder on the back of the bus, adjusted my hat and walked into the sentry's hut.

Inside, the sentry pretended to scrutinize the bus for an overload, or for communist guerrillas, or for whatever he might choose to think was wrong with it. I took my hat off respectfully and placed it on the table next to his clipboard, moved the hat so the *riel* notes in the hatband fell out and pushed the money under the clipboard with my hand.

"Your bus does not look so bad today," the sentry said in a bored voice. "All right, you may go on your way." Kruy was already revving the engine. The wooden bar across the road lifted on its rope pulley, I ran for the bus and hopped on the ladder on the back as Kruy drove on.

I loved my new life. I had no shoes, no change of clothing, and didn't care. As long as I was working on the bus I didn't have to think about the beating my father had given me. The problem was, the bus stopped in the Samrong Yong market twice a day.

When fate caught up with me I was lying on my back on the luggage rack, watching the plume of dust rising behind. The engine noise changed as Kruy downshifted. As the bus slowed I turned my head to look forward. The road was so narrow that two vehicles could pass only if they pulled over to the shoulder and drove at a crawl. A vehicle was coming from the other direction.

It was a black and brown Ford truck.

Uncle Kruy stopped the bus so that his window was directly opposite the window of the truck. My father leaned across and spoke with him.

"Your son is up on the luggage rack," I heard Kruy say.

"Yes, I'd heard he was working for you. Tell him his mother wants him to come home," my father's voice said.

"No problem," said Kruy. "No problem at all. Tell me, brother, did you hear the king's in Europe, negotiating again? Do you think he can get the French out this time?"

"I wish him luck," said my father. "If we have real peace maybe the times will be good and I can get more customers."

"Well, if anyone can get those foreign bastards out the Royal Father can. . . ."

I buried myself deep in the cargo, next to a basket of ducks. I didn't want to talk to my father. He didn't want to talk with me. All he really cared about was his business, just like the rest of the grown-ups. Kruy too. It was all indirect, saying that my mother wanted me to come back. Probably they needed my help at home.

The next morning I dropped off the bus when it stopped at my village and walked warily toward my parents' house. Luckily, the truck wasn't there. When my mother saw me she began crying. She grabbed my wrist and she wouldn't let me go, even when I made a show of pulling away.

That wasn't the end of the problems with my family. Not at all. But it was the end of that stage of my rebellion. It was also the end of bartering in the countryside or working for Kruy. Something marvelous had happened: Just by negotiating, without firing a single shot,

King Sihanouk obtained Cambodia's independence from France. Wild, spontaneous celebrations broke out in the streets of my village. Now we Cambodians could govern ourselves, as we always wanted to do. Now we would have peace, and perhaps we could prosper.

One of Sihanouk's first steps as sovereign leader was to increase the number of free public schools. I entered primary school, sitting with twelve- and fourteen-year-old boys just learning how to read, like me. In that first year I passed through four grades. The next year I passed through two more. From there I went to a public secondary school in the provincial capital, Takeo. In this school most of the classes were in French, because France still culturally dominated the thin layer of Cambodian society that was educated or rich.

I did well in this school, rising quickly to the category for gifted students. One of the reasons was a teacher named Chea Huon, a thin, pale, stoop-shouldered Chinese intellectual. Chea Huon believed in social equality. He invited all the students who wanted extra tutoring to come to his house on weekends for free classes. He was very kind to me. I didn't know about his politics then, and I never imagined the strange and fateful circumstances under which we would meet later in life.

In the last year of this school we had to take exams. Those who passed could begin the next stage of education, *lycée*, the equivalent of high school. I studied and studied. I prayed to Buddha that I would get good marks. When I passed, with high marks, there was only one thing to do.

I shaved my head. I shaved my eyebrows. For the few weeks required by tradition, I became a monk. In the induction ceremony, held in a *wat* or temple outside Samrong Yong, my parents put their palms together in the gesture of greeting and submission that we call *sompeah*. I nearly died of nervousness—my parents, *sompeah*ing me! But they were only saluting the Buddha in me, the holiness that resided in me while I wore a monk's robes.

Each morning I walked barefoot in a line of monks, keeping my eyes fixed on the pavement, silently chanting prayers. Housewives put rice in the bowl I carried in my shawl. The days were spent doing chores around the temple and in prayer. We novice monks sat in the temple on the floor with our palms together in the *sompeah* and our feet respectfully tucked to the side, because pointing our feet is impolite in our culture. We prayed facing the altar, which filled an entire wall. At the base of the altar were flowers and brass boat figurines with votive candles and sticks of incense inside. Above were statues of Buddha in ascending rows, gleaming softly in the candlelight. The largest of the Buddhas sat highest up and farthest back, looking down with a tranquil and mysterious expression.

Buddha was not a god but a wise human being. He left a series of steps for us to follow to lead a correct and moral life. He taught that after life comes death, and after death comes rebirth and life again, on and on in a cycle. If we follow Buddha's guidance, the next life will always be better than the last. Only by following his teachings can we ultimately escape the cycle of birth and suffering and rebirth, which we Cambodians call *kama* and other countries call karma.

A wrinkled old monk made sure I understood the essential points. "What is holy and divine," the monk explained, with his kindly smile, "is life itself, as it runs through your family. You must understand this clearly. It takes a father and a mother to bring a child into the world. They protect him when he is young. It is the duty of the child to honor the parents and to protect them when they grow old. You must also honor all the children of the family who came into the world ahead of you. You must always serve and protect them. Obey your elders, boy. If your family is happy, you will have a good life. If all the families are happy, then the village will be happy. If all the villages are happy, then the land will be strong and content."

I believe what the old monk taught me. And everything he said came true, only in reverse. My family was unhappy, my village was unhappy, and so was the country. And now I look back at it all and think about the connections, and wonder whether I myself was partly to blame.

2

EDUCATION

WITH THE COUNTRY at peace, my father began to make more money
from his trucking business and from the dry-goods store. In 1964 he
bought a lumber mill located between Samrong Yong and Phnom
Penh, just off National Route 2. By Cambodian standards the mill
was technologically advanced—that is, the saw was driven by a motor
rather than pulled by hand. But the motor, which had been taken out
of a jeep, still had a manual crank starter.

The first time I tried to start the engine the crank went around
for a couple of rotations until it built up compression. Then it kicked
back suddenly in the other direction, nearly breaking my wrist. In a
rage, I pulled the crank off and threw it at the engine as hard as I
could. Water spurted from the radiator. My mother's dog, a miniature
poodle, barked and yipped behind me. I turned around and kicked
the dog, which sailed off in the air. My father saw the whole thing.
He didn't say a word. He just turned his back on me and sighed,
shaking his head as he sadly walked away.

I had been a monk but had not yet learned the monks' self-control.

The mill was a success from the time my father took it over. Soon
he had added trucks to haul the logs to his mill. He hired men to cut
trees for him in distant forests. He bought a place to live near the
mill so he could spend most of his time working. Papa knew exactly
what he wanted, which was to become a rich merchant, to have his
sons working for him, and to have grandsons sitting on his knees when
he grew old. He gave generously to charities, like the temples and
the Chinese protective association, because it was expected of him,
but his view of the world was fixed and narrow.

One of the things my father could not do was read and write Khmer, the native language of Cambodia, though he spoke it fluently. My older brother Pheng Huor could read and write Khmer but not well. Neither of them knew French. Most of the government documents were in both Khmer and French. On weekends I bicycled the five miles from Phnom Penh to the mill to help with the paperwork.

It was my duty to work for my family, but I never felt comfortable doing it. Early on, I found that Pheng Huor was tampering with the mill accounts and putting the money in his own pockets. He also signed some of the mill's assets over to his own name, without telling my father. There was no easy way for me to solve this problem, not when I was already known as the family troublemaker. On one hand, my father was the head of the family, the ruler. My brother shouldn't have cheated him. On the other hand, I also had to defer to my brother, because he was older than me. He worked hard at the mill and was nearly as essential to its success as my father.

Two French words, *honneur* and *bonheur*, express what is important to families like mine. Though my brother was violating the *honneur* or honor, at least he was doing it quietly. For me to have pointed it out would result in the family losing its *bonheur*, its happiness or good-hearted feeling. Cambodians will do almost anything to keep the appearances of *bonheur*. We try to stay polite even when we do not feel like being polite, because it is easier that way. To be in conflict forces us to treat one another as enemies, and then we lose control.

In the year 1968, the mill was prospering but my standing with the family was particularly low. I had failed an exam which, if I had passed, would have enabled me to go on to university. My father wanted me to leave school and work for him full time as a clerk, but my mother had persuaded him to allow me to continue my studies. So I was retaking the year's courses that led up to the exam. When I parked my bicycle outside the mill on a Saturday morning and walked in, he turned his back on me and watched out of the corner of his eye as I walked to my brother's office.

"How's the business going, brother?" I asked, dumping my satchel of schoolbooks in the corner.

"We make a little money, in spite of the government," Pheng Huor said gloomily. "But the bastards are getting greedier. Here, look at these papers and tell me what they mean." I picked up the sheaf of papers on his desk. They were written both in the Roman letters of French and in the ornate, looping letters of the Cambodian alphabet, with no spaces between the words. I scanned them quickly.

"You have solved the problem of the government foresters, I notice." On the form listing the number of logs that my father's trucks carried was a figure far lower than the actual one.

" '*Bonjour, mon ami,*' " my brother said sarcastically, quoting one of the few French phrases he knew. *Bonjour* had two meanings. Literally it was a greeting like "hello," but the French practice of shaking hands offered a chance to pass folded money from one palm to another. In Cambodian slang, *bonjour* meant graft. My brother said, "The forester does not have his Mercedes yet, but every time I see him he wears more gold."

I read through the receipts and the taxation forms. How boring. What a waste of time. After I filled in the forms they would lie unread, tied up in bundles with string, in offices whose clerks moved in slow motion under slowly rotating ceiling fans. Government regulations had little effect on businesses like ours. The officials did not make their living from their salaries. They made it from bribes. It was an age-old system: Those in power took from those who weren't. As long as the officials did not take too much, there was no protest. But it made me angry just the same. For most of the week I lived in a world of idealistic students. We were young and believed in progress and honesty and change. We were also Buddhist, and the tradition of *bonjour* conflicted with an even deeper and older tradition of moral behavior.

I said, "If the government lowered its taxes it would be easier to pay the full amount. Then nobody would have to cheat."

"You think so?" said my brother. "The government loves to tax and tax. That's the problem. Look," he said, pointing at a map of Cambodia. "There's a new military checkpoint here and another one here. *Bonjour* and *bonjour*. Worse, the soldiers just bought motorcycles. This week they started going after the logging truck with their motorcycles, after the driver had already stopped at the checkpoints. The soldiers wanted more money." Impatiently, he returned to the table and flicked his fingers across his abacus. The wooden beads made a rapid clacking sound.

"Maybe we shouldn't give it to them," I said, reading through the forms.

"What do you mean?"

"Well, the logging truck is new and powerful. Tell the driver to pay at the checkpoints but to head the soldiers off when they come after him on motorcycles. If the motorcycles try to pass him on the left, he veers to the left. If they try to pass him on the right, he veers to the right. They'll never stop him."

"I think that's a terrible idea," said my brother gloomily. "Come, fill out these papers so we can finish here and go back to Samrong Yong." At the end of work on Saturdays we always returned to our native village, which was still our family's home.

I went back to work with a sigh.

A week passed. The next Saturday morning I rode my bicycle into the mill yard again. The logging truck was there, dust coating the cab and a load of logs stacked on the back. So were several un-marked automobiles belonging to the judicial police. The policemen had gotten out of the cars with pistols in their holsters. They had knocked at the office door. My father was just opening the door.

One of the policemen said loudly that the logging truck hadn't stopped on the road when the soldiers tried to pull it over. He paused for effect before telling my father the reason. "Your driver was afraid to stop because he was carrying communist literature. You have been distributing pamphlets for the North Vietnamese!"

In 1954, after a fierce war, France withdrew from its former colony Vietnam, which split into two countries, a communist North Vietnam with its capital at Hanoi, and a noncommunist South Vietnam with its capital at Saigon. In the early 1960s, the North Vietnamese began trying to take over the South militarily. The Americans sent in troops to protect South Vietnam, and later more and more troops, and by 1968 war was again at its height. Officially Cambodia was neutral, but neutrality was difficult to keep because the war was next door and many Cambodian officials were dishonest.

The police were very clever. Instead of being defensive about collecting illegal bribes, they accused my family of committing crimes against the state. The charge was hard to disprove even though it wasn't true. My father's logging sites were near the Cambodia–South

Vietnam border. The North Vietnamese communists had supply routes through the area. And communist sympathizers occasionally distributed their literature to the common people. I even knew a communist myself. The judicial police had arrested my ex-teacher Chea Huon for subversive activities. I had visited him in jail. But until then I hadn't known he was communist. I didn't have any communist sympathies and neither did my father or brother. They were businessmen. All they cared about was making money.

The police interrogated my father and then Pheng Huor. My father saw me standing around, watching and listening. He told me to go away. I answered that I wanted to stay around to watch in case the police planted communist pamphlets and pretended to find them.

A policeman overheard me. "So you think we are trying to trick you, eh?" he said. He took me outside and threw me into one of the police cars. They put my brother in another car and the truck driver in a third so we couldn't talk to each other and agree on a story. By then they were going through the mill and through my father's house, scattering equipment and upending furniture.

The police drove the three of us to their headquarters in Phnom Penh. They put us in separate cells. Then they began to beat me to try to get me to "confess."

I should explain that Cambodian society has a minor tradition of torture. In the early 1950s, when my father was kidnapped, the government soldiers tied him to a ladder, feet up and head down, and poured anchovy sauce into his nostrils. It was extremely unpleasant for my father, but he didn't suffer any permanent harm. In Phnom Penh, in the late 1960s, the police put my hand in a vise and kept tightening it as they questioned me, but they didn't actually try to crush my hand. When the vise didn't work, because I wouldn't admit to anything, they put me in a rice sack and hit me with sticks, but not very hard. As usual, the real reason for the torture was to raise the asking price for my release.

On the third evening, my parents bought my way out. The truck driver had already "confessed" to distributing the communist leaflets. To get my older brother out they had retained a prominent lawyer friend of Sihanouk's. Day after day, my father went to the lawyer to pressure for my brother's release. Eventually the lawyer, whose name was Penn Nouth, managed to get an audience with Sihanouk, and Sihanouk, who had no part in the scheme, issued a proclamation that my family was innocent. In this way my brother obtained his freedom.

My father was discouraged. He had paid Penn Nouth 1.2 million riels, which was then worth about $85,700 U.S. Presumably Penn Nouth had kept some of the money for himself and spread the rest around to various officials, including the secret police and Sihanouk's hangers-on. Sihanouk himself was not especially corrupt, but he did very little to stop corruption and seldom punished those who were caught. So we could not expect justice from the government.

But at least the family was together again. After my brother and I were released, Papa wanted more than ever to have us living and working together as a unit. He told me gruffly that I ought to get married and come home. It would be better, he said, if I worked full time for the family business.

I answered carefully. "Papa," I said, "I don't have much expertise in business. Perhaps it would be better if I had more schooling first."

I didn't tell him my real thoughts. I hated business. I didn't like taking orders from bosses or giving orders to employees. Above all, I didn't want to have to bribe government officials all my life. If you gave them enough they just wanted more. If you didn't give them enough they put you in jail and beat you.

The eyebrows arched on my father's plump face. "You want to stay in school?" he asked incredulously. He didn't say what he thought either, but I knew. Papa thought the longer students stay in school, the greater fools they become. And in a way he was right. I'd suggested that the truck driver speed past soldiers to avoid paying a few riels, and look what it had cost us.

I told my father that I'd like to study medicine at the university.

"What? Seven more years before you can make any money?" He turned away, unwilling to look in my direction. "You expect me to pay for you to study while the rest of us are working?"

He sent me off and we did not discuss it anymore. I felt terrible. Somehow things were always going wrong and I was always getting the blame. And yet of all eight children in the family, except perhaps for my sister Chhay Thao, who was very religious, I was the one with the best intentions. Of five sons, I was the one who cared most about living honestly, not cheating anybody, and not being cheated in return. I had never stolen anything up to that point, unlike Pheng Huor.

My mother talked to my father and got him to bend his views, against his instinct. Over the next few years my father gave Pheng Huor money to give to me for school. It was never as much as I needed. Even so, Pheng Huor, my rival, gave it to me reluctantly, like a rich man giving a gift to a peasant who does not really deserve it.

So I continued to live in Phnom Penh, where I had gone to lycée. It was a city of wide boulevards, overlooking the juncture of the Mekong River and the Tonle Sap River, which came together like a letter "X" and separated again on their slow, lazy course toward South Vietnam and the South China Sea.* During the dry season the rivers shrunk to narrow channels at the bottom of their banks. In the wet season the water level rose and grew, until at the peak of the floods the water from the Mekong reversed course and actually flowed *up* the Tonle Sap River, filling the basin of the nation's great freshwater lake, Tonle Sap.

I lived in a temple compound, under a monk's quarters built on stilts. There was something rootless about the arrangement, but it cost me little and I liked it. Everything about it struck me as natural and appropriate, from the discipline of sweeping the courtyards, to the sight of the monk's robes hanging on clotheslines in a dozen different shades of yellow and orange, to the wat itself, with its multicolored tile roofs and the curving golden ornaments protruding from the peaks like storks' necks. Most of all I loved the freedom, because the monks let me alone. Indirectly, with only an occasional word of advice, they helped me learn calmness. With my temper under better control it was easier to study.

I passed my exam the second time around and entered the medical program at the national university. The first year was premedical, with courses in biology, physics, chemistry and other basic sciences. The next year was the beginning of medical school itself, six years of clinical work, lectures and labs. All the classes were in French. The curriculum followed the French model, with one important difference: Because of the shortage of doctors in Cambodia, we medical students

*Below Phnom Penh, the continuation of the Tonle Sap River is known as the Bassac.

were allowed to practice before we got our degrees. So within a few years I would be able to get a part-time medical job to support myself. The only problem was getting enough money in the meantime.

I decided to teach. By then I had a thorough grasp of the subjects on the various exams. I became a remedial science teacher at several lycées, squeezing the class time into my busy schedule, racing through the quiet avenues on my bicycle.

I also became a tutor at private homes. A friend of mine from lycée, a girl named Kam Sunary, had two younger sisters who were having trouble with their studies. She arranged for me to teach them.

I arrived at the Kam residence, across an alley from a large temple called Wat Langka, and parked my bicycle. It was early evening. The house was set back from the street, behind a fenced enclosure holding several small dogs. Over the decades the house had settled unevenly on its foundations. The red-tile roof had become weathered and dis-colored. No *bonjour* here.

Mr. Kam, a low-paid veterinarian in the government service, came to the door. I greeted him respectfully and he showed me to a small room down a side corridor. There was a blackboard on one wall. The two younger Kam girls were sitting at a table. At another table was another girl, a cousin, who had come to Phnom Penh from her home in Kampot Province.

I stepped to the blackboard and without any of the usual courtesies began asking the girls why they were having trouble with their exams. I paced back and forth, trying to discover how much or little they knew, asking one question after another. I had to be impartial and correct with them—the door to the hallway was open, and every-thing we said could be heard throughout the house. But I also didn't want to be excessively polite as Cambodians often are, hiding ex-cuses behind the mask of politeness, allowing failure for the sake of keeping face.

The girls didn't know much about the sciences. The Kam sisters, in particular, hadn't grasped the concept of chemical valences. So I stepped to the blackboard, drew a table of the elements, and began explaining how chemicals combine. Three evenings a week it went like this, reviewing basic concepts, steadily making progress. I began looking forward to these sessions more than to my other classes. There was always a glass of tea waiting when I arrived, placed there by the cousin from Kampot. Her name was Chang My Huoy: Chang, her family name; "My" meaning beautiful; and "Huoy" meaning flower in Teochiew, the Chinese dialect most widely spoken in Cambodia, the same dialect spoken by my family.

Once I started teaching those girls I couldn't change my behavior. I was strict with them. They were polite to me. They called me *luk*, a form of address with a meaning like "sir" or the French *monsieur*. All the same, while lecturing them I sometimes felt self-conscious, like a man who accidentally sees his reflection in a mirror as he is walking down the street. Not much to look at, I thought. Acne scars on my face. Glasses. Sneakers. Unfashionable haircut. I looked like what I was, an unpolished bachelor who lived in a temple.

"So if you put carbon, hydrogen and oxygen together to make sugar, how will they combine?" I heard myself saying. I called on the girls for the answer. One of the Kam girls looked in her notes in confusion. The other had the wrong answer.

Chang My Huoy raised her eyes directly to me and said in her quiet voice, "It would be $C_{12}H_{22}O_{11}$, *luk* teacher, for sugars like glucose and sucrose."

"Correct," I said, "though those three elements also combine with others to form an entire class of organic compounds, the carbohydrates. Most edible plants, like cabbages and yams, are composed of carbohydrates along with proteins and minerals. If you burn these vegetables, the same thing happens as when you burn sugar. You drive off the oxygen and hydrogen, and what is left is carbon." I found myself babbling on like that without quite knowing why. Who cared about chemistry? I didn't. They didn't care either. I wished there were a way to take better advantage of being in a room with three attractive young women. I had learned something about women in Phnom Penh, though probably not enough.

Of these three in the class, My Huoy was the most conscientious. She was also the most shy. She never said an extra word, but she phrased what she said precisely, while her two cousins whispered and giggled. She wore Chinese-style pajamas. Ordinary house clothes. Her pajamas—Huoy's, I mean—were white with a tiny pink floral pattern. Though her cousins were pretty, Huoy, with her light, flawless skin and large, round eyes, had something special about her, a grace and gentleness, and something else I couldn't put a name to, though I tried to, late at night, unable to sleep, in my room under the monk's quarters. During the break halfway through the class, she asked if I wanted more tea, and at the end of class she brought oranges for all of us from the kitchen, while her cousins chattered. The other girls were no match for her.

The classes came to an end as the exams approached. Chang My Huoy was going to return to Kampot. After the last class I lingered for a few minutes in the doorway, holding the pay envelope in my hand. The family had treated me well. I wasn't in a hurry to go. In Phnom Penh, I had nobody to go to.

At last I pedaled off through the warm, quiet streets. A Honda 90 motorcycle passed me, pulling a trailer with a cargo of firewood, the noise of the sputtering engine gradually trailing off in the distance. There were few cars. I stopped by a roadside vendor, bought a piece of peeled sugar cane and sat down to chew it.

From a nearby restaurant came the shouting of a high-pitched and unmistakable voice. It was the Royal Father, Sihanouk, giving a speech on the radio. He was a familiar presence. Several times a week he took the microphone of the government radio and talked about whatever was on his mind. Once he started he went on excitedly for hours about the honor and the role of the country.

Tonight the Royal Father was telling us about the dangers of the war in Vietnam. He said Cambodia mustn't get caught between the American imperialists and the Vietnamese communists. Cambodia must remain politically neutral, he said, an island of peace and prosperity. An "island of peace"—that's what he always called it.

Cambodia was the envy of its neighbors, he went on, a highly advanced country. Famous throughout the world. We Cambodians were too intelligent to get involved in the Vietnam war. We were a superior race, better than the Vietnamese and the Thais. After all, he shouted, we were the descendants of the builders of the mighty Angkor Wat, the most beautiful monument in the ancient world! We were fortunate to live in such a marvelous country, one of the most enlightened and progressive countries in all Asia!

All of a sudden in the middle of his speech the streetlights went out. The light bulbs inside houses and the strings of colored bulbs decorating the restaurants went out too, all at the same time. Another power failure. They happened all the time, and we were used to them.

Because of the unreliable power, most radios were battery run, and the radio station generated its own electrical supply. So the Royal Father's voice continued without a break.

He went on shouting in the darkness, but I stopped paying attention. Soon the dim yellow glow of lanterns and candles appeared in the houses. A sputtering of motors gave way to a steady throb as the large restaurants started their private generators, and their colored lights shone once again.

If the Royal Father said Cambodia was an advanced country, I supposed he was right. If he said we were lucky to be Cambodian, he was undoubtedly right about that too. But tonight the issues of national pride seemed remote and unimportant. I hadn't said an extra word to Chang My Huoy. She hadn't said an extra word to me. When she wore her hair up, it lay coiled over the nape of her neck. When she let her hair down, it fell thick and soft to her waist.

We had been teacher and pupil. Very correct.

3

ROMANCE AND COUP

IT WAS a year before I saw her again, and then only by coincidence. She was walking along the waterfront by the confluence of the rivers with an armful of books. "Hello, *luk* teacher," she said shyly, her face lighting up with a smile. I got off my bicycle and walked beside her.

In her home province, Huoy had passed the exam for which I had tutored her. Then she moved back to Phnom Penh to begin training to become a teacher herself. Just now she was returning from a meeting in the Chadomukh conference hall near the Royal Palace. She said maybe I could help her with an assignment, since I was in medical school. She was supposed to make some drawings of human anatomy to use as teaching aids. I said I would help her. Did she have drawing paper? She said she did, in the apartment she shared with her mother.

When we got outside her house, I asked if her mother would mind if I came upstairs. Huoy hesitated. For a man to visit a woman in her house, even for the most innocent reason, had implications. She looked away from me for perhaps half a minute, staring across the street. I watched her closely. Finally she said she would introduce me to her mother.

We climbed up the stairs to the third floor and into their tiny apartment. The mother and daughter had the same light Chinese complexion and large round Khmer eyes. Their surname, Chang, was Chinese. I wondered whether to bow my head to Huoy's mother in Chinese style or *sompeah*. I took a chance and raised my palms together in the *sompeah*. She did the same to me, and I knew they were like me, a mixture of both races and both cultures.

From a glance at their apartment it was clear they were poor. They had a couple of chairs, a dining table, one bed for both of them and a small side table with a statue of Buddha. That was all their furniture. On the wall hung a photograph of Angkor Wat, the pride of the nation, built in the twelfth century, its enormous stone corncob-like towers rising in the air. Very Cambodian. The apartment was very clean. Not just clean but well cared for and comfortable. We began a peaceful and gentle conversation.

An hour passed before I knew it. Huoy's mother invited me to stay for dinner. With classes to teach that evening, the answer had to be no, but she asked me to come back when I could, and I accepted for a few evenings later. On my way out Huoy reminded me about the anatomical drawings, which I had forgotten about completely.

When I came back I was struck once again by how simple and yet how pleasant the apartment was. There were fresh flowers on the dining table and orchids in a vase next to the statue of Buddha. Huoy's mother, whom I politely called "Older Aunt," was even more shy than her daughter. She excused herself so that we two young people could eat together. She served stir-fried beef with ginger, snow peas with water chestnuts and several other dishes to go with the rice. After dinner Huoy and I practiced copying drawings from an anatomy textbook. We didn't flirt. That is, there was nothing we said or did that we couldn't have claimed was perfectly innocent, if we had needed to. But we established an unspoken understanding.

I came back the next evening, and the next evening and the next. Before long I was a regular presence in their apartment. It was the most natural thing, and yet it surprised me. Nothing like it had ever happened to me before. My previous relationships with girls were the kind best not described in public. My friendships with men were based on sports, jokes and quarrels. I was a raw young man. Yet here were two very shy and gentle women who put me on my best behavior.

It was hard to understand. I was hotheaded and stubborn, the kind of person who never changed his mind once he got in an argument, even if he was wrong.

Perhaps the explanation lies in a game that children play in Cambodia; it is played around the world. The two opposing children make their hands into the shape of scissors, paper or rock and show the shapes at the same time to see who wins. Scissors defeats paper, rock defeats scissors and paper defeats rock. I was a tough guy, a rock. My father was another rock. Two rocks cannot defeat each other. My father and I were always battling and neither of us could win. But these two women were soft. They wrapped and cushioned me until hitting had no effect. The rock could not hurt anyone. Sometimes life is like that child's game. Sometimes soft and gentle people win.

It took me months to work up the courage for the next stage, which was inviting the two of them to a movie. When I finally asked, Huoy's mother excused herself and sent Huoy and me off together. Huoy's mother was a widow. A burglar had killed her husband shortly after Huoy was born. Easily frightened and withdrawn from society, she had sheltered Huoy, her only child, but now that Huoy was a young woman her mother wanted her to see something of the world.

Huoy and I had tea in the cafe on the ground floor of her building. We strolled through the smooth evening air down the boulevard to the Angkor Theater. We saw a sentimental love story filmed in Chinese with a Khmer sound track dubbed in. I didn't touch her.

We had begun our romance. We moved slowly, with exquisite and agonizing decorum. Both of us were shy. If we had anything important to say, we didn't say it. We sent messages by allowing our glances to linger, and by sprinkling our conversations with clues for the other person to interpret for hidden significance.

In Cambodia romance is always like that. In our traditional *romvong* dance, men and women move around each other without touching, gracefully waving their hands in the air to the music. Men and women don't demonstrate their affection in public. Even if Huoy and I saw one another every day, we couldn't have held hands on her street without shocking her neighbors and giving rise to sensational gossip.

Most Asian societies are chaste and prudish in their public behavior. The women don't provoke men as much as they do in the West. In Phnom Penh the women wore blouses with ruffles on the front; they weren't trying to show off their breasts. But they could dress modestly and still be attractive. A sarong, wrapped around the waist and covering the legs down to the ankles, or a *sampot*, which is a fancier version of a sarong, shows how a woman is built. Huoy wore a *sampot* most days. I was a normal, healthy young male. I couldn't help sneaking glances at her, imagining what she looked like underneath.

Of course, other men watched Huoy too, and that was the problem. When she walked along the sidewalk by herself, calmly and slowly in the afternoon heat, there was something about her that would have made any sane man want to walk up to her and start a conversation. I began to watch her, from far away, just in case.

I discovered that Huoy did not talk to any other man regularly; she dropped her eyes and found a polite but determined way to walk on alone. But I was young and impatient and I needed to know what was in her heart. I was also tired of behaving well. So perhaps six months after going to her apartment for the first time, we had our first quarrel. I accused her of walking home with another man, even though she hadn't. I itemized the details of his appearance, the color of his shirt and trousers, his glasses. Huoy said it wasn't true but I said I knew it was. "Is he your boyfriend, or what?" I said sarcastically. "If he is, congratulations. He is very handsome. If you get married to him, it will be very good. Congratulations."

Huoy began crying. She had grown up without the teasing and arguing of brothers and sisters, and she had no defenses against the kind of game I was playing. She was very soft. Tears came to her eyes quicker than anyone I have ever known.

I said, "Okay, tonight I have to go teach a class, so I won't be back." I stayed away that evening and the two following.

On the third day Huoy went to the hospital to see me. She arrived at nine in the morning. I was polite to her but let her know by my expression that I was angry and jealous. I let her wait. At ten I summoned her to my tiny office. She was crying again.

"My mother has invited you to the house tonight," said Huoy. "She wonders why you haven't come the last few nights." It was Cambodian style to be indirect like that, using other people's causes to advance our own.

I answered, "Why aren't you in class today?" Huoy was still taking university classes to get her teaching degree.

"I skipped classes today because I wanted to talk to you. Why weren't you at my house?"

"I wanted to go but I was busy. You know, with the patients and all the work at the hospital and the lectures. Please excuse me, I have a lot to do."

Huoy held up her hand as if taking an oath. "Believe me. I have no boyfriend."

I said, "I believe it."

"If you believe it why don't you go to my house? Come tonight. Don't let my mother be sad."

When I went to her apartment that night the food was ready on the table. Huoy gave me a hurt smile. I pretended that everything was normal. When Huoy's mother asked me why I had stayed away, I said I had been busy. She pretended to believe me but she gave me a wise, sidelong look.

She left the two of us to eat together and went into the kitchen as usual. Huoy and I sat down and began to eat. I kept my eyes on the food, not meeting Huoy's gaze.

We had rice with the usual side dishes. As always, excellent home-style Cambodian cooking.

Halfway through the meal, Huoy said, "Sweet, are you still angry at me?"

I helped myself to another piece of fish and put it on my plate next to the rice.

"No," I said.

"Then please, look at me."

"I know what you look like." I was still looking at the plate.

"Don't hurt me," she said.

I still looked down at the plate.

Startled, I felt the touch of her fingers on my cheek. I glanced at her arm reaching across the table and then into her enormous brown eyes. "No, I wouldn't hurt you," I said nervously. "I just asked you—"

"Hush," she said, and the gaze that answered mine held a depth of sadness and wisdom that I had never seen in anyone before. "Don't bring back bad memories."

I reached over to stroke her hair.

Huoy had shown she cared for me. The rock had tried to work loose, but the paper wrapped it even tighter than before.

She went to her classes, I went to medical school and we saw each other in the evenings. We were heading on converging courses, ones that in normal times would bring us eventually to marriage. Engrossed in our daily lives, we could not imagine that an event was about to happen that would set off a chain reaction, push Cambodia into tragedy and affect us to the core of our beings.

In early March 1970 Cambodia was still an island of peace. Politically it was neutral. But all around it was war, or the equipment of war. To the east and southeast was South Vietnam, where the North Vietnamese and the Americans were mired in a struggle that neither seemed able to win. To the north was Laos, mountainous and landlocked, where the communists and royalists waged a smaller war backed by the same outside powers. To the west and northwest was Thailand, where the Americans based B-52s and other warplanes. In the middle of all this was Cambodia, a small country, roughly the size of the state of Washington or one third the size of France.

By Western standards Cambodia was poor and primitive. Most of our people were peasants living off the land. We waited passively for the rains to fill up our rice paddies. We caught tiny fish and foraged for wild foods. Even our wealthiest class, made up of merchants and corrupt government officials in Phnom Penh, wasn't really rich. For all its charm, for all its flower beds and wide boulevards, Phnom Penh was a quiet place where not much happened beyond the morning bustle in the markets and the long lunchtime siestas. And yet how lucky we were, compared to our neighbors! Cambodia was at peace. Nobody had to live in "strategic hamlets" surrounded by barbed wire. We could live where we wanted and do what we wanted. Few were oppressed, beyond the level of oppression and corruption normal for Asian societies. Life ran on in its age-old patterns. In the midmorning, the monks made their silent rounds collecting alms. In the middle of the day, the farmers came in from their fields to rest in the shade under their houses, and old women chewed betel nut and wove their own cloth on looms. At night the villages resounded with the music of homemade instruments and drums.

To me and the people I knew, the war seemed far away. Never mind that the South Vietnamese border was only a few hours' drive from Phnom Penh. We were used to that. Never mind that the Vietnamese communists had a network of hidden roads, the Ho Chi Minh

Trail, along the Cambodia–South Vietnam border. We were vaguely aware of it, but our press didn't remind us of it often. We had had no idea at all that communist supplies were arriving in the ocean port of Sihanoukville, that the Americans had been sending Special Forces teams across the South Vietnamese border or that U.S. B-52s had been dropping bombs in Cambodia for nearly a year. Nobody told us that. Most Cambodians were like me. We were from villages. Our horizons were bounded by rice fields and trees.

We had been at peace because of one man, Norodom Sihanouk. The French appointed him king when he was a schoolboy, expecting that he would be easy to control, but Sihanouk outmaneuvered them, just as he outmaneuvered everyone else. After negotiating our independence in 1953, by hinting at revolution if France refused, Sihanouk abdicated as king and ran for election. He won by a huge margin and continued to be the country's leader. Domestically he kept the support of the dark-skinned ethnic Khmers, who made up the majority of the population, by appealing to their racial pride and by telling everyone over and over how lucky we were to be Cambodians, descendants of the ancient empire at Angkor. But he also protected the rights of the light-skinned minorities, the ethnic Vietnamese and Chinese. In foreign policy he played the communist powers against the Western powers, accepting aid from all of them until 1965, when he cut ties with the United States after what he felt was an insult to his pride. He leaned to the left after that, but officially he kept Cambodia neutral and nonaligned. The American government didn't like him because he wouldn't let U.S. troops come openly into Cambodia to fight the North Vietnamese.

In Cambodia, Sihanouk was immensely popular. We barely noticed his faults, like allowing corruption to go unpunished, and keeping incompetent people in the government. Few of us were educated enough to care. When he spoke to us in his loud, high-pitched voice, shouting and gesturing wildly, eyes bulging with excitement, we listened with respect.

Sihanouk loved drama of every kind. He made movies starring himself. He supported the Royal Ballet; the ballerinas were his concubines. He held huge rallies near his palace, where he heard the complaints of the common people, then called the guilty government officials in and scolded them on the spot. And every year he held a ceremony at the place where the Mekong and the Tonle Sap rivers join and then separate again. At the precise moment when the current reversed and the water began to flow uphill toward Tonle Sap lake, he blessed the waters, which made the water's reversal seem like something he had caused magically (though, of course, the moon's tidal pull on the rainy-season floods made it happen). Foreigners called him "Prince" Sihanouk, because he had officially abdicated, but we still called him "King." Many peasants believed he was a god.

The trouble began on March 11, 1970, when Sihanouk was out of the country and the press was playing up the North Vietnamese sanctuaries along the eastern border. I was attending a lecture when the protest march started. When I caught up to it later, rioting was under way. Young lycée students were throwing papers, filing cabinets, desks and chairs out of the second floor of the North Vietnamese embassy. They tossed bundles of currency on the street below. They lowered the North Vietnamese flag from its flagpole and burned it. They did the same at the embassy of the Provisional Revolutionary Government of South Vietnam, or Viet Cong, which was located nearby. "Vietnamese stay out of Cambodia!" the students shouted. "Don't invade Cambodia again!"

The riot had less to do with contemporary politics than with an old, old racial grudge against the Vietnamese. Cambodia and Vietnam had fought many wars over the centuries. We Cambodians remembered our defeats and waited for revenge—even those of us who were not "pure" Khmer but a mixture of Chinese and Khmer. We all knew the legend of the cooking stones. According to the legend, Vietnamese soldiers took three Cambodians captive long ago and buried them alive up to their necks with just their heads sticking out of the ground. Then the Vietnamese made a fire between the heads and set a kettle on top of the heads as cookstones. Whether this had actually happened or not, most Cambodians believed it as fact. And in this riot, the resentment against Vietnamese of all kinds, communist and noncommunist, from the North and from the South, and even against Cambodians of Vietnamese descent, got rolled into one.

The riot put Phnom Penh in an uproar. Here was the capital of a supposedly neutral country attacking the embassies of its neighbors. Sihanouk cabled from Paris to try to stop it. He knew what people like me didn't—that the rioters, for all their deep feelings, had been manipulated by hidden organizers like puppets on strings. But in his absence officials of his government continued to push the North Vietnamese. The two highest-ranking officials were Sihanouk's royal rival, Prince Sisowath Sirik Matak, and General Lon Nol, who was prime minister and also minister of defense and minister of information. Lon Nol was a dark-skinned man who liked his troops to call him "Black Papa." He was proud of being Khmer, and he hated the Vietnamese as much as the rioters themselves. He gave the Vietnamese communists three days to leave their sanctuaries along the border.

Of course, the North Vietnamese didn't leave. If they could fight successfully against a superpower like the United States, why should they obey a government with a tiny military like Cambodia's? In Phnom Penh the excitement and uncertainty rose. The airport closed. Armored cars and tanks took up positions on the streets. On March 17 there was a big rally and parade. I was in it, carrying a sign, shouting for the Vietnamese to go home. Everybody on the street was anti-Vietnamese and pro-Sihanouk. We all felt the same—students, journalists, police, army. What we had forgotten was that Sihanouk himself had carefully balanced the Vietnamese communists and the Western powers to keep Cambodia neutral. He had also protected ethnic Vietnamese-Cambodians from persecution.

At lunch the following day I was having my usual bowl of sour-and-spicy noodle soup. My friend Sam Kwil, a journalist for one of the newspapers, and I were chatting when there was an announcement on the radio: The National Assembly had passed a vote of no confidence against Sihanouk.

Suddenly the food wasn't tasty anymore.

I looked around the restaurant. Everybody was staring with disbelief at the radio. Overthrow Sihanouk? Impossible! I took the radio from its stand and brought it to my table and turned up the volume. We waited. Then the announcement was repeated, and the hope that we had heard wrong disappeared.

Sirik Matak and Lon Nol were behind the coup. They had the support of only a tiny minority, the Phnom Penh elite, which couldn't become as rich as it wanted because Sihanouk and his family controlled all the top jobs. My journalist friend Sam Kwil, who was very well informed, told me that Sirik Matak and Lon Nol probably had help from the CIA. He said that Lon Nol wasn't smart enough to use racism against the Vietnamese as a way to destabilize the country, and then use the instability as the excuse for a coup. I agreed. But nobody has ever proved that the CIA was involved.

In a short time a new government emerged, with Lon Nol as its chief of state. Soon the government-owned television and radio station and the newspapers that were friendly to it accused Sihanouk of corruption and other crimes. But the attempt to discredit Sihanouk didn't stop there. Back in Samrong Yong, my sister Chhay Thao's husband, a teacher, took me to see a pigsty. There, partially buried under manure, was a statue of Sihanouk, its head severed from its body.

My brother-in-law said the same thing had happened to the statue of Sihanouk in the neighboring town of Chambak. He had helped topple it himself.

"We got orders to destroy it," he explained. "I didn't want to, but the orders came from high up. From *very* high up. We had to obey."

Next, the regime gave an order to all the teachers in the country. Huoy heard about it in her teacher training and became very upset. The teachers were supposed to tell their pupils that Sihanouk was a corrupt traitor. The pupils were supposed to repeat this to their parents. And this was where the backlash began.

All across Cambodia that week, parents scolded and beat their children. It was not just because the parents were loyal to Sihanouk, though they were. It was because Cambodian society was like a family on a big scale. Just like a father who was the head of the family, Sihanouk was the head of Cambodia, the Royal Father. For little children to say that he was bad was disrespectful. Indirectly, it criticized their own fathers.

Anti–Lon Nol demonstrations began. This time the demonstrators were not students but dark-skinned, tattooed farmers and villagers, wearing shorts and kramas and Buddha charms. Sihanouk was their god-king. Even if he could not be restored to power, they wanted his statues restored. They held signs, and some of them had knives and hatchets and machetes, but they didn't have guns. They marched from Samrong Yong to Chambak, and in Chambak Lon Nol's army opened fire on them with machine guns. The dead were carried away in hammocks tied at either end to thick bamboo poles. It was the same in the rest of the country. Near Phnom Penh, the soldiers opened fire on other demonstrators who were waiting next to a bridge. Up the Mekong River in the town of Kompong Cham, an angry mob seized one of Lon Nol's brothers. They killed him, cut his liver out and forced a restaurant owner to fry the liver and feed the slices to the crowd.

Surely the country had run amok. Surely peaceful, sleepy Cambodia was being overwhelmed by the forces of *kum*. But in a few weeks a kind of peace returned. Most Cambodians didn't dislike the new regime enough to fight it. And practically speaking, there was little to be done. Lon Nol, the former commander of the armed forces, used his military to enforce his rule.

Unlike Sihanouk, Lon Nol was on friendly terms with the U.S. government. He let it do whatever it wanted. In late April 1970, without even notifying Lon Nol first, American and the South Vietnamese forces invaded an area along the Cambodian–South Vietnamese border to try to destroy the communist sanctuaries.

At first the invasion was tremendously popular in Phnom Penh; we thought the Americans were strong enough to kick the North Vietnamese out. But we were wrong. After the Americans and South Vietnamese pulled back to South Vietnam, the North Vietnamese remained. A few tall, red-faced, long-nosed American advisers became a daily sight around the central government buildings and in the major hotels, and American equipment began arriving for the Cambodian military in larger and larger quantities.

For me, not knowing what was to come, the greatest worry was not my country but my family. I wanted my parents to accept Huoy. In the past few years my father had built up his business so much that he bought a second lumber mill. He was exporting lumber to Japan by the shipload. With the new American money in Cambodia there was a huge surge in construction, and that meant more orders too. He started a gasoline-delivery service and bought a fleet of trucks. My father was rich. He chose a girl from another rich Phnom Penh family to marry me.

I told my father that I had already met a girl I liked. Afraid what he might think, I brought photographs of Huoy to my sister Chhay

Thao and asked her to show the pictures to my parents, to test their reactions.

My parents glanced at the pictures, but they really didn't care what Huoy looked like or what kind of person she was. They questioned Chhay Thao closely and forced her to admit that Huoy's family was poor. After that, their minds were closed. They felt they would lose ground socially if I didn't marry someone from another wealthy family.

My parents didn't forbid me to marry Huoy. Then again, they didn't give their consent, which was necessary by tradition. And even though I was unhappy I didn't want to argue with them, any more than they wanted to argue with me. This was too important for losing our tempers. The government had left the middle way for the extremes of war, but we would keep the peace in my family. I would negotiate patiently, like Sihanouk used to do before he was deposed.

By the time of the coup I was fairly sure I wanted to marry Huoy. That my parents didn't approve of her made me want her even more. Only I didn't know which was worse: not being married to her already, which would have taken care of some of my frustrations, or that small, nagging doubt. I didn't know what to do. So I devised another test.

Huoy and I were alone in her apartment. We hadn't argued in months. Everything was fine. I told her to sit down. She sat. I paced brusquely back and forth, the way I used to when I was her tutor.

"Today is the last day of our relationship," I told her. "Today we cut things off. But please"—Huoy looked startled and scared—"just answer my questions carefully. This time you must tell me the truth. Just sit there, stay calm and answer my questions."

I was hurting her; I knew that. I loved her very much but didn't know how to say it. Somehow it was easier to pretend to be angry at her for something she hadn't done than to come out with the truth.

"Today you were sitting on the lap of a man in a cyclo," I said. A cyclo was a bicycle-driven taxi, with the driver pedaling in back and the passengers on a seat in front. "He had his hand on your shoulder, and you were talking with him sweetly and laughing. I saw you with my own eyes. It was the same guy you were with before."

Huoy's shoulders were already shaking, and her hand had risen to wipe her eyes.

I persisted. "So now you must tell me the truth. Do you have a boyfriend or not? I don't care one way or the other. I just want to know the truth. After all, I never said I loved you. And you never said you loved me. If you love someone else, no problem. You are free to love whoever you want."

Huoy got up without saying anything and went to the bathroom. When she came back, her head was bowed and she was dabbing at her eyes with tissues. She said, "I don't know how to tell you that I have no boyfriend! Why do you have to keep doing this to me?"

I kept my face set and my voice angry. "You're playing games! You have somebody else, and you want me to be number two!"

"I don't want to hear any more! It's too painful."

I paced the room back and forth. Then I took a deep breath and let it out. The time had come.

I moved close to her until my face was next to hers.

"Sweet, I'm sorry," I said in a soft voice. "Really I am. I promise. I just want to ask you one thing. Just tell me yes or no." I moved even closer and murmured in her ear, "I'll tell my parents we want to get married. What do you say, yes or no? Just one word, yes or no."

For a few seconds she disbelieved me. Then when I told her I loved her, she took my ear and twisted it, fiercely. And hugged me. She didn't say yes with words, but she meant yes, and she was laughing even as the tears streamed down her cheeks.

We embraced. Now I was 100 percent sure that this was the woman I wanted to marry. If she could stand up to my tricks, she would stay with me through any troubles that might come our way.

We heard her mother's footsteps in the hallway. I gave Huoy a last hug and told her to go take a shower so her mother wouldn't suspect. When Huoy's mother came in she and I had a polite conversation about unimportant matters. I asked her to accompany Huoy and me to a restaurant, but as always she decided to stay at home.

At the restaurant I asked Huoy what we were going to do about her mother. Huoy put her glass down and tried not to smile.

"I already told her that you love me," said Huoy.

"But . . . I hadn't told you yet."

"I just knew," said Huoy lightly. "And she knew even before I told her."

How embarrassing. How very embarrassing. They understood how I felt even before I did.

What a fool I had been!

I slapped my forehead with my palm.

Huoy and I went for a walk along the river. It was the dry season, and the water had dropped far down the sloping concrete embankment. We could see big cargo boats and ferries and the huge modern span of the bridge built with Japanese foreign aid, and dozens of sampans plying the water. We saw all those things, but we didn't really see them. They existed as a backdrop for our conversation.

"You and I," I said as we strolled along, "we must build *honneur* and *bonheur* together. We have a big responsibility, to take care of each another and create happiness in our families. We have a responsibility for tomorrow." Huoy didn't say yes to this but she was smiling. In Khmer, "tomorrow" also means "the future." We walked on thinking about our tomorrows together.

"Please understand about my family," I went on. "I have always had problems with them. It is like a war that never stops. They are rich now. They are upset because you are not rich. Tomorrow, someday, we will be married, but at least we already know what is in our hearts."

Huoy nodded, smiling again.

"I know my parents very well," I said. "We must work on them gradually to earn their trust. So if I ask you to do something for my parents, whatever it is, please do it. Do it for us."

"Yes," Huoy said. "Yes, I will." She understood this, that we could be happy only if we made our families happy. In our culture, the family as a whole is more important than the individual family member.

We walked along the promenade, not noticing anyone else. I had my hand around her shoulders and then on her waist and then her shoulders again. Her long hair blew across my chest in the breeze. The moon reflected off the river, and boats shuttled here and there, dark shapes on the surface of the water.

We walked to the Royal Palace and sat on a bench, looking at the river. We talked in low, contented voices about our happy years ahead.

4

CIVIL WAR

AFTER THE COUP, Sihanouk could have chosen to live the rest of his life in his villa in France. It would have been better for Cambodia if he had. But he didn't. The campaign to denounce him and events like the burial of his statues in pig manure injured his public image, or face.

Face is the mask of status and dignity that Asians show to others, who are all wearing masks of their own. It is what makes Cambodia such a polite society in normal times: I respect your face, you respect mine, and we keep our real feelings about each other hidden. In our language, to insult someone publicly is, in the literal meaning, to "break his face." Sihanouk was very proud. He refused to be "broken."

So, not long after the coup, a familiar, high-pitched voice came out of the radio. It was the Royal Father, speaking over Radio Peking. He explained that he had been a victim of a group of "arch-reactionaries." After receiving power and favors from him, he said, they had showed their gratitude by insulting and humiliating him, overthrowing and condemning him as a man who sold out his country. His voice rose even higher as he warmed to his subject. "Such accusations by these ungrateful, ambitious, power-hungry, money-hungry cowards, who didn't hesitate to stab me in the back," Sihanouk shouted, "are unimportant! My personal indignation cannot be compared with the magnitude of my concern for the sad fate of our country!

"These traitors have thrown the country—which had a good reputation as an island of peace—into the furnace of the Americans' war! The freedom and solidarity of the nation have been completely destroyed. Millions of our fellow countrymen will rise up to liquidate the reactionary group of Lon Nol and Sirik Matak and their American masters!" he shouted. "And they will build, after their final victory, a new Cambodia with the power vested in the people's hands!"

Sihanouk announced he was setting up a government-in-exile:

"I call on all my children, both military and civilian, who cannot stand to remain under the traitors' power, and who are courageous and determined to liberate the fatherland, to fight our enemy. If the children already have weapons, I will bring the ammunition and even new weapons to strengthen them. If the children have no weapons and want to undergo training, I will take measures to help them leave for the military school, deep in the jungle to avoid enemy detection. For those children who are in Europe and wish to serve, come to Moscow or Peking to see me. Long live Cambodia!"

Sihanouk had always called the citizens of Cambodia his "children." He had been saying it for so many years that I took it for granted. But the jargon he used now, like "reactionary" and "liberate," rang new and strange to my ears. Sihanouk had always leaned to the left. Now he had joined the left, and not just the powers of Moscow and Peking. Far more remarkable, he had joined forces with his former enemies, the Cambodian communists. For years he had persecuted them relentlessly, throwing them in jail, having them tortured, driving them out into the forests. He had shown them no mercy. He had given them their nickname, the "red Khmers," or in French, *les Khmers Rouges*.

Like the coup itself, Sihanouk's announcement was a sudden about-face and one that could bring no possible good to the country. For him to go over to the communists, even as a figurehead, would give the Khmer Rouge instant credibility. If he said to go to the jungle and join the communists, many Cambodians would obey, particularly the rural people who had worshiped him. They would do anything he asked. Perhaps even more than the coup itself, the date that Sihanouk joined his old enemies marked a turning point for Cambodia. It was the day when the country began its long, ruinous slide into civil war.

But there were at most a few thousand Khmer Rouge in early 1970. They were nowhere near Phnom Penh, and there weren't enough of them to be a serious threat to the new Lon Nol regime. The threat came from the North Vietnamese, whose soldiers were as tough as any in the world.

Until the coup, the North Vietnamese had about forty thousand troops in Cambodia, mostly in the eastern part of the country, near the border. Usually they stayed away from the forces of the Cambodian government, so as not to cause trouble. The overthrow and the brief American invasion along the border changed everything. Pushed back from their border sanctuaries by the Americans, the North Vietnamese spread into territory where they had never been before. When they met units of the Phnom Penh government's military, they attacked. And they almost always won. Within a few months they controlled half the nation.

Until the coup, Lon Nol had been Sihanouk's commander-in-chief. Sam Kwil, the newspaper reporter, told me, "The only reason Lon Nol was promoted was that Sihanouk knew he was stupid. Sihanouk didn't see him as a rival. And it really is true that Lon Nol is incompetent. He takes civilians off the streets, gives them twenty-four hours of training, personally sees to it that they're given Buddha amulets to wear and sends them off to fight the North Vietnamese."

"What's wrong with Buddha amulets?" I said. "You're Buddhist. I'm Buddhist."

"You work in the hospitals," he said sarcastically. "Do you see any proof that Buddha amulets can stop bullets from an AK-47?" Under his fierce glare I dropped my eyes and admitted that badly wounded soldiers with religious tattoos and charms came into the hospital all the time. "Lon Nol's crazy," Kwil said earnestly. "I know. I've followed him around. He's going to get a lot of innocent people killed, and then he's going to rely on the Americans for weapons and air strikes to keep the regime from falling. Take my word for it, my friend—he's stupid. Stupid, I tell you! Stupid! Stupid! He started a war but he will not be able to defend the country!"

Sam Kwil got carried away sometimes—compared to him, I was as calm and reasonable as a monk—but his observations were almost always right. In Phnom Penh during the first years of the war we saw American planes every day, flying in from their bases in South Vietnam and Thailand. Transports landed at the airport with supplies and advisers. Tactical fighters and bombers roared off toward the horizon. If you didn't know what the fighters were used for, you would think them beautiful, like little silver darts traveling incredibly fast and making a loud noise out of proportion to their size. At night, sometimes, in Huoy's apartment, the teacups rattled on the shelves and a sound came from far away like the ocean's roar, only much lower in pitch and barely audible—bombs from B-52s, exploding in the countryside. There were other planes. The Americans gave the Cambodians propeller-driven T-28 fighter-bombers and some transports. In January 1971, the North Vietnamese blew up three quarters of the Cambodian air force's planes at the airport, but the Americans sent in replacements.

Though the North Vietnamese mounted occasional rocket and mortar attacks on the outskirts of Phnom Penh, the war became immediate and real for me on Pchum Ben, the Buddhist day of prayer for the souls of our ancestors, in 1972. Huoy and I were sitting on the floor of a temple, praying with hundreds of people around us, when the explosion came. Everybody ran from the temple in a panic. Out in the street someone told us that the Chhruoy Changwa Bridge had been blown up. This was a huge, ultramodern bridge across the Tonle Sap River at the northern end of the city, built with Japanese aid. We usually called it the Japanese bridge. When we got near the river we could see that the middle spans had fallen down. There was nothing left but immense standing columns and a long stretch of empty water between. Then automatic-rifle fire broke out in another direction, inside Phnom Penh, where guerrillas were attacking a government military position. The government soldiers counterattacked, and the shooting went on for hours.

The following day, the Lon Nol soldiers laid out the corpses of the North Vietnamese and stood over them like hunting trophies. The soldiers grinned proudly, as if they had successfully defended Phnom Penh from the enemy. And when I saw their false pride I felt I finally understood what war is about. Men fight for glory or ideals, but the result is not glorious or idealistic. The main result, besides the suffering, is that civilization is set back many years. Take the Japanese bridge as a practical example: When it was built, travel between Phnom Penh and north-central Cambodia became much faster and easier than before. It was a great improvement. People like me could drive to the ruins of Angkor within hours instead of days. Merchants prospered from the new commerce. So did farmers, who began to grow new crops for the Phnom Penh markets. Relatives visited one another more often. Everyone benefited. The bridge brought the country closer together. Now the largest bridge in the country had been destroyed. We would have to cross the river slowly, on boats, if we crossed at all. Wars do that—they bring societies back into much more primitive ways of living.

In the early war years I belonged to a student group that collected donations from private companies for victims of the war. As a representative of the group, I flew to Kampot, where Huoy was from, and to other provinces. On most of the trips it was necessary to fly because the roads had been cut by the communists. The planes passed over vast stretches of apparently empty forest and uncultivated fields. Once at my destination I distributed blankets, kramas, sarongs, candles, canned foods and other goods to soldiers and their families, and also to refugees.

Some of the refugees lived in camps run by the Red Cross and CARE and World Vision. But most came to the traditional places of refuge in Cambodia, which were the temples. They lived next to the walls of the temple compounds in tents or covered oxcarts or else out in the open on mats woven from palm leaves. Dark-skinned women and children, they were away from their land and they could not farm, though some of them planted garden vegetables. Their husbands and sons were off fighting for one army or another, for Lon Nol or the communists, and to them it really didn't matter which.

If a government official walked among them the women fell silent; but as soon as he left they started complaining about the government's corruption and the incompetence of Lon Nol, and why Lon Nol allowed the war to continue. They all wanted Sihanouk back, because they remembered peaceful times under him. They knew nothing of politics, of the foreign powers behind the war, the Americans backing Lon Nol and China backing the North Vietnamese and the Khmer Rouge. All they knew was they wanted the war over with, so they could go home and live in peace.

Besides bringing gifts to the refugees and to the soldiers' wives, who followed the soldiers from one place to the next without adequate food or supplies, I worked in nearby hospitals and clinics. There were always bandages to change and battlefield wounds to clean and suture. There were never enough doctors to give the soldiers sufficient medical care. But the refugee women and the soldiers' wives needed medical care just as much as the soldiers did, and got even less of it.

In rural Cambodia, traditional health care is provided by spirit doctors, who interpret dreams, cast spells and use magic, and by herbalists, who make their own medicines from plants. Sometimes the spirit doctors are able to help their patients, because the patients believe in the treatments; and some of the herbal medicines are good. (The herbal cure for syphilis, for example, a strong, nasty-smelling tea boiled from bamboo joints, black pepper and about a dozen other ingredients, is reasonably effective, though why it works is hard to say.) But traditional medicine has no concept of infection and no real method of surgery. It is helpless against many of the diseases that are easily treated by Western techniques.

The field of women's health is particularly backward in Cambodia because of all the taboos about the reproductive organs of the body. The refugee women and the soldiers' wives bathed in their sarongs, either in the nearest river or else simply by pouring basins of water over their heads. They were out in the open. Everyone could see them. So they washed their exposed skin, but out of modesty and ignorance, they didn't wash anywhere else. As a result they had a high rate of vaginal infection. When they got pregnant—some of them didn't know exactly what it was that got them pregnant—local midwives attended the births. Between uncleanliness, unskilled midwives, superstition, malnutrition, and lack of medicines, the infant mortality rate for Cambodia was well over 50 percent.

In the hospitals I saw numerous cases of leucorrhea, or white discharges, which seemed to be linked to a high rate of cervical cancer. There were many cases of damage done by rural midwives—primitive Cesarean deliveries that didn't heal right and became infected from herbs placed on the wound, cases of acute shock resulting from placental debris left inside the mothers after childbirth and so on. It was terrible to see the suffering of those women, because most of it was unnecessary. And it was gratifying to help deliver a child and to see that both mother and baby were healthy.

Back in medical school in Phnom Penh, I began specialized training in obstetrics and gynecology. Besides the need for doctors of this sort, I had personal reasons for my choice that went all the way back to the beating my father gave me as a boy. My mother was always kinder to me than my father. My sister Chhay Thao was always nicer to me than my brothers. In Samrong Yong and Phnom Penh and other places I had many good male friends, but none of them meant as much to me as Huoy and her mother. I am a man with an affinity for women. A rock with a liking for paper.

The government required all doctors to work for it but allowed us to take other part-time jobs even before we got our degrees. I took one part-time job in the government's military hospital, a position that made me technically an army officer and gave me the use of a military driver, and another part-time job with a private clinic that did mainly obstetrical and gynecological work.

I stayed busy. From seven to nine o'clock in the morning I worked at the private clinic, near Tuol Toumpoung market, in the southern part of Phnom Penh. From nine to twelve noon I was on rounds at the teaching hospital connected to the medical school. In the afternoon I attended medical school lectures. From six to seven in the evening I worked again at the clinic. After that I saw Huoy if possible, but I was also on call at the military hospital. Sometimes I worked all night sewing up wounded soldiers at the military hospital, then went over to the private clinic to begin the next day.

The war went on.

One Saturday I got a telephone call from an army general ordering me to go to a battlefield outside Phnom Penh to pick up wounded soldiers. The site was "Bridge 13," across the Tonle Sap River and thirteen kilometers out along a road to the east. Because the Japanese bridge had been destroyed, the ambulance had to cross the river by ferry, and that was slow. On the road on the far side, a motorcycle drove past us from the opposite direction, the rider wearing a green paratrooper shirt and carrying a camera bag. It was Sam Kwil, returning from a newspaper assignment.

Eventually we got to Bridge 13, a small wooden structure over a dry gully. We turned down a bumpy oxcart trail leading to a cornfield. The wounded were lying on the ground, moaning, bloody and messy. The medics and I put them on stretchers and carried them to the ambulance. Then the North Vietnamese opened fire.

Brup! Brup-brup-brup! Brup-up-up-up-up! They were hidden in the cornfield ahead of us. *Brup-brup-up!* Then the sound of automatic-rifle fire came from behind us, from a grove of trees. *Brup-up-up-up brup brup!* This time it came from the gully, near the bridge. They had us surrounded on three sides. The Cambodian commander was lying on the ground near the ambulance. He had allowed himself to get outflanked and now he was pinned down in the cross fire.

"Hey, motherfucker! Get us out of here, will you?" I shouted. "We've got wounded to take care of. Call in the air strikes, man! Hurry up! Get the planes here!"

The commander rolled over and looked at me with wide, frightened eyes. He saw I had a lieutenant's uniform on, the same rank as his. Obediently, he lifted the handset of his radio and began talking into it. Around him were his troops, hilltribesmen from northeastern Cambodia, waiting for orders.

I worked my way over to the lieutenant. He was about my age, a light-skinned city boy, probably from the Phnom Penh elite. He was still in shock, holding the radio. It was my first time under fire too, but my gang fights as a boy had been good training. I pointed to the side of the cornfield nearest the bridge. "Have your men attack there, to clear the road. That's the only way we're going to get the ambulance out. Now *do* it! Don't wait any longer! *Do it now!*"

When I got inside the back of the ambulance the hilltribesmen, dressed in motley combinations of army fatigues and baggy trousers, had gotten up from the ground. They were firing their assault rifles as they ran forward barefoot into enemy fire. The driver turned the ambulance around to face the main road and lurched forward. As the North Vietnamese retreated, we bounced along the oxcart trail. Then there was an explosion, and the back of the ambulance lifted up. It settled down and kept on moving. I felt a pain in my stomach, on the left side. The hole in my shirt was only a quarter-inch wide, but there was blood around it and the stain was growing. I yelled at the driver to hurry. Whatever hit us, probably a rocket-propelled grenade, had also torn a hole two feet wide through the metal side of the ambulance, next to the floor. I could see the dirt road surface through it. Then I could see the gravel of the main road, and the ride was smoother. The medics were raising my shirt and wrapping gauze around my stomach and I was yelling for the driver to hurry.

Then there was a loud roaring sound coming toward us, getting louder fast. The medics were looking for shrapnel punctures on other parts of my body. By bending over I could see, out the front windshield, the propeller-driven T-28 fighter-bombers coming in fast and low over the treetops. They roared overhead and toward Bridge 13.

When we got to the flat expanse of the Tonle Sap River we had to wait by the remains of the Japanese bridge. I was furious. There was a long line of cars and trucks and only one ferry. I cursed the Vietnamese for blowing the bridge up, cursed the Lon Nol military for not protecting it, and most of all cursed the inept field commander back at Bridge 13. No leadership at all. I knew the type. He probably felt "above" his dark-skinned hilltribe troops. What brave, wonderful soldiers those hilltribesmen were, charging directly into enemy fire to open up the escape lane! They had saved our lives. They deserved a much better commander than the one they got.

We finally got onto a ferry and made it back to Phnom Penh that afternoon.

At the military hospital, my colleagues operated on me. There wasn't much damage, just the small puncture in my abdomen and minor cuts around my waist and left arm. Only four stitches. It was nothing compared to the wounds on the soldiers coming into the hospital every day. Still, Huoy cried when she saw me, and I couldn't help feeling the pride of the veteran soldier bravely hiding his wounds. My driver, Sok, took me back to her apartment and she made a big fuss.

By this time Huoy was mine. Busy as we both were, we managed to see each other three times a day. First, in the early mornings, I drove from my bachelor place over to her apartment for breakfast, which we usually took in a little restaurant on the ground floor of her building. After breakfast I took her to school on my scooter, a white 150 cc. Vespa, a gentleman's version of a motorcycle and a popular model at that time. If I couldn't drive her myself, Sok took her to work in a car. Sok was friendly and respectful, a man who enjoyed his undemanding role.

The second visit was lunch. At noon, when Phnom Penh was drowsy with heat, everyone who could went home. Huoy and I met at her apartment. There we changed from our Western clothes into comfortable cotton sarongs, which we wrapped about our bodies, sighing with content. We relaxed, enjoyed each other's company, showered and then ate lunch before returning to work at about two. Finally, after work, unless the hospital called me in, I came over to Huoy's for the third time. I ate dinner and stayed until it was time for me to go home to my apartment. We had to follow the outward rules of Cambodian society, like staying in different places overnight, but we were together as much as we could.

And yet I was not truly hers. Not yet. I was not so easy to tame. There had always been a rascally streak in my nature, and my new medical specialty, obstetrics and gynecology, gave me plenty of opportunities. Put it this way: Once my female patients visited me professionally, some of them began thinking about me personally. I had a lot of offers. I didn't always refuse.

One morning I was in my small office in the hospital. Sitting with me was a certain woman patient. We weren't doing anything. Not yet, anyway. We had just been talking. There was a knock on the door. I opened it and found Huoy standing there. I wondered how long she had been listening. Huoy smiled sweetly and said she had no classes that day. She thought she would just drop in to say hello. I introduced Huoy to my lady patient. A sweet feminine conversation ensued. After what seemed to me hours, my lady patient excused herself and left.

"When are you coming home?" Huoy asked me, still sweetly.

"At noon, same as usual."

I went back to Huoy's, memorizing my excuses. But when I got there, Huoy didn't behave as if anything out of the ordinary had happened. If anything, she was even more affectionate than usual. When we changed out of our city clothes she brought me a silk sarong, treating me like an honored guest. We relaxed and had a wonderful time. We showered and eventually we ate. We had the place to ourselves. Huoy's mother was a tactful old soul, and as usual she was out.

That evening after lectures and work at the clinic I went back to Huoy's again. She was kinder than ever. Instead of sitting across the table from me at dinner as she normally did, she put her chair next to me. She had cooked fresh fish, garnishing it with lemon, coriander and other spices. Her mother was off in the kitchen. When my appetite was satisfied I sat back contentedly.

That was then she dug her thumb and forefinger into my thigh. She pulled on the flesh as hard as she could and twisted it. Her frowning face was dark with anger. "What were you talking about with that lady patient this morning?" she demanded.

I had to laugh. She was far cleverer than I'd thought. "Ma!" I called out to Huoy's mother, for we were now on familiar terms. "Ma, help me!"

Huoy hissed, "Quiet! Be quiet!" She twisted the flesh on my leg even farther.

"How can I be quiet?" I said. "Look what you're doing to my leg." I was laughing and in pain at the same time.

Ma came in and asked what was happening. Huoy said, "Please go away, Mother. It's none of your business."

I said, "No, Ma, you have to help me. Huoy is hurting me."

Ma said reproachfully, "Huoy, don't make trouble," and went back into the kitchen.

Huoy put her mouth next to my ear and hissed, "Tell me about the woman patient this morning. Tell me the truth! Who is she? What is the relationship between the two of you?"

"Don't be jealous."

"Oh? With 'treatment' in your office like that? The two of you in one small room with no nurses around? How were you going to 'treat' her?"

"She's just a patient. Nothing more."

"You were lucky this time. I was good to you. I was going to hit her, but I didn't, to keep your face."

"No, no, Huoy, don't hit my patients. Don't do that. It's not good for my practice."

"I wanted to ask her, 'Why did you come here? Why are you trying to take my man away from me? One woman for one man. Not two for one.' You were just lucky I didn't start a fight with her. You were lucky I didn't kill her!"

"Yes, Huoy, I was lucky. Now please let go of my leg."

"No!" she shouted. "Tell me the truth! *Now!*"

"Huoy, she was a normal patient. You're the only one I care about."

"Don't avoid the question!"

"Ma!" I yelled.

Her mother's voice came from the other room, in a tone of warning: "*Huoy!*"

Huoy tried to clap her free hand over my mouth but I turned my head and she got me on the neck. I yelled out jokingly, "Hey, you're choking me! I've got no room to breathe!"

"I'm going to call for Sok," Huoy said in a quiet, furious whisper. "He knows about your girlfriends. Maybe I'm not the only one he drives around for you. Why do I have to wait until I see your girlfriends with my own eyes? Sok, come here!"

Ma walked across the living room and toward the front door. "Huoy, Sok has already gone," she said firmly. She went out into the hall for a second. I could hear her tell Sok to leave.

I got up from the table and walked over to the couch. Huoy came after me, picked up a cushion and began hitting me with it. "I'm going to punish you," she said. "You and Sok both. He knows your secrets. You and he conspire together."

"Ma, help!" I had my hands over my head for protection, laughing as she hit me again and again.

"It's me or nothing! Either me and me only or I'll fix you so you never have another woman again. I'll get a knife from the kitchen and fix you right here!"

"Help!"

"Huoy, Huoy," her mother was saying sadly, shaking her head.

"Save my life!"

"Next time I will *kill* the woman if I find her with you again. So I ask you now: Are you going to see her again, or not?"

"I've stopped. Never again. I'm sorry. Now don't hit me anymore."

Finally Huoy got tired of hitting me with the cushion. She sat on the sofa, stamping her feet on the floor in frustration, tears in her eyes. She turned to her mother. "See! See! He admitted! Sometimes he doesn't come back here for lunch because he's seeing his girlfriends outside."

I moved next to her on the couch. "No, Huoy. I agree with you. I'm a bad boy. I confess. I did wrong. I promise not to do it again." I put my arm around her shoulder, trying to calm her down.

"That's enough, Huoy, enough," her mother said. But her mother was smiling, just as I was.

Huoy pouted. "My own mother, protecting you! She should be protecting me."

"Hush, Huoy," I said. "You'll disturb the neighbors. We'll lose face. I confess I did wrong. I'm sorry."

But inside I was glad. Glad that she was smart enough to wait until evening to accuse me, when I didn't expect it. Glad that she cared about me so much and that she had such a strong character.

From that point on, I was hers.

5

THE CITY OF
BONJOUR

A S   T H E   K H M E R   R O U G E   grew in strength, they began to take the
place of the North Vietnamese communists in fighting the right-wing
Lon Nol regime. In late 1972 a Khmer Rouge force captured the area
south of Samrong Yong. The guerrillas spent the day in nearby forests
and at night came into the village itself.

I drove to Samrong Yong one morning to get my parents out. My
parents packed their suitcases. In the early afternoon, before the Khmer
Rouge emerged from the woods, we drove out of there fast and didn't
stop until we got to my father's other house, near his lumber mill in
the town of Takhmau. This was nearer to Phnom Penh and within
the area that the government troops still controlled.

But my father was still attached to the house in Samrong Yong.
He had built it with his hard-earned money and he really didn't want
to leave. For several weeks he made daytime trips from the lumber
mill to the village and back again, emptying the house of furniture
and possessions. Then his luck ran out. The guerrillas moved into
the village during the daytime and he was trapped.

My father was determined to leave on his own terms. He packed
two big suitcases with the rest of the valuables and waited for his
chance. Then the Lon Nol army counterattacked. An artillery shell
fell out of the sky, hit a big tree right outside the house and blew it
into splinters. My father grabbed a mosquito net, a blanket and a
pillow, climbed on a bicycle and went out the back door. He pedaled
south, away from the artillery, farther into communist-controlled territory, leaving the suitcases behind.

The next day, when I was at school, villagers from Samrong Yong arriving in Phnom Penh told my brother Pheng Huor what had happened. Without waiting for me, my brother got on a motorcycle and drove to the village, which had become a temporary no-man's-land, belonging neither to one army nor the other. He heard that my father had gone to Chambak, and when he got to Chambak he heard my father had gone farther south.

My brother finally found my father, and they began the trip back. They stayed off the paved roads to avoid enemy patrols. They pushed the bike along sandy trails through the woods and drove it on oxcart trails through the rice fields. When they got back to Phnom Penh four days later, we heard the news that a government T-28 plane had dropped a bomb on our house, destroying it totally. But we didn't go back to see.

Papa had already suffered losses in one civil war, in the early 1950s, when the guerrillas and government soldiers took turns kidnapping him. Now in the early 1970s, in the second civil war, which was being fought on a much larger scale because of the outside powers sending in weapons to help Cambodians kill each other, he lost his house and nearly lost his life. He still had the lumber mill, but the end of his business career was in sight. A trip from the mill to Phnom Penh that used to take half an hour now took half a day because of all the soldiers collecting bribes at checkpoints. When he shipped lumber to important politicians or military officers, he did not dare ask for payment. He bribed the local mayor, chief of police and army commander just so they wouldn't shut him down.

Bonjour had always been part of doing business in Cambodia, but it had never existed on this level before. It had grown with the war. Part of the reason was the man at the top, Lon Nol himself. Unlike Sihanouk, who had involved himself in the daily life of the nation, Lon Nol stayed in his office. He seemed to have very little idea what was happening in the countryside or even nearby in Phnom Penh. In 1971 a stroke paralyzed his right side, confining him even more. When he walked, his right arm shook spastically and his right leg shot out stiffly in a goose step. His speech was slurred, and those who watched him closely, like my journalist friend Sam Kwil, believed his thinking was impaired too.

Lon Nol did nothing to stop the corruption. He didn't seem to realize that the *bonjour* and the war were connected—that officers who were interested only in bribes wouldn't fight. He had no real strategy for fighting the communists. He just stayed in his office, making vague, mystical plans for restoring Cambodia to the greatness of its times in the ancient empire at Angkor. He consulted astrologers. He sponsored an organization called the Khmer-Mon Institute, which tried to prove that the dark-skinned Khmer race was superior to the light-skinned peoples like the Chinese and Vietnamese. In Phnom Penh, which was racially mixed and Western-oriented, his ideas were treated like an embarrassing joke. We didn't realize how dangerous he was. Under his regime, racial prejudice against Chinese-Cambodians flared up, and his troops massacred thousands of ethnic-Vietnamese Cambodians.

Even after his fellow coup leaders deserted him and he lost the confidence of the people, the United States continued to support Lon Nol. The Americans gave him the money and weapons to fight with, and since they didn't seem to care what he did with them, Lon Nol cared even less. His generals sold weapons to the enemy. They put extra names, or "phantom soldiers," on their payrolls, and kept the extra pay. They built huge villas for their own use, while their men in the field went hungry for lack of rice. The generals didn't really want to win the war, just keep it going, so they could make as much money as possible before taking the last plane out.

Cambodia was no longer an island of peace. It was a nation at war with itself.

I told my father that he should sell the mill and leave Cambodia. He and my mother could live anywhere they wanted, with enough money to last them the rest of their lives.

My father said no. He liked living in Cambodia. Instead, he suggested I leave. He even offered to send me to France to finish my medical education, at his expense.

This was a change—my father offering to support me through school. But I said no thanks. I told them that even if the communists took over, they wouldn't harm doctors. Not a chance. The Khmer Rouge were communists, but they were also Cambodians. Cambodians wouldn't hurt each other without reason. That's what I believed, and that's what my friends were saying too.

For my father and me and people like us, Cambodia was home,

the only place we had ever lived in. We didn't want to leave. The outside world was unknown. It seemed a greater risk to go abroad than to stay and wait for the war to end. And even though we didn't like the Lon Nol regime, we were doing well under it. For it was one of the strange things about the war that the worse things got out in the countryside, the better life became in Phnom Penh. Not for the refugees, living on the outskirts of the city in shantytowns that grew by the week. Not for the common soldiers, going barefoot because their officers sold their boots on the black market. Not for the rural people, conscripted into one army or the other. But for the *nouveaux riches* and the elite, life was luxurious. The war brought a bubble of prosperity to Phnom Penh the likes of which we had never seen. We had never had so many parties, nightclubs, Mercedes, and servants before.

I myself became rich during the Lon Nol regime. My wealth grew out of an argument in my family—out of another battle, so to speak, in my family's ongoing civil war.

After Samrong Yong fell to the Khmer Rouge, my father decided to live in Phnom Penh. At first he and my mother stayed with my brother Pheng Huor, who had married a businesswoman named Lon Nay Chhun. Pheng Huor and Nay Chhun had three children, including a little boy whom my father loved more than anyone in the world. My father had always dreamed of having grandsons to keep him company in his old age.

My father, in fact, seem to care more about his grandson than the boy's mother did. She liked going to the lumber mill with my brother, counting the money and bossing the employees more than she liked staying home and raising her children.

One day when my father asked her to stay home to take care of her children, Nay Chhun did an extraordinary thing: She pushed him with her hand. My father, who was unsteady on his feet, fell over backward and cut himself on a barbed-wire fence.

In Cambodian society, it is bad manners to talk back to a father or father-in-law. To push him physically is almost unthinkable. It was as bad-mannered, in its way, as it was for Lon Nol to overthrow Sihanouk several years earlier. And like the coup against Sihanouk, my sister-in-law's pushing of my father set a long chain of events into motion.

I took Papa to the hospital and then brought him back to my bachelor apartment. Nay Chhun's parents showed up to apologize and later Nay Chhun herself. I shut the door in their faces. In the evening, my brother came. He stood in the doorway with the same wide face and calm, grave manner as my father.

I told my brother that if he wanted to help Papa he could come in. But he would have to make a choice: He could be loyal to his father or his wife, but not both.

My brother was silent for a moment, listening. I thought he was at least going to apologize for what Nay Chhun had done.

But all he said was, "I have come to bring Papa back."

"So your wife can finish killing him?" I said. "I just came back from putting fifteen stitches in him at the hospital."

My brother turned quietly and went away.

Inside, my father was lying on the couch, pale and old and tired. I could no longer hold back my jealousy and dislike of my brother. "Which of your sons is treating you well, now, Father?" I said. "After all these years, do you know which son really tries to help you and which son has the heart of stone?"

"I know, I know," my father muttered. "But it is best not to speak about such things."

"You know now, Father, but it is too late. Do you remember when you beat me as a small child, when you thought I stole the box of playing cards? Do you know who really stole them? Do you know who has been stealing from you ever since you bought the lumber mill?"

My father turned his face to the wall. He knew.

Pheng Huor's and Nay Chhun's fall from grace gave me an opportunity to do something I had long wanted, and that was to expose my brother's embezzling from the lumber mill.

I called a meeting of the senior family members, including uncles and cousins. They were all in Phnom Penh because of the war. They all showed up for the meeting and my father and my brother did too. I read them the list of my father's properties that my brother had put in his own name: five big gasoline delivery trucks, two buses, a Land-Rover and another house near the lumber mill that my father rented to tenants. As I spoke I held the deeds for these properties right in my hand. How much cash my brother skimmed from the lumber mill wasn't clear, I said, because my brother still had the books.

Next I raised the subject of my father's estate. The inheritance was going to be large. Because I was making a living as a doctor, I didn't need a share of it. Those who did, I said, were our younger brothers and sisters. If their shares were guaranteed, Pheng Huor could have my share. He had done more for the mill's success than anybody except than my father himself. He could have my share if he signed all the stolen assets back to Father.

I looked around the room at my relatives. They were nodding their heads in approval. I was betting on my brother's greed to get him to admit that he had done wrong. But I underestimated Pheng Huor.

Asked why he had put the assets in his own name, he replied calmly, "I worked hard. I deserved them. And I needed to have something for my sons and daughters in case anything happened to me."

"Did you think about other people who have sons and daughters?" I said sarcastically.

My brother folded his hands and shrugged. "Another reason was the government laws," he said. "Papa is Chinese, but he refused to carry a Chinese identity card. There were certain kinds of contracts that it was easier for me to sign."

"That's not true and you know it," I said. "I helped you do the paperwork. There are very few businesses the government does not allow Chinese to go into, with or without an identity card. We may have racial problems in this country, but they have not gone that far."

"This is not a good time to talk about business affairs," said my brother. "I think we should just be glad that I was able to rescue Papa from the communists. Maybe he would not be alive today if not for me."

Try as we could, none of us could get my brother to admit that he had done anything wrong. Each time he managed to turn the questions aside. He would not agree to sign the ownership of the gasoline trucks and the other assets back over to Papa. He ignored my suggestion that he get my part of the inheritance.

The meeting ended unresolved. My father didn't say a word. He didn't know what to do. His daughter-in-law had insulted him by pushing him over. His son had stolen from him. But perhaps he felt it was better to have a son steal from him than anyone else.

A month later my father called his own meeting. All his children were there, except for Pheng Huor, who was his number-two son, and the number-one son, the slow-minded one, who had argued with my father and left the family. There were six of his sons and daughters in the room, all grown, and all married except for me. On a plate were twelve crumpled pieces of paper. We each chose two. Written on the inside of each piece of paper was the license number for a twenty-five-hundred-gallon gasoline delivery truck. The trucks were ours now. So were the delivery contracts, the business connections and the employees. My father had begun giving out the inheritance.

Delivering gasoline turned out to be an easy way of making money. We ran our trucks in cooperation with each other, Pheng Huor included. Before long, I took my profits from fuel, added them to my savings from the part-time medical jobs and bought into the ownership of the obstetrical clinic where I worked. Tacitly, Pheng Huor and I made our peace. I respected him for his ability as a businessman. He respected me for speaking out against him. He never cheated me and we never quarreled again.

I was able to run the fuel business, work two medical jobs and go to medical school because of Huoy. She had her own job, as a school-teacher, but she kept my accounts and watched over my employees. We both worked very hard. She had to overcome her shyness to give orders to employees. She got frustrated adding long columns of numbers together when she was tired. But all in all she was better at business than me. I continued to be the hotheaded one, losing my temper when government officials asked for bribes. She calmed me down and told me when we had to pay and when we could get out of it.

Together, Huoy and I made far more money than we had ever dreamed of. We began eating in restaurants every night. I bought a Mercedes. I bought Huoy French dresses, gold bracelets, diamond earrings. I paid the rent for her apartment, which was only right, since we were going to get married. Our only worry was that we didn't know when the wedding was going to be.

Papa had nothing against Huoy, but according to his beliefs a prospective daughter-in-law had to prove her worth. So Huoy and I sacrificed our long lunch hours together to try to change Papa's mind. At noon every day Huoy went over to my parents' house to make desserts for their lunch. If my father wasn't feeling well, Huoy rubbed his neck or the small of his back.

My father just ate the pastries, accepted the back rubs and ignored Huoy. He had many servants. Huoy was just one more. He also had many relatives who had come to Phnom Penh and were trying to ingratiate themselves. Papa was a rich man, and everyone wanted something from him.

From all over Cambodia, from the towns and the far countryside, people were flooding into Phnom Penh. The original population of six or seven hundred thousand had doubled, and it was on its way to doubling again. The newcomers built huts of corrugated sheet metal or cardboard or thatch. They begged on the streets or took work as servants or laborers at absurdly low wages. If they had relatives in Phnom Penh they moved in, five or ten to a room, or else borrowed money. My father had dozens of relatives show up at the door. His brothers and sisters came from the town where they were born, Tonle Batí, not far from Samrong Yong.

The most persistent visitor was his half sister Kim. She asked my father for a loan so she could set up a new business. My father gave her the money readily. It was the duty of family members to support one another, especially in these times. It also gave my father face to be the one the others relied on.

Aunt Kim could smell money—she was friendlier to my mother than to my sisters, and friendlier to my sisters than to Huoy, all in a neat gradation. But she couldn't be too rude to Huoy because she wanted medical help from me.

I obliged Aunt Kim as much as I could, for the same reasons as my father. I treated her husband for tuberculosis. I also treated their son Haing Seng for minor illnesses. Haing Seng looked up to me. He called me "brother." He told me over and over again how much he appreciated what I was doing.

With the money from my father, Aunt Kim bought military fatigues and T-shirts and sold them in the market. There were hundreds of market stalls like hers with U.S.–made supplies openly for sale: canned food rations, mosquito repellent, mosquito nets, hammocks, cots, knives, ammunition pouches, ammunition clips for M-16 rifles, knapsacks, helmets and fatigues. The olive-green color was everywhere. Barefoot soldiers looked wistfully at the new boots for sale but didn't have the money to buy them. The only thing not for sale in the open-air markets was weapons, because the officers had already sold them to the communists.

Aunt Kim was not satisfied with the living she made from her market stall. She asked me to supply her with government rice. With most of the countryside in the hands of the communists, rice was scarce, so the U.S. government shipped in rice from Korea. Employees of the government, including part-time military doctors like me, could get two twenty-five-kilo bags a month at a price far below its market value. I had never used my ration, because I didn't think it was honest to take rice at a cheap price when I could afford to buy it at a full price from merchants. But Kim pressured me. She pointed out that everybody else was selling government rice in the market. Reluctantly, I gave in. I got two bags for seven thousand riels each and sold them to her at cost. She sold them for fifteen thousand riels each, more than doubling her money.

In Phnom Penh, prices had risen astronomically because of shortages and because of the cost of paying bribes to officials. People used every imaginable angle to make money. When my gasoline trucks made deliveries there was always a shallow puddle of gas left in the bottom of the tank. The drivers siphoned it into wine bottles, mixed it with kerosene, which was cheaper than gas but made engines sputter, and sold it on the street. Fuel vendors like them were on the streets at all hours, waving their bottles, trying to make a living. Teachers became taxi drivers. Doctors, nurses and orderlies were absent from their jobs, working for private clinics or selling medicines stolen from pharmacies. Military officers who needed real, live men instead of "phantom soldiers" sent trucks and troops to wait outside movie theaters in the evening. When the films were over, young men leaving the theaters were thrown into the trucks and driven away, unless they had the money to bribe their way out.

Phnom Penh had become a city of *bonjour*. Nobody was immune to it. One day in 1974 my father went for a walk outside his house with his grandson, Chy Kveng. My father was wearing a faded olive-green military T-shirt, the kind Aunt Kim sold openly in the market. A military policeman drove up in a truck, leaned out the window and said, "Hey, you goddamn Chinese! Stop right there! How did you get that shirt? That's for military use only!"

My father blinked his puffy eyes and said, "No, it's an old shirt. I bought it in the market a long time ago. I'm entitled to wear it."

"No you're not, you fucking Chinese," the military policeman said.

"Then you'll have to close down the market. Don't let people sell military goods. As long as the markets sell the stuff, people will buy it."

"You're breaking the law. Get into the truck."

My father and his two-year-old grandson got into the truck. The military policeman drove around Phnom Penh, threatening to arrest them and throw them in jail. Eventually my father gave him eight thousand riels and was set free.

Kim's son Haing Seng located me at the hospital and told me the news about my father.

My patience for the regime was at an end. After losing Samrong Yong to the communists, after bombing my family's home, after allowing corruption to spread like an infection throughout society . . .

I changed into my military uniform, which I hardly ever wore. By then I had been promoted to the rank of captain, with three bars on the shoulders. I went to the military police headquarters. The man at the desk was a lieutenant, two bars on the shoulders. He saluted and stood at attention.

I said in a deadly calm voice, "I want to know who controls the area my parents live in. Someone in a truck just *bonjour*ed my father for wearing an army T-shirt. And he insulted him for his Chinese ancestry."

"I'll look into it, sir."

"You're goddamn right you'll look into it. And I'll tell you something else. Why don't you people stop *bonjour*ing innocent civilians on the street? What the hell's wrong with you? Don't you steal enough money as it is? Why don't you just *bonjour* the merchants in the market? Better yet, why don't you stop the stealing from military warehouses and fight the communists like you're supposed to?"

"I'm sorry your father was bothered, sir—"

"*Listen* to me, asshole!" I shouted. "I don't care about the money. But I care about the discrimination. *Look at your own skin*. It's the same color as mine. You've got Chinese blood too. You're mixed-race! So why do you allow discrimination? You motherfucking *idiot*! How stupid can you be?"

The lieutenant begged me with the palms of his hands together. He said he realized that his subordinate did wrong. He apologized over and over. He said he would find out who did it.

Finally I left.

Of course, I never learned who the driver was. Nobody was punished. Phnom Penh was like that. Lon Nol was a leader only in name. Under him, incompetence and *bonjour* flourished. The guilty went free and the powerless suffered. Our society had lost its moral direction. And that's why we lost the war.

6

THE FALL

DURING THE YEARS of the civil war I didn't know much about the Khmer Rouge. I wasn't even curious. Like a typical Cambodian, I didn't go to great lengths to learn about things that were beyond my horizons. There wasn't much information available anyway, except for propaganda. The Khmer Rouge had a clandestine radio station, but its broadcasts didn't tell us what the guerrillas were really like or what they really wanted. In Phnom Penh, the Lon Nol regime controlled most of the rest of the media—it owned the TV station and the two radio stations, and through censorship and repression it kept most of the independently owned newspapers tame and obedient. Luckily, there were still a few journalists around who would say what they thought, even though they couldn't always write it.

One of those journalists was my friend Sam Kwil. He was always going off to the battlefields on his motorcycle, so he had learned something about the Khmer Rouge firsthand. He told me the guerrillas were full of tricks. For example, when Khmer Rouge units were defeated, sometimes the guerrillas changed into ordinary civilian clothes, buried their uniforms and weapons and pretended to be innocent farmers. When they lost men in battles, the survivors carried the corpses away so the Lon Nol soldiers wouldn't find any dead. The communists were masters of psychological warfare, Sam Kwil told me. Lon Nol soldiers advancing toward huge, noisy, enthusiastic Khmer Rouge meetings in the countryside would find only loudspeakers and a tape player—and land mines buried around the tree that the sound equipment hung from. Later the Lon Nol corpses would be found eviscerated, their stomach cavities stuffed with grass and leaves. Sometimes innocent civilians were killed and mutilated too, to frighten the survivors.

What Sam Kwil told me about grisly Khmer Rouge practices agreed with rumors that began to circulate around Phnom Penh in 1974. In the markets, it was said that the guerrillas killed people by sawing back and forth across their necks with the spiny edges of sugar palm leaf stems. But this was exactly the sort of gossip that I expected to hear in the markets, repeated and exaggerated from one credulous person to the next.

If I didn't worry about the Khmer Rouge, it was because I didn't believe they could be any worse than the Lon Nol regime. Even Sam Kwil agreed with that. For every story we heard about Khmer Rouge atrocities there were several about the Lon Nol regime—mostly massacres of ethnic Vietnamese civilians, whom the Lon Nol soldiers seemed to hate even more than they did the ethnic Chinese. Every day we heard accounts of government soldiers stealing chickens and livestock from civilians in the countryside, or setting up roadblocks to collect *bonjour*. But we never heard of the Khmer Rouge stealing anything, even a piece of paper or a grain of rice. It was said that the guerrillas kept to a strict and honorable code of behavior—no gambling, no abuse of peasants and, above all, no corruption. After the stench of the Lon Nol regime, the communists seemed like a fresh, clean breeze.

Besides, I knew people in the Khmer Rouge, even if I didn't know them well: my secondary-school teacher Chea Huon, who after being released from prison vanished into the jungle; Aunt Kim's son Haing Meng (Haing Seng's older brother), who had gone off into the jungle in 1967; a few medical colleagues who had vanished after the coup. Huoy had a cousin from Kampot who was an officer in the Khmer Rouge, though she hadn't seen him in years. Almost everybody in Phnom Penh had a friend or relative on the other side.

And then there was Sihanouk. Compared to Lon Nol, who was despised even by those who worked for him, Sihanouk was highly respected. Even if Sihanouk was only a figurehead for the Khmer Rouge, it was hard to believe that the cause he represented was cruel or bad. Sihanouk returned to the "liberated" zones in Cambodia in 1973. He still talked to us over the radio, from Peking. The prime minister in his government-in-exile was Penn Nouth, the lawyer who had obtained my brother's release after the lumber mill incident. Admittedly, there were reports that Sihanouk, Penn Nouth and their entire circle were losing influence in the Khmer Rouge. The real leader was supposed to be a man named Khieu Samphan. That didn't bother me. Khieu Samphan had been a newspaper editor, a member of the legislature and for a time a cabinet minister. He lived a simple life and hated corruption. In the old days I had seen him riding around Phnom Penh on his bicycle.

In 1973 the United States stopped its bombing flights over Cambodia, and after that supplied only weapons and money. By 1974 the Khmer Rouge had almost completely taken over the communist side of the fighting from the North Vietnamese. Most of the Khmer Rouge attacks were small-scale, a dozen killed here, two dozen there, but as they encircled Phnom Penh they ran into entire Lon Nol divisions and attacked in human waves. There were enormous casualties on both sides.

More and more frequently, as part of their psychological war, the Khmer Rouge attacked Phnom Penh itself. They used Chinese or U.S.–made artillery. We could hear the artillery firing in the distance and then the explosions as the shells landed. They also used rockets, which were even more frightening because of the sound they made in the air, a *clukclukcluk-cluk-cluk cluk cluk*, *cluk*, *cluk*, slowing down as it made its descent, and then *pak-kum!* When the shells and rockets landed we ran outside to see what was hit; sometimes it would be a house in the next block, the neighbors already struggling to rescue the victims from the wreckage. Then, typically, the air force sent up its T-28s to stop the shelling, and we would see the little planes across the river diving toward treetop level and releasing bombs, then pulling up sharply and the string of explosions and the palm trees and houses highlighted in the flames and the black smoke billowing up. The government fought back, and its lower-level troops fought well, but each time the Khmer Rouge squeezed in a little closer. Takhmau, the town where my father had his lumber mill, fell to the guerrillas, and my father's business closed forever.

As the roads were cut off for the last time, as the last armed convoy made its way up the river, as the merchants sent their gold and their daughters out of the country and as the planes made tight, spiraling takeoffs and landings at the airport, those of us who stayed tried to adjust. It surprises me now, but most of us pretended that life was almost normal. We made ourselves believe that Phnom Penh was a little island of peace and that it was going to stay that way. Even in March and early April 1975 there were afternoons when barefoot soldiers drank rice wine and fell asleep in the shade. Almost every night, Huoy and I went out to restaurants in the Mercedes. The food was still excellent. There was plenty of cognac. I fully believed that there would be negotiations, that at the last minute the two opposing sides would somehow soften and compromise. Compromise, avoiding conflict, the *sompeah* with the palms together—that gentleness had always dominated the Cambodian way of life. The nasty, violent underside of our culture was something I didn't like to think about.

"Sweet," Huoy said to me over dinner, "why don't you just sell the gasoline trucks and leave now, while you still have a chance? You can buy an airline ticket and go anywhere in the world."

I gave her an exasperated glance. "Because Phnom Penh isn't going to fall," I told her crossly. I had stayed up every night for a week, operating on wounded soldiers in the military hospital. "Look, I'm tired. Do you mind not talking about it? Let's just enjoy the meal, all right?"

Even when the Khmer Rouge ringed the outskirts of the city and the shelling was daily, some mental barrier kept me from accepting the inevitable. On April 12, 1975, the Americans evacuated the city in helicopters. A friend of mine, a pilot in the Lon Nol air force, offered to arrange for me, Huoy and Ma to leave on the American helicopters, but I said no. I watched the helicopters take off in the distance, like oversized dragonflies, hovering and then speeding off with their loud, clattering roar.

On the evening of April 16 I went to the house of an old friend for dinner. He told me, "Tonight is the last night for all of us, and for happiness in our families. It may be the last time we are ever together." We could hear artillery outside, but I still didn't believe him. It was my old stubbornness. Somebody told me one thing and I had to believe that the opposite was true.

After dinner I drove to Huoy's house, arriving around ten o'clock. Huoy was upset. There was heavy shelling in all directions, explosions lighting up the night sky. She begged me over and over again to stay the night. Her mother asked me to stay too. I told them I had some visits to make and said not to worry.

I drove my white 150 cc. Vespa from Huoy's house, near the central market, westward toward my parents' house, near the Olympic Stadium. Ever since the big feud in my family in 1972 I had been on good terms with my parents. I drove them wherever they wanted to go in my Mercedes. I treated them for their high blood pressure and their other health problems. They had gained face by having a son who was a doctor and who looked after them as well as I did. Yes, I was a full doctor now. In February 1975 I had finally been awarded my medical degree. With the new professional status came a softening in my father's attitudes. I had reason to think he was going to let me marry Huoy.

"Stay here tonight," Papa said when I came in, "so we don't get separated." I told him I had to go to the clinic to check on my patients. I repeated what I had said a thousand times, that if the Khmer Rouge got in the city they would never harm doctors. There was nothing to worry about. I had even taped a red cross on the back of my Vespa. Everybody would know I was in the medical profession. Nobody would hurt me.

My older brother Pheng Huor came in from his house next door. "Well, if you have to go," he said, "at least be careful. The rest of us will wait for you here. If something happens, my advice is to get rid of the Vespa. In situations like this, it's safer to make your way on foot."

In situations like *what*? I wondered irritatedly as I drove to my bachelor apartment to get fresh clothes. Some friends of mine were staying at the apartment, sleeping on the floor.

"It doesn't look good," one of my friends said, leaning up on one elbow. "The government cannot last."

"Of course it can. Go back to sleep. Everything's going to be fine."

I changed clothes and drove toward the clinic. In the streets, quiet except for occasional gunfire, my Vespa engine sputtered but kept on going. Bad fuel, contaminated with kerosene. The entire staff was at the clinic, four nurses and four midwives and the guard, but none of the other doctors had showed. "Maybe they were scared of the shelling," said the smallest nurse, whose name was Srei. "I'm scared too, Doctor. If you go someplace, let me go with you."

"Don't *say* that!" I said angrily. "Nobody's going anyplace! We're all going to go on working here as always."

A half-dozen wounded and a few women in labor were waiting for me in the clinic that night. I got to work. As I examined and probed, cut and sewed, my hands seemed to be working automatically. I began thinking. Why was it that everyone I had talked to said the same thing? What instinct did they have that I lacked? What did they know that I didn't? Maybe the city would fall tomorrow. But no. That was impossible.

I spent the night on a cot in the clinic. A little after sunrise on April 17, 1975, I drove my Vespa to my parents' house, where I paid brief respects. Then I drove to Huoy's.

Huoy had dressed for work in a neat white blouse and *sampot*. Her face was pale and tense. We went to the little cafe on the ground floor of her building. We had our normal breakfast, tea and a bowl of Chinese noodles with slices of beef and savory vegetables. "Don't leave school today," I told her, "except to go home. We don't want to be separated. If something happens, come back early so your mother won't worry. But don't worry about me. They won't kill doctors, either side. I'm safe."

By now even I didn't fully believe what I was saying about being safe.

I started my Vespa. Huoy sat sidesaddle on the back seat, the hem of her *sampot* decorously below her knees, her ankles crossed, one foot on the footrest. I drove her to Lycée Sisowath and dropped her off. Then I drove toward my clinic. On the way, artillery shells exploded at random in the residential blocks. All but a few Westerners had already evacuated Phnom Penh. The Cambodian population of the city was up to three or four million. Some were getting ready to welcome the Khmer Rouge; others were afraid; the rest, like me, still hoped to go on living normally.

Because of the rubble spilling into the streets from the shelling it was necessary to make detours, but I got to my clinic at about 7:30 A.M. A crowd of people milled around nearby, watching the market stalls burn and the smoke filling the air. Some of the women with vegetables or meat stalls in the market carried wounded relatives and neighbors into my clinic. I had about a dozen to treat in all, few of them seriously injured.

I had taken care of the worst cases when there was an urgent phone call from a doctor with the rank of army general. He told me to get to the hospital to operate on some soldiers who had been injured in fighting near the airport. Quickly I finished the rest of my patients, and then a military driver came to the front of the clinic with a low, wide, all-terrain-model B-1 jeep. At the military hospital I asked a secretary to telephone the guard at my clinic to ask him to bring the Vespa to the hospital. Then I went to Block A, for major surgery, and glanced through the window into the operating room. The patient was already on the table.

I went to the scrub room and began washing my hands at the sink. An orderly whose name I could never remember helped me into the operating gown and tied the strings for me at the back of the blouse. I went back to washing. "Boss?" he said. "What do you think? The situation isn't too good, is it? Have you heard about the government negotiations with the communists?"

"No, I haven't heard anything about it. I just came in from my clinic."

"Well, the situation isn't good," said the orderly. As if that was news.

I put on gloves. We went together to the operating room. The patient was on the table, unconscious, with intravenous tubes running into his arm, one for blood and another for glucose. The operating staff had already assembled: the anesthesiologist, the nurses and another doctor, whose name was Pok Saradath. The X-ray film was already clipped into place on the translucent glass above the operating table. I went over to look at the film. The patient had been hit by a grenade. There were burns on his face and shoulder and puncture holes as big around as a finger on his abdomen where the shrapnel had entered. His belly was distended from the wounds and the internal bleeding. He was groaning in a low voice. I ordered some more anesthetic injected in the rubber valve in the IV tube.

The orderly left by the front door.

The operating room was quiet. We heard the sounds of gunfire coming from the outside in several directions. Pok Saradath, a long-time friend and colleague, worked beside me, dressed as I was in gown and mask. He made the long incision for the laparotomy and we began talking in the cheerfully obscene language that had always been part of the operating room protocol.

". . . son-of-a-bitch Lon Nol government," Saradath said. "If Lon Nol is incapable, why doesn't he just step down to make life easier for us . . .?"

I glanced up from cleaning the exterior puncture wounds. I raised my right arm and shook it uncontrollably in my imitation of Lon Nol, and Saradath understood, his eyes glinting with humor above his gauze mask. "Because if he steps anyplace he falls," I said.

"And why do you think he is going to fall, medically speaking? You know, I heard he has tertiary syphilis," said Saradath.

"No, he fucks too much. Damaged his spinal cord."

"That corrupt son-of-a-bitch. He holds on to power and everybody else suffers. All the families separated because of the war and nobody making a living."

"Not true. It is very easy to make a living if you don't mind threatening innocent people and demanding their money. There are some very good jobs to be had around Phnom Penh. If you are a policeman or an army officer you can get rich very quickly."

The orderly poked his head between the swinging doors. "I have news: The soldiers near the bridge have surrendered. Everybody is waving white flags. On the streets, on the buildings, everywhere," he said. He withdrew.

We kept on working. The room was quiet. Through the walls we could still hear the boom of artillery.

The orderly stuck his head in the room again. "The Khmer Rouge are now in Phnom Penh!"

I had removed the shrapnel from the patient, and Saradath and I sewed up the wounds in the intestinal walls. I tied off a suture and got a different-size needle from the nurse and then bent back over the patient.

"Well," said Saradath, "let the Khmer Rouge come in and get it over with, so we can reunite with our families."

"Anything would be better than this," I said. "Anything at all."

The orderly came in and said he had seen two young Khmer Rouge jump over the fence and run into the hospital compound, one with an M-16, the other with an AK-47.

There were perhaps a dozen people in the operating room. I told them, "If the Khmer Rouge come in, just be quiet and be careful. We don't know what they're going to do."

Footsteps sounded out in the hall and the doors slammed open.

"Don't move!" an angry, high-pitched voice yelled. "Don't move! Raise your hands!"

I was facing the wall, standing over the patient. I put my needle down and slowly turned around with my hands raised. There was blood on my gloves, but everyone else had their hands above their heads and there was blood on some of their gloves too.

The guerrilla wore a ragged black shirt, black trousers and black rubber sandals made from automobile tires. He was dark-skinned, a racially pure Khmer holding a U.S.–made M-16 rifle. The doors slammed open again and another guerrilla came in dressed the same but with a Chinese-made AK-47. He pressed the barrel of the AK-47 to my temple.

"You the doctor?" he demanded. "You the doctor?"

"No, the doctor left by the back door a minute ago," I said. "You just missed him."

"*Liar!*" He had fiercely bulging eyes and a high voice.

He was, at most, twelve years old.

I didn't move a muscle.

He pushed the string of my green operating cap with the barrel of his rifle. The words came out in a burst. "You *liar*! If I don't find the doctor I'll come back and kill you!"

I stayed calm on the outside. All my instincts told me that this was a time to stay absolutely still and show no fear.

The fierce look in his eyes changed to something like uncertainty.

"Let's go," he said to the other guerrilla. The two of them left by the back door.

We lowered our hands. The nurses were crying.

"Boss, we have to leave," one of the nurses said to me. "If they don't find a doctor outside they'll kill us."

I thought for a second. The patient was lying on the table behind me, unconscious. His intestines were back in place, but we hadn't finished sewing him up.

"Be quiet," I told them. "Nobody move."

We heard the slapping of the guerrillas' sandals recede along the hallway. Thoughts occurred to me faster than I could put them into words. It was like being surrounded in a gang fight as a boy. All of my illusions were gone. They had broken into the sanctuary of the operating room. They were stronger, and we could only try to outwit them. Or evade them.

Half a minute passed. No more footsteps.

"Okay," I told the room, "everybody has to leave right now. Go now and don't wait. The patient stays."

Saradath whirled on me. "You son-of-a-bitch!" he said. "We have to finish the patient first!"

"Finish *what*, mother-fuck? We have to leave now. Get out of here!" And though Saradath and I had the same rank, he gave in because I sounded as though I knew what I was doing. Everybody scurried out of the room except for Saradath and me. We took a last look at the poor young soldier on the table with pale, waxen skin and the long, open incision in his belly. He was going to die. Saradath and I left the room by the front doors and walked rapidly down the corridor together. The corridor was the same as always, yet it looked different, and I couldn't believe what had just happened. I had my arm around my friend's shoulder and I slapped the back of his head and he slapped mine. We got back to the scrub room and my trousers were hanging there but my shirt was missing. Somebody had stolen it. Pok Saradath's clothes were there. There was a woman's blouse on another hook with short tails and three-quarter-length sleeves.

"You don't want this, do you?" I said. He shook his head and I put it on. We dressed quickly.

I went to my office in another wing of the hospital. Everybody there had gone. I grabbed my briefcase and went outside. My Vespa was parked there on its kickstand with the red cross taped on the back of the seat. I put my key in the ignition.

Guerrillas in ragged black uniforms swarmed over the hospital grounds. Most of them held AK-47s, the communist assault rifle with its ammunition clip unmistakably curving out from the underside of the stock in the shape of a banana. They had the same fierce, angry expressions as the two in the operating room. I paused to look at them. There was something excessive about their anger. Something had happened to these people in their years in the forests. They had been transformed. They were not like the Cambodians I had known, shy and a bit lazy and polite.

"Get out!" they shouted. "*Get out!* Everybody has to move! Now!"

I started the Vespa and rode it several hundred yards to the gate. The security guard was gone and the gate was closed. I turned off the engine, opened the gate myself and walked through.

7

THE WHEEL OF HISTORY

THOUSANDS and thousands and thousands of people filled the street, plodding south, where the Khmer Rouge told them to go. Thousands more stood in windows and doorways, unwilling to leave, or else came out from their houses offering flowers or bowls of rice, which some of the guerrillas accepted with shy country smiles and others coldly ignored. Car horns blared. From distant parts of the city came the chattering of assault rifles and the occasional boom of artillery. The fighting wasn't over, but white bedsheets hung from the buildings as signs of truce and surrender.

The Khmer Rouge strode through the boulevard, tired and bad-tempered, armed with AK-47 rifles and clusters of round, Chinese-made grenades on their belts. Their black uniforms were dusty and muddy. They had been fighting all night; some had waded through ditches. A few specialists carried the big tubular rocket-propelled grenade launchers on their shoulders, accompanied by soldiers carrying the elongated grenades in backpacks. Here and there were *mit neary*, the female comrades, firing pistols in the air and shouting harshly at the civilians to hurry up and leave. They were young, the Khmer Rouge, most of them in their teens. Their skins were very dark. Racially they were pure Khmers, children of the countryside. To them Phnom Penh was a strange, foreign place.

Directly in front of me a guerrilla, with the wide-eyed smile of a boy with a new plaything, tried to take a motorcycle for a joyride. He revved the throttle to maximum rpm. As he released the clutch, the front wheel skitted left and right and then the machine lurched forward from under him and into the crowd. He picked himself up from the pavement and walked off scowling, leaving the bike on its side and pedestrians holding their legs in pain.

I put my Vespa in neutral and walked it into the street. No sense starting the engine and wasting gasoline. The crowd was shoulder to shoulder. There was no chance of getting through.

A Khmer Rouge shouted, "You have to leave the city for at least three hours. You must leave for three hours. You must leave for your own safety, because we cannot trust the Americans. The Americans will drop bombs on us very soon. Go now, and do not bother to bring anything with you!"

Was I supposed to believe him? I wondered. After what had happened in the hospital? My instincts told me no. The guerrillas on the street had the same fierce expressions as those who had burst into the operating room. They looked totally unlike normal Cambodians, except for their dark, round faces. And yet a part of me wanted to believe that they were telling the truth.

The harsh voice yelled again, "If you have weapons, put them on the sidewalk. Let Angka collect them. The war is over now and there is no more need for weapons. The weapons are the property of Angka!"

I glanced to the side of the street. Sure enough, a few trusting civilians came out of their houses and put their AK-47s, their M-16s, their pistols on the sidewalk. I wondered: Who is Angka? Or what is Angka?

In the Khmer language, *angka* means "organization." Angka was the Organization—logically, I supposed, the Khmer Rouge command group. What did that imply? That the guerrillas were going to try to organize the Cambodians? That wasn't likely. If there was ever a disorganized people, it was us. Peasants who farmed when and where they wanted, employees who were casual about showing up for work, a society so *laissez-faire* that nothing ever got done. Even Sihanouk hadn't been able to organize us when he was our ruler, and he had tried. Where was Sihanouk now? I wondered. Was he part of Angka? Wasn't he the leader of the Khmer Rouge? When was he going to come back to Phnom Penh? Why hadn't they mentioned his name?

All around, people muttered, "Why evacuate the city? We don't want to go. The war is over. The Americans are not going to bomb us. We don't want to leave." They walked and stopped, took two steps and stopped again. Those with motorcycles pushed them by the handlebars, as I did. Those with cars pushed them with the help of friends or relatives. Nobody started their engines. There was no room on the road to drive. There was no gasoline to spare. When could we buy gasoline again? What would become of my gasoline delivery company?

I trudged south with the flow of the traffic, in the general direction of my clinic. A contingent of Khmer Rouge approached from the opposite direction. In front of them walked a frightened-looking man whose hands were tied behind his back. Shoving him forward was a *mit neary* with a pistol. She was a large-breasted woman who had done everything possible to appear unfeminine. She wore her blouse buttoned to her neck and her sleeves rolled up to the forearms and a checkered krama wrapped around her head. She was as dusty and angry as any of her male comrades. As she neared me, she waved the pistol in the air and addressed the crowd:

"The wheel of history is turning," she declared. "The wheel of history rolls on. If you use your hands to try to stop the wheel, they will be caught in the spokes. If you use your feet to try to stop it, you will lose them too. There is no turning back. World history will not wait. The revolution is here. You must make your choice, to follow Angka or not. If you choose not to follow Angka, we will not be responsible for your safety."

She gave the man in front of her another contemptuous shove. He staggered, the whites of his eyes showing his fear. As they went past me, she waved her pistol again and shouted, "Everybody is equal now! Everybody is the same! No more *sompeah*ing! No more masters and no more servants! The wheel of history is turning! You must follow Angka's rules!"

I pushed on with the Vespa. Whatever hopes I had for the Khmer Rouge were fading fast. They were supposed to liberate us, not tie us up and make threats about obeying Angka's rules. Whoever Angka was.

The air was stifling. The streets were filled from one side to the other. We were no longer residents of Phnom Penh. We were refugees, carrying whatever we could. The wealthy pushed cars or flat-bottomed handcarts, with sacks of rice, suitcases, pots and pans, televisions and electric fans. The poor carried nothing but their rice pots. Grocers carried groceries, booksellers pulled carts with piles of books. It was strange, I thought, the things people treasured. Televisions and fans wouldn't be much use outside of Phnom Penh, where there was no electricity.

A few blocks from the hospital I came to a private medical clinic similar to mine. An exodus of the sick and crippled had begun. All the patients were leaving by order of the Khmer Rouge. A one-legged soldier hobbled on crutches, holding his spoon and mess kit in his fingers. Behind him another man with a bandage over his eyes and amputated legs was being wheeled along the sidewalk on a hospital bed, the IV bag still hanging from the bed rack. Slowest of all was an elderly woman who clutched the front of her sarong with one hand, to keep it from becoming unfastened, and kept her other hand on the shoulder of a female companion for support. The old woman was saying in a feeble voice, "I'm very tired. Please stay here, I'm very tired. I can't go on." Her companion, who was holding the old woman's IV bag, said, "Try your best, dear. Keep walking. Come on now, walk as best as you can. I know you're tired, but you can make it."

I asked the old woman what kind of illness she had. She said she didn't know, she hadn't brought her medical papers with her. Her friend explained that she had a pain in her stomach.

"Let her rest first," I said to the second woman. "Don't rush her. Let her take a few steps at a time, if that's all she can do. But if you can, take her to the Sokchea clinic, next to Tuol Tumpoung market. I'll be there."

Standing in a doorway, I reached for the woman's wrist, to take her pulse. It was faint and slow. Then I pulled her eyelid down to check on her blood supply. The tissue was pale and anemic; if she had been healthy it would have been red. A short young Khmer Rouge with fierce eyes and muddy black clothes came up to us. He shouted, "Go! Don't stay here!" in a high-pitched child's voice. He was not much taller than his rifle.

I said politely, "Yes, we're leaving." The child-soldier walked on, yelling, "You have to leave! Go now!" in his high voice to people in other doorways. He was a few steps away when he raised his AK-47 and fired a burst of ammunition in the air. The old woman trembled and I had to steady her. He walked farther down the sidewalk, yelling and firing in the air.

I gave the two women the directions to my clinic and wished them luck. When I walked on, I was in a terrible mood. Why were the Khmer Rouge making patients leave the hospitals and clinics? What was the advantage of that? Maybe the Khmer Rouge had some reason for emptying the city, but they didn't have to hurry the weak and sick. A picture flashed into my mind of the operating room in the hospital. Of a patient on the table, with a long incision in his abdomen. Of the young soldier I had left to die.

I turned west and then south onto Monivong Boulevard, one of the main avenues of the city. Here traffic was even slower. The mass of people shuffled onward, but it was difficult to move. Around me on all sides were feet and shoulders and heads. Khmer Rouge stood on every street corner, urging us on, and more Khmer Rouge rode scowling past in jeeps and open trucks, waving pieces of red cloth and red handkerchiefs tied to their bayonets. The civilians in the street wore white armbands and headbands and white towels around their waists. There were white handkerchiefs tied to the radio antennas of their cars, and white sheets hung from the windows of the houses. But already the earlier joy, that the war was over, had disappeared, and its place was taken by the smell of fear. On the sidewalk, a man changed from his Lon Nol army uniform into black pajamas.

Something beyond understanding was happening. Between our hopes of liberation and the scowls on the guerrillas' faces, between their order to leave the city "for three hours" and knowing that it took three hours to move three blocks was a chasm that our minds could not cross. We could only sense that some enormous event was unfolding and that we were part of it, and our fates were no longer ours to choose.

I saw an opening in the crowd, ducked into a side street and parked the Vespa, locking both the steering and the ignition. The clinic could wait. I had to look for Huoy and my parents.

I walked on side streets, then north on Monivong. Without the scooter it was easier to maneuver, walking against the flow, dodging the Khmer Rouge, staying out of their sight. But the same bobbing heads and shoulders that hid me made it harder to see. I kept scanning the thousands and thousands of faces. No Huoy. No father and mother either.

I saw families going around blocks on all four sides, walking around and around to give the appearance of moving, hoping that the "three hours" of evacuation would soon end. The women wept, searching for lost children. The men darted back into their houses, remembering another pile of clothing, another sack of rice, another hidden cache of gold. They piled suitcases in the trunks of their cars, ran from their cars back to their houses and back to the cars again and shouted at each other to hurry along.

Toward sundown I returned to the scooter and pushed it south on Monivong to Wat Tuol Tumpoung, near my clinic. The wat compound, surrounded by a high whitewashed wall with a crenellated top, took up an entire block. Worried-looking monks emerged from its ornate gateway, pushing their scanty possessions on a handcart— saffron robes, a few cooking utensils, a rice pot. The Khmer Rouge were making the monks leave too.

Beyond the wat stood a Khmer Rouge cadre who was laughing deliriously as he tried to start a Vespa motor scooter like mine. I glanced at him, then stared. Under the muddy black uniform, surely, was a boy from Samrong Yong. I did not know his name but remembered him from the market and the soccer fields.

He laughed and laughed at the incongruity of having a motor scooter after all those years of hardship in the jungle. The Vespa was a toy for him, a temporary plaything from the city life he had rejected. His smile vanished as he recognized me. I said, "Hello, comrade." He didn't answer. Pumping and pumping the starter pedal, he finally got the engine to start. He got on and drove off without giving me another glance. Perhaps he felt that the people of his village made no difference to him now that the wheel of history had turned.

It was dusk by the time I got to my clinic. From the outside it looked closed and empty, but when I unlocked the sliding grille doors and slipped in, dozens of patients were there. They *sompeah*ed me, raising their palms imploringly to their foreheads. "Please see me first, *luk* doctor." "Please save my life," they said. I *sompeah*ed to each of them in turn, telling them everybody would be seen but that the worst cases would be first. Scanning their faces I felt a stab of disappointment. The old lady whose pulse I had taken on the street was not among them. Well, there was nothing to be done about it.

At the nurses' station I asked Srei, who was my favorite nurse, whether Huoy had left a message. Srei was small and cute and like a little sister to me. She said, with a sort of pouting smile, "Why don't you stop worrying about your girlfriend and take care of the patients? Hurry, we've got a woman in labor inside."

"How far along?"

"Her cervix is dilated to eight centimeters," said Srei. So there wasn't much time.

First we had to get the clinic organized. It was almost dark outside. The electrical system had stopped working and the water system too. The staff was all there but not the other doctor who was supposed to be on duty. I told Srei to find candles and water. She should sterilize the gynecological instruments by putting them in a tray, pouring alcohol over them and setting the alcohol on fire. Srei scurried off, and by the time I needed the instruments she had them ready.

I changed, scrubbed and delivered the child. When it was done, the nurses reminded me about the water situation, which had not been solved. I went out to the waiting room and told the patients that those who were able should slip out of the clinic to collect water and then come back again. Thoeun, the guard, would supervise their comings and goings.

Then I went back to work. My next patient, a civilian, was moaning from a shrapnel wound. The shell fragments had entered his back, and under the dirty krama he had used as a bandage for several days the wound had grown infected. There was no X ray to help locate the fragments, only candles and lanterns. I cleaned the outside of the wound with alcohol and tincture of iodine and injected the periphery with Xylocain to stop the pain locally. Then I explored the interior of the wound as delicately as possible with round-tipped scissors while the man groaned. Eventually I found a couple of large pieces of shrapnel near the spine and removed them.

There were twenty patients that night, many of them women in labor. By some cruel irony they were delivering their infants on one of the least auspicious dates of Cambodian history. The nurses and the midwives and I went from one to the next. We kept the doors locked and didn't allow light from our candles and lanterns to give away our presence inside. Every few hours Khmer Rouge pounded on the metal grille anyway, shouting, "Anyone in here? You have to leave!" None of us answered, not the staff or the patients and their families. After what seemed like a long time we heard the Khmer

Rouge walking away again, ordering others on the sidewalk to keep on moving. Then we peered from behind the shutters at the unending procession of evacuees outside.

After finishing with my patients, before dawn, I slipped out the clinic door and walked northward, toward Huoy's apartment and my parents' house. In the dark it should have been easy to go against the direction the Khmer Rouge wanted us to take. But others had had the same idea. Ahead of me, a man walked into an intersection lit by a streetlight. A Khmer Rouge called out for him to stop and, when the man hesitated, lifted his rifle, aimed and fired. The man fell on the pavement, jerked like someone having a spastic fit and then lay still.

I ducked behind a parked car. Others froze where they were, afraid to move.

"You didn't listen to Angka!" the soldier shouted in the silence to those near him. "You have to obey. The wheel of history will not wait for you. When you move, you have to move in the right direction. You must go to the countryside."

I took a deep breath and walked up to the soldier. "Please, *luk*," I said, using the word that shows respect for a social superior, "I lost my wife and children. I just need to get them. They're close to here, just up the street."

"Stop begging," the soldier replied roughly. "No more begging. And no more *luk*. We're all equal now. We're all the same level. Why do you keep the old ways of society? There is no more old society! Get out of here."

The lie came easily: "Please, comrade, my wife and children will be lost without me."

"*No!*" he shouted. "Angka doesn't allow it! If you try to cross the street I will not be responsible for your safety. Now *go!*"

I dropped back into the shadows, shaken.

Somewhere, Huoy and my parents were wondering and worrying about me. Just as I was wondering and worrying about them.

No use looking for them now, though. Not while this fanatic had a clear field of fire. His target lay on the pavement in a puddle of blood that glistened in the streetlight. Civilians trudging southward across the intersection detoured far around the body. Nobody dared approach to make sure he was dead or to carry the body away.

Staring at the body, my mind's eye kept seeing a patient who had been left to die on the operating table.

By the time I got back to the clinic all the patients had left. Thoeun, the guard, had supervised the packing. Thoeun had been a soldier in the Lon Nol military until a battle wound brought him under my care in the hospital. He had irreparable nerve damage—his eyelids were half closed and his head twitched from side to side in a permanent tic—but he was very resourceful. Since he couldn't go back to the army, I had hired him, and never regretted it.

Thoeun had removed a fifty-five-gallon drum from a water cart and attached it as a trailer behind a Yamaha motorcycle that a patient had left in the clinic. He had piled the handcart with baskets of food and medicine, with candles and lanterns, with a stack of sarongs he had found somewhere. He had piled more on the luggage rack of my Vespa. The nurses had prepared baskets and bundles. They had wrapped their kramas around their heads, country style, to carry loads on top of their heads. They gathered around me in the hallway. "Are you ready to go yet, *luk* doctor?" "Should we bring anything else with us, doctor?"

There were nine of them altogether, eight young and middle-aged women and Thoeun, standing somberly beside the Yamaha.

I told them, "From now on, be careful. If you want me to stay with you, don't call me *luk* and don't call me 'doctor.' Just call me 'brother.' Do you understand?" They nodded their heads, wiping away the tears. "If anyone asks why you're with me, don't say I'm your boss. Just say we're friends. But don't worry, we're going to be all right. We're not going to die. Stop crying, and then we'll go."

We left as the sky was turning gray, locking the door behind us. I wore the woman's blouse from the hospital and had added a krama around my head, to make me harder to recognize. Srei stayed close to me, holding on to the rack on the back of my scooter. We walked south on a small street parallel to Monivong Boulevard.

Again the streets were thronged. Over a loudspeaker, the new rulers repeated their message: "You must leave the city. Allow Angka to take care of the hidden enemies and wipe them out. You must leave the city for three hours. You must leave the city immediately. . . ."

But other Khmer Rouge began to shout to us that we had to leave for three days, without seeming to be aware that they were contradicting the loudspeakers.

We had been up all night and we felt numbed. Like walking through a bad dream. We all knew the Khmer Rouge were lying, yet a part of us still hoped they might be telling the truth. If we could return, whether in three hours or three days, there was no sense in hurrying. We would only have to cover the same distance coming back. So we walked slowly. Everybody else in the street walked slowly too.

The sky grew light. Around us the shapes of people took on color and detail. Alongside me a woman balanced a large bag on her head, steadying it with one hand; behind her walked her young children. I glanced at her and knew her. She had been a nurse in the military hospital. We had worked together for many years.

"Doctor Ngor—" she began.

"I am not a doctor anymore," I said. "Don't call me that. Call me 'brother.' "

"Doctor Ngor," she repeated, with her lower lip trembling. Maybe she hadn't heard me. Or maybe her emotions had taken hold of her mind. And who could blame her? Phnom Penh had fallen. We were all leaving on a journey, destination unknown. She needed to talk with someone she knew. Her face contorted. "We don't know when we will meet together again. Perhaps never," she said. "Maybe we will never see each other again." And she walked off rapidly with her children so I wouldn't see her crying.

"Don't lose hope!" I called out after her. "As long as the sun rises in the east, there is hope!"

Our group of ten came to an intersection and turned east. And just then the sun, huge and red, rose through the smoke on the horizon. We would hope. We would always hope. But the woman was right: I never saw her again. Nor have I seen more than a fraction of the people I knew in the old days in Phnom Penh.

8

EXODUS FROM PHNOM PENH

ON THAT SECOND DAY of the revolution, and on the following days, the weather was hot and dusty. The sky was clear, but from far above came faint sounds like thunder, the sonic booms of jets flying so high we couldn't even see them.

As we stood in the hot sun, shuffling forward with one foot and then the other, the Khmer Rouge fired shots over our heads to get us to hurry, and loudspeakers played radio broadcasts of the government station, which was now under the guerrillas' control:

"April 17, 1975, is a day of great victory of tremendous historical significance for our Cambodian nation and people!" a man's voice declared.

"It is the day when our people completely and definitely liberated the capital city of Phnom Penh and our beloved Cambodia!" a woman's voice responded.

"Long live the Cambodian people!" said the man.

"Long live the most wonderful Cambodian revolution!" said the woman.

"Long live the independent, peaceful, neutral, nonaligned, sovereign, democratic and prosperous Cambodia with genuine territorial integrity!" It sounded to me as if the man was determined not to be outdone.

"Long live the line of absolute struggle, independence, self-reliance and overcoming all obstacles of the correct and clear-sighted Cambodian revolutionary organization!" answered the woman, equally determined to have the last word.

"Resolutely maintain high revolutionary vigilance to defend the Cambodian nation and people at all times!" the man shouted.

"Resolutely maintain the position of struggle to defend the country and people without hesitation!" the woman shrieked.

They went on and on in this strange communist shouting match.

Then marching music began playing out of the loudspeakers. It reminded me of music I had heard on Radio Peking, very stylized and Chinese, with a heavy regular beat and cymbal-and-gong flourishes finishing out the phrases, but the words sung to it were the same jargon the man and woman had been shouting moments before. It was the ugliest music I had ever heard. Imagine, if you can, what it was like for us to trudge along the crowded boulevard under the hot sun while a piercing nasal voice sang "The Red Flag of the Revolution Is Flying Over Liberated Phnom Penh":

The liberation forces have moved forward from all directions like a powerful and stormy fire, killing the abject Phnom Penh traitorous clique and completely liberating Phnom Penh!

(Cymbals and gongs banged away. I asked myself, "Is this *music?*")

The resounding victory cries of our people and army have put an end to the existence of the enemy, liberated the beloved motherland, and definitely ended the war of aggression of the cruel U.S. imperialists, who have all been expelled from Cambodia!

(More banging of cymbals and gongs.)

The red flag of the revolution is flying high over Phnom Penh, the land of Angkor.*

(One step, then another. One step, then another. I wish we had some water to drink. I wish we could lie down in the shade.)

The country's destiny is in the hands of the workers and farmers. This is the reward won by millions of drops of blood shed in the struggle for final victory. . . .

It was all very discouraging. Forced to leave our homes, rifles firing over our heads and terrible music too.

*Note that two unrelated words have a similar sound: *Angkor* was the great Cambodian empire of centuries ago, but *Angka* was the name of the Khmer Rouge ruling organization.

When the music ended, a speech began. "For the past five years," began the speaker, an anonymous man, "our revolutionary army of male and female combatants and cadre fought most bravely and valiantly, crushing the extremely barbarous, cruel aggression of U.S. imperialism and its stooges!"

Like the man and woman who had gone before him, shouting the slogans, and like the singer accompanying the marching music, this man didn't seem to be able to use normal words to say what he thought. Everything was in a special vocabulary of exaggerated praise or hatred, almost like a foreign language. His main point, when he eventually got to it, was that we were now under a new regime, called Democratic Kampuchea. ("Kampuchea" is just the word for "Cambodia" in Khmer.) Under this democratic regime there would be no rich and no poor. We would all be equal. And we would all have to go work in the countryside. "The nation must still pursue the struggle," the speaker said, "with arms in one hand and with tools in the other to launch an offensive of building dams and dikes and digging canals!" He went on and on, telling us that we were going to build the nation into a major power and that we were "gladly going to make sacrifices for Angka." He didn't explain who Angka was.

We walked about five blocks that day.

At nightfall we camped in the shape of a square, with Thoeun and I and the two motorbikes on the outer sides and the nurses on the inside for protection. The nurses took a small ceramic charcoal stove from the handcart and started a fire, and before long they were all squatting around it with pots and spoons, cooking a meal.

I sat with my back against a kapok tree. Around us was a sea of tired people. In the street, on the sidewalks, in the yards of houses, people everywhere. The stately boulevard had been turned into a camping ground, smoky from the cooking fires, yet somehow the change didn't seem remarkable. If this was what revolution was like we were too tired to care. Women and children wept, car horns honked, the Khmer Rouge tried to keep us moving with loudspeaker announcements, but we just sat there.

The nurses served dinner. We talked in low, discouraged voices about finding our families. If we could not remain in the city, our only choice was returning to the safety of places where we were known—to our families and our ancestral villages, for we all came from villages, though most of us had family members lost somewhere in the crowds of Phnom Penh.

I told Thoeun and the nurses that they could go into the streets to search for their families anytime they liked, provided one or two people always stayed with the supplies. Then, after eating, I got up to continue my own search.

I walked though the thick crowd and the smoke of cooking fires, up the boulevard, back, zigzagging across. I stepped over people sprawled asleep on the pavement. The streetlights were still working, perhaps because the Khmer Rouge had not managed to turn them off. Insects flew in swarms under the bright bulbs. To the northeast, an orange glow appeared on the horizon, and later a glow from another direction. Cinders drifted overhead. The Khmer Rouge, it was said, were burning markets, the center of the system they called capitalist and evil; though to us markets had been the center of daily life, the place where we went to buy fresh food and gossip with our neighbors.

By sunrise the crowd was on its feet but at a standstill. From the north came the sound of combat, the high-pitched chatter of U.S.–made M-16s answering the slower repetitive bursts of Chinese-made AK-47s. Somewhere to the north, a Lon Nol commander was still holding out against the Khmer Rouge.

In the south of Phnom Penh, where we were, there was no outward resistance. We did not refuse the guerrillas' orders. Yet we moved forward as slowly as possible, obeying without really obeying. It was passive resistance, Buddhist-style. Why should we go? We had homes from which we had forgotten to take gold and precious possessions. Who would take care of our houses? Why were these dark-skinned peasant boys still pushing us to leave? What was this nonsense about farming? We were city people! The war was over! It was time to reunite, time to find our families.

With my Vespa and Thoeun's Yamaha with the supply cart, it was impossible to move. Impatient as always, I put the scooter on its kickstand, told Thoeun and the nurses to take care of it and took off, slipping through the crowd, working to one side of the boulevard and then the other, climbing up fences and trees to get a better view.

I didn't find Huoy or my parents. What I found was rice. A sudden pushing and shouting developed in the crowd, and by following the surge of running men I found myself in a side street, at a warehouse with wide-open doors. Hundreds of men were already inside, grabbing whatever they could. It was a scene of wild greed. Rice bags stacked high on a wooden pallet had fallen over on one man, killing him outright. His feet were sticking out from the bottom of the jumbled pile, and nobody paid any mind.

I threw a sack of rice on my shoulder with "Donated by the U.S. Government" printed on the label and staggered back to the nurses. Then Thoeun and I went to the warehouse to get more.

In the warehouse and on the streets a new code of behavior had evolved. The new "law" was that it was forgivable to steal as long as we didn't take anything by force or hurt anyone physically. Property left unguarded was property for the taking. At night Thoeun went off and came back to us, grinning, with two live chickens in his hands. We promptly killed, plucked and cooked them and didn't ask him where he had gotten them.

By the fourth day, April 20, the soldiers had given up on telling us to leave for three hours or three days, and now they were ordering us to go into the countryside. "Angka will provide everything for you," they announced through their bullhorns. "Angka will see to it that the people have everything they need."

If we had to leave the city, National Route 2 was the road for us to take. Route 2 would take us to my father's sawmill, where my family and Huoy had probably gathered. If they weren't there, we could follow the road farther, into Takeo Province and right to Samrong Yong. Surely Huoy and my family would go to Samrong Yong if all else failed, I reasoned. And whether or not they did, Route 2 was also the right road for my nurses, who were all from Takeo Province too, from villages farther south of Samrong Yong.

I made my way on foot to the traffic circle at the southern end of Monivong Boulevard, where several roads led out of Phnom Penh in different directions. At the circle, the Khmer Rouge were waving people onto a road that led onto a bridge across the river and onto National Route 1, which was the wrong direction for us. But the other turnoff to National Route 2 was still open and a few people were still taking it.

So we waited. Took a step forward and waited some more. Listened to the sonic booms overhead. Stood in the hot sun and wished we could bathe and change into clean clothes.

The next morning, when we got to the traffic circle at the foot of Monivong Boulevard, there was a barricade across the road to National Route 2. We were too late. "Keep moving," said the bullhorns. "Angka will provide for you on the other side of the bridge." Armed soldiers were watching. There was nothing to do but move on with the sluggish flow of the crowd, even though it took us in the wrong direction.

At the base of the bridge were several sprawling corpses; most, by their uniforms, were Lon Nol soldiers; one, by his shoulder-length hair, a well-known Phnom Penh nightclub singer who had displeased the new authorities. We tried to ignore the bodies and stepped onto the bridge, which formed a shallow arc, sloping upward from the riverbank to a high point in the middle and then back down to the other side.

At the top of the bridge, a bit out of breath from the exertion of pushing the Vespa up the grade, I heard a sudden murmur from the crowd and glanced over their heads. It was one of those events that happens faster than its meaning can be absorbed: a shiny new Peugeot on the far side of the river, driving down the riverbank. It drove into the water with a splash and floated forward slowly, until the river current spun it around and took it slowly downstream.

There were people inside the car. A man in the driver's seat, a woman beside him and children looking out the back with their hands pressed against the windows. All the doors and windows stayed closed. Nobody got out.

Gradually the car sank lower and lower until only the roof was above the water. We just stared, as the car settled lower and the waters closed over the roof.

A rich family committing suicide.

On the other side of the bridge there were, of course, no supplies. Just more Khmer Rouge in black uniforms, shouting at us to keep hurrying. It was noon, the hottest part of the day. Thousands had quietly disobeyed them and had sat down to rest. I led my group under the awning of a locked storefront, in the shade.

Thoeun and I went off to explore. Upriver, out of sight of the soldiers, boats were carrying passengers back across the river to Phnom Penh. In the dry season the river had shrunk to a narrow channel of water between the banks. A few who couldn't afford to pay the boatmen were swimming to the other side. We looked around for soldiers, didn't see any and decided to join them. If we could find more food it would be good, but in any case a plunge into the water was exactly what we needed. It had been days since we had bathed.

When we got to the Phnom Penh side, we walked back to the rice warehouses in our dripping clothes. Most of them had been cleaned out. But in one we found a fifty-kilogram sack of dried beans, too heavy for a single person to carry. We swam back across the river with it.

At the top of the riverbank, other city exiles rushed toward us, offering to buy the beans with bundles of Lon Nol regime riels. I turned them down. We didn't want money from a regime that no longer existed. But when someone offered a bag of sugar in trade for half the beans, I agreed. The nurses cooked rice and green beans that night, and it tasted especially good. Stolen food always does, as I was to discover.

The next morning we left along National Route 1, walking faster than before but not hurrying. The road led eastward across a triangle of land bordered by the Bassac and Mekong rivers. In the crowd, grocers traveled with grocers, jewelers with jewelers, peasants from one province with peasants of the same province. Our group stopped whenever we met medical colleagues from Phnom Penh. We greeted other doctors with traditional courtesy, palms together in the *sompeah*, and exchanged news. I warned them not to tell anyone they were doctors and explained what had happened in the operating room of the hospital. Some of the doctors agreed with me about the danger and others thought I was exaggerating, though they didn't tell me so directly, because they didn't want me to lose face.

The next morning we continued walking. Soon we came to Boeng Snor, Phnom Penh's red-light district, on the banks of the Mekong. The road was up above the level of the land, on a broad dike, but the main brothels and nightclubs were on stilts, to keep even with the road. Lower than the road, on what was land in the dry season, were the floating houses, built on rafts of fifty-five-gallon drums, or sometimes on bamboo. Before the revolution men used to spend time here with their mistresses or prostitutes. They gambled and drank with their friends. It had been a place where everything was permitted for those who had money, a place where the sensuous side of the normally prudish Cambodian character was free to emerge. But not anymore. No painted ladies. Only squatters, and landlords trying to keep squatters out. As a red-light district, Boeng Snor had ceased to exist. Whoring, drinking, gambling, bribery—for better or worse, all these were forbidden under the new regime.

Beyond Boeng Snor, both lanes of the road were still filled with city exiles, pushing their cars or carrying their possessions on springy shoulderboards, all of them headed in the same direction. Yet for the first time there was room enough to move freely among them.

Here and there beside the road lay corpses of Lon Nol soldiers. By now we hardly noticed them. A more surprising sight were the roadside merchants, who were doing a busy trade. From makeshift stalls and from tarps spread on the ground, they were selling cakes, cigarettes, chicken barbecued on skewers, eggs, live poultry, fresh and dried fish, meats, fruits and fresh vegetables of all kinds, books and tape cassettes. The Khmer Rouge might have destroyed the markets but not the market sellers, and it was encouraging to see the merchants making the best of their new situation.

By the end of the afternoon we had traveled three or four more miles, to the edge of a large, crowded settlement of Phnom Penh refugees. It was called Wat Kien Svay Krao, after an enormous walled temple compound of the same name, which sat on the riverbank overlooking the Mekong. Farther inland was a second, smaller wat. There were monks in these temples, picking their way through court-yards packed with people, cars, makeshift tents and canopies. People had camped everywhere—in the village between the temples, under every tree, in the fields nearby, and even on the islands and sandbars of the shrunken river. We decided to stay there too. It was a major node of relocation, outside the city but not too far away for those who hoped to return.

We parked the motorbikes off the road in the shade of a large mango tree. Above our heads were green mangoes, hanging by their stems. In Cambodia we eat green mangoes as a sort of crunchy veg-etable (though they do not taste as good as ripe mangoes, which develop later in the year). So if we wanted green mangoes we could just pick them. There were coconut palms and a grove of banana trees nearby. Farther off there were farmers' fields to forage. If we wanted fish, Thoeun and I could make fishing poles and try our luck in the Mekong. We could also use our beans and rice for bartering. So food and shelter didn't worry us.

What worried us was finding our families. I had met some distant cousins on the road, and some of Huoy's cousins, but none of them knew where Huoy and my family were.

In roaming around every day looking for Huoy and my family I ran into many people I knew. One of them was my old friend Sam Kwil, the newspaper reporter and photographer. Like a lot of journalists, Kwil basically disliked authority. He had never been happy with the Lon Nol regime because of the corruption and the heavy-handed censorship. He was even unhappier with the Khmer Rouge regime, which didn't allow any newspapers at all. Kwil's greatest pleasure had always been finding out what was going on and telling other people. He told me what I had already suspected, that the dull thunder-like sounds from the sky came from U.S. reconnaissance planes flying at incredible altitudes. And he told me what I hadn't known, that next door in South Vietnam province after province was falling to the North Vietnamese. "Soon everywhere will be communist," he told me glumly.

Kwil still had the habits of a journalist even though he didn't have a paper to work for. Wherever he went in Wat Kien Svay Krao he took his duffel bag of cameras, film and notebooks. When he and I walked together to the grove of banana trees by Route 1, he strapped the duffel bag to the luggage rack of his motorcycle and pushed the bike along.

As we were picking bunches of ripe bananas, a convoy of covered trucks came out of the distance on the highway, from the direction of Phnom Penh. I had seen convoys like that before, and I had always wondered where they were going. Sam Kwil had wondered about that too. Along Route 1 there were few settlements of any importance from here to the Vietnamese border.

Between the torn fronds of the banana trees we could make out the front escort jeep and then the long line of Chinese-made trucks behind it. Kwil got his cameras out and stepped forward to get a better view, although he was still hidden.

"Be careful, will you?" I told him, but he didn't answer.

The escort jeep went past us and then the first trucks. As the trucks passed we noticed that some of the tarps covering the cargo on the back were untied and flapping in the wind. When they flapped open we saw what was underneath—chairs, refrigerators, air conditioners, fans, television sets and various sacks and bags. More trucks went past and their cargo was the same. Obviously the Khmer Rouge had taken the furniture and appliances from Phnom Penh. The only question was whether they were giving it or selling it to the Vietnamese.

Kwil moved farther forward among the trees. He had raised his camera to take pictures of the backs of the trucks, and as he turned he didn't see the jeep bringing up the rear, until it stopped suddenly on the pavement beside him.

I ran far back into the banana grove. Sam Kwil was slower to react. Three Khmer Rouge jumped out of the jeep and ran toward him, one to his left, one right at him and one to his right. In a few seconds they had him surrounded.

I could hear their voices through the trees. "Who ordered you to take pictures?" they demanded. "Anyone who takes pictures without permission is the enemy! You are CIA!" Before he could argue, they wrenched his arms behind him in a hammerlock and one of them swung his rifle stock and hit Kwil in the ribs. Kwil collapsed. They half-marched, half-dragged him to the jeep, tied his hands behind him and began beating him with their rifle butts and kicking him. Then the jeep drove off with Sam Kwil inside, accelerating to catch up with the rest of the convoy.

It was quiet when they had gone, except for the chirping of crickets and the loud, irrelevant chittering of birds.

It had been so quick. One minute he had been talking with me, the next he was gone. I stood in the grove of banana trees, trying not to believe my eyes. There was nothing I could have done. Or was there? The jeep got smaller and smaller in the distance until it vanished down National Route 1.

9

WAT KIEN SVAY KRAO

I DO NOT KNOW how many miles I walked that day. My feet had taken control of my body. My body had taken over my brain.

It was better to walk than think. Better to do almost anything than think. Poor Kwil. How they had grabbed him and dragged him away. I had done nothing. Don't think about it, I told myself. Just stay on the move and keep scanning faces of the crowd. If he is not dead now he will be soon. Stay detached, I told myself. Save the emotions for later. Concentrate on staying alive and finding the family. They took him and I did nothing. Nothing to do. Just keep walking and scan the faces. Clubbing him with their rifles. Before him, the suicide of the family in their Peugeot. Before the suicide, the man shot dead for trying to cross the intersection in Phnom Penh. The patient I left on the operating table. We are helpless, helpless, helpless. We cannot struggle against them. We can only evade them and hope someone else dies in our place. Don't think about it. Hide the emotions inside, and keep walking. To survive.

I went back to the mango tree and counted: Everyone in my group was there, nine people stretched out on their mats in the shade, relaxed. No sense upsetting them. They are my responsibility. Back to wandering. National Route 1 was choked with traffic again. Thousands and thousands of faces. Too many on the road and too many in Wat Kien Svay Krao. Too many faces to see.

I walked and walked. In the back lanes of the village late that afternoon, a family was leaving from its camping place, on the ground level between the stilts of a house. Quickly I moved my group there from the mango tree, for better protection from the rains. The nurses chose benches to sleep on and rigged their mosquito nets on strings. I chose an oxcart as a bed, its narrow platform wedged between the pair of tall wooden-spoked wheels. And went back to walking.

I wandered among the barbers who had set up shop with a chair and a mirror nailed to a tree, with the vendors of fish and pork with the flies swarming around, with the fruit sellers. Restaurateurs offered Chinese noodle soup, one bowl for 5,000 riels. The price of the soup was a gauge of the merchants' faith in the currency of the Lon Nol regime: a few months before, a bowl of that same soup would have cost 500 to 600 riels, and a few years before, in 1972, it would have cost 150 riels. But the Khmer Rouge hadn't introduced any currency to take its place.

On the side of the wat, the Khmer Rouge had put up a military recruitment center. They had written a message in chalk, reading: "If you were a Lon Nol soldier before, register your name here and go back to work for Angka. Angka needs soldiers on all levels. Also register if you were a military administrator. Angka will put you back to work. Professors, teachers and students will register later." Lon Nol soldiers in civilian clothing lined up to be interviewed. They looked glad. They hadn't liked leaving the city without their possessions, not knowing where they were going. Now they had a purpose, a direction. Once more they would be serving their country and making a living. When they reached the head of the line, they gave their histories to interviewers holding clipboards. Former lieutenants pretended to be captains, and captains pretended to be majors, to get higher-ranking jobs with the Khmer Rouge. As the trucks arrived to take them off, the men climbed in, happy and smiling. They shouted, "Give the news to my parents! I go back to work for Angka!"

I watched the trucks drive away and it made me suspicious. Why didn't the Khmer Rouge want teachers or students? Or doctors or engineers? Surely they needed all those professions if they were going to rebuild the country. Though I was technically a Lon Nol officer myself, I hung back at the edge of the crowd. So did another former soldier whose friends saw him from the trucks and beckoned him to come on. The Khmer Rouge recruiters quickly closed in on this man and took him by the arm. He insisted he was merely a friend of the soldiers in the truck, but it did him no good. The Khmer Rouge placed him in the line, to be interviewed. He stood there with the expression of a man who was trapped and had no hope of escaping.*

I walked away from the recruitment center, stopping when a Khmer Rouge soldier came up to me. "Let me have a look at your glasses," he said.

I handed him my glasses.

He held them in his palm. "Can you give them to me?" It was as much a statement as a question.

"Comrade, the glasses are not fitted to your eyes," I said. "I am nearsighted. It you take them I won't be able to see anything."

He tried them on, and opened and shut his eyes several times in surprise. "They hurt me!" he said. "Why can't I see?"

"Comrade, they don't fit your eyes," I said. "If they did I would give them to you. Believe me."

As he gave me back my glasses he glanced at my wrist, but I had already removed my watch and put it in hiding. For that matter I had also removed the spark plug from my Vespa, to be able to prove that the Vespa wasn't working, in case someone tried to take that too. The Khmer Rouge code forbade the guerrillas from taking private property, but the guerrillas didn't always obey it, just like they didn't obey the provision of the code against harming the people.

I got away from the soldier as fast as possible and walked to a small dirt road along the riverbank. Below in the river, exiles from the city cooled off, bathing decorously in their sarongs. Large motorized cargo boats pulled out from shore, bringing passengers back to their home provinces in a program organized by the Khmer Rouge. Thousands of boat passengers left each day, without diminishing the number of people living in Wat Kien Svay Krao.

Somehow, without a real turning point, life had become a succession of days spent wandering along the highway and hanging around the village. Phnom Penh was in the past. The news about the future was vague and conflicting. First we would hear that Angka was going to give us land to clear and farm. Then we would hear that Angka was going to push us on to some other location and deal with us later. We never knew what was going to happen. Every day, Thoeun and

---

*Long afterward I learned that the army officers were driven away into the countryside. In a "rest" break they climbed down from the trucks, but the trucks suddenly drove away, and Khmer Rouge in concealment opened fire. Almost all the Lon Nol officers died.

I went out foraging for food. With foraging, fishing and bartering, I had reverted to a way of life I had known in childhood. It was not hard for us. Under other circumstances being in Wat Kien Svay Krao might have been enjoyable. But there was always an edge of anxiety to the waiting.

Then toward the end of April I found a distant cousin who said he had seen my family. I went at once where he directed, to a section of the crowded wat courtyard I had not explored before. I spotted two of the family's gasoline trucks, piled with luggage and crates of live chickens. How could I have missed them before? As I pushed through the crowd Pheng Huor came up to me. "Where were you?" he said with a hint of annoyance, as if I had kept him waiting for a meeting. Then his smile showed through. "Everybody's been looking for you. Did you see Huoy?"

"No, I lost her. Where's Papa?"

Pheng Huor pointed to a makeshift tent made from a tarpaulin suspended beneath a tree. I went inside. My father was sitting at a table. Same old Papa, bags under his eyes and big protruding belly. He was dressed in a faded T-shirt and shorts. His face was spread in a broad smile.

"Why didn't you come home?" he said. "Everyone was looking for you. We waited for you until almost three in the afternoon. We couldn't wait any longer. The Khmer Rouge pushed us to leave home. Are you alone?"

"No, Father, I brought eight nurses and a guard from my clinic, but I haven't found Huoy yet." My brothers and their wives crowded into the tent. My mother came up next to me. Her hair was in a bun and she seemed to have more white hairs than before.

"Yes, we didn't know what would happen to your nurses," my mother was saying in her kindly fashion. "I was worried about them. They don't have any other men to take care of them."

"Do you have enough rice?" my father was saying at the same time. I said we did. He reached in his pocket and counted off fifty thousand riels. I took the money to please him and then asked him if he would like to come live in a house instead of a tent. The family in the house above the nurses and me was planning to leave soon. He said he would like that very much.

In a few days, my parents, three of my four brothers and their wives and children moved into the house above. They were all that was left of the immediate family—my number-one brother had been estranged from my father for several years, and my sisters were all with their husbands' families.

Their new house had a normal rural Cambodian design. It was eight or nine feet off the ground on its stilts. The interior had springy wooden floorboards; a long, low, elevated sleeping platform where they could spread their mats and hang their mosquito nets; and a kitchen in back whose floor and walls had generous-size cracks to allow air ventilation. My brothers and the drivers pushed the vehicles over from the wat and parked them in front of the house—the two gasoline trucks with the empty tanks on the back, plus a Land-Rover, a jeep and a Mercedes. The drivers, their wives and children and most of the servants remained in the wat courtyard, where there was more space.

Now that I was reunited with my family I was nearly content. Family is the glue that holds society together. Life makes more sense for being connected to the past through parents, and to the future through children. Being together also had its practical benefits. For one, more people to rely on in case of emergencies. For another, more food, because my family had stockpiled food and taken it with them from the city. And finally, I had gained face for bringing the family into the house, because I had done my duty as a son; and my father had gained face because I had put him literally above me.

And yet I was not truly content. Huoy was alive. Or at least probably alive, because she was not the troublemaking kind, and the Khmer Rouge would have left people like her and her mother alone. But how could anyone like me, who had seen Sam Kwil hauled away, feel sure of this? And if Huoy were alive, where was she now? What if she had gotten to the Route 2 turnoff before it was closed? Then she would have gone to my father's sawmill, or to my village. She would be waiting for me there. What if she hadn't been swept up in the southern evacuation at all? She and her mother lived along the road to the west, which led to the airport. She could have gone that way. Or she might have gone to the south after all. I might have missed her, just as I had missed spotting my family for more than a week in Wat Kien Svay Krao.

Wat Kien Svay Krao was becoming a less and less attractive place.

The weather was still hot, and most people camped on mats in the shade. At every campfire, people waved vigorously above their plates to keep the flies away. From radios came reports that the North Vietnamese communists were closing in on the capital of South Vietnam, Saigon. The news made us feel more isolated from the outside world than ever. High overhead, the sonic boom of the U.S. reconnaissance planes could still be heard. We had hoped that the United States would come to our aid, but if it let South Vietnam fall, it certainly wouldn't help us in Cambodia.

My father was more stoic than most. "Yes," he said in his deep voice, "it's the end of the old life. Now everyone will be the same class. Just like in China."

He turned to me accusingly. "You should have left the country earlier, when you had a chance. I told you to go to medical school in France, but you wouldn't listen to me."

"Father," I said, exasperated, "when Samrong Yong fell, *I* told *you* to sell all your property and leave the country. You could have lived abroad comfortably for the rest of your life. But now it's too late. And it's all because *you* didn't listen to *me*."

Before long, my father and I were back into our usual arguments. And if the bickering in my family and the tedium of the long days weren't enough, my group of ten from the clinic began to split up. They had become like a second family to me. Srei, who had found her real family, was the first to go. I gave her medicine and rice. I gave her money. Somehow nothing was enough. I was upset when she left, and the rest of the nurses were crying. They had worked together for years in harmony and *bonheur*. And soon after that a second nurse left.

I went back to walking around without a destination and without real hope. Out of habit, I trudged through the dirt lanes of the village to the wat, and from the wat again over to Route 1. By then the crowds coming from Phnom Penh had thinned. I was outside the village, wearing a checkered krama around my head, when a familiar-sounding voice reached my ears. "Sweet!" the woman's voice said. "Sweet! Mother, I've found him!"

How she could have recognized me I do not know. She was on the other side of the road, with her left hand steadying a bamboo basket on her head with two water bottles inside, and with her right hand carrying a plastic-covered pail. "Mother, I've found him. Sweet, sweet!" She was wearing an old green T-shirt and white trousers with a floral print. Her mother was carrying a basket on her head and steadying it with her left hand while carrying a rice pot in her right hand. They looked tired and dusty. Huoy put her basket down and ran to me. We wrapped our arms around each other. She didn't say anything and her chest heaved uncontrollably; she couldn't get any words out. Her mother came up to us with her eyes glistening and said in a choked voice, "We were looking for you."

I said, "I was looking for you too. Where were you? Are you okay?" Huoy nodded but didn't let go.

We moved to the edge of the road. Ma brought the luggage over and then squatted next to us, using the edge of her krama to wipe away her tears, while Huoy and I embraced.

"We looked for you everywhere," said Ma. "We didn't know where you were. We were scared you had been killed by the Khmer Rouge. We saw a lot of bodies with their hands tied behind their backs."

Huoy and I wanted to hug forever, but our culture does not allow such things in public. A crowd had collected around us, curious about the emotional outburst. Someone asked if everything was okay. Another voice commented, "How lucky they are! They met each other again, and I'm still separated from my family!"

I picked up the luggage and we walked through the village to the house. As soon as we got to the house I walked up the steps, kicked off my sandals and stepped inside. My father was resting.

"Huoy is here," I told him.

My mother's aged face creased into a smile. "Prepare lunch for them," she called back to the women in the kitchen.

My father sat up with an unmistakable look of gladness in his face. "Prepare a feast!" he shouted. And he rose to go outside.

Huoy waited at the bottom of the stairs. "How are you?" my father asked, smiling, as he and my mother went down to meet her. Huoy had brought her palms together and raised them to her forehead. With her left foot in front of her right she began to kneel. Her right knee was about to touch the ground when my father got to her and raised her by gently putting his hand under her elbow.

My brothers, their wives and the nurses had all seen Huoy try to kneel in front of my father and it touched their hearts. Everybody was crying. My mother said to Huoy's mother, "You are coming here to live with us. Don't worry. We are safe here." The servants were hurrying out of the house with water and food.

At last I was whole. Huoy was with me. And my family had taken her in.

10

MEDICINE FOR ANGKA

THIS IS what happened to Huoy during the Khmer Rouge takeover:

After I left her at her school on that fateful morning of April 17, Huoy discovered that the school was closed. The other teachers hadn't shown up, the doors were locked and the sounds of gunfire were coming from several directions. By good luck she found a telephone that was still working, and she called Sok, my driver. Sok picked her up in the car and brought her back to her mother's apartment. By then it was about eight-thirty and everybody knew that the city was about to fall. People were waving white cloth from the windows. The guerrillas had entered the streets in their muddy black clothing. Huoy told Sok to go to his own home and bring his family back to her apartment so that everybody could be together, for protection. He agreed and drove off.

While Huoy was waiting upstairs with her mother, the Khmer Rouge on the street started shouting for everyone to leave the city. Huoy didn't want to go, of course. But an hour passed and then another and still Sok hadn't returned. Finally about noon two heavily armed guerrillas entered the house on the ground floor, walked up the stairs banging on the landings and finally knocked on the door of their apartment on the third floor. So Huoy and her mother had only a few minutes to grab some possessions while the guerrillas stood there waiting and yelling at them.

Huoy went into the kitchen and collected all the food she could find, plus a rice pot and two bottles of boiled drinking water. Then she gathered every photograph she had of me, even some ID cards I had left there with my picture on them, and put them in her bag. Last she grabbed a small, soft pillow that she always slept with. Her mother packed a few clothes in a basket. They left and locked the door, the soldiers following them downstairs. Huoy wanted to go to my parents' house, but the street traffic was one way in the wrong direction and they had to go south.

Huoy was determined to find me. With the streets in chaos, her instinct was to go someplace where I would be likely to show up sooner or later. Since she couldn't get to my parents' house she decided to try my clinic. If that didn't work she would go to the sawmill and then to my village. She brought the photos of me so she could show them to people and ask them if they had seen me. That was how her mind worked. It was only later that she realized that she had left her gold and jewelry behind in the apartment. She had completely forgotten about her valuables.

She and her mother got near my clinic but were unable to reach it because of the roadblocks. Like me, Huoy walked back and forth, with and against the flow of people trudging on foot with their belongings, pushing their motorcycles and cars. But when she tried to cut across the flow and dodge into a side street a Khmer Rouge cadre came up to her and waved his pistol in her face: "Do you want to sleep here? I'll give you an appointment to sleep here!" he shouted. Huoy's bravery melted on the spot. To "sleep" meant to die. She allowed her mother and herself to be swept along with the traffic. They were just two more pieces of human wreckage floating out of the city with the tide, and nothing more. They found the turnoff to National Route 2 blocked off, and they were swept over the Monivong bridge and down National Route 1. They were a few days behind me on the same evacuation route out of Phnom Penh.

I listened to her story and sighed inwardly. We were together again—that was the most important thing. Looking at her, dressed in the same grimy trousers and blouse she had worn since the day of the evacuation, I wished that she had remembered to bring more of her possessions. But that's how she was, losing her composure when anybody started shouting. There was no point in being angry with her. And how could I be angry with her when one of the few things she had remembered to bring were photographs of me?

Huoy and her mother moved in—with me, Thoeun my guard from the clinic, and the remaining nurses, under the house on stilts that I had commandeered for my family. We had no privacy. I continued to sleep alone on top of the oxcart. But there was a change. Tacitly, without announcement, it became understood that Huoy and I were the same as husband and wife. Without any formal ceremony, we had become a married couple. The nurses treated Huoy with respect and consideration. My parents, my brothers and their wives all were very kind to Huoy, at least for the time being.

But now that my personal worries were over—finding my family, finding Huoy and finally getting my parents to accept Huoy—I was able to take a larger view of our situation, and I didn't like it. True, we were lucky to be alive and together. Around us in the village of Wat Kien Svay Krao were thousands of Cambodians separated from the people they loved, wandering around lost and unhappy, not knowing what the next hour held or where they would find their next meal. My family was very lucky in comparison to other families nearby. On the other hand, all our efforts to make a place for ourselves over the preceding years had been for nothing. All our hard work at the lumber mill, all my studying at school. We had not been in favor of the revolution. We had not been against it. We didn't even care about politics much. But now that the revolution had come, we had been bulldozed by it, reduced to the same level as the other exiles around us. And there was no new society building. Just the rubble of the old one.

A few months before the takeover I had finally been awarded my degree from the government medical school, the culmination of seven years' effort. Outside of my work for the government, I was the main practitioner in and part owner of a prosperous gynecological clinic. What good was my medical training now, when the Khmer Rouge wanted to kill doctors?

I had also been a businessman, owner of a gasoline delivery service. I had seventeen million riels in the bank in savings, enough at pre-revolutionary prices to buy a couple more gasoline delivery trucks for my fleet. What was that worth now, if it was worth anything at all? The Khmer Rouge did not seem to use any currency at all. Would they let me return to my bank to claim my savings? With every day it seemed less likely. Every day they announced through loudspeakers that we would have to go to the countryside.

Our only usable assets were those we had with us: two gasoline trucks, the Mercedes, the Land-Rover and the jeep. They were all worthless now, unless the situation changed. My little Vespa too. There was no more gasoline to be bought or bartered for. And then it hit me. Barter—that was the key. In an uncertain future, we needed things to barter with. But what did we have to offer?

Gold and jewelry would be useful, gold especially, for everyone recognized its value. Medicine would be valuable too. We needed medicine for ourselves, to protect against infections, malaria and all the other ills of a tropical climate. The medicine we did not use we could barter with. I had brought the medicine from the clinic, but we needed more.

We needed clothes too. Not just for barter but for wearing. I still had on the black trousers I had worn on April 17, along with the woman's blouse I had taken after somebody in the hospital had stolen my shirt. Huoy didn't have fresh clothes either. Already we looked like the rest of the refugees. I had brought a pile of sarongs from the clinic but those wouldn't help much. What could we do? The cars and trucks in front of the house looked more and more like useless sculpture, like monuments to the past. But it was a past I was unwilling to abandon. We had worked too hard to become rich to leave all our wealth behind.

Sitting on the oxcart under the house I realized that, somehow, I was going to have to get back to Phnom Penh.

Every morning the local Khmer Rouge soldiers assembled to recite their code of behavior, which went like this:

1. Thou shalt love, honor and serve the workers and peasants.
2. Thou shalt serve the people wherever thou goest, with all thy heart and with all thy mind.
3. Thou shalt respect the people without injury to their interests, without touching their goods or plantations, forbidding thyself to steal so much as one pepper, and taking care never to utter a single offensive word against them.
4. Thou shalt beg the people's pardon if thou hast committed some error respecting them. If thou hast injured the interests of the people, to the people shalt thou make reparation.

5. Thou shalt observe the rules of the people when speaking, sleeping, walking, standing or seated, in amusement or in laughter.
6. Thou shalt do nothing improper respecting women.
7. In food and drink thou shalt take nothing but revolutionary products.
8. Thou shalt never gamble in any way.
9. Thou shalt not touch the people's money. Thou shalt never put out thy hand to touch so much as one tin of rice or pill of medicine belonging to the collective goods of the state or the ministry.
10. Thou shalt behave with great meekness toward the workers and peasants, and the entire population. Toward the enemy, however, the American imperialists and their lackeys, thou shalt feed thy hatred with force and vigilance.
11. Thou shalt continually join the people's production and love thy work.
12. Against any foe and against every obstacle thou shalt struggle with determination and courage, ready to make every sacrifice, including thy life, for the people, the workers and peasants, for the revolution and for Angka, without hesitation and without rest.

Every morning, when the recitation was over, the same young Khmer Rouge soldier shuffled out of the line and walked to our vicinity of the village, to keep watch over us. He slept each night in a hammock slung from the poles of an open-sided shed behind our house. He wore an old green Chinese-made uniform with a Mao-style hat. His trousers had a hole in the seat. There were rips along the cuffs and more rips at his elbows and collar. There was no pen in his pocket, meaning he was the lowest grade of soldier, like a private.

In spite of his shabby appearance he was full of revolutionary fervor. Several times a day when the mood struck him he fired his AK-47 into the air and began yelling slogans: "Long live our victory! Down with U.S. imperialism! Long live the independent, peaceful, neutral, nonaligned, sovereign, uh, peace, uh, peaceful, neutral Cambodia!" He usually stumbled over the longer slogans because he wasn't very bright and he didn't know what some of the words meant. His rifle fire made us nervous, but gradually we realized that he didn't mean us any harm. He had a wide, round, smiling Cambodian face. Beneath the tattered uniform and the political indoctrination was an uneducated country boy.

I never learned his name, so I just called him *mit*, meaning comrade. He began to hang around the house, attracted to the sight of all the young women. He was never rude or suggestive to them—the Khmer Rouge soldiers usually obeyed that part of their code.

Still, to be on the safe side, I instructed Huoy and the nurses to be careful. They were to do nothing to suggest that I had ever been a doctor. They weren't to talk to him at all, unless he said something to them first. When they cooked food they were to eat immediately, to avoid having to invite him to join. Instead, they were to set food aside for him. When I returned from wherever I had gone, I took the food out to the *mit* and he and I ate together. If there was going to be any trouble for my house, I was going to be the lightning rod.

The strategy worked. If the *mit* had something to say to the household, he said it to me, as the spokesman. We never had problems. And on several occasions he brought us vegetables and pork, in the spirit of "serving the people." The nurses prepared the food, and I made sure he got generous portions.

I tried to get closer and closer to the *mit*. I reasoned that if the Khmer Rouge sent us out into the country to live, he might become our supervisor. If that happened, perhaps he would give us easy work assignments. I tailored the way I spoke with him—polite but friendly, in an accent that closely matched his. Though I never asked him personal questions, I guessed he was from Svay Rieng Province, on the Vietnamese border. Many of the villages in Svay Rieng had been leveled in the fighting and bombing, just as my village had been. He had been swept into the war, like me. The only difference was that he had been swept into the other side.

"What about Angka's plan for the nation?" I asked him one evening as we settled down to eat. He took out his spoon, wiped it on his torn trousers and reached for the rice. Next to his rifle, his spoon was his favorite possession. It was U.S.–military issue, made of stainless steel that would last forever without rusting. Khmer Rouge soldiers, who never used forks or knives for eating, always valued the U.S. spoons highly, which was strange considering how much they hated the United States.

"There were too many people in the city," the *mit* said with his mouth full. "Maybe Angka will have to push them to work as farmers. Angka has a new doctrine, for building a new society."

He wasn't telling me anything I hadn't heard before. I decided to prod him gently.

"Who *is* Angka, comrade brother?" I said.

"I don't know," said the *mit*. The question didn't bother him. He didn't seem to have thought of it before.

"Did you see Angka during the years of fighting against the capitalists?"

"No, I've never seen Angka. But I hear about Angka all the time." He piled more rice and pork on his spoon and put it in his mouth.

That was as much as I ever learned from him about the leadership of the Khmer Rouge.

A few days later the *mit* came around and saw us sitting underneath the house in the shade. Two more of my nurses had found their families. In preparing to leave, they had spread the medicine from the clinic on top of the oxcart and were helping themselves to their share.

"So much medicine, eh?" said the *mit*. "What sickness can you use it for?"

The nurses told him the medicines could treat many kinds of illness. I was sitting nearby, pretending I knew nothing about the matter. The *mit* picked up some glass ampules with clear liquids inside—for vitamin injections, as I could tell at a glance—and asked me what they were for. With a vague wave of my hand I answered that the medicines on the oxcart could treat any disease he could think of.

He sat down next to me. "Do you have any serum for transfusions?" he asked. Serum was the general term for liquids to be injected intravenously into patients, everything from glucose and saline solutions to vitamins to blood products. A picture flashed through my mind of liquids traveling down IV tubes into the arms of unconscious patients. In the hospitals I had hooked up IV tubes countless times.

"We have all kinds of medicines here," I said, as carelessly as I could.

"Can I have some?" the *mit* said. "Angka doesn't have any. When we give transfusions we have to use coconut juice."

I tried to ignore what he said about coconut juice. I told him evenly, "Sure, you can have serum. I've got a lot of it. But I didn't bring it here. If you come to my house in Phnom Penh I will give you as much as you want. If you have some way to get back to town I'll give you any kind of medicine you need. No problem at all."

A thoughtful expression crossed the *mit*'s face. He asked me if I were really serious. "Sure," I said. "Friends of mine gave me lots of medicine. Plenty of it. We kept it at home for our family use. If I had a way to get back to Phnom Penh I'd give you as much as you want."

The *mit* said he would find out about the matter and walked off. I wondered if he actually had a way to get back to Phnom Penh. It was worth trying, anyway.

Then my mind turned to thinking about coconut juice. Flowing into human veins? Coconut juice! Like something monkeys would use if they were playing at being doctors!

Then, as I thought about it more, I realized that coconut juice might work under certain emergency conditions.

When a green coconut is still growing on its tree, and a boy shinnies up the trunk and knocks it down, and then cuts off the end of its husk with a machete, he finds a watery liquid inside, a bit sweet, almost clear. This is coconut juice (as opposed to coconut milk, which comes from grinding and then straining the nut's white flesh). Rural Cambodians drink the juice all the time. It's a wholesome natural product and perfectly clean, except for the germs that come from the machete. If the juice were sweet and sterile there was no real reason why it couldn't be used as a battlefield substitute for glucose solution, to give energy to a patient too weak to feed himself. But—and it was a big "but"—I couldn't imagine the Khmer Rouge sterilizing their machetes. Drinking contaminated juice is not necessarily harmful, because the stomach can cope with many kinds of bacteria. Injecting contaminated juice into the bloodstream is another matter—it could easily be lethal to a patient who was already weakened.

And that wasn't all. The sugar content of the juice varies from one coconut to another. I knew from childhood that coconuts two months old aren't ripe, that coconuts five months old are generally sweet and that at seven months the juice begins to sour, with white strands from the coconut flesh coagulating in it. Would Khmer Rouge medics test the juice before pouring it into the IV bags? Probably not. From what I'd seen, and from the way they'd been looking for doctors to kill in the hospital, they didn't have much respect for standard medical practices. If they wanted Western-style transfusion serum now, it was because they envied it, just as they envied American-made spoons. Not to mention because their wounded soldiers were dying from coconut juice transfusions.

In my mind I saw a lingering, awful image of medics in bloody black pajamas chopping open coconuts and pouring dirty juice down IV tubes.

The next day the *mit* returned. He asked me again if I was sure that I had a lot of serum in Phnom Penh. I answered again that I had plenty and that he could take as much as he wanted if we could get back to Phnom Penh.

He asked me how we would get there.

I looked at him and shrugged nonchalantly. "Comrade, we could go together on my motor scooter, if you like," I said, as if it were the last thing that either of us wanted to do. My old white Vespa was parked under the house by the oxcart, with the red cross on the back of the seat carefully removed. "But I don't have any gas. I'd need four or five liters, at least."

In truth, I did have gas, but I had drained it from the tank and kept it hidden, in case of emergencies, along with my spark plug. Huoy and I had talked it over the night before. We had decided that it was even more important to be able to drive away on a few minutes' notice—if, say, the local Khmer Rouge started slaughtering civilians—than to go into Phnom Penh for medicine and gold. Besides, I didn't want to seem too eager to go back to Phnom Penh.

"We will go to the city tomorrow," the *mit* said flatly. Then he walked off, presumably to report to his superiors.

When he left, I took the spark plug out of hiding, cleaned it and screwed into the Vespa's cylinder. I examined the bike from one end to the other to make sure everything was in good working condition.

In the morning, the *mit* showed up with ten liters of gasoline, twice as much as we needed. What a huge amount that seemed—to me, the former owner of gasoline delivery trucks! I poured the precious fuel into the tank before he could change his mind. With him was another cadre with a torn but neatly mended Chinese-made uniform, a belt holster with pistol and a blue-and-white checkered krama knotted around his neck like a scarf. He also wore one pen in his breast pocket, meaning that he was an officer. One-Pen looked like an ordinary Cambodian, with a face that seemed normal and happy rather than cruel.

Without more talk I pushed the Vespa out from under the house and started the motor. I already felt good: For the first time since the communist takeover I would be riding the bike instead of pushing it. The nurses and my entire family looked on from a polite distance. By the pillars of the house, Huoy gave me a wide-eyed look that implored me to be careful. I winked at her, signaling not to worry. I tied my krama around my neck the way One-Pen did, hoping it would make me look a bit more like a Khmer Rouge. Then I got on and One-Pen behind me and then the *mit* on the back, all three of us jammed together. We drove off, up the dirt embankment and onto the elevated national road. As I accelerated, my krama flapped in the breeze.

A few pedestrians were still walking toward us along the highway. Transients still camped out by the thousands on either side of the road. A truck convoy appeared in the distance, grew larger and passed us, heading toward Vietnam with its mysterious hidden cargo.

I drove on through the morning heat. In half an hour we covered the distance that had taken me days to walk. Near the Monivong bridge, people still milled around, though fewer of them than before. At the edge of the bridge there stood a new checkpoint, a sandbagged machine-gun emplacement with a canvas top for a roof. Beyond it lay a double row of concertina-wire barricades, with space to pass first on one side and then the other.

I stopped at the checkpoint and cut the engine. One-Pen got off. He walked into the tent, promptly returned and got back on the Vespa.

"Comrade brother, they accepted our pass?" I asked as I started the motor again.

"No problem," he said with satisfaction. "When you come with me, it's never a problem."

We drove past the barricades and over the arching bridge. There were no civilians on it. At the highest point there was another sand-bagged machine-gun emplacement, with clear lines of fire over the bridge in both directions and over the river below. At the far end of the bridge we passed through another set of barricades and another checkpoint.

We had entered Phnom Penh.

We drove up Norodom Boulevard, where Phnom Penh's wealthiest families once lived. In a few of the houses, Khmer Rouge soldiers relaxed on upper-floor balconies. Others strolled on the streets, sidestepping the piles of trash and rubble. Debris was everywhere—bottles, books, discarded clothing, mounds of garbage, broken glass, everything imaginable. Motorcycles had been overturned and abandoned for lack of gasoline, or because nobody knew how to use them. In nearly every block we saw burned car bodies and trucks with flat tires and smashed windshields.

I reminded myself to concentrate on the mission. But the sight of the ruined boulevard made me ache with sadness. For all its faults, for all its corruption, Phnom Penh had been a lovely city. And now to empty it, to leave it to the flies—I downshifted to steer around an overturned truck, and tried again not to think about it.

The city was very quiet.

We came to another pair of concertina-wire barricades in front of Lon Nol's former residence. I slowed down, maneuvered through the gap in the first barricade and headed for the second. As I did, the *mit* on the back of the bike merrily shouted "Hello, comrade!" at a soldier on the sidewalk. The next thing I knew, the soldier had pulled his pistol out and was firing it in the air and shouting for me to stop. I braked to a halt by the second barricade.

The new soldier stalked angrily to us. I stood there facing straight ahead, my feet on the ground, my hands on the handlebars. I was only the driver. "What unit do you belong to?" he demanded.

"The 207th," One-Pen answered.

"You do, huh? Well, next time don't call out to me," the soldier said to the *mit*. "This area is under my control. I don't want any yelling from the 207th or any other unit. Do you understand?"

The *mit* said he understood. I took a deep breath and drove off. Behind me, I could hear One-Pen cursing about the units occupying Phnom Penh and how stupid and backward they were compared to his own.

One-Pen ordered me to turn down another street and I did. In the middle of the street, near the abandoned U.S. embassy, a half-dozen civilians were pushing an old car. One-Pen told me to drive up to them and I did. He got off. While the civilians stood there with their heads bowed, he yelled at them to get out of the city, that they were late, that they had to go out into the countryside, and so on. When he finished taking out his anger on these innocent people he got back on the bike. "That's better," he said with satisfaction. "Now go back the way we were going before and show me the city."

So began our tour of Phnom Penh, with me as chauffeur and guide. It was like a ghost city, with its buildings in place but its people missing. In the empty streets my Vespa's engine reverberated like the buzzing of a fly in a closed and empty room. There were no other vehicles on the streets except for the burned and overturned cars. There were no other people on the sidewalks except for the occasional Khmer Rouge walking silently in rubber-tire sandals.

I drove back up Norodom Boulevard, past the Royal Palace and then the old stadium. We came to the French embassy. Here was an unexpected sight—white-skinned Westerners on the embassy grounds, a lot of them. But there were guards outside, and I didn't dare stop to find out what was going on.

I drove past the medical school, to the Central Market and up Charles De Gaulle Boulevard. Finally I stopped the Vespa in front of Huoy's house and turned off the motor.

The street was deserted except for the three of us.

In the ground-floor cafe the tables and chairs were still neatly arranged. Nobody there either.

The city was silent except for the faint sound of gunshots in the far distance.

I locked the Vespa and beckoned the others to come along. To my surprise, I wanted them along, for protection. I unlocked the front door and we climbed the stairs, talking quietly.

As I arrived on the third floor ahead of the others, the door of the apartment across from Huoy's opened a crack. The wrinkled face of an old woman peered through. I knew her. She was the mother of a commercial pilot who had lived there.

She shut the door suddenly when she saw the two soldiers behind me. The old lady must have been hiding there since the takeover.

The Khmer Rouge heard the door shut, but they didn't investigate. They were probably as scared as I was. I unlocked Huoy's apartment, showed them inside and brought them to the glass-fronted display case I had given to Huoy long ago. "The medicine's in here," I said. "I'll get you something to carry it in."

Like someone in a light trance, who acts capably but at the same time watches his own actions with detachment, I found a zippered flight bag for them and a big duffel bag for myself. They squinted at the bottles' labels, which were in French. Meanwhile I reached down to the bottom shelf among the cleaning rags and found a rolled-up black cloth. It was heavy. Inside was the gold.

"What are in all these bottles?" One-Pen said to me.

I palmed the gold and crossed the room to Huoy's dresser with the duffel bag. "I'm not exactly sure, comrade. Why don't we just take what we can now and figure out what it is later?" I wrapped the black cloth in one of Huoy's blouses and stuffed it in the bottom of the bag. Then I found her jewelry box and put that in the bag. I put as many of her clothes as would fit on top of that. I fastened the duffel bag shut. It had taken only a minute. The Khmer Rouge were still taking medicine from the shelves and putting it in the flight bag, but they were hurrying. They didn't want to stay in the apartment longer than necessary either.

On the way out I took a tin of cookies from the table and gave it to the soldiers, as a gift. They wanted to know what it was. I explained that cookies were a kind of Western cake. Poisonous? they wanted to know. I ate a cookie to show them. Then they each had a cookie and smiles spread across their faces. I don't think they'd ever had any kind of sugared pastry before.

We clattered down the steps to the street, ignoring the old lady in the other third-floor apartment. I started the Vespa, put the duffel bag on the floor of the scooter between my feet, and we drove off toward my bachelor apartment while I mentally rehearsed what I was going to do.

When we got there I locked my scooter again, an irrational act considering that nobody was around to steal it. We went inside. Arriving at the medicine cabinet ahead of the others, I reached on top of it and closed my fingers around a heavy gold ring. I put it in my pocket. Then I started shoveling the medicine out onto the floor and suggested that they just take it now and sort it back in the village.

When they were busy once again, I went across to my clothes bureau. In the top drawer were several sets of handworked Cambodian betel boxes, each box with an animal, like a tiger or elephant or crocodile, in raised relief. More barter objects. I wrapped them in clothes and put them in the duffel bag. In another drawer was an envelope with twenty-six hundred dollars in U.S. currency. That too. Then I opened the bureau drawers and stuffed the clothes into the bag—all except for the bottom drawer, which held my military uniforms. Finally I grabbed both sides of the bag, pushed the load down with my foot so everything would fit, and fastened the snap. One-Pen held up a plastic IV bag with liquid inside and asked me if it was serum. I told him maybe, but we could find out for sure back at Wat Kien Svay Krao.

They were squatting in front of a pile of pills, ointments, solutions and lotions, the *mit*'s AK-47 beside him on the floor. They didn't have much room left in their flight bag. I took a towel and selected what I wanted most: antibiotics for infections, chloroquine for malaria, antidysentery and antidiarrhea pills, vitamins, Mercurochrome for cuts, Xylocain and syringes for pain-killing injections. I worked fast, tying the towel into a bundle. One-Pen was picking up one medicine bottle after another uncomprehendingly, puzzling over the letters of the Roman alphabet, trying to figure out what pills did by their shape or color. The *mit* had already given up.

"Have you got water here?" the *mit* asked.

"Yes, comrade. Help yourself," I said absently.

I helped One-Pen finish packing while the *mit* went off to find a drink. Then from the bathroom came a sound of gushing water and the *mit* cursing in a loud voice. I went into the bathroom to look. Sure enough, the *mit*'s chest and shoulders were drenched. He hadn't known that if he turned the faucet underneath the shower head, water would come out. He looked at the sink but decided not to risk it, because the sink had faucets too. Then he spotted water in plain sight and bent down and cupped his hands to drink it. He lifted water from the toilet bowl to his lips and slurped it gratefully. "Tastes just like water from a well," he remarked. Then he bent down with his hands cupped and got some more. When he stood up he was licking his lips, a contented man. He had figured out how to use a Western-style bathroom.

I wanted to laugh. I wanted to laugh out loud, to break the tension. But I kept my jaws clamped shut and said nothing. And at the same time I felt sorry and disgusted that this poor rural boy didn't know what toilets were for.

We left my apartment. I took my medicines from the towel and repacked them in the luggage compartment on the left side of my Vespa. I put the duffel bag between my feet again. We drove off, the engine echoing through the silent streets.

We were on our way back.

In a few blocks we came to an abandoned school. Before the takeover it had been called Lycée Tuol Svay Prey. Now there was nobody in it. Weeds grew knee-high in the schoolyard. We didn't stop there, nor did I give it a close look at the time. But later that year the Khmer Rouge security police took it over and turned it into a prison. They called it S-21, and later it was also called Tuol Sleng. It became a symbol of Khmer Rouge atrocities, just as Auschwitz was a symbol of the Nazi regime.

We drove south on Monivong, the noise of the engine unnaturally loud in the empty boulevard. We came to the Faculty of Law, which the Khmer Rouge had taken over as a barracks. Soldiers were eating meals, squatting in front of cooking fires with their mess kits. They stopped us out in the street. But One-Pen told them, "It's just medicine for Angka." And I nodded my head vigorously and said, "Yes, medicine for Angka."

American-made trucks captured from the Lon Nol regime were pulling up to the Faculty of Law compound just then. Khmer Rouge soldiers stood in back of the trucks, waving to their comrades inside the compound, glad to come into Phnom Penh from the dull countryside. "Bravo! Bravo!" they were shouting. "Long live our splendid victory over the imperialists! Long live the Kampuchean revolution!" This time, I noticed, the *mit* kept his mouth grimly shut, even though he shouted the same slogans in Wat Kien Svay Krao. There was rivalry between his unit and others.

I drove the Vespa down the boulevard, over the Monivong bridge, and onto National Route 1. It was late afternoon. I had accomplished much. I had gotten clothes for Huoy and myself. Gold and silver and medicine for trading. In a subtle way I had even struck back at the Khmer Rouge for what they were doing to my family and to our society. The tension I had felt since morning was giving way to elation.

We ran into checkpoints along the road, but at each of them I yelled, "Medicine for Angka!" and we passed easily.

11

RETURN TO THE VILLAGE

AFTER I CAME BACK from Phnom Penh, Thoeun and the four remaining nurses asked me whether they could return to their villages. To them I was still the boss, the *luk* doctor, which was why they asked permission. The revolution had not yet "liberated" their minds.

I told them to go ahead. And why not? The war was over. The country was at peace. It was time for them to reunite with their families and return to their ancestral villages. Thoeun left first. I saw him off at the riverbank, grinning, his head still twitching from side to side. He pushed his motorcycle down the gangplank and onto a cargo boat and vanished in the crowd of passengers. The boat, with a red flag flying from its cabin, chugged into the Mekong's main current and slowly upstream.

Then the nurses left, on foot, with their bundles balanced on their heads. I wasn't worried about their safety. The Khmer Rouge didn't rape or rob, and everyone else was so afraid of the Khmer Rouge that there was little crime. But I was sad. Their departure tore a little more of the past away, and I preferred the past to the present.

The nurses were taking a roundabout route to Takeo Province: first north on National Route 1 toward Phnom Penh, then west on a dirt road to the Bassac River, across the Bassac by boat and finally south on National Route 2. Many others from Takeo were going the same way, and Wat Kien Svay Krao was gradually emptying.

Now the rest of us had to decide what to do. We had our gold and our medicine. There were no more reasons for staying. It was time for us to leave, to choose a destination before the Khmer Rouge chose one for us.

Huoy, her mother and I decided to go to the Changs' home province of Kampot, southwest of Takeo along the Gulf of Siam. A cousin of Huoy's made regular trips to Thailand by boat, or used to before the revolution. She thought we could go with him. That was our final destination, Thailand, Cambodia's neighbor to the west. It was a Buddhist country, with a culture much like our own. It was also an American ally, in no danger of going communist. If we could only get there, we would be free. We didn't want to live under Khmer Rouge rule, or under any communist regime. We had heard that Saigon, the capital of South Vietnam, had fallen to the communists. South Vietnam, Cambodia, even Laos—one after another, all the countries nearby were falling to communism, except for Thailand.

My father had another plan. He wanted the whole family to go back with him to the lumber mill. He said that the Khmer Rouge would need someone like him, the former owner, to run it. If he couldn't run the mill we would all follow him to the town of his birth, called Tonle Batí, which was near Samrong Yong but had better soil and more water for farming.

I didn't like his plan. Whether we went with him to the lumber mill or to Tonle Batí, it would leave us under Khmer Rouge control. I told him we would go with him to the mill and then decide what to do from there. After all, if we could get to the lumber mill, we were also going in the right direction for Kampot.

The compromise didn't please him. It didn't please me much either. But in truth I was of two minds about staying with my family. The good feelings when Huoy returned had given way to the usual quarreling. My brother's wife, Nay Chhun, barely spoke to me, and she was always being nasty to Huoy because Huoy and I weren't officially married. The whole family was on edge, and the reason was uncertainty. We did not know what life under the Khmer Rouge was going to be. It was just as well that we were leaving.

We left in the morning—the entire Ngor family, the two Chang women and I, plus the entourage of servants and drivers and their children. We were thirty-odd people in all, with two trucks, two four-wheel-drive vehicles, a car and a motor scooter. Behind my motor scooter was the cart that Thoeun and I had taken from the clinic.

Each vehicle had half a tank of fuel. We pushed them along National Route 1, to save gas. Later, we turned onto the dirt road and the wheels got stuck in sand, we started the motors. The men pushed harder, the motors roared, and the wheels spun around, sending plumes of sand to the rear. Once the vehicles were free, we turned the engines off and pushed again. I pushed the Vespa by the handlebars, and Huoy pushed it from the back of the trailer, which carried our luggage. It seemed like a dream, that I had actually ridden the Vespa to and from Phnom Penh.

It was hard work, pushing. The weather had that almost unbearable humidity that comes in the last months before the rainy season, when the sky turns hazy white and the sun is like an oven. Slowly we passed blown-up houses and decapitated palm trees. The landscape was empty of people except for city exiles like ourselves, walking or pushing cars along the dusty road.

On the third day we reached the Bassac River, a lazy, muddy channel sunk far down in its banks. We camped by the riverbank next to a house belonging to my aunt on my father's side. The roof and the upper story of her house had been destroyed in the war and she was living on the ground floor in a tent supported by the concrete columns. My aunt was glad to see us. She prepared the best meal she could under the circumstances, using fish from the river and fresh fruit picked from trees.

Next we had to find out how to cross the river. Pheng Huor went out on a bicycle to explore, and he found four pirogues, about the size of canoes, whose owners were willing to work for us. But the boatmen wouldn't accept Lon Nol currency in payment, no matter how much he offered. They wanted fifteen cans of rice per boat trip, using cans from Nestlé's evaporated milk as a measure. It was the first time I had heard of using rice as money, but it made sense. Everyone needed and used rice. It was the perfect medium of exchange.

Because the boats were small, we could take only the lightest vehicles across the river. Papa decided to leave everything but the jeep behind with his sister. Pushing them had been exhausting anyway. He also decided it was time to let the drivers and their families go off on their own. He gave them money and food and they went off after saying their farewells. And it was a sad, scaled-down expedition that traveled across the river: the jeep, with each wheel riding in a separate small boat, the boatmen poling their way across; the Ngors and the Changs and all the extra gasoline and the supplies; and finally my Vespa and its trailer.

By the time we unloaded everything on the other bank we were tired and short-tempered. We camped and made a fire. When Pheng Huor's daughter Ngim upset a cooking pot, I cuffed her on the head. The girl's mother, Nay Chhun, shook her finger in my face, which is very rude in our culture, and told me never to touch her children again. I said that if her children needed lessons in behavior I had the right to teach them. I lost my temper, she lost hers and soon we were shouting at each other at the top of our lungs. A Khmer Rouge soldier came over to stop us.

"No yelling!" he said. "Angka doesn't allow people fighting each other! If you don't stop I will bring both of you to *Angka Leu.*"

I had never heard of Angka Leu. It means "higher organization" in our language, and nothing more. But the way the soldier said it suggested that Angka Leu was something to fear. Nay Chhun retreated, muttering and flashing nasty glances. When I had calmed down, Huoy told me not to discipline Nay Chhun's children even if they needed it. Whatever Angka Leu was, Huoy said, it was best to avoid it.

We never did get to my father's sawmill. There was a bridge between it and National Route 2, and the soldiers wouldn't let us cross. Papa tried telling them that he wanted to get the mill working to help the regime, but they wouldn't even listen.

Even before we reached the bridge, however, I had decided to leave. I had no problem with respecting the family hierarchy, in theory. Life means being part of a family. The older members are in charge, and every individual works together harmoniously to benefit the whole. But in practice it was one problem after another. If I wasn't quarreling with Papa it was with my older brother, and if it wasn't with him it was with his wife. Much of the quarreling was my own fault, but that didn't make it any easier. For all my maturing as an adult, inside I was still the hyperactive, hot-tempered boy with the short fuse. My instincts told me to get away from my family, just as my instincts told me to get away from the Khmer Rouge. I had to live on my own terms.

As Papa sat glumly by the roadblock, I explained to him that we had to go. Reluctantly he gave his permission. When the good-byes were over, Huoy, her mother and I found ourselves walking down National Route 2.

We had walked for an hour when three Khmer Rouge with rifles stopped us. They were children, maybe ten years old. They didn't search our bodies—that was against their code—but they went through the luggage in the cart behind the Vespa. They didn't find the medicine, which I had hidden inside the rice supply, but they did find my camera, some medical equipment and my medical textbooks.

One of the child-soldiers opened a textbook and saw the type printed in the Roman alphabet. My medical books were all in French.

"You are CIA," he remarked in his high-pitched voice.

It took me a second to follow his train of thought: Since I had a book in a foreign language, I was working for foreigners. This made me an agent of the CIA.

"Eh?" I said. "What does it mean, 'CIA,' comrade? I have never heard of it before."

"Where did you get the books?" he demanded suspiciously. He picked up a speculum and some surgical clamps. "And what are these for?"

I said, "I don't know. People were throwing them away on the street, so I picked them up and kept them. The same with the books. If you want any of them, keep them. I don't know how to read anyway. I was just going to use the paper from the books to wrap things in."

One of the other soldiers said to the first one, "Ah, yes, good idea. We can use the paper for rolling cigarettes."

The first one tossed my pharmacology textbook and two pathology books to his comrade, who ripped out a page, tore it into quarters, sprinkled tobacco on the paper, rolled a cigarette and lit it with a gold lighter.

"Angka needs these too," said the first soldier, grabbing a handful of medical instruments.

Then they let us go and began to search people who had arrived after us.

We walked on. We came to other checkpoints and were told to turn off the highway, to begin farming nearby. Fortunately I knew the names of all the villages, and at each checkpoint managed to convince the soldiers that we were going to the next village farther on.

The next afternoon we reached Samrong Yong. At the north end of the village, a few houses still had parts of their roofs intact and others had walls or concrete supporting columns, but none of them was whole. The market in the center of the village was gone, except for a few smashed wooden benches among the knee-high weeds. The old French-built blockhouse wasn't there and neither were the trees. Everything had been flattened. All the landmarks had vanished. I couldn't even find my family's home.

Then I saw it: concrete walls that had toppled over and lay flat, like giant playing cards. Grass grew in the cracks of the walls, and the garden was buried in weeds.

We camped that night on the fallen-over walls. There were no other people nearby. No dogs to bark, no roosters to crow. The village was as quiet as if it had been abandoned a hundred years before. A lone Khmer Rouge, a child, sat at the road intersection with his rifle.

Before the revolution, most Cambodians felt a strong loyalty to their home villages. Even those who moved away to a big city like Phnom Penh continued to identify with the place of their birth, which inevitably had an accent all its own, different even from the accent of the next village over. Samrong Yong was home. It was an extension of my family. To see it destroyed was almost like seeing my own family dead. I tried to keep my grief hidden from Huoy and her mother so they wouldn't be saddened, but they must have known what I felt.

From Samrong Yong we went to Chambak, the next town. There was nothing left of it except staircases rising into empty air.

An hour's walk beyond Chambak we came to another checkpoint, manned by young, barefoot Khmer Rouge. For the first time they asked me my profession. I said I had been a taxicab driver in Phnom Penh. Then they asked Huoy if she had worked for the Lon Nol government. Huoy lost her presence of mind and I broke in, saying that she used to sell vegetables in the market and that her mother used to take care of our baby. Huoy, hesitating, added in a small voice, "Yes, I was a vegetable seller. My husband was a taxi driver. What he says is true."

The soldiers searched the cart again. They didn't find the rest of the medical instruments, which I had hidden underneath the cart by the axle, but they did find some of the other reference books. They took the books and threw them violently on the road. "No more capitalistic books now!" they shouted. "Capitalistic books are Lon Nol–style, and Lon Nol betrayed the nation! Why do you have foreign books? Are you CIA? No more foreign books under Angka!"

I gave them the usual story about finding the books on the road, but they didn't listen.

"Angka says no more traveling!" the soldiers said crossly. "Wherever you think you're going, whatever village you are trying to reach, it will be the same as the villages around here. They are all destroyed. So you have to stop here and go to work."

"No, please," I begged. "We have a newborn child. We got separated from it in Phnom Penh, and my sister took it to Kampot. Please, comrade, the baby has no milk! She needs her mother!"

"Angka only says once!" the soldier thundered. "No more traveling! No is no! If I chose to let you go, I would let you go, but no is no!"

We sat sadly by the side of the road as the soldiers checked families arriving at the checkpoint after us. The soldiers gave them the same treatment, the interrogations, the confiscation of their goods, the raised voices and the angry, suspicious glares. It was depressing. It was a mentality I had seen many times before, and not just under the Khmer Rouge. It was typical of uneducated Asians who were used to obeying orders from those above and giving orders to those below. There was no place in their minds for reasoning with equals. For them, even listening to us would mean deferring to us, and they could not do this without losing face.

They sent us off on a side road with the other families and with two soldiers as escorts. The dirt road quickly degenerated into a sandy oxcart path, uneven and twisting. I strained to push the cycle and the trailer through the sand and then it became easier and I looked back and saw Huoy pushing too. She was tired and sweaty, and there was a wild look in her eyes that told me she had taken a psychological beating and was on the edge of breaking down. I asked her to let me push by myself, but she said no, she wanted to help. I told her again in a firm voice not to worry, to let me push alone. Eventually she let go of the Vespa and walked with her mother, who was tired and afraid too.

The soldiers led us to a small village on the edge of the jungle. The houses were on stilts in the rural style and had not been damaged in the war. The inhabitants were *moultan chah*—"old" people or "base" people—meaning that they had consented to Khmer Rouge rule while the civil war was still being fought. Their early decision not to oppose the Khmer Rouge put them in a middle category of revolutionary society, below the Khmer Rouge themselves but above people like Huoy and me, who were *moultan thmai*, or "new" people, and at the bottom. The midlevel status of the "old" people enabled them to stay in their homes, without having to evacuate. The "old" people of this village showed us traditional Cambodian hospitality and were very kind to us. They brought us palm-tree sugar cakes to eat, and they listened with sympathy to my tale of wanting to get to Kampot to reunite with our baby. But they didn't have enough influence with the Khmer Rouge to enable us to leave.

In the morning Huoy and I were ordered to go to work, along with the other "new" people. Leaving Ma behind in our camping spot, under another house on stilts, we walked for about an hour to a mountain called Phnom Chiso. It was a place of boulders, bare rock outcroppings, scrubby brush and trees whose leaves had fallen off in the heat of the dry season. One part of the mountain was a rock quarry. I knew it well, for my father had often driven there to get loads of gravel for his truck when I was a child, and sometimes I had gone along for the ride.

The supervisor issued us ordinary-size hammers, took us to piles of fist-size rocks and told us to break the rocks down into gravel size. The gravel was going to be used as ballast on railroad tracks, he said.

We began. Chips flew off the rock when we hit it, and I told Huoy to wrap her krama around her face so it covered everything but her eyes. I did the same, and I had the additional protection of my glasses. We found that the rocks had a grain running in one direction and there was a knack to hitting them to make them split. We hammered rocks all morning and tried to avoid hitting our free hands or our faces with flying chips. There was no shade on the mountain and it was very hot.

In the early afternoon they gave us our first meal of the day, a bowl of salted rice porridge, or rice that has been boiled into a sort of mushy cereal. There was nothing else in it, no meat or vegetables to give it flavor. "Angka is poor, so you must sacrifice for your nation," the supervisor explained apologetically. "We are starting to rebuild the nation, to make it rich. We just got free from the hands of the capitalist oppressors."

I looked at my hands. At my capitalist hands. Blisters had erupted across my palms and on my fingers. Huoy's blisters were even worse. As a schoolteacher, she had never held a heavier tool than a piece of chalk. She was not used to physical labor. All morning long while she broke rocks she had been crying quietly, not just because of the hard work but because our entire universe had been turned upside down. She was a soft, shy, maternal woman, and she wanted nothing more than to have babies and stay home and run a clean, well-ordered household. And that's what I wanted for her.

We went back to work, squatting on the mountainside in the afternoon heat, hitting the rocks with our hammers. When we built up a pile of gravel I hauled it in a basket to a nearby truck. As a boy I had waited in trucks just like that while other men broke the rocks and brought them over. Back then I had taken those men for granted, but now that I was in their place I remembered them with new respect. I knew now how hard it was to break rocks for a living.

At the end of the afternoon we walked back to the village of the "old" people. Dinner was a bowl of rice and some soup with vegetables and bits of fish, not enough to replace the energy we had used, but better than lunch. We settled back to massage our blisters and rest our tired bodies, thinking that the day was over. Then a soldier came up and told us, "Angka invites you to a *bonn*."

Bonn is an ancient religious word meaning a celebration or ceremony at a temple. I asked the soldier for time to bathe and change clothes and prepare food to bring to the monks. He told us to come as we were. Huoy and I obeyed rather reluctantly, because we were dusty and dirty. He led us to a clearing in the forest and turned us over to a *mit neary*, a female comrade, who was about eighteen years old. She took us down a path farther into the forest to another clearing where about twenty other "new" people were sitting. We sat down with them in front of a big clump of bamboo.

Like the others of her kind, the *mit neary* made no attempt to look feminine or attractive. As she faced us in the fading light I saw a young woman who aspired to conform. If she had ambition, it was to obey Angka with perfect zeal. Her appearance was standard, her tunic buttoned to her neck, her hair cut short and parted in the middle with the sides tucked behind her ears. She had that same contemptuous expression toward us "new" people as most of her comrades.

She addressed us in a harsh voice, without any opening remarks or pleasantries:

"Angka won the war," she began. "Not by negotiation. Not by *sompeah*"—she gestured scornfully with her palms together—"to the Lon Nol government, or to the U.S. government, or to the other capitalists. We won by fighting!

"At the beginning we had only empty hands," she declared. "We had no rifles, no ammunition. Then we got slingshots. Bows and arrows. Crossbows. Wooden traps. Knives and hatchets. We used hoes and sticks. And we fought until we won against the capitalists! We were not afraid of the American government or the other big powers!"

What kind of folk tale is this? I wondered. They had AK-47s. They bought heavy weapons from corrupt generals of the Lon Nol regime.

The *mit neary* raised her fists and shouted, "We were like an ant that bit an elephant! The U.S. government looked down on the small ant and laughed! But then the big elephant died from our poisonous bite! We are not afraid of elephants! Or anyone else!"

A mosquito whined in my ear and settled on my cheek. I slapped it.

I had never heard anything as ridiculous as an elephant dying from an ant bite.

"We have won the revolution but the war still goes on!" she said. "Now we are in a new phase of struggle. We warn you that it will not be easy. We must maintain a mentality of *struggling against all obstacles*. If Angka says to break rocks, break rocks. If Angka says to dig canals, you must dig canals. If Angka says to farm, you must farm. Struggle against the elements! When there are obstacles, smash them. Only in this way can we liberate the country and liberate the people!"

In the brief silence that followed, I nudged Huoy and she leaned close. I whispered to her, "When do we go to the *bonn*?"

Huoy whispered back, "Be quiet."

The *mit neary* went on:

"Don't think back. Don't think about houses, or big cars, or eating noodles, or watching television, or ordering servants around. That age is over. The capitalists destroyed the country. Right now, our economy is underdeveloped and we must build it up. You must maintain a revolutionary attitude, and you must keep your mind on the guiding principles, the 'Three Mountains.' They are:

" 'Attain independence-sovereignty.' That is the first principle.

" 'Rely on our own strength.' That is the second.

"And 'Take destiny in our hands.' Those are the 'Three Mountains.' "

By then it was totally dark and mosquitoes were everywhere. I rubbed my hands over my ankles and arms and neck to protect myself. The *mit neary* talked on and on about the development of the economy and how we would all have to sacrifice. She used the same jargon over and over again about starting with an empty hand and struggling with the elements, and about the ant that killed the elephant, in case we didn't understand the first time.

It was a long evening.

When we got back to the village, at about midnight, there was no water to wash with. I felt unclean.

"Sweet," I said to Huoy, half-jokingly, "we have just taken the first step on the road to hell. We have gone to a *bonn* where all they talk about is war and economics."

For another few days, Huoy and I went off to break rocks in the mornings and we went to the so-called *bonn*s at night. But I had already begun to plan our escape. From the beams of the house above us hung a bamboo shoulderboard. I found some braided cord in a neighbor's yard and stole it. I made friends with the one dog of the village, patting him on the head and stroking his fur. On the fifth day, when the supervisor told us that Huoy's mother would have to begin working, I made the decision to leave. Ma wasn't strong enough to work with us in the quarry. And if she went off to work with us someone would be certain to search our luggage and discover the truth about our pasts.

That night, long after everyone else in the village was asleep, we packed our essential belongings into two giant bundles to hang from the ends of the shoulderboard and into smaller bundles for the women to carry. With regret, I decided to leave the Vespa and the trailer behind.

We crept out of the house in total darkness. I went off to calm the dog, who growled but didn't bark, while Huoy and her mother went on ahead. When they were out of hearing I shouldered the heavy load and hurried after them. I came to a fork in the road but didn't see them. I whispered, "Sweet! Sweet! Where are you?" The two women, who had taken the wrong fork, reappeared and we set off in the right direction. When we walked beyond the trees of the village and into the open rice fields we found ourselves in bright moonlight. The moon, which was nearly full, was over our shoulders, distinctly illuminating the checkerboard pattern of the dikes in the rice fields.

We cut across the fields. In the distance, at an angle, the headlights of truck convoys bobbed along National Route 2. Directly in front of us was a dark island of trees: another village. We detoured far around it. The dogs of the village heard us, and barked in the stillness of the night, and continued barking until we were on the other side of the village and far away.

Near National Route 2 we took a break, resting in the tall grass. The muscles on top of my shoulders were sore from carrying the heavy loads. Still, I was encouraged. I knew where we were and where the checkpoints were likely to be. The women were tired but did not complain. They trusted me to lead them. And they cared about me. Huoy's mother wrapped my shoulderboard in cloth, to cushion it, and we went on.

We walked through Chambak on the road, and then through the flat wasteland of Samrong Yong. The young Khmer Rouge who had stood sentry at the main intersection was nowhere in sight. As dawn approached we hid in the ruins of a temple outside the village. Huoy rubbed my shoulders, which were red and badly swollen on both sides.

We rested only an hour, then began walking again, up the deserted highway and then across the fields and through the forest. My shoulders hurt so much that I had to stop every few hundred yards to rest and shift the load to the other shoulder. Huoy gave me cold water compresses with her krama to soothe the pain. She was upset and it worried me that she was upset, but she kept herself under control.

We walked on and off and rested in the fields. The next morning we got to Tonle Batí, and who should we see by the ornate village gate but my father and the rest of my family and the jeep. Much had happened since I had seen them last. We had camped on the ruins of the old family home. We had tried and then abandoned our plan to leave the country by ship, because of all the checkpoints. We had begun forced labor, attended *bonn*s and escaped from the village of the "old" people. It seemed like a lifetime, but we had only been apart from my family for a little over a week.

12

THE CROCODILE LOSES ITS LAKE

THE ANCIENT TOWN of Tonle Bati lies alongside a long, thin lake of the same name. Within Cambodia, the town is famous for its temple or wat, a marvelous example of its kind. A reflecting pond with lotus plants and goldfish surrounds the wat on three sides, and on the fourth a grand stairway leads up to the entrance, with railings in the curving shape of *naga*s, or holy seven-headed serpents; the *naga*s have their hoods spread and mouths open wide to frighten off evildoers and protect those who worship inside. Next to the wat is the *sala* or hall, open on the sides, with pillars supporting a multilevel roof. Nearby stand temple outbuildings, some of them dating back to the ancient empire at Angkor seven centuries ago and made of reddish stone blocks with sculptures carved in deep relief. In one of those Angkorian buildings sits a huge, bronze Buddha figure, recently but exquisitely made. It was the statue my father brought back from Thailand on his truck when I was a boy.

The temple had the same importance to us that a large cathedral or abbey would have had in the Middle Ages in France. Parents sent their sons to the temple to learn to read and write, and to become monks temporarily in the rite of passage to manhood. The monks in turn went out in the community every morning collecting alms. In both religious and secular matters, the temple had been the center of Tonle Bati for more generations than anyone could remember. But by the time my family and I arrived there, in mid-May 1975, the

Khmer Rouge had forced the monks out of the wat, stripped them of their saffron robes and made them change into black pajamas. They said that by accepting alms the monks were parasites living off the labor of others. Or, as a *mit neary* explained to us, "The monks use other people's noses to breathe. It is Angka's rule: Breathe by your own nose."

Buddhism was the old religion we were supposed to discard, and Angka was the new "religion" we were supposed to accept. As the rainy season began—normally the time when youths from the surrounding villages would shave their heads and join the monk-hood—soldiers entered the empty wat and began removing the Buddha statues. Rolling the larger statues end over end, they threw them over the side, dumped them on the ground with heads and hands severed from the bodies, or threw them into the reflecting pond. But they could destroy only the outward signs of our religion, not the beliefs within. And even then, as I noticed with bitter satisfaction, there was one statue they did not destroy. It was the bronze Buddha, still gleaming inside the small Angkorian outbuilding. It had taken all my father's ingenuity to maneuver the heavy statue inside the narrow stone entrance. The Khmer Rouge couldn't figure how to get it out, much less smash it. They didn't have the intelligence, or the tools.

In Tonle Batí the Khmer Rouge made us go to *bonn*s, or brain-washing sessions, the same as in the village Huoy and I had just come from. They were always at night and usually in some mosquito-infested clearing in the forest. One evening, however, the Khmer Rouge leaders held a special *bonn* in the *sala* or hall next to the temple itself. We in the audience sat on the cool, smooth wooden floor. Soldiers had rigged a loudspeaker system powered by truck batteries. Standing near the microphone were cadre with the usual black cotton trousers and shirts, plus red headbands and red kramas tied like sashes around their waists. Outside, a light rain fell. One of the costumed men stepped to the microphone and spoke.

"In Democratic Kampuchea, under the glorious rule of Angka," he said, "we need to think about the future. We don't need to think about the past. You 'new' people must forget about the prerevolu-tionary times. Forget about cognac, forget about fashionable clothes and hairstyles. Forget about Mercedes. Those things are useless now. What can you do with a Mercedes now? You cannot barter for anything with it! You cannot keep rice in a Mercedes, but you can keep rice in a box you make yourself out of palm tree leaf!

"We don't need the technology of the capitalists," he went on. "We don't need any of it at all. Under our new system, we don't need to send our young people to school. Our school is the farm. The land is our paper. The plow is our pen. We will 'write' by plowing. We don't need to give exams or award certificates. Knowing how to farm and knowing how to dig canals—those are our certificates," he said.

"We don't need doctors anymore. They are not necessary. If someone needs to have their intestines removed, I will do it." He made a cutting motion with an imaginary knife across his stomach. "It is easy. There is no need to learn how to do it by going to school.

"We don't need *any* of the capitalist professions! We don't need doctors or engineers. We don't need professors telling us what to do. They were all corrupted. We just need people who want to work hard on the farm!

"And yet, comrades," he said, looking around at our faces, "there are some naysayers and troublemakers who do not show the proper willingness to work hard and sacrifice! Such people do not have the proper revolutionary mentality! Such people are our enemies! And comrades, some of them are right here in our midst!"

There was an uneasy shifting in the audience. Each of us hoped the speaker was talking about somebody else.

"These people cling to the old capitalist ways of thinking," he said. "They cling to the old capitalist fashions! We have some people among us who still wear eyeglasses. And *why* do they *use* eyeglasses? Can't they see me? If I move to slap your face"—he swung his open hand—"and you flinch, then you can see well enough. So you don't need glasses. People wear them to be handsome in the capitalistic style. They wear them because they are vain. We don't need people like that anymore! People who think they are handsome are lazy! They are leeches sucking energy from others!"

I took off my glasses and put them in my pocket. Around me, others with glasses did the same. My eyesight wasn't too bad, just a little nearsighted and astigmatic. I could still recognize people at a distance, but missed some of the details.

The speaker retreated from the microphone and stepped back into the line of cadre dressed like him, with the red kramas around their waists and the red headbands. A hiss in the loudspeaker system gave way to tape-recorded music, a strange march with chimes and gongs finishing out the phrases, the same kind of music I had heard in the exodus from Phnom Penh. Definitely music from Peking, I decided. The cadre began a stylized dance to it, raising their hands and dropping them in unison, as if using hoes. When the second stanza of the music began they changed position and mimed pulling on the handles of giant wrenches, as if tightening bolts on industrial machinery.

I watched in surprise. I had never seen a dance that glorified farm work and factory labor.

Another speech began, about the development of the economy and how we were all going to have to work hard for Angka and how laziness was our enemy. "Angka says, if you work you eat. If you cannot work you cannot eat. No one can help you." The country was going to be self-sufficient in filling all its needs. It was not going to rely on the outside world for anything.

Then the second dance began, with the same sort of alien music. This time the female comrades danced in unison, moving with masculine vigor instead of feminine grace, mimicking rice harvesters slashing rice stalks with their knives. Then came another propaganda speech, and after that came another dance, one after the next.

At the end of the last dance all the costumed cadre, male and female, formed a single line and shouted "BLOOD AVENGES BLOOD!" at the top of their lungs. Both times when they said the word "blood" they pounded their chests with their clenched fists, and when they shouted "avenges" they brought their arms out straight like a Nazi salute, except with a closed fist instead of an open hand.

"BLOOD AVENGES BLOOD! BLOOD AVENGES BLOOD! BLOOD AVENGES BLOOD!" the cadre repeated with fierce, determined faces, thumping their fists on their hearts and raising their fists. They shouted other revolutionary slogans and gave the salutes and finally ended with "Long live the Cambodian revolution!"

It was a dramatic performance, and it left us scared. In our language, "blood" has its ordinary meaning, the red liquid in the body, and another meaning of kinship or family. Blood avenges blood. You kill us, we kill you. We "new" people had been on the other side of the Khmer Rouge in the civil war. Soldiers of the Lon Nol regime, with the help of American weapons and planes, had killed many tens of thousands of Khmer Rouge in battle. Symbolically, the Khmer Rouge had just announced that they were going to take revenge.

Tonle Batí was my father's birthplace, and the place where five of his brothers and sisters returned after the fall of Phnom Penh. Papa had been very generous to them during the Lon Nol years, loaning them large amounts of money that they weren't really expected to repay. He had given the most to his younger half sister Ngor Pheck Kim, the one who had opened the business of selling American military supplies. I had helped Aunt Kim too, by giving her children and her tubercular husband free medical treatment and by allowing her to take my government-subsidized rice supply and sell it for a much higher price on the black market. I had regretted giving her the rice ever since, because I had come to think of her as a grasping, greedy and unpleasant woman.

In Phnom Penh, Aunt Kim had played up to us and flattered us. In Tonle Batí she played up to a man named Neang, an "old" person who acted as village chief for the Khmer Rouge regime. True, her friendship with him helped us at first. She got him to give my family a house to stay in until we could build houses of our own.

But Kim made me uneasy. The extended Ngor clan held a meeting with all my uncles, aunts and cousins present, many of whom I didn't really know. Kim's husband sat apart from the rest, sickly and skinny, with his long, drawn-out tubercular cough, the phlegm never clearing from his throat. One of my cousins asked the question that was on all our minds, whether it was possible to escape from Khmer Rouge rule and go to another country. Almost all of us wanted to leave Cambodia. "Oh no, you can't go," Aunt Kim said, pointing right at me. "Ngor Haing here tried to escape, and they caught him. He wanted to sail to Thailand, but he never even got to the seacoast. If they caught him, it is impossible for us."

Curious faces turned to me. I kept my own expression blank, but inside I was angry. Foolish woman! I didn't want anyone but my parents and my brothers to know that I had tried to leave the country. Now all of Tonle Batí would know. And if I couldn't trust Aunt Kim to keep quiet about my escape attempt, I certainly couldn't trust her to keep quiet about my being a doctor. If the Khmer Rouge found out about *that*, it was the end.

Thinking back on it, it seems likely that Aunt Kim resented the favors my father and I had done for her, because accepting the favors put her in a lower position. In her mind she thought she had repaid the favors, or more than repaid them, by arranging for us to stay in a house on stilts. The new house was similar to our house in Wat Kien Svay Krao, airy and large, with springy floorboards. My family crowded into it and under it as we had before. Next to it, in a neat row, were plots of empty land that had been assigned to each married couple to build on. Aunt Kim and her sons had plots in the same row as my father, my brothers and me. A few days a week, we all got time off from our regular work for the Khmer Rouge to build our own houses. We went off into the forests, my brothers and some of Aunt Kim's sons and I, chopping down trees and carrying the poles back to Tonle Batí. Each of us made piles of the poles we had cut.

One morning Aunt Kim's pile of poles was missing. Her son Haing Seng, whom I had befriended in Phnom Penh, came up to the house on stilts and pointed his finger rudely at me. Haing Seng was furious. He asked if I knew where the poles were. His tone made his question seem like an accusation.

"Haing Seng," I said quietly, "do you know who I am? I am the man you used to call 'brother.' "

"No more 'brother' business now," said Haing Seng. "I want to find out who stole the fucking wood."

"Okay," I said, "no more 'brother' business. No problem. But Haing Seng, don't cuss at me. Go look at my woodpile if you like."

We walked to my woodpile about fifty yards away. My pile was bigger than the others because I had cut more trees. He looked at my pile and shoved it over with his foot.

"What did you do that for?" I demanded.

"Ingrate. Stealing after all we've done for you."

Tonle Batí was Haing Seng's home territory. He thought we should behave as if we were obligated to him, because his mother had found us the house. He thought I should show him special respect. But it was too late for that. I shouted that he had no "race," which means that he didn't know who his mother and father were—that he was a bastard. In Cambodia this is a deadly accusation.

He stalked back angrily to tell his mother.

I restacked the woodpile. My father had heard the argument from the upper story of the house and was coming down the steps to see what had happened. But my father was old and slow, and my aunt got to me first.

She slapped my face twice, hard. "Why do you tell my child he has no race? I have race! And I am related to you! So why do you say that?"

I turned to call out to my father, who was huffing and puffing toward us. "Papa, you see by your own eyes that she slapped me. I forgive her the first slap because she is your sister. I forgive her the second slap because she is older than me. So I'll let her get away with it. But"—I turned to Aunt Kim—"don't do it again."

She pointed her finger at me. "You came as a stranger to this village!" she screamed shrilly. "If it weren't for me you wouldn't have land here. You have totally forgotten the good things I did for you." She spat at my feet and quoted an old Cambodian proverb: " 'The crocodile has lost its lake!' "

She meant that I had forgotten the place that had nourished me, and now I was in trouble, like a crocodile far away from the water.

"Are you finished?" I said. "Are you finished cussing me?"

"What is it to you if I'm finished or not?"

"You filthy cunt!" I roared. "What is this about a crocodile that has lost its lake? When you came to Phnom Penh my family fed you. We gave you money. I treated your children. I gave medicine to that miserable husband of yours. I know which crocodile lost her lake!"

My father finally came up to us, breathing hard. "Kim, Kim, my whole family is in your hands," he pleaded. "We are in your world. If you feel you must do something against my son or my family, we cannot stop you. We are powerless. But do not forget all the good things we did for you."

Haing Seng returned with three or four of his brothers, and they were all holding sticks and knives. "Come on, motherfucker," he said, motioning me toward him, "let's fight." I told him to go away. He stood a few yards away, biting his lower lip, his eyes flashing, waving a stick in his hand.

Where were my own brothers when I needed them? They were nowhere in sight.

There was a tug on my arm. It was Huoy. "Come on, sweet, come on," she said, trying to pull me away.

Her mother took me by the other arm. "Don't fight them," she said. "If your cousins want the wood, let them take it. No fighting, please."

Aunt Kim looked contemptuously at Huoy and said something about a "taxi girl." I lunged forward, but my father blocked my way, and Huoy and her mother grabbed my arms more tightly and I allowed myself to be restrained. There was a long standoff by my woodpile, trading insults back and forth, until finally Aunt Kim and her sons went away.

By the time the anger had drained out of me, the sun had risen high. It was another hot, humid day, and I was late for work.

"That's your sister for you, Papa," I said. "Feed her, give her money and what does she do? This is her repayment for all your good deeds."

My father heaved a deep sigh and said, "Son, let it pass. Forget about it." But there was worry written on his heavy, intelligent face. He was upset at his sister for being two-faced. Upset at me for endangering the safety of the family. It was bad enough that the Khmer Rouge were threatening to avenge blood with blood. Here were relatives, members of the same clan, on the edge of shedding each other's blood.

My father turned away and walked slowly back to the house.

The local Khmer Rouge administration divided Tonle Batí into sections of "old" and "new" people. They put us in a subsection of two hundred "new" people who were ethnic Chinese, even though my family was a mixture of Chinese and Khmer.

Our neighbors were former shopkeepers from Phnom Penh. They had pale skins and straight hair, and like most Chinese they privately looked down on those with darker skins, including the Khmer Rouge. Twice a day, at lunch and dinner, we stood in line at a common kitchen built near the temple. We each got a bowl full of salted rice porridge, sometimes with bits of vegetables inside. After eating the meals with a bowl and spoon in Khmer Rouge style, our neighbors went back to their houses and discreetly cooked meals of their own with supplies they had brought from Phnom Penh. They had real rice—steamed rice—and sometimes salted pork or salted fish. They ate with chopsticks, lifting the bowls to their mouths and shoveling the rice in while making a sucking noise, and burping afterward to show their appreciation, in traditional Chinese style.

The two hundred of us made up one large work crew. Sometimes we went out in the fields, planting a rice crop, but most days we worked on a canal that was supposed to bring irrigation water to the fields. We began digging near the lake, hacking rather lazily at the reddish clay with our hoes, filling baskets with dirt and passing them leisurely from the bottom of the canal to the top. We didn't work very hard. When there were no soldiers in sight, we didn't work at all. We just sat down, in the shade if possible, and talked. Our civilian overseer, an "old" person whose way of thinking hadn't changed with the revolution, sat down and talked with us. He saw no reason why we should work hard in the hot sun, and neither did we. Nobody had, in traditional Cambodia. During break time, which sometimes lasted half the morning, the Chinese shopkeepers complained, "Why should we exert ourselves? There is no reason. They give us the same amount of food every day, whether we work hard or relax." Our foreman shrugged and said he didn't understand what was going on any more than we did.

The regime's controls were very loose in this period, when the Khmer Rouge were still consolidating their rule and making their plans for reshaping society. In Tonle Batí, only one person of each household had to report for work each day. Huoy could work in my place if I needed to do something else, like cut poles for our house. Furthermore, it was easy to fake being sick. On some days nobody from our household went to work at all.

I used part of my free time to barter in nearby villages of "old" people. It was exactly what I had done as a child. I walked through the same paths through the forest and found that many of the villagers remembered me, even though it was my first visit to them in almost twenty years. I brought them odds and ends to trade, like the stack of cotton sarongs from my clinic in Phnom Penh, and the silver betel boxes I had taken later from my apartment. The villagers had rice, vegetables and other goods. In the village where I had gotten drunk on palm beer as a child, I traded for a sturdy white plastic tarp, knowing that it would be especially useful during the rains.

When I wasn't trading or gathering wild foods, I worked on building my house. I nailed the poles together for a clumsy frame. My father, the ex-lumber tycoon, made rectangular panels for the roof and walls by folding palm tree leaf pieces over long slivers of bamboo and sewing the sides together. Papa's craftsmanship was so much better than mine that it made me feel ashamed. For all my education in the city, for all my training to be a doctor, there were many practical skills I had never learned.

The finished house was no more than a one-room hut. I made a low platform with a top surface of split bamboo, and laid the white plastic mat on the bamboo for Huoy, her mother and I to sleep on. The three of us got along very well. Huoy and I treated her mother with respect because she was old, and Ma made herself useful around the house with small chores. Once a week or so, Ma went to the evening *bonn* in my place, so Huoy and I could have privacy. It was the only good thing about these *bonn*s, that because of them Huoy and I could occasionally behave like husband and wife.

One night when we were all under our large mosquito net together, Huoy between her mother and me, a faint creaking noise came from the pathway outside. Immediately I was wide awake. It was a bicycle, I decided. Then the creaking stopped and there was a soft knock at the door. I got up to peer through the cracks. It was Neang, the chief of the village.

"Yes, what do you want?" I said.

"Ngor Haing, I know you are a doctor," he said. "Please help me save my child."

I was silent. And afraid.

"I am not a doctor," I said at last.

"Your aunt told me you were a doctor. She said you were a doctor in the military, with the rank of captain. I don't care what you did before, but now my child has a fever. He's very sick. So come save my baby boy. He's only eleven months old."

I thought, that bigmouth Kim told the village chief.

"I was only a student," I said through the door. "Never a doctor."

Neang was losing his patience. "Everybody here knows you were a doctor. Now come on, and don't be scared. Angka doesn't know about your past and I will never tell. Come on. I'm the leader here. I'll take care of you."

"Please give me a minute."

I did some quick thinking. Neang had come alone, without soldiers. He had a reputation as a good-natured man. Earlier that day he had asked our work group at the canal site whether any of us had fever medicines, but nobody had answered. He knew I was a doctor even then, but he hadn't singled me out in public. He had waited for dark instead.

Huoy sat up in the mosquito net. "What's wrong?" she whispered. "Are they going to take you away?"

"Don't worry," I whispered back, changing from my sarong into trousers. "Everything's going to be all right."

I followed Neang to his home, which was lit with lanterns inside, the light showing through the cracks.

Neang had called on some other medical practitioners before me, and they were standing around the baby. Two of them were traditional rural healers. They were dark-skinned, heavily tattooed and wore only shorts. They had prepared a green liquid medicine, grinding palm sugar, black pepper and various leaves together in a mixture with unboiled water. They had fed it to the baby with a spoon. They had also sprinkled what was supposed to be holy water on the baby's forehead. When I came in they were chanting to drive away the evil spirits.

Two young female Khmer Rouge doctors were also there, in the usual black uniforms and short haircuts. One of them was drawing a white liquid from an ampule marked "Thiamine" into a syringe.

Oh no, I thought. Please don't.

The baby was lying on a table, wrapped tightly in blankets. I pulled the covers back to look. A swollen belly. Skin hot to the touch. Occasional tremors in the body. Without lab tests it was hard to be sure, but my guess was meningitis as a secondary condition brought on by the fever.

"How can I save my son?" Neang asked me.

"Take the blankets away," I said. "Your son is too hot. You need to cool him down. Moisten a cloth with cold water and pat him with it."

"No," commanded the *mit neary* with the syringe. "The baby has a fever because it is cold. Don't take the blankets away."

She was wrong, but I did not want to assert myself. She and her comrade were in charge. The one with the syringe wiped the needle between her fingers and approached the child. I winced. It was not just a matter of an unsterile needle. Thiamine, or vitamin B_1, is sometimes used in Western medicine as an ingredient in multivitamin treatments but only in tiny quantities. It is never injected alone. The *mit neary* had drawn five cc's into the syringe. I doubted that she could read the label on the ampule, which was in French, or that she knew that she was administering an overdose.

She jabbed the needle into the unconscious child and pushed the chamber until all the liquid was inside the little boy's body.

The traditional healers chanted in a monotone. The Khmer Rouge women waited, sullen and bored. Neang looked at me anxiously, but I kept silent and stayed in the background. The oil lamps cast our shadows on the wall.

Outside, the crickets chirped and the bullfrogs on the lake made their deep croaking noise.

The child began shaking, not with light tremors but with deep, terrible convulsions. It fell into a coma with its unseeing eyes wide open. It twitched for another five or ten minutes and then it was dead.

I excused myself and went outside.

I took a deep breath. The chorus of crickets and frogs was louder here. Their sounds came from all directions, filling the night air.

I wanted to scream.

How I hated it all! If I had told Neang that the child shouldn't get the injection, the Khmer Rouge medics probably would have ignored me. If I insisted, they would have reported me for interfering, and then I would have been taken to Angka Leu. To them, anything in an ampule was medicine. If a patient died after getting an injection, it was the patient's fault. What was the purpose of a revolution like that? I wondered. What was the gain, what was the progress, when a society went from ignorant herbal healers to monkeys like the Khmer Rouge? What about the kind of knowledge that was taught in medical school? Wasn't it worth anything? Were we supposed to forget that it existed?

Maybe, I thought, just maybe, if I had been more forceful the child wouldn't have died. If I had told the medics to stand back, if I had put confidence and authority into my bearing, they might have obeyed me. Then I could have removed the blankets, cooled the baby down and prevented them from giving the injection. In doing so I would have risked my own life, but I would have saved the child's.

I hadn't done it. I had protected my own life instead.

How I hated it. The country was ruled by the ignorant. Already there were unnecessary deaths. To avoid our own deaths people like me were doing things we knew were wrong. And as we scrambled to protect ourselves, or sought to gain favor with the new powers, the old relationships were torn apart. Doctors broke their professional oaths. Families argued. People like my aunt became collaborators, and used their influence with the leaders to satisfy old grudges.

I stood in the dark thinking about the new regime. I had already seen more of it than I wanted. What I did not know was that everything that had happened so far was mild and harmless, compared with what was still to come.

13

NEW DIRECTIONS

A WEEK after the death of the village chief's child, at one of the nightly *bonn*s, we were told that Angka had a "new direction" for us. "We have almost finished our projects here," a *mit neary* declared, though in fact the canal was barely begun, "and soon we will have to begin other projects. You will still be struggling against the elements to help develop the country, but someplace else."

This news, that we were going to leave Tonle Batí, was unpopular at first with the "new" people. We had planted crops but not yet harvested them. But later it was announced that we would be allowed to return to our native villages. We would walk to a collection point, and then trucks would take us to our destinations.

With that the idea of leaving looked much better. What an opportunity! Except for a few families, like Aunt Kim's, who had been longtime residents of Tonle Batí and who would be staying, the Khmer Rouge didn't know where we were from. I revived my plans for going to the seacoast, and from there to Thailand by boat. My parents planned to go to Battambang Province, in western Cambodia, and from there to Thailand by land. Everybody in my immediate family was ready to leave except for my number-four brother, Hong Srun. I had just helped his wife deliver a baby, and it was too soon for them to travel.

Huoy, Ma and I left our little hut with few regrets. We carried a smaller number of possessions than before, in two big baskets suspended from my shoulderboard and the rest in bundles the women balanced on their heads. My father left his jeep behind, the last vehicle of his fleet. We were all traveling lighter.

The trip was supposed to take half a day. We set out on foot through the extensive sandflats next to Tonle Batí. With the weight of the load on the shoulderboard, my feet sunk into the sand. I took off my shoes, but the sand was hot on my soles. Huoy trudged on in her leather sandals, looking as urban and fashionable as a woman could under the circumstances. Her mother, plump and unpretentious, wore rubber shower sandals, the most sensible of us all.

Soon the trail led out of the sandflats and into the forest, up and around and down and up again. Thousands of us walked on it in single file, heading generally northwest. We were not just from Tonle Batí but from many villages around. In the early afternoon, long after we were supposed to arrive at the central collection point, we turned onto another trail leading south. "This is what the communists mean by 'new direction,' " I thought. "Taking the long way around for no apparent reason."

By evening we had reached a small valley with a railroad station. A crowd of other "new" people was already there with bundles, bags and suitcases. Wood-burning steam locomotives came chuffing along the track but kept on going without stopping. Behind the locomotives were old wooden boxcars full of passengers, who were standing in the boxcar doorways, peering out from the slats along the sides, or sitting on the boxcar roofs. They didn't wave to us and they didn't look happy.

By now everybody knew that we weren't going to be allowed to go back to our home villages. The Khmer Rouge had told us that just to get us to leave the places where we had been.

We waited by the railroad station for four days while trains went by, each one with a cargo of thousands of human beings, shipped like farm animals out of eastern Cambodia. It looked as though the Khmer Rouge were evacuating the entire region.

There had been a mix-up with our shipment, however. We never did get on a train at that station. Instead, we were led on foot to another village nearby, and the next day a convoy of empty Chinese-built military trucks drove in. Now the "new" people nervously called out the name of the places they wanted to go. The soldiers said to shut up and get in the trucks. So we got in feeling both afraid and stupid. It was amazing that we had believed even at first that Khmer Rouge would really let us return to our home villages. We had been naïve to think they might be telling the truth, after the lies they had told us to get us to leave Phnom Penh.

Packed into the back of the trucks, we bounced down the rutted road and then onto National Route 3, heading north. It was the same kind of war-wrecked landscape we had seen elsewhere. Houses flattened except for occasional walls. Coconut trees with their tops blown off. Mango trees blackened by fire. Lon Nol military bases with overturned trucks and jeeps, and tanks with metal treads hanging loose and broken.

Our truck was in the middle of the convoy. As we neared Phnom Penh along the airport road a murmur of hope swelled and we could hear the yelling of enthusiasm from the other trucks. We entered Phnom Penh at twilight and drove through the streets at top speed. There were no people and no lights anywhere; it was the same city of ghosts that it had been in April after the evacuation. As we drove to the northern edge of Phnom Penh all hope died and then the trucks were speeding along north on National Route 5 in the countryside again. The road ran parallel to the Tonle Sap River, visible from time to time as a flat, silvery surface in the gaps between the trees.

After a stop to camp overnight we got on again the next morning and reached the town of Pursat around noon. At Pursat, a provincial capital, National Route 5 and the railroad line came together, then ran parallel for some distance to the northwest before separating again at another town, called Muong. Pursat was empty of regular inhabitants—nobody in the market, sliding metal doors pulled shut across the storefronts—but a crowd of travelers like us filled the streets nearest the railroad station. Loudspeakers announced that Angka was giving away food, and the crowd surged forward to get supplies. I stood in line and eventually got rice and salt and some dried fish.

By then it was late afternoon. A few blocks from the railroad station there was a pond with water lilies and other aquatic plants. My family chose a quiet spot on the far side of the pond, back in a grove of banana trees, where there were no other people. Here we built our fires. Huoy cooked rice. Her mother was tired but did not complain. We were windburned from the long journey in the open truck, and all of us were tired.

When Ma had eaten her fill she stood up, rewrapped her sarong around her waist and went off to the pond to get water. Huoy and I picked at our food. My father and mother and my two remaining brothers, Pheng Huor and Hok, ate with their families close by.

"Where's my mother?" Huoy asked after a few minutes had passed.

"She's probably talking to somebody. I'll go look for her if you like." I stood up and walked through the trees to the pond. There was nobody along the shore of the pond except for a few people on the far side. I squinted to see if I could make out a plump figure in a sarong.

Where was Ma?

Then I looked lower and my eyes caught a bit of bright color on the bank. I walked closer and even before I was sure it was Ma's rubber shower sandals my heart was beating fast.

I checked again, but there was nobody wading or swimming in the pond.

I shouted to Huoy that her mother had fallen into the water, and then I dove into it and began thrashing around to try to find her. The pond was cold and full of slippery plants and there were leeches on my arms though I barely noticed them. My father heard and he waded into the water too, old and slow but doing his best. I dove farther out from the bank and then felt something soft under the water lilies, and I pulled Ma out of the water and up on the bank. She wasn't breathing. I lifted her up so her belly was on my shoulder and I jumped up and down. Water came out of her mouth and some rice too, but she still wasn't breathing. Her limbs were soft and pliable but she had no pulse. I tried artificial respiration with my mouth over hers, then thumped her chest hard with my two fists together to start her heart, and then went back to artificial respiration.

I kept trying.

There was a ring of faces around me but it was no good.

"Attention, comrades!" said a voice echoing out of the loudspeakers by the station. "You will now board the train. Angka wants you to collect your belongings and get on board!"

Ma was dead. Huoy was frantic. I was numb. If there was anything more to do, I didn't know it. My brother Pheng Huor took over. He carried the limp body to a shed and put it up on two boards. He built a fire underneath. It is a Cambodian folk belief that the spark of life continues as long as the body is soft, and the heat from a fire can bring it back. The part of me that had been trained in Western medicine was not strong enough to object, and I waited there like the rest, hoping for a miraculous recovery.

Two soldiers with rifles were watching.

Pheng Huor added wood to the fire and built up a blaze and massaged Ma's arms and legs. But Ma didn't respond.

"You have to leave. Time to leave now," the soldiers were saying behind us. "No crying. Angka does not allow it."

We could either bury Ma in the Chinese tradition, or else cremate her according to the Cambodian Buddhist tradition. We could do it either way, but it didn't seem possible that we had to make the choice and that she was dead. I had my arms around Huoy, but Huoy was beyond consolation.

Nearby, in the banana grove, a large hole had already been dug for planting trees.

My brothers carried the body on planks and placed it next to the hole. Huoy smoothed her mother's hair and began kissing and hugging her as if she were still alive. Huoy wouldn't release her mother until my father patted her gently on the back and told her to let go, and then Huoy began beating the ground with her fists and her feet and her elbows and knees.

We had no candles, so we set a couple of sticks from the fire in the ground. Huoy and I prayed out loud on our knees in front of her mother with the rest of my family behind.

"Mother, you left me! You left me all alone!" Huoy bawled. "Were you angry at me, Mother? Tell me how I can serve you. You can ask me for anything you want. Just wait for me in paradise so I can be with you in the next life. Mother, oh Mother, I want to be with you. Please, please, take me with you!" And Huoy fell sobbing with her head on her mother's breasts.

"If she is dead it doesn't matter anymore," the soldiers said crossly. "You must hurry."

Weeping without restraint, we prayed with our palms together in the *sompeah*, and then placed our palms on the ground in front of us and rocked forward, touching our foreheads to the backs of our hands.

"And if you cannot wait for me in heaven," Huoy wailed, "come back into our family. I want you to be reborn as my daughter, so I can treat you well again."

"You have to go now," said the soldiers. "You will be punished if you miss the train."

We put Ma in the ground and covered her with earth. We left the site and walked toward the railroad station, not believing that it had happened and that we were leaving her behind. It was unreal. She had been with us around the cooking fire and then two minutes later she was gone. Nobody had seen her. She must have stepped into the pond to get water and then slipped on the steep bank and drowned. But she was such a smart old lady that it couldn't have happened to her by accident. Perhaps, I told myself, Ma had her reasons.

The train was at the station and the wooden boxcars were full. The last few passengers were climbing up to the roof, and some people helped push us up with our luggage and Ma's too. Huoy sat next to me and it was all I could do to keep her from jumping off the train and running back to her mother's grave.

The locomotive let out a piercing whistle and began slowly pulling out of the station, *CHUFchufchufchuf CHUFchufchufchuf CHUFchuf-chufchuf* with the wheels making a rhythmic clicking on the track. We drew out of Pursat. I sat with my arm around Huoy, protecting her from the wind, holding her together. Huoy had never outgrown the need for her mother's love and advice. She had depended on Ma, even more than she depended on me. Now I was all she had.

The train chuffed along in a straight line. The landscape was utterly flat, rice fields reaching right to the bluish hills rising out of the plains near the horizon. The earth was dry and bare, the dikes war-damaged, the fields unplanted. Maybe that's why they had sent us here, I thought, to grow rice in western Cambodia.

The late-afternoon light turned a rich yellow and then orange and then the sun set. A full moon rose behind us. There was no comforting Huoy.

The train took us beyond Muong and finally stopped at a station called Phnom Tippeday, at the base of a mountain rising out of the plains of Battambang Province. Huoy and I walked away from the crowd to be alone. Next to the ruins of a rice mill destroyed in the war, we found a pile of rice hulls, and there we spread our white plastic mat. We improvised an altar with bowls of rice and water and with candles given to us by kindly strangers on the train.

We lit the candles, kneeled and prayed to Ma's soul.

14

THE PLOW

WE CAMBODIANS believe in *kama*, or karma—a religious concept meaning something like destiny, or fortune. A person's *kama* depends on what he has done in this life and in previous lives. If he has done bad deeds he will suffer, sooner or later, in this life or the next. Similarly, if he has done good deeds he will have better fortune, sooner or later, in this life or the next. The cycle of births and rebirths goes on and on, and souls carry their *kama* forward with them.

Ma's *kama* was excellent. She had always been kind. She had made much merit for herself through religious devotion. Her next life would be better. We missed her and we wanted to be with her again, but we weren't worried about her soul.

It was our own lives, Huoy's and mine, that we were more worried about. We couldn't help wondering: Was there something in our past existence, some terrible deeds we had committed, that caused us to be punished by this regime? Plenty of Cambodians thought so, but they tended to be people who belonged to rather mystical and super-stitious sects of Buddhism. They believed that old prophecies were coming true and that Cambodia was being punished for sins com-mitted long ago. They submitted to the Khmer Rouge sadly but without objection, as if surrendering to their fates. I didn't agree. To me, whether we had good *kama* or bad *kama*, it was important to fight the Khmer Rouge. If we couldn't fight them openly and physically then we would fight on the inside, on the battlefields of our minds. As Huoy and I walked along the railroad track the next morning, two doctor acquaintances of mine joined us. We began a conversation.

"Yes, we are religious," one of the doctors, an ophthalmologist, was saying, "but we are university-educated too. Our minds have the power to observe and draw conclusions. It is easy to blame it all on *kama*, but the fact is that real world events made this new regime. When he was in power, Sihanouk kept us on a neutral path, but after him we went from one extreme to the other. First we went to a corrupt rightist like Lon Nol, and now we have gone to crazy leftists. If we are being punished for anything, it is that we have abandoned the middle way."

"I agree with you," said Huoy. "We are educated and we must always use our minds. But in all the history I have read, about Europe and about Asia, I have never heard of a regime like this one. The last place we lived in, they said our projects were finished, but the canal we were working on was barely begun. Then they told us we could leave to return to our villages, but instead they sent us here. They are always lying. When was there ever a regime like this before?"

We continued walking down a path along the railroad tracks.

"Ngor, your wife is right," the other doctor, a pediatrician, said thoughtfully. "Even the other communist regimes don't lie as much as the Khmer Rouge. Look at China. The communists there seized private property and sent city people out into the country, but the Chinese are always talking about having the support of the people. You don't get the sense that the Chinese government turned against the people the way the regime has here."

"Without China the Khmer Rouge could not survive," the ophthalmologist, himself a light-skinned ethnic Chinese, said gloomily. "Peking gives the Khmer Rouge all their weapons and uniforms, so it should expect something in return. At the very least, Peking could put Sihanouk in charge of the regime here."

"But my good friend," said the pediatrician, "you make a mistake if you think China has any control over the Khmer Rouge. The Khmer Rouge are always talking about independence. They want to control their own revolution."

I said, "But *you* make a mistake if you think the communists control their own revolution. Look at all the confusion when everybody had to leave Phnom Penh. All the unnecessary suffering, like the patients having to leave the hospitals. That costs the Khmer Rouge popular support. So does the lying. I tell you, the people at the top of the Khmer Rouge, like Khieu Samphan, are highly educated, but the people under them cannot even read and write. They don't know where their revolution is going. They don't even know they are communists."

"Of course they do."

"No they don't," I said flatly. "When have you ever heard them mention the word 'communist'?"

"That's true," said the pediatrician after a moment's thought. "But then what are they?"

"*Kum-monuss*," I said, and they all laughed. It was a play on words: *kum*, a long-standing grudge that finally explodes in disproportionate revenge, and *monuss*, meaning people. "That's what they are at the lower level," I said, " 'revenge-people.' All they know is that city people like us used to lord it over them and this is their chance to get back. That's what they are, communist at the top and *kum-monuss* at the bottom."

We continued to walk slowly down the railroad track in the morning sunlight, talking about communists and *kum-monuss* and the fate of the country. It was the central question in our lives, what the Khmer Rouge would do now that they were in power; it was the mystery we could not solve. We crossed over railroad trestles with brown, muddy puddles underneath. Several times we stopped to help sick people resting by the tracks. Most of them had intestinal ailments from drinking dirty water. But even though we were doctors, there wasn't much we could do for them. Not without medicines.

By noon we came to our destination, Phum Chhleav. Thousands had arrived ahead of us, and more were on the way—a census later showed seventy-eight hundred in all. Phum Chhleav had a railroad siding but no railroad station. About a hundred yards from the siding, where a bridge crossed a dry irrigation canal, stood three houses on stilts. The Khmer Rouge soldiers and administrators lived in those three houses. The area assigned to us "new" people, on the other side of the tracks, had a double line of mango trees but no buildings at all.

We were told to choose land and build our houses. I borrowed a knife and went off and cut some spindly bamboo and some reeds and lengths of vine, and brought them back to a shady spot under a mango tree. Huoy and I stood the bamboo and the reeds on end and tied them with the vines to make our walls. We traded one of Ma's silk *sampot*s for some panels of thatch, and the thatch and our white piece of plastic made our roof.

When we finished and stood back to look at the hut there was little to admire. Our new hut was even worse than our first one back in Tonle Batí. This one was a tiny, low-ceilinged, one-room hovel that looked as though it would blow over in the first strong wind. You could see though the reed walls to the inside of the hut, so of course the water could get through too. The "kitchen" inside the hut was a triangle of three rocks to put the pot on. We made a mattress out of reeds and put tufts of grass on top to make it softer. Nearby, my father and brothers made huts that were a little better, but not much.

After a few days, when flimsy structures had risen throughout Phum Chhleav, turning farmland into a crowded slum, the Khmer Rouge called a meeting. All the heads of families were supposed to attend.

About a thousand of us showed up and sat on the ground near the railroad tracks, waiting for the speaker to arrive. It was early morning but the day was already hot. The land was brown and dry and the sky was milky white. Far off to the south rose the Cardamom Mountains, remote and wild. To the west, behind the Phnom Tippe-day train station, dominating the skyline, rose a mountain with a long, uneven ridge. On a plateau below the ridgeline were two white spots, the smaller one a *stupa* or funeral monument, the larger one a Buddhist temple. Below the mountain in the flat, uncultivated rice fields, a man was riding a horse in our direction. He rode bareback, without saddle or stirrups. His lean, swaybacked horse picked its way over the low earthen dikes, without hurrying.

Gradually the horse and rider approached. The horse's hooves clip-clopped on the hard soil. The man drew up, slid off the bare back of the horse and stood in front of us, a skinny, dark-skinned old fellow with no shirt or shoes.

He looked around and smiled at us. There were a few teeth in his lower jaw, but his upper jaw was as bare of teeth as a newborn child's.

"Welcome to Phum Chhleav," he said. "Angka has let you come here to help build a new society. You must work hard, but you must be patient. At the present time, Angka is poor. Angka will provide food, but sometimes it will not be enough. And sometimes the food will be late."

We listened with sinking hopes. The Khmer Rouge hardly ever admitted their faults. If they said there would not be enough food, it could even mean starvation.

"You must understand," he said, "that we only got free recently from our capitalist oppressors. Sihanouk"—there was a sudden rustle in the crowd at the mention of the name—"helped liberate us from Lon Nol and his lackeys. We are free now, but the economic situation of the country has not yet improved. So we must sacrifice. We will follow the principles of 'The Three Mountains.' We will attain independence-sovereignty, rely on our own strengths and take destiny in hand. What this means to every one of you is that if you work hard, you will eat. If you cannot work, you will go hungry."

I waited to see whether he would say anything else about Sihanouk. Like everybody else, I hoped that Sihanouk would reappear and take control of the government from the Khmer Rouge. But the old man only mentioned Sihanouk that once in passing. To him, Sihanouk was no more than a minor figure from history. He talked instead about how important it was that we city people learn from the peasants, that we build our own houses and grow rice. We were going to start with empty hands and build up the country. I sat still and pretended to pay attention. But I had heard it all before.

The old man, whose name was Comrade Ik, had the bearing of a man who was used to being obeyed. For a guess, he had been the headman of a rural village before becoming a civilian administrator for the Khmer Rouge. He wore a faded krama around his waist, black *culottes*, or shorts, and over his shorts a sarong doubled up above knee level. It was a peasant style of dress except for his sarong, which was made of silk. Before the revolution few could afford silk unless they grew the silkworms themselves. But now, those who had joined the Khmer Rouge could get silk kramas and sarongs free from frightened "new" people. For the Khmer Rouge, silk was a status symbol, and a lot of them in Battambang Province wore it.

The old man had a Battambang accent. Within Cambodia, Battambang was well known for its rice crop. With its flat land and rich soil the province produced enough rice to feed the whole country. Or it used to, before the war.

Surely, I thought, that's why they brought us to Phum Chhleav, to grow rice for the regime. To restore Battambang to its position as rice bowl of Cambodia. We were near the railroad, which made it easy to send the rice out, but far away from the temptations of any city or town. Yes, they were going to isolate us here. I had only to look at the wrinkled old man, with his bare chest and bare feet, to be sure: From now on, our lives would be more rural than ever.

Work began the next day. We went out into the long-neglected rice fields with hoes and began breaking up the hard soil surface. It was a long day and at the end of it there was no food. If the Khmer Rouge didn't give us enough to eat, I reasoned—their rations averaged about a can of uncooked rice per person every two days—there was no sense in working at all. This was easy in the confusion of a big new settlement like Phum Chhleav.

The following morning, shortly after sunrise, my wife and I and another couple walked away from Phum Chhleav and into rice fields that were not being cultivated, keeping a careful eye out for soldiers. Once we were in the fields we were essentially out of sight. Rising from the bottoms of the paddies like islands in the sea were hillocks topped by brush or trees or sprays of bamboo. The hillocks were actually termite mounds, a common feature of tropical landscapes. They were as high as our waists or our heads, and anywhere from a few yards to tens of yards long. It was impossible to see through the vegetation growing out of the hillocks, and there were so many of them scattered around the fields that the view was limited to the middle distance, usually from fifty to a couple of hundred yards. However, the mountain ridge with the temple was in clear sight above the hillocks, giving me a reference point to steer by.

The purpose of our outing was to gather wild foods. In Cambodia we have a humorous saying about food: "Eat anything with two legs except a ladder, anything with four legs except a table, and anything that flies except an airplane." The point is that when you live off the land you cannot be particular. The Cambodian peasants, who are geniuses at living off the land, sometimes eat termites for protein, though there are many other foods they prefer. Until the rains came—the rains arrived later in Battambang than in eastern Cambodia—there were no termites aboveground anyway.

We began by looking for field mice. We hovered near the mouse holes in the dikes in the rice fields and tried to trap them with a piece of fishnet. The problem, as I realized after several hours without catching any, was that mice always have a second entrance to their burrows. I had acquired some skills at hunting and gathering in childhood, but mice-hunting was not among them.

Next we went looking for red ants, which live in sandy forests, weaving fibrous nests in the branches of trees. Rural Cambodians put red ants in soups to add crunchy texture and protein. They also cook the ants' eggs, which are soft and white and sour, a kind of poor man's caviar. The challenge is collecting the ants without being bitten. When you approach, the ants rise up with their forelegs waving in the air and their mouthparts scissoring back and forth in their eagerness to bite you. When you move left, they move the same way. When you move right, they follow. For their size they are the fiercest creatures I have ever seen. Unlike the stories we heard in the *bonns*, ants cannot kill elephants, or even humans—their bite isn't poisonous—but their sting leaves a mark like a needle puncture. Fortunately, after my embarrassing attempts to trap mice, I knew how to hunt red ants. I held a plastic pail with some water in it and tipped the nest in with a stick. A few of the ants crawled onto the stick and onto my arm to bite me, but I had rubbed ashes onto my hands and arms. The ants fell off harmlessly when they reached my skin.

While collecting ants in the forest we heard a sound from nearby—*to-kay, to-kay*—the first syllable higher-pitched than the second.

Tokays, as they are commonly called, are lizards about a foot long. When cooked, their flesh tastes a bit like chicken. We followed the *to-kay* sound to a tree not far away. When we got close there was a flash of tail as the tokay darted into a hole in the tree trunk. I climbed up after it and put the scrap of fishnet over the hole. The four of us shook the tree until the lizard fell out.

At the end of the afternoon we wandered back toward Phum Chhleav with red ant nests, several tokays and quantities of bamboo shoots, water convolvulus and other edible plants. We had foraged off the land like peasants and we looked like peasants ourselves. I was barefoot, with no glasses or wristwatch, carrying a bundle of food tied up in my krama. Huoy wore her krama wrapped around her head like a turban. The other couple looked about the same. We were nearing the railroad track when Huoy suddenly whispered to me,

"Sweet, sweet! Get down! Soldiers ahead!" I dropped to the ground ahead of her, crawled to a hillock and peered through the bushes on top. "Stay down!" Huoy commanded behind me.

"Don't worry," I whispered back.

On the path beside the railroad track two civilians were walking with two soldiers behind them, all in a line. The soldiers wore black uniforms with green Chinese hats and Ho Chi Minh–style black rubber sandals, and they carried their rifles slung over their shoulders by the straps. The two civilians had their elbows tied tightly behind their backs. A rope traveled from the first civilian to the second civilian and from there to one of the soldiers' hands. The two civilian prisoners walked slowly, with their heads hanging low.

I recognized them with a shock.

"My two doctor friends," I whispered back to Huoy.

Huoy crawled forward and onto the hillock next to me. We watched together. There was something so irrevocable, so final about the sight that we felt our own ends had come as well. "These two friends of mine weren't troublemakers," I whispered to her. "The soldiers are taking them away because they were doctors. Tomorrow it will be my turn. Everybody knows I am a doctor."

The two doctors walked along very slowly, weighed down by the knowledge of their approaching deaths. We watched them walk farther and farther away along the railroad track until we couldn't see them anymore. Then we still waited, expecting to hear rifle shots, but the shots never came.

"Maybe you're wrong," Huoy said at last. "Maybe they're being taken away because they didn't work in the rice fields."

I thought this over. She had a point. Maybe the two other doctors had avoided work so they could go gather food, just as we did. Maybe they had been caught at it.

We never knew for sure, because we never saw the two doctors again, or heard anything about their arrest. But after that Huoy always insisted that I show up for work, and I did. As she pointed out, if we worked we didn't have enough food, but it was better to be hungry than dead.

I was sent off to repair roads. About thirty of us from our section of Phum Chhleav left together, walking with hoes over our shoulders down a winding path through the rice fields and the jungle. In previous years a series of floods had cut huge gullies through an old dirt road. We set to work with our hoes, filling up baskets with dirt and carrying the baskets on shoulderboards. There were no other people around, and no villages. We worked eight days without much food. When we trudged back to Phum Chhleav at last, Huoy was sitting on the ground outside our hut, waiting for me.

"You lost weight," she said.

"A lot, sweet."

She rose and hugged me tenderly, and hung on without letting me go. She had been alone when I was away. Alone and worried about me and grieving for her mother. And even after I came back it would take her a day or two to recover.

"Did Angka beat you or punish you?"

"No," I said. "We just worked a lot."

"I have food for you," she said.

"What kind?"

"Guess," she said, and it had to be something special.

"I don't know."

"I have cooked mice for you. Field mice. I knew you were coming today."

It was as if I were returning from a business trip and she had fixed me a steak or an especially nice fish as a wifely gesture. She had traded for the mice with some more of her mother's clothes. She was taking care of me as best she could, and it made no difference that we would never have considered eating mice when we were living in Phnom Penh. Here in the countryside mice were a treat.

We ate the meal, and what little there was of the mouse meat was tasty, and I was touched by what she had done and worried to see that her sadness still lingered.

The next day I went to work in a rice field near the railroad track. Huoy and I were assigned to the same group of about a hundred "new" people. The Khmer Rouge gave hoes to Huoy and the rest of the women and told them to break up the topsoil where it hadn't been broken before. Two teenage soldiers with rifles took us men to paddies that had been hoed already. There were about eight wooden plows and three or four oxen by a hillock. "We don't have enough oxen now," one of the soldiers told us, "but we have to plow the fields. If we don't plow and plant rice, we won't have anything to eat."

"Oh no," I said to myself. "Are we going to use *human beings* to plow? Is this what we have to do to build this advanced society they're talking about—go back to prehistoric times?"

The soldier's face combined the dull gaze of limited intelligence with an obvious contempt for us city people. He held a long whip of plaited leather in his hand. "You," he said, pointing at one man. "Go to the plow. You too, and you." I hoped he wasn't going to point at me. The ethnic Chinese in the group were cursing in Teochiew dialect, saying they just wouldn't do it.

He pointed at me.

I walked over to the plows.

"You," said the soldier. "Take this plow and get on the right side."

I stood on the right side in back of the crosspiece and all I could think about was *kum-monuss*. On my left an old female ox stood, making a sideways chewing motion with her mouth and swishing her tail to keep the flies away.

"Now go," said the soldier, cracking his whip overhead.

I began to push forward against the crosspiece. The ox walked forward in its harness. The soldier walked behind the plow, guiding it. My bare feet passed over clumps of clay with weeds growing out of them. The first light rains had softened the clay but only on top, and the ground was still cracked from the long, hot dry season.

When we got to the edge of the field, the soldier sunk the tip into the earth below the depth the hoes had reached. The plow nearly came to a halt. By pushing harder I could still make it move forward, but the ox was stronger and the plow swerved off to the right. I had to push with all my strength to keep it going in a straight line.

We plowed down one side of the field, the early-morning sun shining into my eyes. It took a long time to reach the end of the field. Finally we turned the corner and began down another side.

A rhythmic clicking noise came over my shoulder and then to one side. I turned my head and glimpsed a miniature flatcar traveling down the railroad track. Four men stood on it using long bamboo sticks in unison to pole themselves along, two of them on each side. They sped effortlessly along and soon they they were out of hearing.

I leaned forward again and kept pushing but the wooden crosspiece was too high, about the level of my neck. I wished it were lower. Reaching up to it strained my shoulders and the small of my back.

Blisters had formed on my hands from the road repair work and I could feel them pop open and the fluid running out.

I looked around at the other paddies and saw other men plowing with oxen and farther off the crews of women with their hoes rising and falling. I could not see far into the fields because of the hillocks, but in every direction men and women were working. Above us all, above the treetops to the west, rose the mountain with the two white dots. Lord Buddha help me, I thought. Help us all. Give us the strength to make it through the day.

The plow had veered to the right and it was heading toward the dike at the edge of the field.

"Faster, faster!" came the soldier's voice behind me. "If you can't go faster I will whip you!" He cracked the whip above the ox and me, in the air.

I bent forward to the work again. The neck and head of the ox filled the left side of my field of vision. The ox was making its sideways chewing motion, and spittle was drooling from its whiskered chin. It twitched its ears to keep insects from landing nearby, but when insects bit its foreleg the ox lowered its head and licked the spot with its enormously long, thick, sandpapery tongue. I heard its slow, regular breathing and the swishing of its tail on its back. How could anything that stupid be so strong? I wondered.

The sweat rolled down my armpits and chest. I took my hand from the crosspiece and dabbed with my krama to keep the sweat out of my eyes, then went back to pushing.

Why are the gods so blind? I thought. Did I do something wrong in a previous life that I have to do this now? Is there something terrible in my *kama*?

Life had been so good back in Phnom Penh. So relaxed and prosperous. My patients *sompeah*ed me and spoke to me politely. Huoy and I were happy. We had no worries. We ate in restaurants nearly every night and always ate enough. But not anymore. Now we have no fried noodles. No fish cooked with lemon and coriander. Every evening Huoy talks about her favorite recipes. She remembers the sweet desserts she used to make for my parents and says she wishes we had more food. Huoy's cheeks have lost their roundness. She is losing weight.

I struggled to keep up with the ox, but my breath was labored. I heard my breathing and my footsteps and the ox's footsteps and the twittering of the birds.

Listen to the birds singing like that! Whenever they want they fly from one tree to another. They go wherever they want. When they find food they can eat it. It's harder for people. We are draft animals like the oxen. So maybe our *kama* is very, very bad.

Ma must have known that life was going to be like this. She was always intuitive. So she chose to drown herself in the pond. That's why she died. What a wise old lady she was. I hope in her next life she—

SNAP! A searing pain across my back.

"Hey!" I yelled angrily. "How can I push if you're whipping me? Let me rest first and then I can go back to working."

"Finish the field and then rest," the soldier replied. But after a few more lengths of the field he stopped to roll and smoke a cigarette and I took a break too. I looked around. A woman in the next field was holding a hoe in one hand and looking at me. She was standing absolutely still and her other hand was clasped across her mouth as if she were trying to stop herself from screaming. It was Huoy, but without my glasses I could not see the expression on her face.

When the soldier finished his cigarette we went back to plowing. The sun was still low in the morning sky and the day was humid and hot. I could not imagine why the sun was taking so long to move across the sky. The soldier whipped me a few more times and after what seemed like days somebody far away rang a gong. Lunchtime. The soldiers went back to their kitchen in the row of three houses by the old canal, and some *mit neary* in black brought us out our meal, a cloudy broth with some grains of rice at the bottom.

I had blisters on my palms, on the first and second joints of my fingers and between my thumbs and forefingers. My shoulders and my back and my calves ached, and my Achilles tendons were sore. But the whip marks hurt the most.

"You eat my portion, sweet," Huoy said.

"No, I'm okay. I don't really have an appetite."

"Please. You eat it for me. You need the strength. I cannot eat it."

After lunch the soldier and I took the plow off the rig and put a wide rake or harrow in its place, to break up the clods turned up by the plow and to smooth the furrows. The soldier didn't especially want to talk.

"Not even one field plowed," was all he said to me.

All afternoon he stood on the harrow to drive the points in, and with his weight it was even harder to drag the harrow than the plow. We went around and around the field. Along one side there was a view of the mountain with the white dots but it meant nothing to me now. I kept looking at the sun, which stayed motionless in the sky.

Late in the afternoon, the railroad maintenance crew came back along the track, poling vigorously toward the Phnom Tippeday railroad station, traveling faster than the breeze.

Near sundown, the gong rang again and we quit. We had not plowed or harrowed a single rice paddy.

In our flimsy hut, Huoy heated water and made a hot compress with strips of cloth and put them on the whip welts, which curved over my shoulders and neck to the top of my chest. She was crying. She felt my pain more than I did. I was too tired to feel much of anything. "Today I prayed to my mother to take us with her," Huoy said. "I don't know why we should go on, being treated like this. The Khmer Rouge should just kill us now and get it over with."

I didn't know what to say. To myself I thought, Ma was smart to commit suicide.

It rained that night, a long, drenching rain with flashes of lightning and rolling thunder and water leaking inside the hut. In the morning I went back to plowing, but the ground was softer than before. And even the soldiers had admitted their mistake. Now they paired two men against each ox, or four men if there were no oxen.

The rainy season had finally arrived in Battambang. The rain was cold and nearly continuous. After a few hours in it my fingers were white and wrinkled, like staying in bath water too long. We plowed in the rain. Snails appeared on the ground, and when I picked one up the soldier whipped me across the back. "If you have time to pick up snails like that, how can we finish the fields?" he shouted. "Don't you like the food Angka is giving you? Isn't it satisfying enough?"

There was nothing to say to that without insulting Angka. I kept quiet. But I didn't see why we shouldn't pick up snails.

At night I used a tiny oil lamp inside a can with reflective sides to look for food. But there were only tiny frogs and snails to be found nearby. Bursts of rifle fire came from near the soldiers' houses, and I was afraid to go out into the rice fields and to the canals and ponds, where the fish and the frogs would be large and plentiful.

From my normal weight of 135 to 140 pounds I dropped to 110 to 115 pounds. Then I began having to excuse myself while plowing to go to the bushes. At first I thought it was a case of ordinary diarrhea. Then I noticed white mucus on the ground and later yellow mucus and dark, purplish blood. And then I knew I was very, very sick.

15

SICKNESS

I wasn't the only sick person. Not at all. In Phum Chhleav more
people were sick than healthy. The hard work, the food shortages,
the unsanitary conditions and the near-absence of medicine combined
to cause illness on a scale I had never seen before in all my medical
training. In the rice fields the remaining "new" people worked in slow
motion; in the huts they lay down with fevers or swollen limbs or
uncontrollable bowels. Every day, processions wound through the
pathways of the village on the way to the burial grounds.

The greatest single factor in this public-health disaster was malnutrition. The Khmer Rouge fed us a bowl of salty broth with a few
spoonsful of rice at the bottom for lunch, and the same for dinner.
That was all. They didn't allow us to gather wild foods for our private
meals, though sometimes we did anyway. Without proper nutrition,
we weakened.

There were other factors. We were city people, unused to hard
labor. Chronic fatigue—the kind of tiredness that comes from pulling
a plow twelve hours a day—lowered our resistance to disease just as
malnutrition did. We had hardly any resistance at all. Because we
were from places like Phnom Penh, we hadn't built up natural im-
munities to the microorganisms of Battambang—to the bacteria in
contaminated drinking water, for instance. To make things worse, we
didn't have proper latrines or bathing facilities. We didn't have much
medicine, and the Khmer Rouge didn't let doctors like me practice
openly.

Until I got sick, I practiced anyway. So did my two doctor friends,
before the Khmer Rouge took them away, and so did a clever little

fellow named Pen Tip, whom I will tell you about later. I visited my patients' huts at dawn or dusk with my stethoscope and blood pressure cuff concealed in my clothing. Without laboratory tests I could only base my diagnoses on their symptoms and tell them what medicines I thought they needed. They had to buy the medicines themselves on the black market, either with rice or with gold.

The most common symptom of illness was edema or swelling. It was related to the lack of proteins in our diet and possibly to the high proportion of salts in the broth we drank at meals. Instead of getting thinner as they starved, the people with edema became bloated with fluid, usually first in their legs. In the most extreme cases, the victims were unable to close their legs together; the men got huge, distended scrotal sacs. The cure was very simple—food—but anybody who had extra food was hoarding it.

The range of infectious illnesses was amazing. Cuts filled with pus and wouldn't heal properly. Skin lesions were common, especially fungal infections; we "new" people were always outdoors in the rain, and our skins didn't have a chance to dry. There were cases of malaria, pneumonia and tuberculosis. Almost everyone in the settlement got common diarrhea, and many got amebic dysentery, a much more dangerous infection of the intestinal tract. That's what I got, dysentery, presumably from drinking contaminated water when my resistance was low.

By the time I got sick, I had used up all my antibiotics and dysentery medicines treating my father and my brothers, who had been sick before me. Huoy went out to get medicine from people I knew. She looked and asked, but there was nothing available. Finally she traded a *damleung* of gold, or 1.2 ounces, for fifteen 250-mg. tablets of tetracycline, a standard antibiotic.

I took one capsule of tetracycline twice a day as long as the supply lasted. In normal times I would have prescribed double the dosage, for a total of 1,000 mg. a day, plus an antidiarrhea medicine such as Tifomycin.

To supplement the tetracycline I tried folk remedies. When rural Cambodians get diarrhea or dysentery they eat the tender, bitter leaves at the branch tips of guava trees. There were guava trees nearby. Huoy collected the leaves and made me a tea out of boiled guava leaves and bark. Nothing happened. I stayed home and shuttled back and forth from the reed mattress to a latrine she had dug for me near our tiny garden. I couldn't think clearly without an effort, and then only for moments at a time.

As my dysentery grew worse, my world shrunk to the hut and the garden. I was too weak to go anywhere else. Whatever I knew of the outside world came to me: the sound of the steam whistle of the railroad trains hooting far away and then the metal wheels rocking and clicking on the metal tracks and the driver wheels going round and round *CHUFchufchufchuf* as freight trains went by. I heard the rapid, rhythmic clicking of the maintenance crew as it poled its way along, twice a day. And every morning through the cracks in the hut I saw the burial processions. The dead were wrapped in plastic tarps or cloth and carried on wooden boards suspended at either end from a long piece of bamboo, which rested on the mourners' shoulders.

Sometime after the first week with dysentery I had just come in from the garden when Huoy came back from work. All the tetracycline was gone. "Please, sweet," I begged her. "Sell some more things. Ask around again."

In my confused, weakened state I didn't even trust her. I wasn't sure she was doing all she could.

"Don't you believe me?" Huoy said, standing over me and looking down with her sorrowful eyes. "Trust me. I am trying my best to get the medicine." She went out again but still she didn't find any.

There was one other remedy to try: eating carbon from burned food. It works by trapping gases, like the activated charcoal in certain kinds of cigarette filters. For the most part, the carbon only reduces the symptoms of diarrhea or dysentery, but sometimes it has a marginal effect on the infectious agent itself.

The problem with burned food was that we had hardly any food to eat, or burn. My father brought some strips of pork to the hut. He and Huoy carefully trimmed off the fat, then grilled the pork in the fire until it was black on the outside. I ate it but vomited it up.

I was long past feeling any shame about my dysentery, even though it is an ugly and humiliating disease. I was simply too weak to care about modesty. Day and night, several times an hour, I shuttled between my pallet in the hut and the hole in the yard, where I lifted the edges of my sarong and squatted. When I got up I glanced at the pus and blood and liquids I had left behind to see whether I had gotten any better, but by the end of the second week I hadn't. When I lay down there was a sloshing, gurgling noise inside my intestines. Sometimes I even saw my intestines moving from the gas expanding inside. There was a war going on, with amebas on one side and my bodily defenses on the other. My body was pouring its resources into the battle, getting used up, wasting away.

By the seventeenth or eighteenth day I felt nothing. Lying on my side I had diarrhea and didn't even know it until I reached around with my hand and discovered the wetness.

I had eight sarongs left from the stack I had taken from my clinic. I used them like diapers. By the twentieth day I couldn't walk. I had to crawl out to the garden on all fours. Huoy went to the authorities to get permission to stay away from work to take care of me.

She was a perfect nurse. She bathed me day and night. She cooked the little bit of rice we had and fed it to me a spoonful at a time, with my head in her lap. After feeding me she kissed me and stroked my hair. A wondering, sorrowful expression came over her, and I knew her thoughts: If I died, a part of her would die too.

With my head in her lap I saw only her face. The large, round, dark eyes. The lush, thick eyebrows that had never needed makeup. The hollow cheeks. When I lay down my eyes saw the woven reeds of the wall and the light filtering through.

The other huts nearby, my parents' and my brothers', now seemed incredibly far away. It was impossible even to think about going there. My brothers visited me once but they didn't come back, and this made me angry. I had given them medicine, but they wouldn't use their gold to buy medicine for me. Family ties meant nothing to them now. Everybody was looking out for himself. And then I stopped resenting my brothers. I was too weak to care.

Day by day, as the invaders and the protectors fought their battle in my intestines, I lost more and more weight. My clavicles protruded. Every rib showed. My legs were like matchsticks, except for my knees and ankles, which bulged out, big and knobby. My weight was down to about seventy pounds.

I lay on my side and a fly landed on my face and I did not move. I felt the fly walking on my cheek, felt the little legs as it moved around, and I knew it would head for the moisture at the corner of my eyes. And then I sensed Huoy's presence as she moved close and then felt the air as she fanned the fly away. Huoy lowered the mosquito net around me. I focused on the gauze of the mosquito net and then on the light coming through the cracks in the reed wall.

I heard the grumbling of the thunder and the freshening of the wind as the storms came in. Raindrops fell on me and I didn't move. Huoy went out in the rain and tied a krama to the outside of the walls to stop the rain from coming in.

I was very detached. If I wanted to lift my leg I thought about it and then my mind wandered and later I remembered and watched myself do it. My leg seemed very far away and I looked at it objectively, as if it were somebody else's. It didn't look like my leg. It was too thin.

I dozed but didn't sleep. My intestines were bubbling with liquids and gas and every few minutes some more spurted out the back end. Nothing could stop it from happening. The poisons kept coming out and coming out but inside the bubbling and the gurgling and mixing went on and it always produced more. Food only made it worse. Maybe if I had a huge amount of pure bland rice I could have quieted my stomach, but Huoy and I were down to one can of rice. That was all the food we had. Huoy ate nothing but the salty broth from the Khmer Rouge. The rest she fed to me.

Up through the thirtieth day, some deep intuition told me that I was going to outlast the infection.

Then, on the morning of the thirty-first day, something changed. I decided to take my pulse, but before I could do it my mind wandered. Where was Huoy? I couldn't hear her in the hut. I turned my head and then twisted it farther and then through the cracks in the hut saw her outside, taking the clean sarongs from the drying line. What was I thinking about? Oh yes, my pulse. I'll have to move my right hand to my left wrist. If I tell my hand to move, it will obey. If I do it now, I won't forget. Better do it while she can't see.

I watched my right arm swing over and the fingertips of my right hand probe for the pulse in my left wrist. Not there. There. Yes. The beat is very slow.

My heart is slowing down.

In a few more hours it will stop.

Huoy came in with the folded sarongs and put them away. Then she knelt by me and smoothed the hair back from my forehead and wiped my face with a damp cloth.

"I don't feel well," I said. "I think I am going to die. Please, bring my father here."

"You aren't going to die," she said firmly. "We're going to live together a long time, you and I." But she herself didn't believe what she was saying. Huoy went to get my father and they both came back and sat beside me, Papa looking down at me with his wrinkled face. I could remember when he was much younger and fatter.

I told my father that I was going to die in the next few hours. I asked him to take care of my wife. Huoy, I said, had taken good care of me but just didn't have the means to save my life. "If anybody says anything bad about her, don't believe it. I want you and Mama to take her in. Don't let her live with anyone else in the family. So take care of yourself and take care of Huoy and the gods will bless you."

My father told me not to worry, that I wasn't going to die. But when he went outside he set candles and incense on the ground under the mango tree and got ready to pray.

Huoy sat next to me. "Keep being strong in your mind," she said, over and over. "Keep being strong and you will never die." She stroked my face and cleaned my face and body with a damp towel. The tears rolled down her cheeks and she didn't hide them.

"Be happy if I pass away," I answered.

Outside my father was saying in a loud voice, "Let him go to a wonderful paradise! Let life be good, the next place he goes. Let there be enough food and enough medicine."

I said to Huoy, "Even if I die I will still protect you. I will take care of you all your life."

My mother joined my father and they knelt and prayed together. Then Mama came into the hut and sat next to me, massaging my limbs. She looked truly old now, old and gray. Together my mother and my wife stripped me of my sarong and tried to dress me in a new shirt and a new pair of trousers to die in.

"Please don't," I said. "It's a waste to put me in new trousers. You can trade them for something after I die."

"I don't care about trading," Huoy said as they put my feet in the trousers and pulled them up. "There's nothing to trade for. If you die, I die."

I lay on my side and waited.

In the early afternoon there was a sound of footsteps and a big loud voice.

"Come get your yams! One person from every family, come to my house! We've got yams! Come get your rations! Get your yams!" It was the civilian leader of Phum Chhleav, a burly man who reported to the man on horseback. With him were the section leaders of Phum Chhleav and a crowd of excited followers, talking and waving. It was the first food the Khmer Rouge had distributed for private use in three days.

I sent Huoy to get our ration. My father had already disappeared to get his.

I lay back and began thinking about yams. They are long, crooked tubers, quick to grow in a tropical climate. They contain minerals and vitamins, but they are basically carbohydrate. Put in a fire, they burn. They turn into charcoal.

Huoy had left the fire going beside me, with a tea kettle on the three stones. When the water boiled I pulled the ends of the wood away from the fire, but I didn't have the energy to make tea.

After a period of time had passed, how long I do not know, Huoy returned. She showed me the ration: one small yam the size of her fist.

Huoy was looking at the yam with a glazed, intent expression. How long had it been since she had eaten a real meal? Two weeks? Three weeks? Had she eaten well since the dinner with the field mice?

I said, "Sweet, please give me the food to eat. I think if I eat it, it will help my stomach. I know you are hungry like me, but we still have rice. You eat the rice."

We still had not touched our one last can of rice. We were saving it, though I do not know why. Our hunger could not have gotten worse.

Huoy looked at me with a sad smile and nodded. "Whatever you want, I will do it. I want you to stay alive. As long as we both are alive we will be happy."

I told her to burn the yam without cooking it first. She put it in the fire. When it was completely burned, she took it out to cool, trimmed off the wood ashes, and cut it into small pieces. The yam was black all the way through except for some small soft yellow specks. She put my head in her lap and she fed it to me with a spoon, one piece at a time, until it was gone.

I felt stronger.

My trips to the garden diminished from five times an hour to three. The next day they decreased to two an hour, and the day after that to once an hour. The burned yam had helped turn the tide. It enabled my natural resistance to grow.

Within a few more days, I could eat solid foods.

After another week had passed, Huoy picked me up, draped my arm over her shoulder and gave me a long stick to use as a cane. She helped me walk. I had to reteach my legs to obey.

We only took a few steps. But the next day we walked around the hut.

It was fifty yards to the railroad track. It became my goal. Every day I walked nearer, and when I finally made it I had to stop to rest three or four times along the way.

Huoy and I sat on the railroad tracks, near a trestle with water underneath. I was tired but triumphant. Huoy was happy and smiling. We talked as we always had in the old days, calling each other "sweet."

A healthy young woman from another village came walking down the railroad tracks, carrying a sack over her shoulder. She walked past us, then turned around in surprise. In those times, even husbands and wives were supposed to call each other "comrade."

"Is that your husband?" the young woman asked Huoy. Her tone was pleasant and courteous, her accent from Phnom Penh.

"Yes, he is," Huoy answered with a smile. "He was very sick, but he's better now."

The young woman put her sack down. She reached in it and pulled out a piece of fruit. I knew the fruit, though I have never discovered its English name. It has a very thick rind, and like guava leaves it is a folk remedy against stomach ailments. "Older sister," she said to Huoy, "give him some of this. It will be good for his health." She broke it open on the railroad track and gave us half.

I put my palms together and raised them to the middle of my forehead.

She asked whether we were from Phnom Penh. I said yes, told her my real name and said I used to be a doctor. She asked me whether I knew her uncle so-and-so. I said yes, he was my professor in medical school. We began a conversation, using all the terms of politeness in the Khmer language, talking about old times in Phnom Penh.

Before she left, she dug in her sack again and gave us an ear of corn. It lifted our spirits, meeting this courteous young woman who, incidentally, we never saw again. It reassured us that in spite of the Khmer Rouge, compassion still existed and Cambodian high culture still lived. We watched her walking down the tracks and disappearing in the distance.

I said, "Sweet, I'm going to live."

The sun sent low rays across the landscape. The air was cool. I ate a portion of the outer fruit as medicine and gave the rest to Huoy. We went underneath the trestle to bathe, and Huoy scrubbed the dust and dirt off me.

That evening we cooked the ear of corn. I made Huoy eat every kernel, as a small gesture of repayment for the yam she had given me. I loved and respected Huoy more than ever. I put her above me. She had saved my life.

16

THE PARADE OF
THE SELFISH AND
THE DYING

WHEN MY WEIGHT rose to about a hundred pounds I was sent back
to work in the rice fields. I didn't mind. Just being out in the fertile
fields of Battambang made me feel better. The rice plants were large
and bushy, higher than my waist. From the middle of the paddies
the dikes were invisible, except as gaps in the thick carpet of green.
When a breeze came through the rice, the smell was so sweet and
clean that it made my stomach rumble with hunger. So much rice!
In a few more months, in the harvest, we could eat bowl after bowl
of steaming white rice, as much as we wanted. That's what we had
been promised.

By now, toward the end of the rainy season, the hard work—
plowing the fields and transplanting the seedlings—was over. Only
light tasks were needed, like regulating the water levels. It was easy.
A few other men and I walked around on the tops of the dikes with
our hoes. The dikes were eighteen inches to two feet high. Wherever
the rainwater was in danger of flooding over the dikes we began
chopping holes, letting the water spill from one paddy into the next
and then the next, until the extra water reached the edge of the field.
Then we rebuilt the dikes with the hoes and our hands.

We were wet and muddy all day long, but the job was a good
one. We had little supervision. No Khmer Rouge soldiers standing
over us with whips. The soldiers hardly came into the fields at all.
Even better, we were able to collect food while working.

Whenever there is water in rice paddies there is life—frogs, snails, tiny shrimp, small fish or crabs. In Phum Chhleav the crabs were the easiest to catch for those who knew the trick. It was no use trying in the early mornings or the late afternoons, when the water was cool. Then the crabs were out among the rice plants, holding on to the stalks with their claws. If they heard you coming they dropped to the bottom and swam sidelong away. But in the middle of the day, when the water was warm, the crabs retreated to their burrows in the dikes. You could catch them by reaching into the burrows with your hand—the quicker the better, because they bit with their pincers, sometimes hard enough to draw blood. I put the crabs in my shirt pockets. They couldn't climb out. I always wore the same shirt in the fields, a Lon Nol–era camouflage-colored parachutist's shirt with big pockets and extra pockets that Huoy sewed on the inside. I worked in the fields with my shirt tails out and my pockets bulging with live crabs.

We cooked the crabs in our hut in the evening, after the regular dinner of thin rice gruel and the political meeting that usually followed. Sometimes Huoy and I ate fifteen or twenty crabs each. Every family in Phum Chhleav had someone working in the rice fields, and everybody ate crabs in secret. The few times that Huoy and I managed to get meat or fish, we cooked and ate the flesh first, then put the bones back in the pot, waited until the bones were soft and ate them too for the calcium and the proteins and the nutrients in the marrow. We wasted nothing.

Food was power. For all the talk about a revolutionary society in which everyone was equal, those at the top ate reasonably well and those of us at the bottom were chronically malnourished. Every day, when the gong rang for lunch, *mit neary* brought a vat of watery rice to a hillock in the fields and ladled watery rice into bowls for the "new" people. Meanwhile, the soldiers went off to the Khmer Rouge headquarters, the row of three houses near the railroad tracks. The rest of us had seen oxcarts laden with supplies pull up to those three houses. We saw the smoke from the cooking fires every day. We didn't need to be told what was happening inside. But when the soldiers came back to the rice fields, licking their lips, looking well fed and content, they pretended not to have eaten anything at all. They took up bowls and ate watery gruel the same as we did. They spooned the liquid into their mouths with loud slurping noises and said, "Look. We eat like you. Exactly the same food. It's enough for us, so it should be enough for you. You people really are lazy. You must work harder, to show your gratitude to Angka."

With or without their rifles, the soldiers had an aura of power about them, like big, muscular village bullies. We were weaker and afraid of them. We weren't strong enough to fight back, so we kept quiet and ate our crabs in secret and waited for the rice harvest to come so we could eat all we wanted. But the Khmer Rouge had other ideas for the rice crop.

One morning I straightened up from opening a dike in the rice fields to see a lone figure in the distance. It was the old man on horseback. He rode slowly along the trail by the railroad tracks, coming toward us from the railroad station at Phnom Tippeday. He looked the same as before, his silk sarong doubled up to his waist and the edge of his black culottes showing underneath, his krama around his middle. He rode leisurely along the path until he got to the three houses, then dismounted and went inside.

Comrade Ik didn't come to Phum Chhleav unless he had a reason.

A few hours later, after lunch, he led his horse out on the dikes of the rice fields. He walked this way and that, inspecting the rice plants and the water levels in the paddies. Whichever way he moved, I unobtrusively moved in the opposite direction, so the two of us wouldn't meet. Finally he reached the edge of the fields, mounted and slowly rode off.

There goes bad news, I thought.

Comrade Ik's orders filtered down the Phum Chhleav hierarchy and eventually to the leader of my work group, who was, a "new" person. He told us the news the next day while I was standing in a paddy in water up to my knees, leaning on my hoe. "We will move from Phum Chhleav fairly soon," he announced pompously. "We don't know precisely when, but Angka will tell us the date later on."

I didn't allow emotion to show on my face. I didn't trust the group leader, even though he was from Phnom Penh like the rest of us. He was heavier and stronger than we were, with clear, healthy skin. I wondered where he was getting his food. My coworkers didn't trust him either. He had scarcely turned his back when they began to complain.

"See? See? They're doing it again!" said a man I had known in Tonle Batí. "They always say, 'If you work hard, you can eat.' Now that we've worked hard and planted the crop, they want us to move away! Where will we go now? Whose crop can we eat now, if we cannot eat our own?"

"Yes," said another one bitterly. "Some armies kill with bullets. The Khmer Rouge kill with rice! I cannot believe it: We have rice all around us, but we cannot eat it! I have never seen so much rice in my whole life, and I have never been so hungry."

I said nothing, though I agreed with them. With so much rice, with so many people sick, it was the cruelest of crimes to take us away before the harvest. But it didn't surprise me that they were doing it. To me, the only question was whether they were doing it to kill us intentionally, or whether they were doing it by mistake. For if there was one thing sure about the Khmer Rouge, it was that they knew nothing about planning. They were always starting projects but not finishing them, then going on to the next.

Discouraged, we slowed our pace in the fields. If we could not eat the rice around us, we were not going to work hard to produce it.

As things turned out, the Khmer Rouge didn't trust our group leader either. A couple of days later we saw soldiers lead him away with his arms tied behind his back—caught for running a business after work, trading gold to "old" people for meat.

The following morning the exodus began. Huoy and I removed the white tarp from the roof of our hut. We packed the tarp, the mosquito net, the mats and the clothes into bundles once again and attached them to the shoulderboard. Another journey. We had been on the move ever since the communists took over. From Phnom Penh to Wat Kien Svay Krao. From there, the failed attempt to escape the country, which brought us to Tonle Batí. From Tonle Batí by truck and train to Phum Chhleav, with Ma's death on the way. And now this. The Khmer Rouge said we were going to the "front lines" but didn't explain what or where the front lines were. For all we knew we were going to the moon.

With a groan, I hoisted the bamboo stick to my shoulder. The load was heavy. My weight and strength were still below normal because of the dysentery, and I had stubbornly packed the rest of my medical reference books in our luggage, even though Huoy had asked me to throw them away. Huoy carried the teapot in her right hand, and with her left hand she steadied a bundle on her head. We entered the muddy pathways of the crowded settlement. In many places the paths were six inches deep in water. Garbage and human wastes flowed downhill over the paths and in and out of houses. Phum Chhleav was on low ground, and when the rains came it caught the runoff water from higher land nearby.

Around us, the other inhabitants emerged from the huts they had built of thatch and reeds and pieces of plastic, and started down the paths. It was a cold morning. The "new" people wrapped their kramas around their shoulders to stay warm. Those who didn't have kramas or extra shirts shivered and rubbed themselves with their hands. We walked down the paths toward the railroad tracks, but not everybody in Phum Chhleav was lucky enough to leave. Through the open door of a hut, we saw an old lady lying unconscious against a wall. Her legs were grossly swollen with edema. She stank with wastes and was covered with flies. Unable to walk and too heavy to carry, she had been left behind.

As we climbed onto the railroad track, which was elevated a few feet above the nearby ground and was the only dry place in the landscape, we looked around at the pitiful spectacle. And then I understood why the rice fields had been so empty of workers. It was as if all the patients I had visited in their huts had been multiplied many times over and put in a parade before our eyes. People with shrunken faces and haunted, vacant eyes, with legs and arms as thin as sticks or else puffy and bloated with edema. Leaning on canes or on relatives' shoulders, or alone, they walked with that terrible economy of movement that signals the approach of starvation. As Huoy and I watched, a thin, scrawny, middle-aged woman put down the end of the hammock she had been carrying, slung under a bamboo pole. The man inside the hammock called out weakly, "Sweet, sweet, bring me with you! Don't leave me behind!" But the woman shook her head and trudged off down the railroad track. After a moment of indecision the man carrying the other end of the hammock abandoned it too and hobbled off after her. No one went to the hammock to help the man. I didn't. Even if I could have helped him, there was no way that

Huoy and I could have carried him. If we tried to carry him we probably wouldn't make it ourselves. So we walked on.

The sun cast our shadows in front of us, onto the railroad track. I put the shoulderboard down, shifted it to the other shoulder and went on. To me, every hundred yards seemed like a mile. To other people, every ten yards was a mile. Around us the malnourished, the sick and the near-dead shuffled on in groups of two and three, dressed in whatever rags they owned. Everyone was muddy. Some had wet their crotches or soiled the seats of their pants. They stopped to rest, covered with flies, and some who rested just stayed there, giving in to gravity. A teenage boy ahead of us tried to get up from a sitting position. He put his palms on the ground and pushed but wasn't strong enough. He tried again, pushing as hard as he could with his matchstick arms. With a great effort he got his buttocks off the ground and then brought his legs underneath and shakily rose to his feet. He took a step, almost fell and then took another faltering step as we passed him.

What made it worse, what made it more appalling was that some-how it was ordinary. You put one foot in front of the other and you kept on walking. You heard the cries of the weak but you didn't pay much attention, because you were concentrating on yourself and your own survival. We had all seen death before. In the exodus from Phum Chhleav, the atrocious had become normal.

No one took count, but my guess is that of the seventy-eight hundred who walked in to Phum Chhleav, a little over half walked out, and some of those were dying on the way. Those who lay down and didn't get up had plenty of company, for scattered along the railroad track were corpses from the previous days and weeks. What happened to the corpses is what always happens in a tropical climate. Their skin had swollen, turned purple-black and burst through their clothes. Most of them had one leg or one arm raised stiffly in the air. They stank badly. Their eyes were half open. Flies clustered around the mouths and anuses and eyes. For them I felt sorrow more than revulsion. It was not the dead's fault that they were lying there. It was the Khmer Rouge's fault for causing the deaths, and the relatives' fault for not burying the dead. And that made me angry.

How fast man changes! How fast he sheds his outer humanity

and becomes the animal inside! In the old days—only six months before—nobody abandoned the dead. It was part of our religious tradition that if we didn't cremate or bury the bodies, and if we didn't pray, the souls would wander around lost. They would be unable to go to heaven, or to be reborn. Now everything had changed—not just our burial customs but also all our beliefs and behavior. We had no more monks and no religious services. We had no more family obligations. Children left their parents to die, wives abandoned their husbands and the strongest kept on moving. The Khmer Rouge had taken away everything that held our culture together, and this was the result: a parade of the selfish and the dying. Society was falling apart.

My own family was falling apart too. Of my father's eight children, only three of his sons were still with him, and I was barely on speaking terms with the other two and their wives. My brothers had done nothing for me when I was sick. They had been willing to abandon me to die. Huoy and I kept my parents in sight as we trudged along the railroad track, but we didn't walk together.

In the late afternoon we all made it to the railroad station at Phnom Tippeday. There the Khmer Rouge gave us two cans of rice apiece, enough for a couple of undersized meals. We trudged on, following the crowd along the road to the south.

We went through a village called Phum Phnom—literally translated, "village of the mountain." It lay at the base of the mountain ridge that dominated the western skyline. It was empty except for some Khmer Rouge soldiers and those of us "new" people who were passing through. Near the old town hall, which the Khmer Rouge had taken for their regional headquarters, the road split in three directions. We took the left fork, following the other stragglers from Phum Chhleav.

That night we camped on a hillock in the rice fields—my parents, my brothers and Huoy and I. A Chinese family shared the hillock with us. The night was noisy with frogs and crickets and the treetops stirring in the wind. I couldn't sleep. I got up several times to sit in front of the fire, feeling its warmth, rubbing my hands, watching the flames. Huoy, who was worried about my health, kept asking me to come back next to her and sleep. Finally I did. In the morning we discovered that the Chinese man on the other side of me had died. In the dark nobody had noticed.

With this, something inside me snapped. It was too much to accept—the death march, the hunger, the uncertainty of going to another unknown destination. I brought Huoy and the rest of my family to a shady spot on the side of the road and asked them to stay there. Then I went off, exploring, without any clear idea of what I was going to do.

The first person I ran into was Pen Tip. Pen Tip had practiced medicine in Phum Chhleav, though he was not a doctor. Even then there had been something familiar about him, and I had searched my brain for the reason. Finally I placed him: Around 1972, at the hospital in Phnom Penh where I had gone for my radiology rotation as a medical student, Pen Tip had been a radiological assistant, positioning patients for the X-ray camera. He was a tiny man, less than five feet tall, sure of himself and quite clever. We knew each other by sight, but this was our first conversation.

Pen Tip told me in a self-satisfied way that he had gotten permission to stay in a hamlet nearby. He said it was better to stay there, close to the railroad, than to move even farther into the countryside. Anything was better, he declared, than going to the front lines.

"I was thinking the same thing," I said. Whatever the front lines were, I didn't want to go to them. "Besides, in the mountains to the south there is sure to be more malaria."

"I agree, Doctor," he said.

"Don't call me 'Doctor,' " I said. "But thank you for the advice."

I left Pen Tip and wandered off. The next person I talked to was an "old" person who turned out to be originally from Chambak, just down the road from my home village, Samrong Yong. Because I came from a village near hers, she was very kind to me. She took me to see a man whom she thought might take me in. His name was Youen. He was an "old" person and section leader of another hamlet nearby.

Youen was a dark-skinned man with short, wavy hair and broken teeth. He wore only black culottes cinched around his waist with a cracked leather belt. As we talked, he took out a pouch with locally grown tobacco and soft, brown flexible pieces of banana leaf inside. He sprinkled tobacco on a rectangular piece of banana leaf and rolled it into a cigarette, with one end slightly larger than the other. He flattened it between his fingers and lit the larger end with a lighter.

I told him my name was "Samnang" (a common nickname whose literal meaning is "lucky"). My wife was "Bopha" (which means "flower" in Khmer, just as "Huoy" means "flower" in Teochiew Chinese). I said I had been a taxicab driver in Phnom Penh. I came from a humble background. "Bopha" and I wanted to work for him. We would do anything he asked if we could stay there. We wanted to serve him and in this way serve Angka. If he let us stay there it would save our lives.

"Tell me more about your background," he said.

I explained how I had lived in Samrong Yong all my life, just a simple man of the countryside, until the war drove me into Phnom Penh. My wife and I had been poor under the Lon Nol regime, barely able to find enough to eat. "Bopha" had sold vegetables in the market, but corrupt officials took everything she earned.

Apparently he believed that Huoy and I came from a proper class background, because he agreed to let us stay under his care. I thanked him effusively and went back to find Huoy and my parents.

I was happy. Here was a little backwater, outside of the main current of hunger and revolution. Here we could stay and get enough to eat. Youen would protect us. I told my parents they probably could get a place with him too, if they came along.

My father and my brothers exchanged knowing glances.

I had pointedly invited my parents to join Huoy and me, but not my brothers and their wives and children. On the surface, my reason was practical: We could not all hide with Youen; as a group we would be too conspicuous. But the underlying reason was my anger at my brothers. Had they helped me? Only my father had visited when I was sick. We were all family, but my strongest obligation was to my parents, to the top of the hierarchy. Toward my brothers I felt little; toward my sisters-in-law, nothing. Neither of them had been nice to me or to Huoy.

We talked it over, my father and my brothers and I. Papa agreed that he and my mother would go with Huoy and me.

But fate had not finished playing its hand. The Khmer Rouge had finally realized that they were losing too many workers on the exodus. They sent oxcarts to help the survivors along. My brother Pheng Huor got one of the oxcarts and put his family inside.

My parents were standing beside me with their luggage. Pheng Huor and his wife, two daughters and son drew slowly away with a great creaking of the oxcart's wooden axle. Then Pheng Huor's three-year-old son looked back, saw his grandfather there and began to cry.

It was too much for my old father. The little boy was his favorite in the entire family, the only son of his favorite son.

"Wait! Wait!" Papa shouted. Pheng Huor stopped the oxcart. Without another word, my father and mother ran to the oxcart with their luggage, leaving Huoy and me behind.

17

REORGANIZATION

YOUEN, the chief of the hamlet outside Phum Phnom, was not a man of much ability. He knew how to farm, he knew how to obey orders, but he was not particularly clever or strong. Still, he had agreed to protect Huoy and me, and as long as he did that he would have our loyalty.

His hamlet was full of "old" people. Not much had changed there since prewar times, though the chaos of the revolution was all around. A short walk away, in Phum Phnom, was the Khmer Rouge regional headquarters. In another direction lay Phum Chhleav, a place we were glad to leave behind; and somewhere off in a third direction were the mysterious "front lines," which Huoy and I were trying hard to avoid.

In exchange for Youen's patronage, Huoy and I became his servants. We worked at his house, and at the houses of his sister and his daughter nearby. Huoy helped with the cooking and housework. I swept the yards, filled the water jars and took the oxen out to graze on the stubble of the harvested rice fields. Whenever I walked past anyone in Youen's family I bent over to keep my head lower than theirs. Even if they were sitting down, I tried to stay lower than them. In Cambodia this is the normal deference shown by servants to their masters.

It was amazing, really, what had happened to us. In Phnom Penh, as a doctor, I never would have stooped before an illiterate farmer like Youen. He would have lowered himself in front of me. Now everything was reversed. I offered him water with my eyes downcast, the cup held in both hands. I called him *puk*, which means "father."

As far as Youen and his family were concerned, I was Samnang, the ex–taxi driver. Bopha was my wife. Those were our identities. Huoy and I kept to our roles night and day, except when we were alone together, and even then we whispered, so nobody would discover our true backgrounds.

The strange thing was that Huoy and I were happy. We were like people who had fallen from a cliff and landed on a ledge halfway down. We got used to the ledge and didn't complain about being lower than before—we were glad enough that we hadn't fallen all the way to the bottom. Life wasn't too bad. We didn't have to work very hard. And our health had gotten better, because we had enough rice.

When we first moved in with Youen, he gave us a few cans of rice from his personal supply. Soon he put our names on the ration list, the first step in making us permanent members of his community.

He sent me to a Khmer Rouge depot to get a rice ration. I came staggering back with a 25-kilogram bag of paddy rice on my shoulder and a jubilant smile on my face. Imagine getting so much food from the Khmer Rouge! Imagine knowing that we had enough food for weeks ahead!

Each grain of paddy rice is covered by a tough brown husk with raised ridges. The husks are inedible, so they have to be removed. Youen's sister, whose name was Yin, lent me a hand-operated rice mill. I poured the paddy rice into the mill and turned the crank around and around, grinding the rice between the two flat stones. Out came a mixture of white rice and empty husks, plus some broken bits and pieces.

Next, Huoy poured the mixture of rice and husks on a large flat basket and began tossing the grain up in the air and catching it again. She had never tried it before, but it was really quite easy. The white rice landed back in the basket but the lighter husks or chaff floated away in the breeze.

The rice was edible now, but some of the grains were still covered with a brown layer of bran. Yin showed us how to polish the rice in an old wooden device in Youen's yard. The polisher was like a large-scale mortar and pestle, except that the pestle that struck the rice grains was attached to a foot-operated lever.

This was the old-fashioned way of processing rice in the country-side, milling it, winnowing it and finally polishing it. It was all new to Huoy, who like most city people always bought white rice in the market. But once we had polished the rice she was in her element. She put rice and water in a pot and rubbed the rice between her palms to release the dust and the impurities. She reached in with her fingers to pick out the bits of husk and other impurities that floated to the top. Then she drained the water from the pot, added fresh water to the level of the rice and a little higher, checked the level with her forefinger to make sure, covered the pot and put it on the fire to boil. Once the water had reached a full boil, she pulled wood from the fire to reduce the heat until the water was simmering quietly. Then she let it cook covered and without stirring until all the water had boiled off and evenly spaced steam holes appeared in the surface of the rice.

It was perfect—the grains separate and fragrant-smelling, not too wet or dry. Before eating, Huoy took three sticks of incense from our luggage and lit them, to honor her mother. She prayed aloud, waving the incense in her palms three times in Chinese fashion. "Mother, we have good food now," she said. "We are thinking of you, and we miss you. You eat first."

After the offering we began our meal. We had nothing to serve with our rice and didn't care. We just ate and ate and ate. We ate so much it hurt, and we were still happy.

After we were on the ration list, Youen's sister Yin suggested that we take the next step toward permanent residence, which was building a house. She, Youen and I were standing in Youen's yard, next to the tree that Huoy and I had been sleeping under at night. I didn't say anything, because it wasn't my place to, and studied Yin discreetly. She was a remarkable woman—divorced, in her forties, a gruff-voiced cigarette smoker with thick, muscular arms like a man's. She was physically stronger than Youen, smarter than him and more of a natural leader. Her brother scratched his head as the idea of my building a house slowly sank in.

Yin said impatiently, "If Samnang doesn't know how to build a good house, I will show him." With that, she picked up an ax, handed me another ax and took off at a fast stride. I glanced at Youen, who nodded his permission, and followed her.

I followed her on a path through some rice fields and into the forest. She had enormous, muscular calves and wide, splayed-out feet, and it was all I could do to keep up with her. Finally we reached a dense grove of trees on a hillside and stopped. To give herself maximum freedom of movement, she stood with her legs apart, took the hem at the front of her sarong and twisted it around and around, brought the twisted cloth through her legs and up, and then tucked it into her beltline at the back of her waist. This way her sarong was like a pair of shorts, revealing her stocky thighs. Yin swung her ax. She felled a tree and I felled another one, but it took me longer. She watched me critically as I finished chopping the tree down and then we carried the tree trunks back to the village. Every few minutes I had to stop to put my log down, but Yin strolled on without changing pace, her log on her shoulder, a half-smoked cigarette tucked behind her ear.

We went again the next day, collecting timber to use for the house. She began to talk in her gruff voice as she walked ahead on the pathway. "You eat and eat until there's nothing left," she said. "You will have no seed to plant next year." I kept quiet, afraid that Huoy and I had offended her by eating our rice so greedily. Then I realized that she was talking about "new" people in general and indirectly criticizing the regime.

Yin had watched the relocation march from Phum Chhleav. "I saw you people walking past here to the front lines. Never seen so many sick people before. Never," she grumbled. "Don't know what things are coming to. Before, when you worked you got money. You could take your money to the market and buy medicines. Cure yourself. But not now. No markets. Can't buy anything. No money either. New government doesn't even have money."

She turned around as if with an afterthought, swinging the log on her shoulder as if it were weightless, and looked at me with narrowed eyes. I was panting hard.

"Never seen anything like this watery rice they feed you people. Hardly any rice in it at all. People like you get weak and skinny. You're not good for much when you're weak. Not good for much at all." I looked down at my body and had to agree with her. My shirt was open in front and all my ribs were showing.

"Yes," I said humbly, "it is true that there has not always been enough to eat. But Angka says we have to sacrifice until we build up the nation."

Yin looked at me as if I were a fool, and spat vigorously to the side. "Used to grow more rice around here," she said. "Much more. Now, people living here don't work as hard as they used to. No reason why they should. Can't plant what they want. Can't eat when they want. So they grow less. Problem is, there's a lot more people to eat it now. Like you and your wife."

"Auntie Yin," I said, using the polite prerevolutionary form of address, "I apologize for the food my wife and I eat. We do not mean to be a burden."

"Not your fault, son. Angka runs things around here. Angka owns all the fields. Owns everything. I planted mango trees—I've got to ask Angka for permission to pick the mangoes. Never seen a government like this one."

Yin continued down the path, shaking her head. "Never seen a government like this one," she repeated, and spat again.

I hurried after, smiling to myself. Her skeptical grumbling was full of common sense. Yin could live in her house without going to the front lines. She didn't go hungry. But she still didn't like the revolution, and I found comfort in that.

When Yin and I had cut enough wood for the house frame, we gathered reeds that had been growing on the edges of the rice fields and made thatch by sewing bundles of reeds together. Soon we had the house finished, a sturdy, waterproof, one-room affair. It wasn't beautiful, but it was far better than the hut in Phum Chhleav and better than my first hut in Tonle Bati. Huoy and I moved in, buried my medical books and other secret possessions under the dirt floor and spread the white plastic mat on top.

With the house, we became members of Youen's community. But I sensed that our situation was not permanent. From time to time emaciated stragglers from the mass relocation marches came wandering through the landscape, as sick as anybody who had been in Phum Chhleav. And all around Youen's hamlet the Khmer Rouge were busy. Every day, messengers on bicycles and motorcycles drove by, coming from or going to the headquarters in Phum Phnom. The leaders went past us on horseback and jeep, on their inspection tours. The Khmer Rouge had big plans. They were mobilizing the whole countryside.

All too soon, the day came that I had dreaded. Youen assembled everyone from the nearby houses, and announced, "Angka needs all childless couples to go to the front lines."

The news was like a body blow. Huoy and I thought we had an understanding with Youen. We had become his servants. We had worked for him. He was supposed to protect us.

Youen said the two of us and another couple would be going. "Better get ready," Youen told me. "They say you should have a hammock, a hoe, some rope and some baskets for hauling dirt. You won't need anything else."

I felt betrayed. "How can I go to the front lines?" I told him. "I don't have any of the equipment. It's ridiculous. I won't go."

Youen hadn't expected me to talk back to him, and he was slow to react. "Well, maybe Angka can supply you with what you need at the front lines," he said.

"No. I need the equipment here," I said. Indirectly, I was both resisting the order and challenging his authority. Besides, I knew that Youen had a son who was married but childless. He hadn't made his son go. He had protected Huoy and me for a short while, but when the pressure was on, he got rid of us.

Youen raised his voice and spoke to everyone. "This is Angka's rule, not my rule. Everyone who must go, must go!"

Yin came up to me and stood with her back to her brother so he couldn't hear. "Son, we have no choice," she whispered. "I don't want to push you out. I wish you could stay. You and your wife are nice people. But really, you must obey. If you don't obey, it will mean trouble for everyone."

I knew that she was right. Yin was a smart, good-hearted woman, and my respect for her was great. But I argued until Youen gave me two old hemp rice sacks to make a hammock with, and one hoe and a rope. Then I asked him for another hoe and the baskets, not because I thought he was going to agree but because I was stalling for time. Huoy was in our house getting our secret possessions from the hole in the dirt floor. By the time she came out of the house with our luggage, the *bonheur* between Youen and me was gone. I didn't care.

Huoy and I and the other couple got ready to walk. An escort of soldiers with rifles had come in to show us the way. The soldiers motioned to us to start. We began to walk slowly down a path to the south, to rejoin Angka's experiment of social reorganization.

We walked for less than an hour. We were still in sight of the big mountain ridge behind the Phnom Tippeday train station, but on its back side, out of sight of the wat on the plateau. Though I had no way of knowing it, this was the area where we would remain for the next three years. None of the places we had already been in this part of the country—from the railway station at Phnom Tippeday, to Phum Chhleav where I had pulled the plow, to Phum Phnom where the Khmer Rouge had their headquarters—or where we would go, among the transient labor camps of the front lines, was more than a few hours' walk apart. Our new universe was about ten miles square.

The soldiers took us to a hillock where the front lines "cooperative," as it was called, had its field kitchen, warehouses and administrative quarters. We were given the rest of the tools we needed and sent off to another wooded hillock, where we would sleep.

With her quick, expert fingers Huoy sewed a double hammock out of the rice sacks. We rigged the hammock between two trees and strung the mosquito net overhead to protect us from the mosquitoes, gnats and flies. We were part of a section of about two hundred young married "new" people, some with children, most without. Between two and three thousand other "new" people camped out on neighboring hillocks in the dry rice fields.

The main task of our cooperative was digging canals for irrigation and water control. Every week or so, as work on the canals progressed, the location of the cooperative was moved. Every day we dug as long as there was light to see by, and usually long after. At night we attended political meetings. I had never worked so hard in my life, nor slept and eaten so little. We had no days off, no holidays, no celebrations.

It was here on the front lines that I truly understood, for the first time, the Khmer Rouge's far-reaching plan for the reorganization of Cambodian society. They had led us to it in stages, first with the evacuation of the cities, then with the gradual tightening of their rules, then with the second and third exoduses where necessary. In February 1976, on the front lines, they were trying out their revolutionary theories in purest form.

The key concept for the new society, as we were told all the time in propaganda sessions, was "independence-sovereignty." One word made out of two, independence-sovereignty. For Democratic Kampuchea, this meant being absolutely free of other countries—free of their aid and even of their cultural influence. We Khmers would make it on our own. By reorganizing and harnessing the energy of our people and by eliminating everything that distracted from our work, we would become an advanced, developed nation almost overnight. And that rapid development, or "great leap forward," as it was called, required our "correct revolutionary understanding" of many other concepts and terms. For us it was almost like learning a new language.

For example, there was the concept of "struggle." I had been hearing about "struggle" ever since the takeover in Phnom Penh, but it was only on the front lines that I fully understood how it fit in with the rest of the ideology. "Struggle" was military talk, like "front lines." It reflected the idea that the nation was still at war. On the front lines we didn't just work, we "struggled," or else "launched offensives." We were to "struggle to cultivate rice fields vigorously," "struggle to dig canals with great courage," "struggle to clear the forest," and even "struggle to solve the manure problem." We were to "launch an offensive to plant strategic crops," and "launch an offensive to perform duty with revolutionary zeal."

The goal of this struggling and launching of offensives was "victory," or "mastery." We were going to achieve "victory over the elements." We would become "master of the rice paddies and fields and forests," "master of the earth and water," "master of the canals," "master of the flood problem."

To become masters, to achieve the "great leap forward," we had to sacrifice. That meant working hard without complaining, no matter what the obstacles. No complaining, even though we worked eighteen- or twenty-hour days, with only thin rice gruel to eat. They wanted us to be single-minded work fanatics, never slowing our pace. They wanted us to be revolutionary zealots. As a song on the Khmer Rouge radio put it, "We are not afraid of the night, the day, the winds, the storms and rain and sickness. We gladly sacrifice for Angka to show support for the revolution."

We had to sacrifice everything from the old regime, including material possessions. "Get rid of all the Western goods you still have with you," a cadre told us. "Because if you keep those things your minds will still be on the old times and you will not be able to work hard. Discard the makeup, the fancy clothing, the books, the gold. You do not need them. Get rid of your cooking pots and utensils too. If you cannot discard these things, you are the enemy. You will still be serving capitalism, and not serving the community. You do not need any property now."

They abolished private property. Everything belonged to Angka now. Luckily, the Khmer Rouge code kept the soldiers from searching our bodies for property, because that was where Huoy and I kept our gold and where all the "new" people hid their valuables. And they never found my medical books and instruments because I buried them underground. But they went through our luggage. Missing, when we came back from work, were some of Huoy's silk blouses and *sampots*, some of her brassieres, her makeup kit, most of her mother's clothes and our cooking pots, except for the teapot, which we were allowed to keep.

They had already abolished religion—disrobed the monks, destroyed the Buddha statues. On the front lines they abolished the family too. They wanted us to renounce personal attachments of any kind, because those relationships interfered with our devotion to Angka. Children had to leave their parents, the elderly had to leave their sons and daughters, and if work assignments required it, husbands and wives had to split up too. From Angka's point of view this was "liberation," because it freed us from the time of caring for others and gave us more time to work. To maximize working time they abolished individual meals too. Everyone ate meals in the common kitchen.

"How lucky you are!" Chev, the front lines leader, exclaimed to us in an evening meeting. "You come back from work and the rice is already cooked for you! You have no cares, no worries. Your children are taken care of. Your parents are taken care of. Everybody is happy! Everything is provided to you by Angka. The young people don't even have to go to school! Under Angka, the 'school' is the farm. The 'fountain pen' is the plow. The 'paper' is the land. You can 'write' all you want. Anytime. Everything is free. No money for tuition. You don't need to pay for anything now.

"How lucky you are!" he said. "Under the regime of the arch-fascist, arch-imperialist, arch-feudalist Lon Nol, you were oppressed! You never knew any happiness! You were not masters of your country then! You were slaves! Everywhere was corruption! The greedy merchants and the fascist military took over the land! Now under the glorious reign of Angka you are masters of your own destiny. You are masters of the water and the land. The entire people, united in solidarity, join in building the country. Life is much better now. There is no more corruption. No more gambling or prostitution. You are learning from the peasants and workers, who are the source of all useful knowledge. Only the peasants and workers possess it. The monks don't possess it. The only wise man is the one who knows how to grow rice."

The Khmer Rouge wanted a complete change of society, from top to bottom. Gone was everything that had governed our lives in the old times. Lon Nol was gone, airlifted to America before the fall; Sihanouk was gone, his fate a mystery. The monks were gone. ("The monks are bloodsucking imperialists. If any worker secretly takes rice to the monks, we shall set him to planting cabbages. If the cabbages are not full-grown in three days, he will dig his own grave.") The families were broken up, the children and the elderly sent off to live in their own groups. There were no more cities. No more markets, stores, restaurants or cafes. No privately owned buses, cars or bicycles. No schools. No books or magazines. No money. No clocks. No holidays and religious festivals. Just the sun that rose and set, the stars at night and the rain that fell from the sky. And work. Everything was work, in the empty, primitive countryside.

In place of the old regime there was a new government whose upper layers could only be guessed at. Angka—whoever that was—was at the top. Logically, Angka had to be a person or group of people, but many found it easier to believe that Angka was an all-powerful entity, something like a god. "Angka has eyes like a pineapple," Chev told us, repeating a common saying of the regime. "It sees everywhere. So you must behave correctly." The mystery of Angka's identity added to its power, because "Angka" also meant the regime at all levels, from the topmost leader down to the lowest spy. In fact, Chev sometimes told us that we were Angka too.

Below the topmost officials was (I guessed) a layer of "zone" leaders, with the "zones" roughly corresponding to the old provinces. What used to be Battambang Province was now a part of the Northwest Zone. The identity of our zone leader was unknown to me, but his top local official was a man who sped around the dirt roads on inspection tours, always sitting in the passenger seat of a jeep. I had seen this man several times, riding with his right arm sticking out the window and his hand resting on the roof, though I had never been close enough to see his face. Below him in the civil administration was Comrade Ik, the old man on horseback, who had addressed us in Phum Chhleav. Below Comrade Ik were the village leaders. The leader of Phum Phnom, and overseer of Youen's hamlet, was Chev; but Chev also had a parallel role as leader of this cooperative on the front lines. Other village leaders and a few military leaders reported to him on the front lines, and below them were section leaders, who usually were not Khmer Rouge but trusted "old" people. Beneath the section leaders were group leaders, who usually were "new" people directing the work of about ten other "new" people like me.

Sometimes, as I stood by the canal, hoe in hand, I had to admit: Angka, the Organization, had indeed reorganized the countryside. Before the takeover, nobody could have thought that the land would look as it did now, with thousands of people marching to work in orderly single-file lines. And Angka did more than set the tasks. It had provided a complete philosophy, parts of which were obviously true (the corruption under Lon Nol had indeed been terrible), and other parts of which appealed to patriotism (we needed to rebuild the country after the civil war). With loudspeakers attached to poles near the common kitchens, our new leaders blared a new music that carried far across the rice fields. And when I listened to that marching music, with its strong and vigorous beat, and when I saw the huge red flags flapping in the breeze and didn't look too closely at the lines of people, I found myself believing, for at least a few moments at a time, that the Khmer Rouge had done it. They had succeeded in remaking the country to their bold plan. They had erased the individual, except as a unit in a group. They had given us a new religion to devote ourselves to, and that religion was Angka.

But when I looked more closely, the illusion fell apart. The people working in the canal were tired and malnourished and their clothes were torn. Just like me. Their hoes rose and fell slowly, without energy, and their faces expressed a terrible futility and sorrow.

That's all it took, a moment's glance, to know that the country had turned in the wrong direction.

The Khmer Rouge pushed their own beliefs to extremes, and in doing so turned them into lies. They wanted us to work—then they worked us so hard that we produced less and less, because we were weak. They wanted to purify the country of everything that was not Khmer. Buddha was an outsider, from India, so they destroyed the Buddhist temples. The cities were too tainted with Western imperialist ways, so they made us leave. They wanted to eliminate everything that was not Cambodian. But they were hypocrites. Except for their dark skins, everything about the Khmer Rouge was alien, from China. They borrowed their ideology from Mao Tse-tung, like the concept of the great leap forward. Sending the intellectuals to the countryside to learn from the peasants was an idea of the Chinese Cultural Revolution. Their AK-47s and their olive green caps and their trucks were Chinese. Even the music they played from the loudspeakers was Chinese, with Khmer words.

The Khmer Rouge's greatest strength was propaganda. They knew that a small lie can be caught and that a big lie is easier to get away with. Their system was so different from anything we had known before, and so complete, that we gave in without really knowing how to resist. Even if we had been allowed to speak out publicly, which we weren't—and if we did, they tied us up and marched us away—there was something inadequate about trying to counter their words with arguments of our own. It just didn't help. For example, I could say to Huoy, in a whisper, that any government that oppressed as many of its people as the Khmer Rouge would eventually weaken itself. I could say that to her, and believe it, and she could agree with me, but it wouldn't do us any good. When the whispering was over the regime was still there and we were still digging with hoes and feeling tired and hungry and not even able to remember the last time we felt any different. There was no way out of the situation. We were only left knowing in our bones that we were being abused.

There was a medical clinic on the front lines. The nurses there used dirty needles and didn't care one way or another if their patients died. At mealtime during a visit there, I heard one nurse calling out to another, "Have you fed the war slaves yet?" It was a chance remark, but it stuck in my ears because it explained the Khmer Rouge better than anything else. All the talk about being comrades in a classless society, building the nation with our bare hands and struggling to achieve independence-sovereignty didn't mean anything. The Khmer Rouge had beaten us in the civil war. We were their war slaves. That was all there was to it. They were taking revenge. And on the front lines, day and night, they ran our lives with bells.

18

BELLS

THEY RANG the first bell at four o'clock in the morning.

Still exhausted from the day before, Huoy and I rose out of our hempen hammock, got to our feet, rubbed our eyes, groped for the water jar and washed our faces.

Around us other couples, seen as silhouettes moving against the starry sky, did the same, or else tried to steal another few minutes of sleep. But there was no escaping the bell. It was a penetrating, relentless noise. A command to be obeyed.

After the bell fell silent, a hiss came out of the loudspeakers by the common kitchen, followed by the music of the national anthem. A chorus of men's, women's and children's voices sang:

> Bright red blood that covers towns and plains
> Of Kampuchea, our motherland,
> Sublime blood of workers and peasants,
> Sublime blood of revolutionary men and women fighters!
> The blood, changing into unrelenting hatred
> And resolute struggle
> On April Seventeenth, under the flag of the revolution,
> Frees us from slavery!
>
> Long live, long live, Glorious April Seventeenth!
> Glorious victory with greater significance
> Than the age of Angkor Wat. . . .

Another day on the front lines had begun.

At four thirty they rang the bell again. Slow, separate beats to start with, then gradually faster until the notes ran together: *DING*

. . . *DING* . . . *DING* . . . *ding, ding, ding, ding, ding* . . . *ding-ding-ding-dingdingdingdingding!!!* Then a pause, and they rang it again. Another pause, and they rang it a third time: *DING* . . . *DING* . . . *DING* . . . *ding, ding, ding, ding* . . . *ding-ding-ding-ding-dingdingding-dingding!*

Always, they rang the bell in series of three. Before the revolution the monks had beat their drums in the same pattern, dull, single booms at first and then faster and faster into a drum roll, then a pause and then starting over again, in threes. With that signal, the monks had called the faithful to prayer. Unconsciously, perhaps, the cadre banging his stick against the metal car wheel hanging near the common kitchen was replaying a rhythm of his youth. Or perhaps, in the new "religion" of Angka, work had come to mean something like prayer, as a way of purifying ourselves and showing our devotion.

By the second series of bells, Huoy and I had joined our separate groups, ten people in each. Different groups joined together, depending on their work sites, and set off across the landscape in long, single-file lines.

I carried a hoe on my right shoulder. From the right side of my belt hung my hatchet; from the left side hung a small metal U.S.-made field cooking pot, curved to fit against my hip, with a tightly fitting lid on top and boiled water inside. From a cord around my neck hung my spoon. Hidden in tiny pockets inside my waistband were a Swiss watch, several pieces of gold and a worn Zippo lighter with an extra supply of flints. I was barefoot. My long-sleeved shirt was ripped and unbuttoned. I wore a brimmed palm-leaf hat to protect against the sun, but the sun hadn't risen yet. There was a grayish light above the eastern horizon, just enough to see by.

When we reached the canal my group split off and went to its site, marked with wooden stakes. The canal was a dry trench deeper than I was tall and twice as far across, with sloping sides. Along the top but set back from it were dikes made from the clay we had dug, giving the canal a height of several feet above the surrounding land, to contain floodwaters. I climbed down to the bottom of the canal, sighed and swung my hoe. I didn't swing it hard; my muscles were stiff. I swung again. The trick was to warm up gradually, then work at a steady pace without straining.

I swung again, putting fractionally more into it. With the edge of the hoe, I scooped the loose earth into a mud basket; the others picked it up and handed it in relays to the top of the canal.

In the gray light the canals stretched in a straight line as far as the eye could see. Elsewhere, crews dug other canals to meet at right angles with ours, plus smaller ditches or minicanals to tie the entire network together. The canals, the Khmer Rouge assured us, would collect the runoff water in the rainy season and hold it until the dry season, when the water would be used to irrigate the fields. Yes, I thought bitterly, the Khmer Rouge had great faith in their canals. "We will grow three rice crops a year!" an enthusiastic cadre told us at a political meeting. "Nobody will ever go hungry again! And if the Americans attack us again we will dig a canal across the Pacific Ocean and invade their territory!"

The band of orange above the horizon thickened and turned to pink as the sun rose. Next to me in the bottom of the canal a skinny man gave off deep, unconscious sighs as he worked. I knew what he was thinking. No days off, no gaiety, no incentive to work hard except to stay alive. Or half alive, which is what we were.

Don't think about it, I told myself. Just swing the hoe and let it fall. Don't wear yourself out but get the job done. Look at that wooden stake. When we dig that far we will finish and they will send us somewhere else. But where will they send us? To flat ground or to a hillock? Flat ground is easier to dig, but hillocks are better. So much life in the hillocks' soil. Last week that snake slithering into its hole and all of us tearing the hillock apart and finally killing it with our hoes. How Huoy smiled when I brought my share to her. First time she's smiled that I can remember.

Chop. Chop. In either direction, the sound of hoes chopping into clay. Another hot, cloudless day. Working steadily, the sweat running down from my armpits.

When the sun shone across one wall of the canal and into the edge of the bottom, a shout rang out: "Comrades, take a break!" Everyone dropped tools and climbed out of the canal. Huoy waited for me in the shade of a *sdao* tree nearby. I reached above her and snapped off a branch, then stripped off the leaves, putting them in my pockets, before sitting down. We shared water from my canteen. She sat with her back against the tree trunk. I sat with my back against her shins, rubbing the red, itchy sores that were spreading up my ankles and onto my legs.

Breaks were for smoking. The common kitchen distributed locally grown tobacco to the group leaders, who distributed it to workers like us. I took a wad of tobacco from my pocket and rolled a cigarette with a piece of banana leaf, lighting it with the Zippo. I took a few puffs without inhaling, then let it die out and put the rest in my pocket. There. Anybody watching would see I had smoked, and I would continue getting the ration. And I would trade most of my tobacco ration for food, because there were some tobacco addicts on the front lines who would rather smoke than eat.

There were also a few marijuana smokers. Next to us in the shade of a tree, an old man sucked noisily on a bamboo water pipe and held the aromatic smoke in his lungs as long as he could before exhaling contentedly. Marijuana smoking was an age-old tradition followed by a small percentage of rural men, and by a few others who had started smoking in Lon Nol's army. The smokers themselves didn't attach any particular meaning to the drug and neither did the Khmer Rouge, who didn't bother outlawing it. When the marijuana smokers got up from their breaks they seemed to work even harder than before. I tried smoking it once, hoping it would do the same for me, but instead I felt an almost overpowering urge to lie down and sleep, so I never smoked it again.

"Back to work, comrades!"

I climbed down to the bottom of the ditch again and picked up the hoe. And I sighed.

In the late morning, when there was no more shade in the bottom of the canal, they turned on the loudspeaker system at the common kitchen. The music came to us faintly but clearly across the fields. It began with the national anthem:

> Bright red blood that covers towns and plains
> Of Kampuchea, our motherland,
> Sublime blood of workers and peasants
> Sublime blood of revolutionary men and women fighters . . .

"The blood," I sung grimly to myself, ". . .frees us from slavery!" I knew every word. The rise and fall of every phrase, the timing of every gong and xylophone flourish.

. . . We are uniting to build
Splendid Democratic Kampuchea
A new society with equality and justice
Firmly applying the line of independence-sovereignty
    and self-reliance
Let us resolutely defend
Our motherland, our sacred soil
And our glorious revolution!

. . . And our terrible revolution, I sang in my mind.

Long live, long live, long live
Democratic, prosperous and new Kampuchea
Let us resolutely raise high
The red flag of the revolution
Let us build our motherland!
Let us advance her with a great leap forward
So she will be more glorious and marvelous than ever!

After the national anthem came a song called "Hooray for the Courageous, Strong and Marvelous Revolutionary Soldiers' Group." After this came "New Safety for the Small Town Under the Light of the Glorious Revolution," and then "Our Splendid Fighting Comrades Struggle to Study the Revolutionary Way of Living." I knew them all, and hated them. They were all so un-Cambodian. I pictured an imaginary loudspeaker on the bottom of the canal, swung the hoe and smashed it. Swung again and smashed it again. And then found that I was swinging the hoe to the rhythm of the music. There was no way to avoid it. Not when I knew every phrase, every beat.

After "Revolutionary Soldiers' Groups Protect the Safety of Democratic Kampuchea" the loudspeakers mercifully fell silent. Once again the sighs of the workers and the chittering of birds accompanied the sounds of hoes chopping into clay.

Then "The Glorious Seventeenth of April" started out of the loudspeakers again.

Bright red blood that covers towns and plains
Of Kampuchea . . .

———

At lunchtime they rang the bell: *DING . . . DING . . . DING . . . .* Before the first bell had stopped, we fell into a line and trudged off, merging with other lines that converged on the common kitchen.

This kitchen site, on a large hillock nearly cleared of trees, was only a few days old. The kitchen crew had erected a framework of wood and bamboo over the fire pits and had put the first thatch panels up on the roof. A few soldiers had slung their hammocks between the poles at the far end of the framework. Outside, mounted on top of a bamboo pole, were the loudspeakers, facing four directions, with wires running down the pole to the tape player and a truck battery near the soldiers' hammocks. From a branch of one of the remaining trees hung a metal car wheel: the bell.

Nine of us sat on the ground in a circle while the tenth, our group leader, went to the kitchen to get our rations. Toward the others of my group I felt little emotion. No hostility, but no real liking. People were always leaving the group for other work assignments or coming in from the villages of the "back lines." You never knew them long enough to trust them, to become friends.

Our group leader was a "new" person like us, with torn trousers and sweat-matted hair. He stood in a long line that edged slowly close to the ration table. At the table was a *mit neary* with the blackened teeth of a betel chewer, about forty years old. Her left arm steadied a baby riding on her hip. She had been nursing the baby, and as she moved, the nipples on her enormous breasts were covered and then uncovered again by her unfastened blouse. With her right hand she served portions of watery rice with a coconut shell ladle. As our group leader came near her in the line, she put the ladle down. Using her thumb and forefinger, she wiped the thin red streams of betel nut juice that had dripped from the corners of her mouth. Then she wiped her hand on her buttock and took up the ladle again.

This particular *mit neary* was well known in the cooperative for stealing from "new" people's luggage. At night in her hut, she and her fellow female comrades tried on the mascara and rouge and lipstick and the Western-style bras they had stolen and pranced around in front of mirrors, admiring their looks. In the morning they reverted to the usual *mit neary* look, hair pulled back of the ears, breasts pushed flat against the body by traditional Cambodian vests, and no makeup. All but this woman, who wore twin circles of bright red lipstick on her cheeks.

Haing Ngor's father, Ngor Kea, in happier times before the revolution. *(Haing Ngor Collection)*

The only picture of Chang My Huoy, Haing Ngor's wife, in the gold locket he had specially made. *(Haing Ngor Collection)*

Haing Ngor (in sunglasses) with three classmates from medical school. None of the others survived the Pol Pot years. *(Haing Ngor Collection)*

Prince Sihanouk *(center)* in Laos, 1972, flanked by the communist leaders of Laos and North Vietnam. *(Roger Warner Collection)*

Saloth Sar, better known by his revolutionary pseudonym, Pol Pot. *(David Hawk Collection)*

Three Khmer Rouge boy-soldiers. Smoking was encouraged by the Khmer Rouge; even forced laborers were given cigarette breaks. *(Roger Warner Collection)*

Forced labor on the front lines as depicted in *The Killing Fields*.
Haing Ngor is in the center. *(Haing Ngor Collection)*

An incoming prisoner in Tuol Sleng, or S. 21, extermination
center where twenty thousand were killed. *(David Hawk Collection)*

Blindfolded skulls from a mass grave; under the Khmer Rouge more than a million Cambodians lost their lives. *(David Hawk Collection)*

Vietnamese "liberators" invaded Cambodia in late 1978 and drove out the Pol Pot regime. They have been engaged ever since in a guerrilla war with the Khmer Rouge and other resistance groups. *(Roger Warner Collection)*

Cast members take a break from filming *The Killing Fields (from left to right:* John Malkovich, Sam Waterston, Julian Sands, Haing Ngor). *(Haing Ngor Collection)*

Haing Ngor in 1985 at the Chinatown Service Center in
Los Angeles. *(AP/Wide World Photos)*

Haing Ngor with a sick child
on the Thai-Cambodian
border. *(Roger Warner Collection)*

Because of the great number of land mines in Cambodia, amputees are a common sight. (*Roger Warner Collection*)

Haing Ngor, Elie Wiesel, and Dith Pran at a meeting to endorse bringing Khmer Rouge leaders before an international tribunal. (*David Hawk Collection/Larry Busacca*)

Finally she ladled the portion of watery rice into the pan that our group leader held. By the time he returned to the circle with the pan and a stack of rusted bowls, the rest of us were sitting expectantly on our haunches with our spoons out.

"Stir it well this time," growled the skinny man who worked next to me. "Be fair."

The leader stirred it obediently. Ten pairs of eyes focused on the thin, whitish gruel as he spooned it into the bowls. "All right, let's eat," he said when he had served the last drop.

"No!" barked the skinny man. He went on all fours to examine the bowls from above. "You didn't stir it right. Look! This bowl has much more rice in the bottom than the others! Everybody can see!"

We all leaned forward, licking our lips. The broth was semi-opaque, with long strands of mucus-like rice matter lying in it, but the white rice grains were visible at the bottom, one layer deep. There was a bit more rice in the bowl he was pointing to than in the rest.

"Not true!" complained the woman in front of whom the bowl had been placed. She turned toward the skinny man. "You're always saying I get more rice, and I'm tired of it. The portions are fair, and I'm going to eat mine!"

"Hold it! Hold it!" the rest shouted, and somebody grabbed her wrist so she wouldn't eat. The woman and the skinny man began arguing, and it lasted until the leader spooned broth and a few grains out of the woman's bowl, over her protests, and sprinkled the drops around the circle. Then the leader put leaves on the ground next to the bowls and sprinkled salt as equally as he could on top of the leaves, though not equally enough to stop the bickering.

Without eating, I got up from the circle, carrying my bowl and salt, and went over to Huoy, who rose from her group and joined me. We walked off the common kitchen's hillock and past other groups sitting in their circles arguing over food and past other crowded hillocks. Finally we found a shady spot where we could be alone.

I spooned some gruel into her bowl. "Eat," I told her. "Keep your strength up." I took the *sdao* leaves out of my pocket, rinsed them with boiled water from the canteen and put them between us. Huoy spooned gruel from her bowl and put it back into mine.

"Men need more food than women do," she said. "You work harder than me."

The work groups all argued over food. Husbands and wives quarreled over food, each trying to take more than the other. Huoy and I argued but we were always trying to give each other food instead of taking it away. It was a special closeness in our relationship that began, I think, when she had nursed me through my sickness in Phum Chhleav. I had never forgotten that she had given me the yam, and I was always trying to make it up to her.

In the end we compromised, as usual, and spooned equal portions of watery rice into our mouths and munched the bitter *sdao* leaves. *Sdao* tastes like quinine, which is probably not a coincidence, since *sdao* is at least a semi-effective substitute for quinine as a malaria medicine. I didn't mind *sdao*, but it was the rice I savored. I swallowed each mouthful slowly, crushing the soft grains against the roof of my mouth. I could feel it giving energy to my body. Even the watery broth was good, because rice had been cooked in it. When I came to the last spoonful I paused, not wanting to eat it, because when I did the meal would be over.

A cadre banged on the metal car wheel with a stick, and everyone rose to their feet to bring the rusted bowls to the common kitchen and reform the lines.

DING . . . DING . . . DING . . . Everyone in the cooperative was standing near the common kitchen. We could all hear him perfectly well. Why he couldn't just ring the bell once I do not know, unless it was to punish us.

DING . . . DING . . . DING . . . DING . . . ding, ding, ding, ding, dingdingdingding . . .

The afternoon was the same as the morning, only longer. There was no breeze in the bottom of the canal. I swung the hoe, but it seemed heavier than before. The group didn't make much progress. We hadn't dug as far as the wooden stake. They gave us a tobacco break, and then they played music again to make us work faster. I would have done anything they asked if they had only played different music. But they didn't. The cooperative had only one tape.

Bright red blood . . .

The worst part of the day was late afternoon. That was when the soldiers came to take prisoners. We never knew ahead of time whether they would come, or who they would choose, or how many. The uncertainty made the waiting worse.

As one side of the canal fell into shadow, and then the bottom and part of the other side, and I set down my hoe to carry a basket of clay to the top of the dike for the thousandth time that day—that was when I saw them. Three soldiers, walking across the fields directly toward me. I climbed down to the bottom of the canal with the empty basket, my heart pounding. Maybe it's my turn, I thought. Maybe the time has finally come. I came up with another load, but by then the soldiers had veered off to a spot farther along. When they walked away from the canal, there were two "new" people in front of them, with their heads bent in utter sorrow and their arms tied tightly behind their backs.

What had the prisoners done wrong? We knew not to ask. Asking wouldn't bring them back. It only endangered those who dared to question. There were no laws under the Khmer Rouge except the law of silence. There were no courts except Angka Leu. Maybe the prisoners hadn't worked hard enough. Or they stole food. Or a *chhlop*, a spy, overheard them making remarks about Angka. People disappeared. That's all we knew. And I knew that someday I would be one of them.

It was after sunset, the orange light fading quickly from the western sky, that the bell rang next. I climbed out of the canal, walked briskly to a minicanal with water in the bottom, and jumped in fully clothed for my bath. Dripping wet, I rejoined the line as we walked back to the common kitchen.

At dinner it was too dark to see the rice at the bottom of the bowls, and there were fewer quarrels. The food was also better: In addition to the watery rice and salt we were given water convolvulus, the Cambodian equivalent of spinach, gathered from the wild by the kitchen's food-foraging team. Huoy and I ate together. We hoped to go back to our hillock, make a quick fire, put the tea kettle on and cook some more *sdao* leaves and a few snails Huoy had found during work. But we didn't get the chance. The bell rang right after dinner.

At that hour the bells were a summons to a political meeting. They were like the *bonn*s that we had been to earlier, but on the front lines they were called by the English word "meeting," pronounced with the emphasis on the second syllable: *mee-TING*. We had three or four a week.

The entire collective assembled in a field next to the common kitchen. The first speaker was Chev, the leader of the cooperative. He had a soft, mild voice, and he paused often to smile at the audience. Everybody was afraid of him. Chev said the digging of the canal was going much too slowly. We would all have sacrifice and work much harder to get it finished in time for the rainy season.

"Some people here are very lazy," said Chev. "They do not want to participate in the revolutionary activities because their minds are in the past, on capitalist times. They slow the project down. They would like to stop the wheel of history. But we don't need these people. We don't want them. They are counterrevolutionaries and CIA agents. Am I wrong or right?"

"Right! Yes, right!" we answered, and applauded to show our approval.

Chev said that such people were our enemies and we must hunt them down and eliminate them, and asked if this was wrong or right. We clapped and said yes, he was right. He told us how lucky we were to be living under Angka. The Cambodian people had been waiting thousands of years for such an opportunity, and was this wrong or right?

Huoy and I sat at the rear of the crowd with our backs against a tree trunk. It was truly dark. I pulled the brim of my hat low over my forehead and shut my eyes. The state of rest that I allowed myself was not sleep. It was more like a controlled doze, since part of my mind stayed alert, like a soldier on sentry duty.

". . . or right?" Chev demanded.

"Yes, right!" I answered, clapping my hands together without opening my eyes. I had been to enough meetings not to have to pay any more attention than that.

After Chev, lower-ranking cadre took turns speaking. Out of their mouths came words that their brains didn't understand: ". . . waging a continuous offensive to launch a struggle to achieve a very spectacular great leap forward for mastery of the elements. . . ." Their real purpose was not to say anything new but to demonstrate their orthodoxy. In a regime where individuality was discouraged, they showed their enthusiasm by imitating their leaders. They talked and Huoy and I leaned against the tree trunk, gathering strength for what was still to come.

The bell rang again.

Wearily, we lined up in the darkness and stumbled off again to the canal.

We worked by the light of the moon and the stars. Or a few of us worked, in slow motion, just enough to keep the guards away. We dug a few basketsful of earth and no more. The rest napped on the ground. We could have used the time better to sleep in our hammocks and then be refreshed for the next day, but there was no telling this to the Khmer Rouge.

At midnight the bell rang for the last time, a welcome signal traveling through the chirping of crickets and the hooting of owls far across the fields. We trudged back to our hillocks, navigating by the silhouettes of trees. Huoy and I fell into our hammock. Four hours later, the bell woke us up again.

Food and sleep were all we cared about. If we could only get enough sleep, if we could only fill our bellies, if the soldiers would only stop taking people away—then we could have thought about other things. Like setting off along the unknown routes toward Thailand. Or joining the freedom fighters, called the Khmer Serei or Free Khmer, who were said to live along the Thai border. But escape seemed infinitely unlikely. The Khmer Rouge posted guards around the cooperative at night, and no one that I knew tried it.

Sleep was more important than escaping. I was so tired I wanted to sleep for a week. Food was even more important than sleeping. All the weight I had gained in Youen's village had dropped off. Once again I was down to about a hundred pounds.

The *sdao* leaves, the snails and the other food we found on the job helped but weren't enough. So in those evenings when no meetings were held, I went out foraging again, in the rest period between dinner and night work on the canal. I tried to gather the wild food in the evening and hide it in the bushes of the hillock where we were staying. At lunch on the following day, Huoy and I would get our usual bowls of watery rice, bring them back to the hillock and start a quick fire with straw and twigs. We would put the rice and our wild food in the teapot, so we could pretend to be making tea if the authorities came around. Tea, particularly medicinal tea, was still permitted.

But it was hard to gather wild foods at night. I began foraging in the early mornings, which was easier. By the time I returned to our hillock, after the first bell, the sky was beginning to grow light. It didn't seem like much of a risk. There were other foragers too. One morning about a month after we got to the front lines, I filled a broken mud basket with arrowroot, hid it in the bushes near our hammock and went off to work with the hoe over my shoulder as usual. When Huoy and I came back to the hillock at lunch, the basket was missing. We asked the other couples who were camped with us on that hillock, but they knew nothing about it. So Huoy and I ate our watery gruel and then lay down in our double hammock.

The next thing we knew, two boys were standing next to the hammock and looking down at us. They were both smoking cigarettes rolled from banana leaves. They twirled the cigarettes in their fingertips in an identical manner, perhaps copying the style of some older smoker they admired.

They frowned over the hammock at me.

"Comrade!" they shouted in their high voices. "Angka wants to see you! Hurry!"

I sat up.

Now I knew who they were. They weren't just ordinary boys. They were spies. *Chhlop*.

19

ANGKA LEU

THEY WERE a little old for spies. About twelve, I guessed. They wore baggy black culottes, nothing else. In our part of Battambang many boys their age wore Khmer Rouge uniforms and carried rifles. Maybe the parents of these two were cadre nearby and had used their influence to delay their sons' departure from home. Yes, maybe that was what had happened.

It was strange, I thought, in that long moment when the *chhlop* were peering over the hammock at me and I had not yet gotten up: Nowadays you became a spy when you were a young boy, and then when you were half grown you became a soldier. There was no such thing as childhood anymore. Before the revolution these boys would have been learning rice farming from their fathers, or going to school, or making themselves useful to the monks in the temples. They would have learned to respect their elders.

"Hurry up, comrade!" That shrill, high, irritating voice. If they had been my sons, I would have beaten them for their rudeness.

"Please," I said, getting up out of the double hammock, "I'm just putting a shirt on. I'll be right there."

"My husband is *going*," said Huoy in an exasperated voice. As a schoolteacher she had scolded many children that age. "Why are you *accusing* him? He's just putting on a shirt. He is going now."

"I'll be back," I told Huoy.

I walked off at a relaxed pace, the two boys behind me. I wasn't worried. If I had done anything seriously wrong, Angka would have sent soldiers to get me, in the late afternoon. The *chhlop* were too young to be trusted with anything important.

The "Angka" the *chhlop* were taking me to turned out to be Chev, the cooperative's leader. Chev was sitting in a black hammock in a Khmer Rouge–style house, which was just a thatched roof on poles, without sides, near the common kitchen. He sat upright with his feet on the ground, barechested, now and again puffing on a cigarette that he rotated slowly in his fingers. He was a skinny, dark-skinned man with soft, straight hair, big fleshy lips and a wide mouth. His eyes were not cruel. He was smiling.

"Comrade . . . ?" he said tentatively.

" 'Samnang,' " I said, supplying him with the name I used.

"Very well. Comrade Samnang, you have to tell Angka the truth. This morning our *chhlop* went to look at the hillocks to see who had food. They checked. They found you had a big basket of arrowroot. My question is this: If you had the food, why didn't you bring it to Angka for the collective meal? Why didn't you give it to the community? Why did you plan to eat it by yourself?"

So. The spies had stolen the food. I should have guessed.

"Comrade Chev," I said, "last night I went to find some food, but it was only a small quantity. It wasn't enough for the community."

"You just wanted private property," he said in his gentle, chiding voice. "And that is forbidden."

I didn't answer. No point getting into an argument with him.

"And another thing," Chev said, still smiling. "The *chhlop* say that you call your wife 'sweet.' We have no 'sweethearts' here. That is forbidden."

Two soldiers hurried toward us, as if late for a meeting they wanted to attend. Chev sat calmly in his hammock, smiling at me with his big lips and wide mouth. He had pointed out that I had broken some minor rules. I was getting ready to tell him I wouldn't break them again.

The soldiers' voices rang out in a deep, authoritative baritone. "Who gave the comrade permission to go out to find something to eat? Comrade, who allowed you?"

"Nobody allowed me, comrade," I answered. "I did it without permission. I did wrong. I'm sorry."

One of the soldiers said contemptuously to me, "You see? You have too much liberty. You think you are as free as a bird, but you are a reactionary."

"Comrades, I had no such thoughts in my mind. I always respect Angka's rules. If Angka says that I am wrong I accept it, and I will not do those things again."

From his hammock, Chev said mildly, "Yes, you recognize yourself that you did something wrong, but this is not enough."

"Comrade Chev, send him to Angka Leu!" urged the soldier who had been doing the talking. "Send him to Angka Leu! To Chhleav!"

Huoy had been watching from a distance. She ran up when she saw Chev nod and the soldiers begin to tie my elbows tightly behind my back. Huoy asked Chev what was happening, and Chev replied, "Your husband betrayed Angka. Now we are sending him to higher authorities for judgment."

Reflexively, Huoy put her palms together and *sompeah*ed to Chev. It was the age-old gesture of respect, but it was out of place, a sure sign of her unrevolutionary background. "Don't kill my husband," she pleaded. "Please let him come back. You decide what to do with him yourself, but don't send him to Angka Leu. He didn't do anything to Angka Leu."

"No," said Chev with that unchanging smile he wore like a mask. "I cannot decide. It is up to Angka Leu."

Huoy stood next to me. "Then if you send him to Angka Leu, send me too. I will stay with him."

"No. Samnang did wrong, not you. 'His hair is on his head. His hair is not on your head.' Anyone who steals is responsible for himself. Nobody else is responsible. You stay here."

I had not struggled when they tied me up. I told Huoy to take care of herself, and a tone in my voice caused Huoy to step back, with her hand to her mouth in fear. She understood what I really meant, that there was no use in her getting involved.

The soldiers led me away.

We walked on a path through the woods and over the fields in the direction of Phum Chhleav. The soldiers walked behind, holding a long rope attached to me. My arms grew numb from the tight cords around my elbows, which restricted my circulation.

We neared Phum Chhleav but didn't get as far as the railroad track, or the cluster of flimsy huts where I had lived a few months before. Instead we stopped at a collection of buildings I had never seen before, in a clearing back in the woods. The prison itself was a long thin structure with a thatch roof and walls made out of split bamboo and thatch and pieces of corrugated metal. The soldiers told me to sit down and wait.

I sat.

They left.

Here I must interrupt my story for a warning: Many people find the truth about Khmer Rouge prisons extremely upsetting. Readers with sensitive feelings might want to skip over the next few pages and begin reading again toward the end of the chapter.

Muffled sounds of human activity came from the prison, and an unpleasant smell drifted toward me in the breeze. Some wrinkled black objects hung from the eaves of the roof but I was too far away to see what they were.

In about an hour a prison guard came out for me. He led me to a large grove of mango trees. The trees were tall and well formed, spaced at regular intervals. At the base of each tree sat a prisoner, tied to the trunk.

The guard and I walked down a row of trees. We walked past a middle-aged woman lying face down on a wooden bench with her arms and legs spread apart. Metal clamps secured her wrists and ankles to the corners of the bench. Her *sampot* or dress was torn, revealing her indecently, and her blouse was ripped with one of her breasts showing. As we went by she turned her head and looked at us with an unfocused stare.

"Please save my life," she moaned in a low voice.

She hadn't noticed that I had my arms tied behind my back, or that the other man was a guard. Red ants were crawling on her hands and her arms, and her fingertips were bloody.

The guard took me to the next tree, about thirty feet away. He loosened the rope around my elbows and the circulation returned to my lower arms. He tied a longer rope to my wrists and then around the tree trunk. I sat with my back to the mango tree.

He left.

I said my prayers.

If I have to die, I thought, at least let me die with dignity and composure.

Something crawled onto the skin on the back of my neck. Then it bit.

Damn—red ants! I craned my head backward and twisted it from side to side to try to crush the ant. Another ant crawled onto my shoulder. They were coming down the tree. My wrists and elbows were tied behind me but I could still move the rest of my body. A lot of them were on me now. They were on my wrists—I crushed them with my fingers. On my upper chest and shoulders—I swept them aside with my chin. On my calves too—I rubbed my calves together, then brought a foot up to help. They bit my scalp—I rubbed the back of my head against the tree trunk, but more ants came down the trunk to get me. They were in a fighting mood, waving their forelegs in the air and working the sideways pincers in front of their mouths, daring me to attack.

The more I struggled, the more they swarmed over me. I strained against the confinement of the ropes, scratching and moving my feet in a frenzy, unable to move enough. I imagined them biting even when they hadn't bitten me.

This was torture enough.

When the afternoon sun sank low enough to shine under the branches and onto me, a sturdily built man with curly hair walked into the mango grove. He wore new black clothes, black rubber-tire sandals, a wristwatch. Under his black shirt I glimpsed a flash of blue. A Montagut shirt, I guessed. In Phnom Penh before the revolution Montagut shirts had been a status symbol, like wearing an alligator shirt. They were French-made, cool and comfortable in tropical weather. And now Montagut shirts were status symbols for the Khmer Rouge, like the silk kramas they stole from the "new" people. Emblems of an old society that they hated but also envied.

The curly-haired man carried a hatchet and pair of pliers in his hands.

He walked down the row. He sat on the wooden bench by the spreadeagled woman.

"Where is your husband?" he asked her, the sound of his voice carrying to me. "You have to tell Angka the truth. What rank was he under Lon Nol? A captain? A lieutenant? Tell the truth."

The woman slurred her words together. "I still don't know where he is," she said. "And he was not a soldier. He wasn't a captain. He wasn't a lieutenant. He wasn't anything like that."

"You still lie to Angka?"

The burly man stepped up on the bench, put a foot down on her hand, bent down with the pliers, pulled hard and came up with something in the pliers' jaws.

"AAAEEEEIIIIIIIII!!! AAEEIII!!! AAAAEEEIIIIIIIIIIIII!!!" the woman screamed, but he paid no attention.

"If you don't tell me the truth, I'll take another fingernail tomorrow," he said. "If you tell the truth now, Angka will release you."

The woman writhed on the bench, her *sampot* up around her hips. "AAAAEEEIIIIIIIII!!! Kill me soon! Now! Why do you do this to me? I have nothing to say. I am telling the truth. Oh, Mother, Mother, Mother, save my life!"

When we Cambodians are in danger, we call out to our mothers to save our lives. We believe their spirits watch over us protectively.

The burly man came over to me. I was right: It was a blue Montagut shirt under his black tunic. In his tunic pocket two pens showed.

He stood over me and said, "Tell me the truth. Who gave you permission to go out and find something to eat?"

"I went on my own, comrade. I was hungry."

"Angka doesn't provide you with enough food?"

"Yes, enough food, but I was still hungry."

"Then why did you go out, when other people don't go out? You're supposed to work. If you don't work you do an injustice to others."

I began to say something but he paid no attention and broke in, demanding to know whether I was Vietnamese or Chinese. I said I was neither.

"What did you do before? Were you a soldier? A teacher? High-ranking job? What did you do in the Lon Nol regime?"

"Taxi driver."

"What kind? What model car did you drive?"

" '404.' A Peugeot model 404."

"Where did you go?"

"Mostly long-distance drives. From Phnom Penh to Takeo, or to Battambang. Wherever they wanted to go, until the roads were closed because of the war. Then just around Phnom Penh."

"*NO!!!*" he roared. "You were not a taxi driver! I can tell you are *lying!*"

"I was a taxi driver, comrade. Really. Not a high-class person.

My wife sold vegetables in the market. If there were no vegetables she baked little cakes and sweets and sold them."

"*NO!* You're not that kind of person! You've got to tell Angka the truth! If you tell Angka the truth you can go back to your wife right now."

"I am telling you the truth, comrade," I insisted.

He called out for someone else, who arrived quickly. They tightened the rope around my elbows and pushed me over on my side. While the second one held my neck down in the dirt, the burly one put my right hand on top of a mango tree root and then stepped on my wrist with his foot. He dropped down and swung the hatchet. There was an excruciating pain in my little finger, and the shock of it spread throughout my body. Automatically I gasped and stiffened, but no matter how hard I clenched, the pain was there, from the tip of my finger up my arm exploding into my brain.

"The next time," the burly man said, "don't steal food. If you do it again, Angka will show you no mercy. Angka will not allow you to do it again."

They let go of my neck and hand and shoved me upright, but I pulled against the ropes and fell partway over until the rope restrained me and my back landed against the tree.

"Why don't we cut off a toe?" said the second man. "We shouldn't let him walk. He's too greedy."

"Right," said the man with the two pens. "Good thinking. Hold his leg here, will you?"

The burly man aimed at my right ankle and swung the hatchet, not as hard as he could have, because that would have severed the joint, but hard enough to lay bare the bone underneath.

His face swam into focus near mine. "One more thing," he said. "Don't call your wife 'sweetheart.' Call her 'comrade woman.' She can call you 'comrade brother.' "

Then they left.

I could see my ankle, the white bone exposed in the middle of the wound, the flesh red and bleeding around the edges. I couldn't see my hand, which was tied behind me. I tried to wiggle my little finger and, even with the pain being so general, knew that the fingertip wasn't there anymore. Drawn to the blood, red ants swarmed over my hand and bit like hot, stinging needles, but that didn't matter.

The thought occurred that the wounds were going to get infected and I had to stop the bleeding. I rubbed the heel of my good foot in in the dirt and coated my ankle wound with dust and did the same thing with my good hand and my finger wound even though the nerve ending in my finger was naked and raw.

Of the late afternoon and sunset I remember little. My ankle hurt. My finger throbbed. When the darkness came I dozed until red ants bit me around the eyes. I got the ants off by turning my face to the side and rubbing my eye sockets against my shoulders.

It was a long, long night. The woman on the bench moaned and whimpered. She had defecated and urinated, and the smell drifted to me.

The next morning, the burly interrogator came out, untied my hands and gave me a bowl of watery rice.

For the first time, I could see what he had done to the little finger on my right hand. He had chopped it off halfway. One and a half joints were still there, the stub coated with dust, the bone showing white in the middle. The other one and a half joints with the fingernail were gone.

He told me to stay there. I did. I didn't have the strength to run away, and besides it seemed as though they might release me. When he left I turned around in a sitting position to look behind me and saw my missing fingertip with ants crawling over it. It wasn't part of my body anymore and it didn't frighten me. Then I turned back to my original position, sat and thought.

With my good hand, my left hand, I felt the lymph nodes in the inguinal crease, between the top of my thigh and the trunk of my body. The lymph glands were bumpy and swollen from fighting the infections. I tore strips of cloth from my shirt and tied the bandages around my finger and my ankle.

In the afternoon the guards retied my ropes but not too tightly. Then they brought a new prisoner down the line of mango trees, a pregnant woman. As they walked past the woman I heard her saying that her husband wasn't a soldier. It seemed to be the most common offense in the prison, being the wife of someone in the Lon Nol military. She begged them to spare her life. They told her she was still lying. They tied her wrists around a tree not far away from me, then tied her ankles and left.

Later a new interrogator, one I had not seen before, walked down the row of trees holding a long, sharp knife. I could not make out their words, but he spoke to the pregnant woman and she answered. What happened next makes me nauseous to think about. I can only describe it in the briefest of terms: He cut the clothes off her body, slit her stomach, and took the baby out. I turned away but there was no escaping the sound of her agony, the screams that slowly subsided into whimpers and after far too long lapsed into the merciful silence of death. The killer walked calmly past me holding the fetus by its neck. When he got to the prison, just within my range of vision, he tied a string around the fetus and hung it from the eaves with the others, which were dried and black and shrunken.

Each tree in the orchard had its prisoner, and each prisoner had a different means of punishment or death. The sturdy man who chopped off my finger and the other who disemboweled the pregnant woman were only two of the specialists on the prison staff.

Never had I seen deliberate killings before, carried out by professionals, in front of terrified spectators who knew that their own turns to die would come soon. Never, never, never. There had been cruelty in the Cambodia of Sihanouk and Lon Nol. There had been torture in their prisons. Lon Nol troops had done barbarous things to civilians of Vietnamese descent, and also to captured Khmer Rouge. But I knew of nothing like this, no cold-blooded pleasure in such a broad range of torture and murder techniques.

I stayed awake that night, ants biting me as they wished. The faint light of an oil lamp filtered through the thatch wall of the prison. The tree trunks with the prisoners tied to them were black outlines in the silvery moonlight. Owls hooted. Crickets sung in their chorus, and from one place and then another in the mango orchard prisoners moaned.

In the depths of the night, a pack of *chhke char-chark*, similar to wolves but smaller, drifted into the mango grove and sniffed the air. They trotted toward the corpse of the pregnant woman and began tearing at her flesh, eating it noisily and greedily. I could see them in the moonlight, three or four of them, tugging at her, pulling backward, snarling and growling at each other in warning. If the wolves wanted to attack me there was nothing I could do. I let go—pissed in my pants and shat, surrendering all control.

The burly torturer came again the next morning and tore another fingernail from the woman on the bench, but he left me alone. In the afternoon two new guards came. They asked what I had done before the revolution, and when I told them I had been a taxi driver they seemed satisfied. They untied me from the tree and told me to get up. I tried and I fell over. I tried again and got to my knees and then they jerked me up to my feet.

We left the prison by the same footpath I had entered. My right foot was swollen from my toes up to my calf. Every time I stepped on it the pain flashed all the way up to my hip. To walk I put all my weight on my left foot, brought my right foot a little ahead of my left foot, set my right foot lightly on the ground, then hopped onto my left foot again.

We were out of sight of the prison, in a mixture of woods and uncultivated rice fields.

"Up there at that next hillock," said one of my escorts, "you will tell us the truth. Or else you will sleep there for a long, long time."

If they wanted to kill me by that hillock, it was okay by me. As long as they got it over with quickly.

I hobbled to the hillock, a long mound with trees and brush on top, and then past it. They didn't tell me to stop.

"We'll stop at the next hillock on," they said after a while. We passed that hillock and then they said the same thing about the next one.

The three of us walked very slowly on dikes between rice paddies. Our course lay at an angle to the dikes. They told me when to turn right and when to turn left on the dikes, and we made slow progress across the fields.

I knew they weren't going to let me go. This was part of the torture, to let me think I was going to get away. But I really didn't care. One hillock was as good as another.

I concentrated on walking, one short step and then a hop, one short step and a hop. The guards were behind me. They were going to do whatever they were going to do, and I couldn't prevent it.

"Stop here!"

I stopped.

We were next to a hillock.

They kicked me from behind and I fell on top of the dike.

They stood over me, looking down. "Why don't you tell the truth? Hurry up! We will kill you now!"

I said slowly, "I was a taxi driver. That is the truth."

They said I was still lying and they kicked me in the side. I fell down the dike onto the dry stubble of the rice field and lay there with rice stalks poking me in the face until they hauled me on top of the dike again. One of them put his foot on my neck and twisted his foot back and forth like stubbing out a cigarette. Then they took turns kicking me in the ribs.

"Do you want to die or to live? You'll die in the next minute if you don't tell the truth!"

I lay there without saying anything, breathing hoarsely.

They squatted a short distance away with their rifle butts on the ground.

" 'If he lives there is no gain,' " one of them muttered to the other, quoting a common Khmer Rouge expression. " 'If he dies there is no loss.' "

When they had rested they pulled me to my feet and I limped a few more yards to the next hillock.

"Stop."

I stopped again.

"Do you want to go home, or what? Do you want to be reunited with your wife?"

I turned around to face them but kept my eyes lowered, like a servant does to his master. "Yes," I said. "If you allow me to go, I will. But if you don't allow me, if you kill me, it's up to you."

They untied me and removed the rope. Apparently I had given them the right answer. I had told them they had power of life and death over me. Hearing me admit this gave them almost as much satisfaction as killing me.

"Don't look back," they said. "Just keep on walking. Go home."

I looked above the treetops and saw the mountain ridge with the two white dots below the summit. From them I took my compass bearing.

"Home," the most recent location of the front lines cooperative, was in a southerly direction, about a mile away. I was in no condition to hurry. It hurt to breathe. The stump of my finger was swollen to three times normal size. But now that my hands were untied I could bend my right arm at the elbow and elevate my hand so it wouldn't throb so much. I found a stick of bamboo and picked it up. I hobbled slowly along, using the bamboo as a staff in my left hand to help support my weight.

I came to a canal with muddy water in the bottom. I took my clothes off and sat down heavily with a splash. With my good hand I washed myself and cleaned the dirt from the wounds as best I could. Blood still seeped from what was left of my finger. There were large bruises on my ribs but nothing broken. Shit and piss stained my trousers. I rinsed my clothes with one hand, but there was no way to get them really clean. I put them on wet and rolled the waistband of my trousers so they wouldn't slip down.

I walked. Left foot; then a short, light step with the right foot and most of the weight on the bamboo staff; then the left foot again.

Right foot. Left foot. Right foot, left foot.

I stopped to rest. Then started again. My body was stiffening from the bruises. The sun was setting.

When I came into camp it was dusk. Work had finished for the day. On the hillocks, other "new" people saw me but weren't sure whether to help, and I didn't ask them to. Huoy was in our hammock, gazing at something far away, thinking. When the neighbors told her I was coming she jumped out of the hammock and ran to me. She took the bamboo stick away and draped my left arm around her shoulders and helped me walk the rest of the distance.

Everybody from our hillock crowded around asking questions, until they saw me up close. Then they fell silent. They knew the answers to their questions just by looking.

Huoy brought me to the hammock, but I didn't want to sit in it because I wasn't clean. Someone brought a pallet of split bamboo and I lay down on that. The neighbors had gathered around, everyone silent except for Huoy, who was crying.

They boiled water, and Huoy and the other women used their kramas like washcloths to clean me. By then most of them were crying, because they knew what happened when people disappeared and there could be no more pretending. What had happened to me could happen to them. They brought gifts of medicine, a capsule of ampicillin from one, a capsule of tetracycline from another and from the rest a couple of aspirin and some herbs. I opened the antibiotic capsules and sprinkled half of each directly on my wounds, saving the rest for later.

One of the older ladies who had brought herbal medicine finally said what had been on everyone's mind.

"Samnang," she said, "maybe you did something bad in a previous lifetime. Perhaps you are being punished for it today."

"Yes," I said. "I think my *kama* is not so good."

20

THE WAT

CHEV gave me time off from work to recover from my injuries. I lay in the hammock, suspended from two trees on a hillock, resting and watching.

I tried not to think too much about my experiences in prison. The pregnant woman, the wolves, the burly man with the Montagut shirt—I tried to suppress them all from my memory. But the bruises on my body, the infected cuts and the stump of my little finger were reminders of something that could not be ignored. I began to analyze what I knew of the Khmer Rouge system of justice. Or rather, injustice.

I had not known that the prison existed until I was taken there. I had never heard of it. The reason was perfectly simple. Few who went there ever returned. Why they had let me off so easily I did not know. Nor did I know why they had gone to the trouble of taking me there at all instead of simply taking me out to the woods and killing me, which is what the soldiers usually did with their victims in the late afternoons. Why were some taken to prison and the rest to the woods?

Maybe, I thought, prison was the punishment for political crimes, and death in the woods was the punishment for breaking simpler rules, like loitering at the work site. But that couldn't be true. Why was gathering wild food a political crime instead of a minor infraction? Why was being married to a Lon Nol officer a political crime? More to the point, why was either of them any kind of crime at all?

But that question had no answer.

Perhaps, I thought, there were two parallel systems of punishment. A prison system, part of a bureaucracy that needed to be fed to justify its existence. And another, informal system that gave the cooperative leader freedom to hand out the punishments, though the effect on the prisoner was ultimately the same.

In either case, the prison or the woods, the key man was the cooperative leader, since everyone on the front lines took orders from him. In our cooperative the leader, Chev, didn't do any of the killing himself, or at least didn't kill anyone that we saw with our own eyes. Nor did he allow his soldiers to kill anyone in public. That was another holdover from the Khmer Rouge code of the old days, when the guerrillas were still trying to gain popular support: "Thou shalt behave with great meekness toward the workers and peasants, and the entire population," the code said. Now that the Khmer Rouge had won the war and their contempt for the "new" people was so obvious, it was strange that they even pretended to stick to their rules. In effect, the new rule was, "Do not kill anyone in plain sight."

And in fact Chev *was* a killer himself. More than once, as I recovered from my wounds, I watched Chev accompany the soldiers to the afternoon arrests. He stood around pretending to inspect the canals until the soldiers and prisoners were out of sight. Then he nonchalantly followed them with a hoe over his shoulder, stopping now and again with the pleased expression of a man who is enjoying his afternoon stroll. There were never any gunshots later. Chev used his hoe to kill. The next day he was invariably in a cheerful mood, walking around energetically without his hoe. He killed to feel good about himself. If he purged enough enemies, he satisfied his conscience. He had done his duty to Angka.

Why? Why did they kill so many? For the Khmer Rouge in general, from the lowest-ranking soldier to the burly interrogator who had chopped off my finger to the ever-smiling Chev, the act of killing other human beings was routine. Just part of the job. Not even worth a second thought. However, there were differences in their backgrounds, and in their motivations. The low-ranking soldiers, for example, were young and uneducated. Few of them had any independent sense of right and wrong. In the civil war they had been trained to kill Lon Nol forces. When they were ordered to kill "new" people on the front lines they obeyed automatically, without thinking much about the difference. For some of them, of course, and for the prison interrogators, there was an element of *kum-monuss* in what they did. But the prison interrogators were older and higher-ranking than the soldiers, like the two-pen rank of the burly man who chopped off my finger. Officers like that didn't kill just to obey, or to get revenge. They enjoyed it. They were sadists: Torturing others was the ultimate proof of their own power.

But for Chev and other front-lines leaders there was a more sophisticated reason for killing, and that was political necessity. When they talked about sacrificing everything for Angka, they meant it. Whatever got in the way of Angka's projects had to be eliminated, including people. To them, though, we weren't quite people. We were lower forms of life, because we were enemies. Killing us was like swatting flies, a way to get rid of undesirables. We were a disappointment to them because we never finished the projects on time, because we didn't work hard for twenty hours a day, because we were constantly wearing out and getting sick.

The worst thing was that the killings seemed so normal. Maybe not normal, but inevitable. The way things were. To us war slaves, the old way of life was gone and everything about it half forgotten, as if it had never really existed in the first place. Buddhist monks, making their tranquil morning rounds, didn't exist anymore. Three-generation families, where the grandparents looked after the little children, didn't exist anymore. Shopping for food in the markets and staying to gossip. Inviting friends over to eat and drink and talk in the evening. It was all gone, and without that pattern we had nothing to hold on to. Demoralized, split apart, like atoms removed from their chemical compounds, we let the Khmer Rouge do what they wanted with us. We didn't fight back. In the fields we were two thousand men and women with hoes, and Angka was only two or three brain-washed teenagers with rifles. Yet we let the soldiers take us away. Why? Because it was in our nature to obey leaders. Because we were weak and sick and starved. Because it was *kama*. We did not even know why, but we submitted to them.

There had been an evening, before I went to prison, when a few of us talked about rebellion. It was one of those rare evenings when we did not have to go back to work after the political meeting. About a dozen of us from the old elite sat around a fire. We swore an oath of secrecy and talked about an armed uprising against the Khmer Rouge. Our leader was a "new" person named Thai, who had once been a Lon Nol soldier. Also there was Pen Tip, the tiny X-ray technician from Phnom Penh whose path often crossed mine. We talked about seizing weapons. We talked about heading for the border of Thailand to join the freedom fighters, the Khmer Serei, who were supposed to live there. But that's all it was, just talk. Gradually, as the evening wore on, we stared for longer and longer periods into the flames, not saying anything. Resistance was hopeless and we knew it. The Khmer Rouge had already won. We looked into the fire and our thoughts were sad and far away. Just like every evening, at every campfire on the front lines. Gazing into the flames and feeling tired and defeated.

But even though we were defeated, and even though we could feel ourselves slipping farther down into slavery, we didn't lose hope. Or a lot of us didn't, anyway. Take Huoy and me, for example. I had been to prison, but I had survived. That was something to be grateful for. And while I was away in prison something very good had happened to Huoy: She had been transferred from hauling mud baskets in the canal to preparing food in the common kitchen. The kitchen staff didn't have to work in the evenings, or work very hard at all. Most important, they could always get enough to eat. While I was recovering from prison Huoy brought me rice twice a day, hidden in the rolled-up waist of her sarong. It was real rice, a welcome change from watery gruel—the same rice, she told me, that Chev and his soldiers ate at every meal, as much as they wanted.

Once again, like the time when I had dysentery, Huoy proved to be a perfect nurse. Besides bringing rice and preparing meals, she mended my clothes. To cheer me up, she sang to me in her clear, soft voice. Without soap or antibiotics she couldn't stop my infections, but she changed my bandages twice a day, and boiled them in water to sterilize them before hanging them up to dry. Since leaving Phnom Penh I had seen a new side of Huoy, and it made me respect her more and more: Whenever anything needed to be done, she taught herself how to do it, without any prompting. She was good at everything she did. Except for losing her mother, which grieved her every day, she had adapted to the hardships of the new regime better than most people, and much better than me. Of the two of us, I was supposed to be the strong one, but it wasn't turning out that way. I was the one who was always getting in trouble or getting sick.

When I had recovered enough to walk without a cane I was sent back to work with a mobile crew of eight people, none of whom I had known before. On our first day we were summoned to the common kitchen, where Chev addressed us. Huoy was only a few yards away, pouring rice into huge vats, signaling to me with a frown that I should keep my mouth shut. She didn't have to worry about that —I was far too afraid of Chev to say anything. But there was no way I could hide from him. He knew with a glance at my bandaged ankle, at the bandaged stump of my finger, what had happened when he sent me to Angka Leu. I kept my face blank and my eyes averted. My usual expression.

Chev smiled and nodded at us pleasantly.

He said the cooperative needed to build a bridge. Because we had no lumber, our task would be to go the old temple on top of the mountain, tear it apart and bring its lumber down. "I'm sure you agree that this is an excellent plan. Am I wrong or right?"

"Right," everyone in the group said.

"Exactly," said Chev. "It is better to destroy the temple, which is useless, than to have no bridge. We don't need Buddha. What we need are bridges for the people's transportation. The gods cannot build bridges for us. We must take our destiny firmly in hand."

My face registered agreement. But I thought, We don't need Buddha at this point in history? Are you crazy? Now we need him most of all.

Chev was still smiling at us with his wide, full lips.

Motherfucker, I thought, did Buddha ever do anything bad to you? If you destroy Buddha's temple, Buddha will get you back. Maybe not in this lifetime, maybe not even in your next lifetime. But someday. And I hope it's soon. Because I want to see you suffer. I want to see you die an awful death, like the prisoners at Chhleav.

Nobody moved.

He looked at each of us in turn. He peered closely at me. He was testing me, to see whether I had learned my lesson in prison.

Finally he dismissed us.

Our group walked without escort from the common kitchen to the road and from there to Phum Phnom. A path near the Khmer Rouge headquarters led into the forest to the base of the mountain ridge.

We climbed up the switchbacks in the trail. As the land flattened at the edge of the plateau, we saw some concrete monks' quarters on stilts, still intact. Farther on we passed the remains of wooden quarters already torn down by scavengers like us. Above we heard the faint, tinkling sounds of wind chimes.

It was a clear day toward the end of the dry season. The landscape was bright with yellow flowers. Pigeons and brown-speckled turtle-doves flew from branch to branch in the nearly leafless trees. Over the treetops on the lower slopes we could see the alluvial plain spread out far below. A steam train whistled in the distance. It came along the tracks, the miniature locomotive belching a cloud of black smoke, the long line of cars moving through the curves like a snake. A train like that had brought us to Battambang, a long time ago.

We rested. It was an odd sensation not to have anyone supervising us, to sit down when we wanted. We listened to the train as it chuffed along, the clicking of its wheels and the hooting of its steam whistle growing fainter and fainter. And then above us we heard the tinkling of wind chimes again.

We walked up to the wat. To the side of the wat and perhaps two thirds its height was the large *stupa*, or funeral monument, that had appeared as the smaller of two white dots when I was plowing in Phum Chhleav. Seen close it was a graceful example of its type, two square layers at the base, then a large bell shape with convex and concave circular bands, and finally a tapering spire on top. Within the large stupa lay the ashes of some prominent person, perhaps the person who had given the money for the wat to be built.

The wat itself was ten or twenty years old, with walls of concrete and wooden beams, and planks supporting a roof with faded colored tiles. The building was not so much ruined as purposely destroyed, a sight that swelled my heart with grief. Outside, Buddha statues lay toppled over, their parts scattered. The grounds were grown up with weeds and vines and littered with scraps of saffron cloth, the kind the monks had used for their robes, and also the kind tied around the trunks of holy *bodhi* trees.

Most of one wall was missing, the concrete broken up for the metal reinforcement rods inside, which the Khmer Rouge used for making nails. The thick, intricately carved wooden doors found in all temples were missing. So were the door frames, the windows and the window frames, leaving ugly, gaping holes. The ornamental railing leading up the stairs from the terrace in the shape of a holy *naga* or snake had been smashed, also for the reinforcement rods. The scavengers had wrecked the lower part of the roof, taken the wood away for the lumber and left the colored roof tiles in broken heaps on the terrace.

We went inside. Debris and bird shit covered the floor. Pigeons flew in and out of the holes in the roof. At the far wall, once filled with Buddha statues in ascending rows, all the statues were gone, except for the largest Buddha at the top. The vandals had cut off the statue's head and right arm, but they had been too lazy to destroy the rest.

To my ears came the polytonal tinkling of the wind chimes, from the eaves outside.

We stood there, eight ragged, barefoot men.

Without a word, we dropped to our knees and prayed.

Lord Buddha, I said silently, forgive us for what we are about to do. We do not wish to tear down your temple. Our hearts are not in the work. Our hearts belong to you. We obey only to save our lives, because we are weak and afraid. Please do not punish us. Please protect us. Punish those who give us these orders. Punish those who do not let us come here to worship or to clean the grounds to make merit.

There was nobody else around the temple, nobody watching. The previous scavengers had left bamboo ladders outside. Slowly, reluctantly, gesturing apologetically to the headless Buddha, we climbed the ladders to a part of the lower roof where the tiles were already broken and the wood exposed. We pried rafters loose with our axes, as few of them as possible. Then we left the temple quickly and slid the rafters down the steep mountain slope.

Fortunately we didn't have to go back to the temple the next day. Or ever. The authorities were always changing their minds.

Instead we were sent back to canal work. It was the same dreary routine as before. Bells day and night. Walking out to the site before dawn in single file, enduring the taped music from the loudspeakers, working until the lunch bell rang, walking back to the common kitchen in single file, on and on. Too much work, not enough sleep, not enough food. No real friendships. I was luckier than most. For me, the lack of friends was no problem, as long as I had Huoy. We shared everything. There was a bond between us as instinctive as the bond between animal mates.

What was hard was the terror. I had already been to prison once. Every morning I wondered if I would make it through the day. Every night I wondered if I would make it until morning, or whether a shrill child's voice would bring a circle of accusers. It was the same for all the "new" people. We never got used to the terror, we just kept it inside, in our hearts. Our arms and legs could be as thin as bamboo. Our hair could be turning brown or white, but we didn't show the terror on the outside. Inside, we were thinking all the time, maybe the next hour. Maybe tonight. It was always on our minds that the soldiers would take us away.

"Be careful—bodies disappear." That was one of the sayings that sprung up among the "new" people as a warning not to attract attention. Another saying was *Dam doeum kor*, which literally means "Plant a kapok tree." The word *kor*, however, also means "mute," as in "Keep your mouth shut." Stay quiet. Plant a kapok tree. Bodies disappear. The warnings were muttered and indirect, but the meaning was clear: Avoid the soldiers completely. Don't give them a reason to single you out from the crowd. Whenever my work group walked anywhere, we changed directions if there was any chance of crossing paths with soldiers.

Except to answer questions, I hadn't spoken a word to soldiers since the ride to Phnom Penh and back on my Vespa. On the front lines the low-ranking soldiers seemed very much like the *mit* of that trip: dark-skinned, illiterate, not very clean, unfamiliar with modern objects like engines and toilets and televisions. They spoke in the accent of the Battambang hill people, with a singsong intonation. They could walk forever. Their feet were too wide for their rubber-tire sandals, but they were proud to be wearing them, and their uniforms, and their silk kramas and Montagut shirts, because most of them had never been fully dressed until joining the Khmer Rouge.

On the canal site we "new" people moved with a feebleness that made us seem old. No wasted movements, no spring to our step, no playing around. Here and there were those of us who had lost their minds. They sang snatches of old songs and then broke into tears. Or sat down on the clay when it wasn't break time. The soldiers took them away, six one day, two the next, none the day after, three the day after that, culling the insane and the politically suspect from the ranks in the late afternoons. Bodies disappear.

I worked harder than ever, because Huoy asked me to. She said our best chance lay in being model workers. If I worked hard, she pointed out, it might prove to Chev that I had reformed my ways after being sent to prison. At her suggestion, I cut back on food-foraging too. Now that she had her job in the kitchen we didn't need wild foods as much anyway. I only continued foraging at all to keep my fellow workers from suspecting how much food Huoy was bringing home.

Because of my energy on the job (made possible by the food Huoy stole from the kitchen), I was promoted to group leader, a supervisor of nine other workers. There were no extra rations or privileges that went with the position. Now I was the one who got blamed for being unfair when I spooned the portions of watery rice into the bowl. I went to meetings with other group leaders to listen to our bosses, the section leaders. Invariably I agreed with whatever the section leaders said, even when it didn't make sense.

The other group leaders were also "new" people who inwardly opposed the revolution but who obeyed to stay alive. There was only one group leader I wasn't sure about, and that was Pen Tip, who had been promoted just like me.

Pen Tip was an odd-looking man, with a duckfooted walk like Charlie Chaplin. He liked to hang around with "old" people and Khmer Rouge. He joked with them and flattered them, and somehow he got away with it—other people who got close to the soldiers were taken to the woods. Pen Tip knew how to manipulate people, how to make them feel obligated. He conveyed the impression that since he was well connected to Angka we other group leaders needed to stay on his good side. I began to avoid him whenever possible.

I knew Pen Tip couldn't tell Angka about the clandestine evening meeting about joining the resistance. He had been part of that too. However, he could conceivably tell Angka about my background. Pen Tip had seen me in hospitals in Phnom Penh. He knew I was a doctor. But he didn't know any details. He didn't know my real name.

He called me over one day when he was sitting on a bamboo bench that soldiers sometimes used, near the common kitchen. He was so short that his legs didn't reach the ground. He swung his feet back and forth like a child and rotated his cigarette in his fingertips.

"Tell me something, uh, 'Samnang,' " he said, pronouncing the name with deliberate irony. He had a way of lifting his eyebrows in surprise or puzzlement, and darting his eyes around without looking directly at me. "Uh, tell me the truth. You were a doctor back in Phnom Penh, but"—he took a puff on his cigarette—"you're a nice guy and, uh, I like you very much."

He didn't finish the thought. He didn't need to. He was threatening to expose me if I didn't give him a bribe.

"Look, Pen Tip," I said, "I helped sick people in Phum Chhleav, same as you. You weren't a doctor, I'm not a doctor. We were just concerned about public health."

"I hear you have had, ah, problems before with your own health," he said. His eyes rested on the stub of my little finger, then darted away. I found myself suddenly perspiring.

"I really don't have time to talk now, Pen Tip," I said. "I've got to get some more mud baskets for my crew. But you're mistaken about me. So *dam doeum kor*, eh?"

"People disappear," he replied.

I walked away, calm on the outside, angry inside. It was bad enough to humble myself to the Khmer Rouge. I wasn't about to humble myself to another "new" person. And I didn't like people who played up to the Khmer Rouge. Aunt Kim in Tonle Batí, Pen Tip here—people like that made me sick.

Over the next few weeks Pen Tip managed to extract concessions from all the other group leaders, food or tobacco or other signs of respect, but I held out. It became a contest of wills. I didn't tell Huoy about it. There was no sense upsetting her.

Then one afternoon during tobacco break, when several groups were resting together on a hillock near the canal, Pen Tip made the struggle public. There were no soldiers or high-level supervisors around. We were smoking our tobacco cigarettes and relieving our depression by joking about what we had done under the old regime. One man said he used to be the king, but he had resigned to be a toilet inspector. The next man told him how lucky he was, that he had been only an assistant toilet inspector. We all laughed and tried to outdo each other with the most ridiculous stories.

"You want to hear something funny?" Pen Tip said. "I'll tell you something funny. Samnang was a doctor." The tone of his voice made everyone fall silent.

"No, Pen Tip," I said wearily, "that's not true. And don't call me that. Angka might kill me."

"Don't worry," Pen Tip replied. "Everybody knows you're a doctor."

"*Comrade* Pen Tip," I replied, "don't say that. If you play around like that and Angka believes you, I'm in a lot of trouble. Don't play games."

The break ended and we all went back to work. From that time on it was common knowledge that I had been accused of being a doctor, though nobody knew whether it was true or not.

A week or so later I was resting on a mat and Huoy was lying in the hammock when two teenage soldiers came up. I had never seen them before. They were not the soldiers usually assigned to our co-operative. One of them held a rope in his hand. It was all I could do to persuade them to wait for me to change into fresh trousers. There was gold in the trousers I was wearing and, since it was obvious where I was going, it seemed better that Huoy keep it. They tied my elbows behind my back again. Then they kicked me as I stood on the edge on the hillock. I fell on my face in the rice stubble. Huoy was hysterical. They marched me away past the common kitchen in full view of hundreds of people. If Pen Tip was watching, I didn't notice.

21

THE KING OF
DEATH

A WARNING: This chapter tells of the very depths of suffering that people like me saw and experienced under the Khmer Rouge regime. It is an important part of the story, but it is not a pleasant part. So if you wish, or if you must, skip this chapter and go on to the next one.

The soldiers directed me to turn left and right on the paths, and soon there was no doubt that we were heading toward the prison at Phum Chhleav. Then they told me to stop. We waited for about an hour, until six or seven more prisoners and their guards came up. We prisoners were tied together in a line and began walking again.

When we reached the prison another group of tied-up "new" people was waiting, like us the victims of a roundup that had been planned in advance. Our guards tied the two lines together but loosened the bonds around our elbows, enough for the circulation to return to our arms. We sat with our backs to the prison wall, which was part thatch and part corrugated metal, and tried not to look in the direction of the mango trees, where other prisoners were in various states of torture.

"What did you do wrong?" I whispered to a woman next to me.

"Nothing. I don't even know why they took me here," she said. "I've been working very, very hard for them in the front lines." She was pregnant, one of five obviously pregnant women in the line.

None of the others knew why they had been arrested either. Quietly, in whispers, up and down the line, we agreed not to tell the Khmer Rouge anything.

A young guard, fifteen or sixteen years old, asked us disdainfully if we were hungry or thirsty. When everyone said yes, he brought a large bowl full of water. He held it in his hands and the first person leaned over and put his mouth in it and drank like a horse. Then the guard put the bowl in the first person's hands, which were tied behind his back. The first person turned, holding the bowl behind him so the second person could drink like a horse, and then the second person took the bowl in his hands and held it for the third person and so on down the line.

" 'No one will take care of you,' " the guard said smugly, reciting one of the regime's favorite expressions. " 'You have to take care of yourselves.' "

We spent the night inside the jail, a long, narrow structure with an aisle in the middle and a row of prisoners to each side. We lay on our backs with our heads to the wall and our feet locked into leg-irons attached to a long piece of wood running next to the center aisle. Low wooden partitions gave us each a space to lie in, like a private pigsty, already dirtied with wastes. The air reeked of shit and piss and an odor like ammonia. It was hard to breathe. For me, it was impossible to sleep. There were about eighty "new" people in the jail, and some of them were always moaning.

Early the next morning the noise of a motorcycle came to our ears. The motorcycle approached, downshifted, stopped nearby. I thought: Somebody important has arrived. In the Phnom Tippeday region, messengers and low-ranking cadre usually rode bicycles or horses, middle and upper-middle cadre rode motorcycles, and those at the very top rode in jeeps. A motorcycle rider would be someone like . . . like an officer in the state security apparatus, I decided. Yes, that was about right. It had been prearranged, the fresh capture of political prisoners and our interrogation the following morning.

Our group of eighteen prisoners was taken outside, past a parked Honda 90, into a neighboring building, where my guess about the visitor was confirmed.

In Cambodian folk religion one of the main mythological figures is known as the King of Death. He is a judge, the one who assigns souls to heaven or hell, and he knows all about everyone's good and bad deeds. Nothing is hidden from him. The souls he sends to hell become *pret*, spirits of the damned, the victims of gory and everlasting tortures brought upon them by their own misdeeds. Looking around the room at our group of eighteen prisoners, all of us afraid, dressed in ragged, stinking clothes, I decided that we were already *pret;* our fates had already been decided. The Khmer Rouge who had ridden in on his Honda 90 and who sat smiling at us now—he was the King of Death.

He was muscled and well fed, holding paper files and a black notebook under one arm. He wore a green Mao cảp and an old green-and-white krama around his neck. His black clothes and rubber-tire sandals were dusty from his motorcycle ride. He sat down in a chair at a small table and asked us to sit. We sat on the floor while he scanned the files. Several guards with holstered pistols stood at his side.

The King of Death was calm and sweet. He was like Chev, but more sophisticated. For a guess, he might have finished high school, or lycée.

"Please tell Angka the truth," he told us. "If you do, you will not be punished. Angka never kills people unnecessarily, or kills the innocent. Those who tell the truth will merely be re-educated."

One by one the prisoners went before him, sitting at his feet. He read from their files. He knew some of their names. Their crimes were: being a CIA agent, a Lon Nol officer, the wife of a Lon Nol officer, a ranking member of the Lon Nol government. All of the prisoners denied that the charges were true. At a signal from the judge, which I could not detect, even though I looked for it, the guards came around the side of the desk and kicked the prisoner. The guards did not kick everyone, but they kicked the pregnant woman next to me in the ribs and in the stomach for denying that she was the wife of a captain in the Lon Nol army. They dragged her back to where the rest of us sat, and then it was my turn.

I sat in front of the judge with my hat in my lap and my krama neatly folded on my knee. From where I sat I could only see his trouser legs and his feet with their black rubber-tire sandals.

"Samnang, Angka knows who you are," the King of Death began gently. "You were a military doctor. You held the rank of captain.

So please, tell Angka the truth. You will make it much easier on yourself."

Now I was certain that Pen Tip had informed on me. In Phnom Penh, few knew I was in the military, because I hardly ever wore a uniform. Since then I had not told anyone about it. Only a former hospital insider like Pen Tip would know that a government doctor my age would have held a captain's rank. The only thing Pen Tip didn't know was my real name. And Angka didn't either.

I didn't say anything.

"If you tell the truth," the King of Death said, "Angka will forget the past and give you a high-level position. Angka will let you operate on wounded soldiers, and teach medicine to students of the younger generation. The students will look up to you for giving them this knowledge. You will be a hero. But," he said, "if you don't tell Angka the truth, you will be held responsible."

I cleared my throat.

"Good comrade," I said, "I was not a captain, or a doctor. I was a taxi driver. My taxi number was 213755." (The numbers were from my motorcycle license plate.) "I went to Takeo, Battambang, Kampot, anywhere the passengers wanted to go. I'm telling the truth. This is the second time I've been to jail, and still Angka doesn't believe me. I work hard for Angka. I struggle to master the elements for Angka. I do everything for Angka, and I never make trouble. Why doesn't Angka believe me?"

"Because you are a liar," the judge answered in his calm, soothing voice. "Please tell Angka the truth. If you do, Angka will give you an excellent job. You are an educated person. You can lead people. You can help the country develop. You can help the country build its independence-sovereignty."

I said, "Comrade, if I were a doctor I would tell you so. I want to help Angka. If you don't believe me, go to Phnom Penh and check the files at the medical school. If you find I am really a doctor, Angka can do what it wants."

BAM! The kick came to my ribs. I fell over on my side. Then the other guard kicked me with the hard edge of his rubber-tire sandals. *BAM!* I arched my back in agony. The guards took turns with me, first one, then the other. Then the judge rapped on the table and the guards stopped. They dragged me by the legs back to the line.

By the time I counted my bruises the judge was already interrogating the next prisoner. The guards had kicked me in the rib cage, in the shoulders, the thighs and the back of my neck. They were professionals. They knew what they were doing. A beating like that would have been hard even on a healthy man.

When all eighteen had talked to the judge, the guards led us outside. We walked in single file, away from the mango orchard, through another grove of fruit trees and into an uncultivated rice field.

There we saw wooden structures with uprights and crosspieces, like soccer goalposts, except narrower and higher. There was a double line of them, each one the same. On the ground in the middle of each, where the goalie would stand, was a pile of rice hulls and wood. In front of each goal lay a wooden cross with a length of rope.

At first I couldn't figure it out. Then I looked farther down the rows, which stretched over several dikes and far down the field. At the far end of the rows, prisoners were being punished in a manner I had never heard of before. They were tied to the crosses, the weight of their bodies sagging against the ropes. The crosses were upright, hanging from the goalpost crossbars. Smoke and flames rose from the fires around the prisoners' feet.

The soldiers stood crosses behind each prisoner and began tying us up.

I thought, I hope Huoy never knows about this. I didn't tell her about the worst things of prison last time, about how they cut the poor woman open. I don't want her to know. It would hurt her. She is so tender. She saved my life. I love her so much. If I am gone, who will take care of her? Please, gods, save Huoy and keep her away from this kind of punishment. But she has little chance. The soldiers will probably come for her anyway, because they are after the wives of soldiers and doctors. It is just a matter of time, unless the gods intervene.

And please, gods, I prayed, when I have gone either to hell or to paradise, keep me away from Khmer Rouge. When I am reborn, don't send me near them. I don't want to be anywhere near Cambodia. If I did something wrong in my last life I will pay for it now, but please, gods, surely this is payment in full. In my next life let me be happy.

I was still on the ground and the soldiers were tying my wrists to the cross. "Just shoot me!" I shouted at them. "Just shoot! Get it over with!" I fought them, but they were much stronger and they outnumbered me. They tied my upper arms to the cross and then my thighs and my feet. Then they threw the rope attached to the top of the cross over the goalpost and hoisted me up until my feet were above the pile of wood and rice hulls. I swayed there, back and forth, with a view of the double line of goalposts and the uncultivated rice field.

After the guards tied all of the prisoners they went around to each pile of rice hulls and lit it with cigarette lighters.

Rice hulls have a consistency like sawdust. Fires with rice hulls give off thick, stinging smoke and burn slowly, for days.

When the cross stopped swaying I was facing the double row of goalposts at a forty-five-degree angle, twisted around to the left. Judging from the position of the sun I was facing due west; the rows ran southwest to northeast. Behind me was the grove of fruit trees we had walked through from the prison. To my far left, at the edge of my vision, was a rooftop of a separate building where teenage girls were imprisoned for "crimes" against Angka, like premarital sex. In front was the rice field, weeds covering the flat patches and the raised paddy dikes, and the horrible, unavoidable sight of the other prisoners hanging like me.

Of those who had been crucified longer, some had already died from starvation or thirst—generally women, their heads dropped against their chests, their bodies sagging heavily against the ropes, their feet burned and blistered. Their sarongs had dropped to the first tight circle of rope around their thighs. They didn't have underwear. Unable to control their bodily functions, they had soiled themselves. Beneath them the fires smoldered.

Oh Huoy, Huoy, I am glad you are not here to see this.

My feet were about six feet off the ground and three feet above the pile of wood and rice hulls. The fire had not yet spread to the wood underneath, but the smoke rose into my nostrils and eyes.

Our group of eighteen prisoners didn't do any more talking. We were too thirsty to talk out loud. We were too busy praying.

Hot sunlight struck me on the back of my neck. The weight of my body dragged down on the ropes around my arms and legs. My feet had no feeling at all. My fingers were numb but I could still wiggle them. Iridescent green flies whooshed around my head. I shook them off but they returned and settled on the wetness at the corner of my eyes. I shaped my lips and blew air upward but they just buzzed around and landed again on my face, and on my back where the skin was bleeding from the beating.

The buzzing of the flies was the loudest sound in the landscape. To my right, a woman in her twenties moaned, begging her mother to save her. She was pregnant, with a full roundness in her belly. I did not think she could last long.

Gradually the fire spread below the surface of the rice hulls to the wood. There were no flames, but there was a new smell. I looked down. The hair on my legs was shriveled and burned. My feet must have been blistering and burning, but I could not feel them. My eyes formed tears from the smoke. The guards had built the fire for heat and smoke more than for flames. Their purpose was not to burn us to death but to prolong and intensify the pain of being tied to the crosses.

Late that afternoon, when my eyes were shut against the direct rays of the sun, I felt myself swinging around on the cross. The wind had changed direction. I opened my eyes. The wind blew the smoke away from me, at an angle, but it also pushed the red line of fire farther through the rice hulls. The fire grew hotter, and the heat rose up my thighs. To my left came a quiet sputtering as the man on the next cross peed in his pants hoping to dampen the fire, but it was no use. The drops of urine fell from his feet to the fire, vaporized and rose up again, and the fire burned as strongly as before. The flies attached themselves to my arms and legs, waiting for the wind to die down.

The sun inched toward the horizon and sank. It was then, at dusk, that the wind stopped and the mosquitoes came out.

The mosquitoes came in close, their high-pitched whine near one ear, then the other. I didn't even bother chasing them away.

Oh Huoy, you saved my life when I was sick. You saved my life. May the gods and the winds bring you this message from me, that I am alive for now, that my spirit will always be watching over you.

The moon was nearly full that night. When it rose above the trees behind me, it cast an elongated shadow of the goalpost and of me hanging from the cross in the middle. When the wind picked up, the coals glowed underneath and the fire grew hotter; and when the wind slacked, the mosquitoes came back, whining in my ear and biting my flesh, where I could still feel my flesh. The moon rose silent and calm, and the shadows of the goalposts shortened. The wind stirred the treetops, and the crucified hung like strange butchered animals from the goalposts.

Oh Mother. Oh Huoy. Please save me.

You gods—any gods who can hear. Hindu gods. Jesus. Allah. Buddha. Spirits of the forests and the rice fields. Spirits of my ancestors. Hear me, gods: I never killed anyone. Never, never, never. I saved lives. I was a doctor and I saved the lives of Lon Nol soldiers and Viet Cong and didn't care who they were. So why make me suffer?

Spirits of the wind, I prayed. If the gods cannot hear, then carry the news to them. To any god who has power. Tell the gods what is happening to me.

How Huoy would cry out if she were here. I am glad she cannot see me. Please, gods, do not punish her. She is innocent. Do not let her know what I am going through. I am one of the damned, a *pret*. I am already in hell. And I do not know why. I never betrayed the nation. If I killed anybody in a past life, or tortured people, then punish me and get it over with. If this is vengeance finish it, so my next life will be free.

But I do not think I killed people in past lives. And I do not really know why they are torturing me. This has got to be worse than Hitler and the Jews. Hitler thought the Jews were different from him, like another race. But the Khmer Rouge kill their own race. And the gods do nothing to stop it.

In the morning the guards took down those who had been crucified before us. They put plates of rice in front of the ones who were still alive and asked them questions. Then they tied plastic bags over the prisoners' heads. The prisoners began kicking spastically, to get free. I was too weak to look for long. Or to care. All I knew was that the sun was hot on the back of my neck and my mouth was dry and my lips were cracked. Whatever was happening between the guards and the prisoners seemed incredibly far away, though it was in plain sight. When the guards dragged the bodies away and put fresh people in the goalposts, I barely noticed. What was left of me was a core—a heart that still beat in my chest, a mouth that breathed, eyes that stung from the smoke and the sun. And a brain that prayed.

After four days and four nights with no food or water they let me down and untied the ropes. The circulation returning to my arms and legs brought a pain that was worse than the numbness and hotter than the fire. I fell over on my back and didn't move.

They tied my hands and feet. They tried to make me kneel, but I fell over and they grabbed my hair and shook my head until I saw the plate in front of me. On the plate was fresh rice with two small salted fish on top.

"Are you a doctor?" a faraway voice asked. "A captain?"

I tried to form words, but my mouth wouldn't work. In front of me was the plate heaped with rice.

"No," I whispered. "Give me water. Then shoot me."

"If you tell the truth. Just tell Angka the truth, and you will have water and rice."

Blood had trickled into my mouth from my cracked lips. "Just *shoot*," I croaked. "Please, I can't bear it. Please, Angka, if you don't trust me, just shoot. I will be happy to die. Just shoot."

"Bigmouth!" the guard exclaimed. He shouted to other guards, telling them to come over. They pulled me to a sitting position. Just before they put the plastic bag over my head, I glimpsed the pregnant lady next to me. She already had a bag over her head and she was kicking convulsively with both feet. They tied the bag around my neck, I couldn't see anything, and they pushed me and I fell over again. I tried to breathe, but the plastic got in the way of my mouth and there was no air and I went wild, struggling to get the bag off, but I couldn't and my feet were kicking and I couldn't see. Then they pulled the bag off and I took great gasping lungfuls of air.

They took the bag off the pregnant lady next to me, but it was too late. She had died of suffocation. A guard ripped her blouse apart and pulled down her sarong. Then he picked up his rifle, which had a bayonet attached. He pushed her legs apart and jammed the bayonet into her vagina and tried to rip upward but the pubic bone stopped the blade so he pulled the bayonet out and slashed her belly from her sternum down below her navel. He took the fetus out, tied a string around its neck and threw it in a pile with the fetuses from the other pregnant women. Then he reached into her intestines, cut out her liver, and finally sliced her breasts off with a sawing motion of his blade.

"Good food," he remarked to the other guards. Then he bent down between her legs where the wound was still quivering and he said, "Ha! Look at this! Her cunt's laughing." The other young guards came and looked and stood around, grinning. The flies whooshed around the body of the poor woman, whose crime had been marrying a Lon Nol soldier.

I lay on my side without moving. They would disembowel me next, just for fun. It was nothing for them to cut someone open. Just a whim. They would come for me soon. But the seconds turned into minutes and then they walked away with the woman's liver and breasts. "Enough food for tonight?" said the nearest one, and another said in a voice that was fainter and farther away, "Yes, I think so. Probably enough."

Time passed. Five minutes or five hours, I did not know the difference. A rubber-tire sandal shoved my shoulder and then I was on my back looking up at a guard. He said, "This one isn't dead yet. Give me some water to pour up his nose."

Another guard came over and I found myself staring at a thin, brown-colored waterfall descending from a pail.

The muddy water splashed down near my nostrils and some of it went into my mouth, which was partly open. I started to choke and cough but at the same time my mouth began to work and I swallowed. I had never tasted anything so good. A change come over my body, a stirring of strength. He kept pouring and pouring in a thin, steady stream to get into my nose, and some of it did, but I tilted my head back and it filled my mouth and I swallowed again and again. The water also got in my eyes, but I blinked and concentrated on the brown water pouring down.

When the guard emptied the pail and walked away, I felt much better.

At twilight, the guards untied us and helped us walk back to the jail. Of our group of eighteen, only five of us were still alive, and none of the women. My feet and legs were covered with blisters, which popped underneath as I walked.

They gave us watery rice, and after four days with no food it was like a banquet. Then they dragged us by the arms into jail and locked us into the pens again. The next day I expected to be killed but they gave me a bowl of watery rice again, and the same the day after that.

They made me work around the prison. I gardened and raked and saw the "new" people coming in and only a few of them leaving alive. In the daytime vultures wheeled overhead. At night, the wolf-like *chhke char-chark* snarled and growled as they ripped the flesh of corpses outside.

Then they loaded me into an oxcart and drove me to another jail with thatch walls. Here the prisoners plowed rice fields and tended oxen and ate the rations of watery rice. It was like the front lines, except harder, and we were all terribly emaciated, with arms and legs like sticks. I spent two long months at this place, living from one day to the next.

Then I was released. Soldiers escorted me and some other prisoners back to our cooperative, which was in a new and semipermanent location.

They took us to the common kitchen and told us to sit down. The soldiers went in to report to Chev.

Huoy had seen us coming but she hadn't recognized me and I didn't want to say anything. She was cutting vegetables for cooking. When she finished she sat on the ground with her back to me and began cutting thick slices of banana trunk. Before the revolution banana trunk was pig food, but on the front lines it was used to add bulk to our rations.

Chev came out and the soldiers read off the list of names. When she heard "Samnang," Huoy froze, then turned around and stood up. She was shaking. She called out in a choked voice, "My husband is here! My husband is here!" in spite of her attempts at self-control.

Chev told me, "You can go see your wife. She's waiting."

We walked rapidly toward each other but we were afraid to embrace. I put my arm around her shoulders like a casual friend and took her aside.

I whispered, "I have survived. Don't worry. I will stay here with you."

Huoy was barely able to say anything. "What did they do to you?"

"Don't talk right now. I have survived."

After dinner, when she got off work, Huoy brought me to a canal. Somehow she had procured a bar of real soap. She bathed me and scrubbed me, fighting back the tears when she saw how tight the skin was on my rib cage. The infection on my ankle was worse than before. Sores covered my legs and neck and chin. She asked me what had happened. I said, "Sweet, don't ask. I don't want to see any more tears."

Huoy insisted. She wanted to know why I was so skinny, why I had so many blisters, what they had made me do.

I said, "If you love me, don't ask. I love you and I don't want to tell you."

Huoy let my old clothes float away in the current of the muddy water. I put on a sarong and we walked slowly back to where she had been sleeping, in a long, narrow hut with a thatched roof and no walls. She had a single hammock. Someone gave her a rice bag and she made a double hammock for us with needle and thread.

That night she snuggled next to me. She kissed me again and again. Then she put her lips next to my ear and whispered that she had been sure I was dead. There had been a big purge, she explained. Hundreds of people had been taken away by the soldiers, tied up, a few at a time, without any reason given. Few had returned. Their places had been taken by people from other cooperatives, including —and she whispered names to me.

I lay back in the hammock, staring in the darkness. Around us were hundreds of people in close quarters, in hammocks or on the ground. We couldn't really talk now. That would have to wait.

I was amazed. Amazed that I had lived, that the gods had let me survive a second time, against the odds. To have my arm around my wife's soft female form, to feel her breathing. To hold her. She was so giving, so comforting. She was alive. And she had told me joyous news: My father was alive too.

22

CANDLES

THE LAST TIME I had seen Papa, he and my mother were hurrying after the oxcart holding Pheng Huor, Nay Chhun and the children. From there they had all gone to a front-lines cooperative much like mine, only farther south, near the foothills of the Cardamom Mountains. They had not fared well. First the three children had been taken away—sent off to a youth group, to be brainwashed into forgetting their parents and loving Angka. Then my aged mother had been sent off to another work camp in the jungles. They had not heard from her since.

Three adults remained: Papa, Pheng Huor and Nay Chhun. By the whim of Angka, or the gods, they had been transferred to my collective while I was away in prison. My father was put in a longhouse, a thatched roof on poles, with barely enough space to lie down between his neighbors. Pheng Huor and Nay Chhun were put in a second longhouse and Huoy was in a third. There were twelve of these longhouses in all, with roughly two hundred people in each for a total of approximately twenty-four hundred people.

My father was assigned to a work group of elderly people. He fixed hoe handles, wove baskets, made bamboo shoulderboards and did other light tasks. It didn't take him long to spot Huoy in the common kitchen. Her grief-stricken face told him what her lips could not, that she thought I was dead. My father consoled her, urged her to keep hoping. Every afternoon he went to Huoy's longhouse to visit. When Huoy came back from work he was already there, sitting on the white piece of plastic next to her hammock.

A bond grew between them like father and daughter. The time

they spent together was their favorite part of the day. Huoy told him stories, mended his clothes, kept his spirits up. After meals in the common kitchen where she worked, Huoy cleaned the fifty-five-gallon steel-drum rice pots but purposely left a crust of rice grains along the side. Papa came along later and scooped the crust with his hands. For a man who used to be a millionaire, pot scrapings don't sound like much, but they made a real difference to his health.

Life on the front lines had one good effect: It stripped away everything unimportant and allowed us to see each other's true worth. Papa finally saw what kind of woman Huoy was, that she didn't care whether he was rich or poor and that she had never asked for anything from him, except the chance to show him love and respect. And Papa began to compare her to Nay Chhun, my brother's wife. Nay Chhun had been very nice to my father as long as he owned the lumber mill, but she didn't have much time for him when he was a war slave.

The morning after I returned from prison I was resting in the hammock when Papa walked up. He was even thinner than before, with hollow cheeks and a flat belly. He wore only a faded black T-shirt and a pair of light blue culottes that had been skillfully patched in several places; I recognized Huoy's handiwork. When he saw me, tears came to his eyes.

When Papa asked what had happened in prison I left out the details, as I had with Huoy. He listened. He shook his head, sighing. He wept. He got up, walked around and paced back and forth, taking deep breaths.

He had changed, I decided. When I was growing up he had always been tough and stern and skeptical. In old age, he was softer inside, more sympathetic. But he was still the leader of the family. He sat on the plastic mat beside the hammock and gave me advice:

"Son," he said, "I just have to look at you to know you have suffered. People hardly ever come back when they are taken away. You have come back twice. From now on, keep your mouth shut. Plant a kapok tree. *Dam doeum kor*. No matter what happens, don't give them any excuse to take you away again.

"When you were a young boy you were very hothearted. Since meeting Huoy you have become less so, but you are still too angry underneath. You must cool your heart even more. Keep your emotions under control, so they will not show on your face. You have fooled many people but not everybody. If you were as smart as you think you are, they would not keep taking you away."

"Yes, Papa," I said.

"And another thing," said my father. "Pen Tip. You have not spoken of taking revenge on him, but it is written all over you. Forget it. You are an educated person; he is not. He has done you wrong, but let the gods punish him. Do not attempt it yourself. If you do, the Khmer Rouge will find out. Then they will kill you, and Huoy will be a widow again. If you see him, pretend nothing has happened."

This was harder to accept, but thinking it over I slowly began to see that he was right. "Yes, Papa," I said.

"The Khmer Rouge are crazy and uneducated," he went on. "To survive them you must be patient and very, very smart. Use your brain, son. Look around you. The canals they are building will fall apart when the rains come. You know that yourself, because you have worked in them. They will not hold up to the rains of Battambang. Everything the Khmer Rouge try to do will fail. And they do not have the support of the people. So plant your kapok tree, son. Be patient, be quiet and stay calm. One day, sooner or later, the revolution will be overturned. The regime will be replaced and we will be free again."

I listened carefully. He was certainly right about one thing: The regime could not last forever. The best way to fight it was to lie low and allow it to self-destruct. Not taking revenge on Pen Tip was going to be harder. Many nights in prison I had lain awake thinking what I was going to do to Pen Tip for informing on me. I had not learned about pain without wanting to inflict it. I had not endured torture without wanting revenge. My thoughts were so dark and gruesome that I never would have mentioned them to anybody, but my father guessed them. And he was right again. It was more important to avoid future suffering than to take revenge for the past. And to avoid more suffering I was going to have to become a better actor than I had been before. I was going to have to control and conceal my emotions.

The visit of my sister-in-law Nay Chhun that afternoon gave me a chance to practice. Nay Chhun and I didn't like each other. We hadn't had a real conversation since before the revolution. She had never visited me when I was sick in Phum Chhleav. But this was a chance to repair the damage and forge a new relationship. When she asked how I was, I answered, "Not too badly, thank you." She said I had lost weight, and I said with a smile, "Who hasn't?" I asked her how she and my brother were. We had a superficial but polite conversation.

What absorbed my attention was not Nay Chhun but my father, who went silent and cold when she approached. On the front lines he avoided her, except when she was with my brother. Papa had finally seen into her character. Yet when she left he heaved another sigh and wiped a tear away—glad, I supposed, that she and I were finally on speaking terms.

Such changes in my father! In the old days, when he was rich, he barely noticed Huoy when she came into his house. That I had chosen a poor woman like Huoy embarrassed him. Because of him Huoy and I never had the wedding we wanted, with the monks and the ceremony and the families coming together and the great feast with half of Phnom Penh invited to the tables. Huoy had paid a price for not being married, with insults from Nay Chhun, Aunt Kim and my other relatives—insults to which she never replied.

But the past didn't matter anymore. We were all on the same level now. My father brightened visibly when Huoy came back from the kitchen that afternoon. His entire manner changed, and a smile creased his wrinkled face. That was what I had been waiting for, to know that he welcomed her into the family.

But it was my fate barely to recover from one disaster before being hit with another.

I went back to work. The first sporadic rains had fallen. The weather was hot and muggy, as it always is before the real rainy season begins.

Chev assigned my group to create paddies for large-scale rice farming—diked fields much longer and wider than those of the pre-revolutionary peasants. It was a good idea in theory, because big paddies would allow us to put more land into cultivation than before, with proportionately less maintenance. The problem was with the plan for the dikes. Instead of just taking half of the old dikes out to create fields twice as large, which would have been a sensible plan, Chev told us to tear all of them out and then build new ones. It was an enormous job, with no practical benefit, and it had to be done in a hurry. Perhaps Chev wanted us to show how zealous we could be in proving our devotion. I worked in mud up to my shoulders. The air was hot, the mud was cool, and I went back and forth. I was exhausted. From the woods nearby came swarms of mosquitoes.

When I came down with shivering fits twice in one day, and then with fits at the same times the next day, it seemed almost like a blessing. It was a perfect excuse for getting out of work without faking it. There was plenty of malaria around. Everyone knew the symptoms.

Released from work, I set out to find medicines. My first choice was Western medicine, either quinine or a similar drug like chloroquine. I didn't have any myself. I looked and asked, but there was none to be found on the black market. There were people moaning and shaking with malaria in all the longhouses—crowded, unclean places that stank of urine and buzzed with flies.

Next I tried the regime, which had three levels of medical care. The top cadre could go to a reasonably good, Western-style hospital in Battambang City, but that was off-limits for me. Ordinary Khmer Rouge and "old" people could go to a smaller regional hospital in Phum Phnom, but I couldn't get in there either. There was only the front-lines clinic, the place where the nurses called the patients "war slaves." This was an ordinary house on stilts next to a yam garden. When I went there, the clinic staff announced a meal, and the war slaves, who were pathetically thin, crowded in line and started pushing each other to get to the food table first. One patient started a fight, and a *mit neary* broke her serving ladle over his head getting him to stop.

In this clinic there were only two medicines: vitamin injections and homemade malaria pills. The multivitamin solutions seem to have been made in Phnom Penh by someone with a basic knowledge of pharmacology. They were stored in old Coca-Cola bottles. Following standard medical procedure, the nurses sterilized the hypodermic needles in boiling water, but before they gave the injections they ran their dirty fingers along the length of the needles to make sure the needles were firmly attached to the syringes. As a result, almost all the patients developed abscesses at the injection site. Few of them recovered from the illnesses that brought them to the clinic in the first place.

The malaria pills were made at the clinic from yams grown outside in the garden and *sdao* leaves. The mixture was ground up with a mortar and pestle, baked in sheets and stamped into pill form with M-16 shell casings. The pills were popularly known as "rabbit turds" because of their circular shape and tan color. I was given a handful of rabbit turds and walked away quickly, before the nurses could give me an injection. The *sdao*, I thought, would be mildly helpful against malaria; *sdao* was one of those folk remedies that had a basis in fact. But it was the yam in the pills that appealed to me. Yam was food.

As the malaria infection attacked more of my red blood cells, I grew weaker. I lay on the white plastic mat in the longhouse and waited. I felt cold and unable to stop shivering. The next thing I knew, Huoy was sitting astride my waist holding my arms, and my father was holding my feet. I was drenched with sweat. They said I had been unconscious, flailing around convulsively with my arms and legs. I didn't remember any of the fit. All I knew was that I was thirsty. I drank what seemed to be gallons of water without stopping.

Huoy and my father took care of me together. When I had used up the rabbit turds my father gathered *sdao* leaves and bark. I ate the leaves, and Huoy brewed the bark into a tea for me to drink. My father roamed through the forests at dawn, looking for new, tender bamboo leaf shoots with the dew still on them. This was a traditional Cambodian cure. He also made a Chinese medicine for me with shavings from a piece of animal horn he had brought with him from Phnom Penh.

Huoy was worried too. Every day she went off looking for Western medicines. Finally she found eight 300-mg. quinine tablets and bought them for a *damleung*, or 1.2 ounces, of gold. I took half a pill in the morning and half at night, along with the *sdao* leaves and the *sdao* tea and my father's traditional cures. With the medicine and with the devoted attention of Huoy and my father, I recovered.

Then it was back to work. The rains arrived. Water flowing down from the hills filled the canals and poured across as if no obstacle were there. The paddies were submerged except for a few of the higher dikes, which protruded like the lines on a checkerboard, and the hillocks, which were like checkers, some of them in the middle of the squares and the rest out of position on the dikes between squares.

Chev came to inspect, carrying his hoe. He was muddy from head to foot. Under the water surface, invisible from sight, were the delicate green shoots of the rice seedbeds.

"The seedlings will die in a few hours if the water does not go down," Chev remarked. He spoke calmly, but as I followed his gaze to the flooded fields I felt weak. It wasn't our fault! The canal hadn't been deep enough to contain the water. We didn't have the manpower to build dikes to protect the seedbeds. We had only four in our group—two out with malaria, another two taken away to the woods.

"You must take your destiny firmly in hand," Chev told us as he began to walk away. "If you lose this battle, you will be responsible."

We went back to rebuilding dikes with a desperation made worse by knowing that whatever we did would not be enough. I prayed while I worked. The others did too. And that afternoon, by the kindness of the gods, the rain stopped. The runoff water ceased flowing. The water level in the paddies subsided and the green shoots of the rice seedlings reappeared.

But the next day the rains fell again. Every day the work was urgent. Dikes washed out, patches of rice were swept away. I put everything in my work. It was a matter of saving my own life and also raising rice, so the cooperative would have food to eat.

Chev decided to reorganize the cooperative with two common kitchens a mile apart. My father and brother were assigned to the new kitchen, but I still saw them often. A major purge began. The soldiers took captives morning and afternoon. Instead of marching them away immediately, the soldiers made public examples of them, tying them to trees and shouting to anyone who would listen what they had done wrong. I tried not to look or listen. I had enough on my mind just getting through each day.

So I wasn't really paying attention when I trudged back toward the longhouse at the end of an afternoon early in the rainy season of 1976. There were puddles on the footpath. I walked around the puddles half-noticing how they reflected the sky. "See the enemies here! See the enemies!" a teenage soldier was shouting, like an announcer at a carnival. "Angka caught them for stealing food! They stole food from all of us! See them now, while you have a chance! Learn from their example!" Near the soldier's feet sat several captives with their hands tied around a tree trunk. Their faces were angled away. I was wondering how much the dinner rations were going to be when something caught my eye: One of the captives was my father.

I froze.

My father turned his face and looked sadly into mine. His lips moved. He wanted to explain something to me. He wanted my help.

"Why have you stopped?" the soldier yelled at me. "Go on!"

The people behind me had almost collided into my back. They turned to look at the prisoners and their muttered comments came to me from far away. "They are already old. Why make them suffer?" said one voice. Said another, "That's a nice old man there, the skinny one. Why kill him?"

"Go!" roared the soldier.

It was like looking into a tunnel, seeing my father's eyes widened in sorrow and fear and not being able to see anything else. He signaled me to go. Numbly, I obeyed.

Huoy's face was already swollen from weeping. She knew. She had heard that a high-ranking official visiting the new kitchen had seen my father scoop rice from the sides of a fifty-five-gallon drum. He had asked Chev why the "new" people were scavenging for food while they should be working. Chev arrested Papa on the spot.

Around sunset the procession walked slowly past our longhouse. Papa was roped to two other prisoners. A soldier walking behind them held the end of the rope in his hand. As they came close, my father lifted his head and looked at me. There was no accusation, merely an immense sadness. From where he was going there was no coming back.

Plant a kapok tree, he had told me.

I went outside the longhouse and sat on the ground. There was a lump in my throat and the tears rolled down my cheeks, but I didn't say anything. Plant a kapok tree.

When three days had passed, Huoy and I brought our evening rations back to the longhouse with some candles. Our neighbors knew what we were doing and left us alone. Late at night, Pheng Huor and Nay Chhun arrived. We lit the candles. My brother and his wife went first, because they were older. They *sompeah*ed to the improvised altar, put their palms on the ground three times, bowed down until their foreheads touched the backs of their hands another three times and prayed. Huoy and I sat behind them until they had finished and it was our turn.

I prayed that my father be reborn away from Cambodia.

Day after day the purge grew worse. Some were taken away for complaining, most for stealing food to stay alive. We tried to learn why the Khmer Route were killing so many but found no real reason. It was just something they did, a craving they could not satisfy. They created enemies to devour, which increased their appetite for enemies.

Shock, horror, grief—with the death of my father, part of us died too. Under control of an alien force we responded, but without energy to spare. We were beings so imperfect and fragile in manufacture that we wore out constantly, or were destroyed for being defective by those who did not care. Everything was gone. Society was destroyed and monks and temples destroyed and markets and families and the bonds between humans destroyed. There was no hope.

Two weeks later, my brother and his wife were taken away with their hands tied. I never learned why. They never came back. Huoy and I had a service, the same as we did for my father, *sompeah*ing, bowing, praying. We lit the same candles, which were already burned down to stubs. There were only two of us to pray for their souls. We wondered who would light candles for us.

23

THE RAINS

THE SKY was clear at dawn.

By midmorning the first clouds had sailed in from the west, puffy and white, like the cottony fibers of the kapok tree.

The clouds billowed and grew and spread out until they blocked the sun.

From far away came the sound of thunder, a low rumbling, like bombs from a B-52. The air turned cold. The wind rose, the rice flattened in the fields and the trees bent over on the hillocks with their leaves flying off horizontally.

Small tornadoes of dust and rice stalks spun through the fields and onto the bare ground by the longhouses. Clothes flew off clotheslines. Thatch panels flapped on the roofs and wood frames creaked. The people tied their kramas tightly around their heads, and clapped their hands over their faces to protect themselves from the dust.

For a minute or two, the wind paused and the trees and the rice straightened. It was as dark as twilight. In the stillness the birds chirped with unusual loudness and clarity. Swallows dipped and rose through the air, hunting for insects.

Then the sky closed in. The wind blew and the trees leaned over and the rain fell diagonally from the black undersides of the clouds, stinging my face. I ducked my head but the wind pushed my hat brim against my cheek, and when I raised my head the brim flew up and the rain stung me again. The droplets made a tinkling noise when they struck the water in the rice paddies, and splashed upward again like tiny fountains. I could see the man next to me swinging his hoe, and beyond him there was another one less distinctly. Beyond that there was nobody at all, no people and no landscape, only a veil of water.

I loved the rains. They made the greens in the landscape brighter, the clay redder. The coolness they brought was like the answer to a prayer. Leaves sprouted on the trees, rice paddies turned green, insects and fish and crabs multiplied. Life was better. On the front lines we were given more food. We didn't have to work at night. There were fewer evening meetings, because the leaders didn't like getting wet. The water dripped from the eaves of the longhouse with a sound like the softest music. It splashed from roofs and trees onto the ground, flowed down the paths, cut snaking, twisting channels where it chose. In the longhouse Huoy and I put the white plastic tarp above us, but that didn't keep us dry. Lightning flashed, as bright as day. Thunder boomed like artillery, and Huoy wrapped her arms around me and buried her head in my chest for protection. It rained for days and then turned foggy, with a shower so fine and thin it was nearly invisible.

During the rainy season of 1976, from about July through September, I worked with a mobile crew, filling in wherever help was needed. We built more dikes. We plowed fields, planted and transplanted rice. Sometimes we tended oxen and water buffalo. But our biggest job was road repair. On the road leading toward the Khmer Rouge headquarters at Phum Phnom, the runoff water had carved a gully thirty yards long. Brown, muddy water poured through like a river, and the rice fields beyond were like a lake.

We hadn't seen the sun in a week. With new members there were eight men in our crew, each with a hatchet and hoe. We cut saplings near the roadside and put the trunks vertically in the ground as a stockade against the water flow. We laid logs and branches behind to buttress it, and packed it full of mud entangled with roots and plants. The rain was falling steadily, neither hard nor soft.

I told the others which trees to chop, where to get the mud, even though I was not the official leader. My father used to say, "Think like a boss, not like a worker." He meant that it is better to use your brain and be active than to be sullen and passive, as most workers are. I worked harder than anyone in the crew because it kept my mind sharp and because it kept me from thinking about other things.

For hours at a time, if I was lucky, I would not have a mental picture of my father's face when he was tied up, or my brother and his wife when they were being marched away.

I chopped down a sapling and threw it like a spear across a small canal, where the others were building the vertical stockade. They moved in slow motion, their tiredness a form of protest. Only one worked as hard as me. His name was Seng, and he was overseeing us that day. He was short and muscular, maybe fifty years old, with Buddhist tattoos on his chest. He was a village chief on the back lines and one of Chev's assistant chiefs on the front lines.

From farther up the road, out of sight, came a noise interrupting the quiet of the rain. It sounded like an engine whining at high rpm and tires spinning in the mud. Seng raised his head to listen, then walked off to investigate.

I chopped another sapling down without slowing my pace. It was funny about Seng—"Uncle" Seng, as he liked to be called. He was the only one of the Khmer Rouge who seemed fully human. The last time he supervised us, we had been tending livestock. While I sneaked off to cook a meal in a hillock, a pair of oxen wandered off into the forest. I looked for them all night and didn't find them until morning. Chev would have killed me for carelessness if he had known, but Uncle Seng only warned me not to do it again. He had never ordered anybody killed.

That wasn't to say I trusted him. If he thought I was a model worker, fine. If he liked me as a person, even better. Neither he nor anyone else knew that I led a double life. They didn't know that almost every night I crept out of the longhouse to steal. I took vegetables from a nearby village. I carried my hatchet as a weapon, ready to attack anyone who caught me. I was willing to die. They had already taken everything else away from me except for Huoy, and Huoy and I had decided that if the time came we would commit suicide together.

"Hey! All of you!" Uncle Seng's reappearance broke my train of thought. He was waving for us to follow him. I plunged into the canal and swam across it with my hoe and hatchet. When I climbed out I was no wetter than I had been before.

I trotted down the road with a few others just behind me and the rest hurrying to catch up. When we got close to Seng we saw a low, wide, model B-1 jeep with a cloth roof.

Only one jeep looked like that in the Phnom Tippeday region, and that was the one belonging to the highest-ranking civilian Khmer Rouge. I had often seen it driving around, the leader's right arm sticking out of the passenger window, his hand on the roof.

One of the jeep's wheels had become stuck between logs lain across the road below the surface. The motor roared, the tires spun and a plume of slippery mud shot to the rear. The driver, a soldier with a green Mao cap, sat blankly behind the steering wheel and revved the accelerator while two other soldiers pushed the jeep from behind. Nothing happened. The tires spun and the wheel sank even farther between the logs, tilting the jeep at a crazy angle.

"Stop, please," a voice said mildly, and the driver lifted his foot from the accelerator. I walked behind and saw a man bending down to examine the wheel. He wore the same black pajama uniform and Mao cap as the soldiers, but there was something about him that suggested authority. He was good-natured, with narrow Chinese eyes and a wart on his cheek. It's Chea Huon, I said to myself. Then I thought: No, it can't be.

"What should we do?" he asked the driver, but the driver was too shy to answer. Better to act stupid than risk contradicting a superior—that was the driver's attitude. Typically Cambodian. If Chea Huon said the best way to get the jeep out was to spit on the tires, the driver would have started spitting. But I was not sure it was Chea Huon. He had the same slight build, hunched shoulders and bad posture. The same wart. If it was not Chea Huon it was his twin. What was he doing here?

"We'll do it for you, comrade," Seng said deferentially to him. "We're already muddy. No need for you to be muddy too. Come on," he said to our group. While Chea Huon watched, the rest of us and the two bodyguards started pushing the jeep. If he noticed me glancing at him, then away, then at him again, he didn't react. He looked as if he wanted to oblige Seng, to cooperate with what was asked of him.

The rest of us pushed, but the tires spun and the jeep sank even lower. We weren't getting any traction.

"Uncle Seng," I said, "maybe we could try putting tree branches under the tires. It might give them something to catch hold of."

Chea Huon had started walking slowly down the road. "Good idea," he said over his shoulder.

At Seng's nod, we picked up our hatchets. "Get long tree trunks if you can," I called to the others in the group. "Branches too, and rocks if you find any." Two of them immediately started hacking at a tree by the side of the road. I followed Chea Huon and passed him. He was pointing at a sapling farther on. I started to hack at its branches. He came even with me.

There was nobody else in earshot.

I spoke in a low voice, without looking at him. "Excuse me, *luk* teacher. I may be wrong, but your name is Chea Huon. You were a teacher in Takeo. I recognize the mark on your cheek."

"You know me?"

"You taught me in 1962 and 1963."

I removed the last of the branches, bent down, and attacked the trunk.

"Yes, you're right," he said after a moment. "And I now know who you are too. You got your doctor's degree, right?"

"Yes, *luk* teacher."

The rain fell. He stood with his hands on his hips, nodding his head up and down to show he understood. Then he came closer, patted me on the shoulder and said in a kind and friendly voice, "Just keep working and stay quiet."

The two bodyguards came up before he could say more. They walked within earshot and then stood a respectful distance away. I bent over, chopping at the trunk of the sapling. Only a few more blows to go. It was up to Chea Huon, to keep on talking or not.

". . . And how is the rice coming along?" he asked me, as if we were continuing our conversation. "Is the irrigation under control?"

"It goes very well, comrade," I answered, a little louder than necessary. "Right now we have a heavy flow of water coming down from the hills and cutting the road, but under Uncle Seng's leadership we have launched a road-repairing offensive. We have already repaired many washed-out spots."

"We must fight on all battlefields," Chea Huon replied piously. "We must struggle to control nature."

With that he walked farther down the road to inspect the rice fields, followed by the bodyguards. I carried the pieces of the sapling back to the jeep.

I got on my hands and knees in the mud and jammed the branches underneath the tire. Then I directed the others to bring the branches and the rocks, while making sure that Uncle Seng approved of the way things were proceeding so he would appear to be the one in charge. The driver wasn't very bright and didn't understand that he had to rock his jeep forward and back so we could work the branches in. I had to be polite about telling him what to do, because his rank was much higher than mine and I didn't want him to lose face.

Covered in mud from head to toe, I thought about those long-ago days when I went to Chea Huon for free tutoring in mathematics. He lived a simple, spartan life. In his house on stilts outside Takeo he wore a sarong, like a farmer. When we students were thirsty we dipped a bowl into the earthern water jar. He was very pure and intellectual and treated everybody the same. I never suspected he was communist until later, in 1967, when I visited him in jail in Phnom Penh. Yet when I looked back, it all made sense. He was typical of the idealists who joined the communists in the 1960s and then vanished into the forests. Yes, he was about the right age and background to be at his level of the Khmer Rouge hierarchy.

I pushed more branches in the tire's hole. When the driver rocked forward and back we wedged the poles farther and farther in.

Chea Huon knew I was a doctor. Somehow I was certain he wouldn't turn me in. But everything else about him left me confused. "Just keep working and stay quiet," he had told me. And that was all. What was that supposed to mean—that he wasn't going to help me? He had a brain, he had eyes! He *saw* the unhealed sores on my arms and legs and face. He *knew* I was a doctor. It was in his power to order me to set up a real clinic, to treat the sick on the front lines. He had a higher rank than Chev. He could save even me from being a war slave, if he wanted. He could take me off the front lines!

Why didn't he?

We rocked the jeep forward and back, wedging more and more brush underneath. Finally the jeep popped out of the hole and onto the level road surface.

Chea Huon returned from inspecting the flooded fields. He was soaking wet, but unlike the rest of us he was not muddy. He thanked everybody and looked at each of us briefly in turn, nodding and smiling. He turned to Uncle Seng. "That one there," he said, pointing at me, "is a good worker. He shows initiative. Take good care of him."

Then he climbed in his jeep and drove off, disappearing in the drizzle.

We stood there, holding our hatchets and hoes. The road was emptier than before. The rain was cold on our skins.

The rest of that day, and the next day, and for many to come, questions and attempts at answers crowded my brain:

Chea Huon is educated. He is smart. He is not like the rest. Why then does he allow those like Chev to kill people like my father and brother? Does he know about it, or not?

If he does know, why doesn't he stop the killing? He is smart enough to realize that the revolution will fail if it doesn't have the support of the people.

If he doesn't know of the killings directly, he must have heard about them. If he hasn't heard, how could he be so stupid? But I know he isn't stupid, so he must have heard of them.

He is the head man in the entire region! Doesn't he have enough power to stop the killing? And if he doesn't have enough power, why doesn't he go to someone higher up who does?

I must go to his headquarters to talk to him and ask why there is so much killing. He would receive me. He knows me from the past. If I could get through to him, it could change the entire situation on the front lines. The upper-level Khmer Rouge just need to realize what a disaster they have created. Then they would change it.

No, they wouldn't. They wouldn't do that at all.

I must think this over carefully.

Dam doeum kor.

I don't want to go to Khmer Rouge headquarters. It is too dangerous. I cannot trust Chea Huon, because he has killed many, many people. He must have. He is one of them! The last thing the Khmer Rouge want is suggestions for change. They would call it complaining or having a capitalist mentality. They would kill me for sure.

I am afraid.

And—I think—Chea Huon is afraid too.

24

RICE FARMING

WHEN THE HEAVIEST of the rains was over and the roads were fixed, my group went back to rice farming.

Farming was our reason for being on the front lines. Directly or indirectly, everything centered around it. We dug canals to have irrigation water for the dry season and to prevent flooding in the rainy season. We built paddy dikes to grow rice on a huge scale. We tended oxen and water buffalo so they could pull our plows. We guided the plows and harrows around and around the fields. We went to propaganda meetings so the Khmer Rouge could tell us how glorious farming was.

For anyone whose mind had been sharpened by education, farming was easy to learn. When another man in my group broke a wooden plow tip, I walked into the forest, chopped a tree down and made a replacement part. In an hour he was plowing again. When someone stole the reins for my oxen, probably to eat the leather, a common practice on the front lines, I didn't get upset. I went into the forest again, cut vines, quartered them and braided the outer strips. The new reins were as tightly woven and strong as anything the old peasants could make. And I cursed the Khmer Rouge for saying that anybody could practice medicine. It had taken me seven years of training to get my degree as a doctor. There was no single skill of farming that I couldn't learn in a day. What nonsense, to say that only the peasants possessed worthwhile knowledge!

Yet I liked farming. I liked working with the rice plants most of all. When the seedbeds were plowed and harrowed and a few inches of rainwater covered the soil, we put seed rice (rice with the husks on, or paddy rice) in pails for a few days to sprout. We took handfuls of sprouts and scattered them into the water, which had been fertilized with manure. A day or two later, narrow, whitish shoots showed above the water. A few days more and the shoots had turned a pale green, and then a delicate green that is difficult to describe. This was the most critical phase of rice cultivation. A hard rain could cover the young shoots with water and kill them in a few hours. A lack of rain could deprive them of water and do the same. We stood by the seedbeds with our hoes to let water in and out of the dikes as needed.

A month after planting, the rice seedlings were a foot high and densely packed together, like a lawn. There is no sight in the world as lovely as a young rice field with the sun shining through. It is like light shining through stained glass, only more natural, and more refreshing to the eyes. The rice has a clean, fragrant smell. Walk close to it and you can see the clouds and the sky reflected on the water between the stalks, or the reflection of your own face, until the wind ripples the water surface and stirs the rice shoots in waves.

It was on sunny mornings in the rice fields that I felt happiest. The air was fresh. The scenery was beautiful in every direction. Working in the fields did something to me, like awakening an ancestral memory. My parents had farmed rice when they were young. I was descended from people who had farmed rice generation after generation, as far back as there had been a human race. It was almost enough to make me forget what had happened under the Khmer Rouge and forgive them. Almost, but not quite. If only I had time to fish and to gather foods openly, if only they didn't kill us, if only men like me had time to make love to our wives and raise our families with dignity and take care of our old parents—if, if, if—I would have accepted my fate, and become a rice farmer with all my heart and soul.

The most backbreaking part of the cycle was transplanting the rice from the crowded seedbeds to the rest of the fields. Most of the collective was mobilized to help with it. We used an ancient technique for uprooting the seedlings: Standing with our knees bent to take the strain off our backs, we grabbed a few rice shoots at a time with a circular motion. The shoots came up easily and we put them in our left hands. When our left hands were full we swished the roots around in the water to loosen the mud, lifted our left feet and whacked the roots against the instep to make the mud and water fly off. Then we stacked the clean, neat bundles of shoots in the water behind us and moved forward. To either side were people doing the same; we were in a long line, making patient progress across a field.

Then came replanting, another ancient technique. Carrying bunches of shoots in the crooks of our arms, taking care that the roots always stayed wet, we tranferred the shoots one at a time to our right hands and planted them with a swift thumb-and-forefinger motion, first poking a hole in the mud with our thumbs, then lowering the roots into the hole, then tamping the mud around the stalk with our fore-fingers. Two plants in a row, then a step forward and one in the next row, then two again, planting in equilateral triangles. Again, I was part of a row of people working its way slowly across a field. The fields seemed to go on and on without end. It was an extremely ambitious planting program.

Everything about the front lines was ambitious. There wasn't much planning or careful follow-through. The canals on which we had worked such agonizing hours were never a success. The rains had rounded the edges and silted the bottoms. In some places the water surged right over the canals, tore away huge patches of rice plants and carried the plants off with the current. For the fields that survived, and well over half did, the crews were too small to keep up with the maintenance. We went out there with our hoes, to weed and to regu-late the water levels by tearing down or building up dikes, but we were like tiny human figurines in a vast landscape. Chev threatened us, but we simply couldn't do it all. Most "new" people didn't even feel like trying. Whether we were diligent or not, we knew we would get the same amount of rice at harvesttime. There were no incentives. It was not like the old days, when the peasants worked much less and planted smaller crops, but ate more because they knew what they were doing and could keep what they produced.

I worked hard to keep my mind sharp, but the others in the crew were sullen and slow and did as little as they could get away with. When there were no guards in sight we caught crabs in the rice paddies, then sat down and talked about food. The conversations were always the same:

"Ahhhh . . ." (a big sigh). It was a man named Som, who had one withered arm and who was our most outspoken critic of the regime. "Look at all this rice. We can plant it but we cannot eat it."

"Of course you can eat it," I said. "Just start chewing on a stalk, the way an ox chews on grass."

"Do you remember Phnom Penh?" said Som. "Rice every day? Anytime you wanted it you could step into a restaurant. You could have it with anything you wanted, fried rice, steamed rice—"

"I'd rather have some noodles," another man said. "Every afternoon, I had noodle soup with curried beef and fish balls. Very spicy and tasty—"

"No, fried noodles are better, with ginger and beef—"

Everybody was talking now.

"Fish fried with ginger and lemongrass was my wife's specialty—"

"What I wouldn't give for some fried catfish. Or pork."

". . . or some juicy grilled chicken stuffed with herbs—"

". . . so juicy, so tasty—"

"How about fruits?" said Som. "Do you remember papayas? Mangoes? The tiny fried bananas in the market? I used to buy a bag of those every morning—"

". . . so delicious, so good—"

We sat in the paddies and reminisced, licking our lips while our stomachs rumbled.

"No, noooooo! Don't remind me! Enough of this!" said our group leader. "We've got to get back to work."

"Or cognac with ginseng," said Som. "I used to drink that before going to a whorehouse. Put my brain to sleep but woke my dick up—"

"Be quiet, will you? I don't have the strength to think about sex. Let me get my belly full of food first."

"Back to work, comrades," said the group leader. "I think I see a guard coming."

". . . fried rice with pork and lots of soy sauce . . ." Som muttered as he picked up his hoe.

When the rains stopped the rice paddies still held a foot of water. The plants branched and swelled to the sides—"pregnant" was how they were usually described. They gave off a sweet, fertile smell. As the water in the paddies dried, seed buds appeared and the plants turned a tawny gold.

As the harvest approached, Uncle Seng assigned us to make scarecrows for the paddies and to chase birds away when the scarecrows failed. We were also supposed to guard the fields against thieves. Naturally, we field workers were the biggest thieves of all. We just had to be careful, because we never knew when *chhlop* might be watching. I ducked down between the rows of rice plants and stripped the seeds off lower branches. I stored them in whatever container I could find, then went back to pick it up at nighttime when nobody could see me.

Finally, in November 1976, the harvest began. Everyone had high expectations. Chev said the regime was going to trade the surplus rice to other countries for tractors and bulldozers, so we could grow even more rice the next year. We "new" people had hopes of eating bowl after bowl of real rice, the full year around, instead of the thin gruel with a spoonful of rice the common kitchen served at meals.

Everybody in the collective was mobilized for the harvest. Even Huoy, who worked in the kitchen, came out to the fields and worked beside me in one of those long rows that stretched from one side of the field to the other and was just one of many rows in sight. We cut hour after hour, placing bundles of rice behind us, which others piled on oxcarts and drove off to the threshing ground.

As soon as the first rice was threshed, the common kitchen began serving real rice at meals. We weren't satisfied. The rice was *ours*. We wanted more. We helped ourselves to the rice in the fields. Smoke rose from quick, furtive fires on every hillock. We used sticks and holes in the ground as makeshift mortars and pestles, milling the husks away, then cooked the rice and ate it as fast as we could. Little children sat by the fields, pounding sticks into holes, sometimes just imitating the elders in play, but usually with actual rice in the bottom of the holes, milling the husks from the white inner seeds.

The soldiers tried to stop the stealing. To set an example, they took a four-year-old child who had been milling rice and tied him to a post in front of his parents. They made the parents watch their little boy without touching him or giving him any food or water until a few days later, when he died of dehydration. But even the horror of that punishment didn't stop the rest of us from stealing.

As we cut the stalks in the fields, revolutionary songs blared from the loudspeakers, alternating with news broadcasts from the radio. The news programs announced the "glorious victory over the elements" that had resulted in a harvest larger than ever before. "Soon we will begin the struggle again to put more fields into production!" said the announcer, who started reading a long list of rice tonnage statistics in which Phnom Tippeday was mentioned. "The women and men there are very active and working vigorously in the harvest! And they are very happy, singing in the rice fields and coming home to plenty of rice to eat!"

That was what the Khmer Rouge radio said. But in reality there was no singing. Our faces had become pained and sorrowful. A month after the harvest began, while we were still cutting the fields, the rations were cut back again. Not to watery rice, but to a loose porridge with five or six spoonsful of rice in each bowl. Next year, Chev promised us, we would get to eat more.

From a distance, with aching hearts, we watched the activity at the threshing grounds. Soldiers poured the rice into large hempen sacks and loaded them onto trucks. The trucks drove off. A few were unloaded at nearby warehouses under heavy guard. Most drove away and vanished. And by early January 1977, when the harvest was half through, we were eating watery rice again.

25

THE DAM

THE KHMER ROUGE always held meetings before the start of new projects to make sure we had the correct revolutionary understanding of our tasks. In January 1977 they called a mass meeting and gave us half a day off to attend it—a very unusual step for a regime that never gave weekends, vacations or any other relief from the work routine.

On the day of the meeting I collected my ration of watery rice, put it in my field cooking pot and started walking. The paths and roads were crowded with "new" people heading toward the same destination. Huoy was waiting for me there. We sat down on a hillock, spread her krama over both our heads as a sunshade and took out our food. I brought leaves of water convolvulus and several aquatic plants called *truoy snor* and *slap chang wa* and *kamping puoy*. Huoy had fixed a traditional dish of crabs ground up with tamarind and peppers. We ate with our spoons, reaching into the watery rice and then the crabs and the leaves. It was a good rural-style meal under the circumstances, though with real rice it would have been much better.

Around us sat war slaves in ragged clothes, eating watery rice with whatever they had found to add to it. It was the largest gathering I had seen on the front lines—more than ten thousand people, by my guess. Yet we looked small in comparison to our surroundings. To the east, drab clay flatland stretched for miles, broken by the humps of two hills. To the north, the mountain ridge rose almost vertically, the ridgeline hiding the old temple, which lay on the far side. To the west, the ridge curved around and southward to a point in front of us, where it was joined by the start of an earthen dam.

The completed segment of the dam was a slope of orange clay

about a hundred feet high and a hundred feet long. When finished, the dam was supposed to connect to the first hill, from there to the second hill and from there to the big curving mountain ridge, making a reservoir in the shape of a ring.

Huge red flags hung limply from poles on top of the dam segment and on top of the ridge. Armed soldiers walked from one flagpole to the next, keeping a lookout for trouble that would never come from unarmed people as tired and beaten-down as we were. Where the dam and ridge intersected, a stage had been set up, with more red flags and palm fronds around the dais and on top of the roof. A jeep was parked off to one side of the stage, and next to the jeep a horse was tethered. A throbbing generator powered the loudspeakers.

On the stage sat Chea Huon, his subordinate Comrade Ik—the old man who rode the horse—and the village chiefs, including Chev and the kindly Uncle Seng. The lesser leaders had already made their speeches, expressed their allegiance and repeated revolutionary clichés. The master of ceremonies was at the microphone.

"Today is an historic day," he was saying. "We have an opportunity to listen to our leader speak about the new dam-building offensive. He will talk about the revolutionary spirit of struggle and renunciation! Let us show him how firmly we take our destiny in hand! Let us demonstrate our solidarity with Angka's goal of rebuilding our nation! Here's Sama Mit Vanh! Please give him a big hand!"

Everybody clapped dutifully as the thin, stooped figure stepped to the microphone. Of ten thousand people, only Huoy and I knew his original identity: Chea Huon. To the rest he was Sama Mit Vanh. "Vanh" was his revolutionary *nom de querre*. "Sama Mit," meaning "Equal Comrade," was a title given only to high officials. I always wondered why the bosses were called Equal Comrades; it was another one of the Khmer Rouge's crazy inconsistencies.

"LONG LIVE THE KAMPUCHEAN REVOLUTION!" Chea Huon bellowed into the microphone, his amplified voice echoing off the mountain walls.

We scrambled to our feet and answered, "Long live the Kampuchean revolution!" pounding our right fists over our hearts, then raising our fists in the straight-arm salute.

"LONG LIVE THE KAMPUCHEAN REVOLUTION!" he repeated. We gave it back to him. "LONG LIVE THE KAMPU-

CHEAN REVOLUTION!" he said a third time, and we answered. Then he recited other revolutionary slogans, three times each, and we echoed, as automatically as the mountain, and saluted with our fists.

"Long live the great solidarity!

"Down with the American capitalists!

"Long live the great leap forward!

"Long live the great prosperity!

"Long live the great splendor!"

When everybody sat down again, Chea Huon began his speech. He spoke in a mild voice, though to emphasize his points he waved his two clenched fists. It was a gesture I remembered from the classroom in Takeo.

I still couldn't get over it. My former teacher, who had helped me when I was an adolescent, was now the leader of my enemies.

It wasn't so much that Chea Huon had killed my father and my brother. He didn't deserve all the blame for that. Chev, who sat smiling and nodding onstage, had been much more directly responsible for their deaths. Of course, Chea Huon could have stopped Chev from killing so many, but on the front lines the cooperative leaders had a great deal of autonomy. It was our bad luck to get Chev as a leader rather than a basically kind man like Uncle Seng.

No, what amazed me most about Chea Huon was the change in his character. He was the first intellectual I had ever known. He was very smart. But if he was smart he couldn't possibly believe what he was saying to us now, in the dam dedication ceremony.

He had begun with a recital of the victory over the American capitalists. How the patriots had fought the American invaders, first with "empty hands," later with hatchets and crossbows, and driven them out of Cambodia. It was a lie. And he knew it was a lie. The Americans had hardly ever engaged the Khmer Rouge in head-on combat. American ground troops had been in Cambodia for only a few months, in 1970, fighting the North Vietnamese. The U.S. bombing had stopped in 1973, two years before the communists took over.

But Chea Huon wasn't interested in facts. The myth of defeating the Americans was something that the Khmer Rouge repeated over and over again until they believed it. They needed to believe in it, because it was the basis of their programs to develop the country. To them, defeating a superpower proved that they, the Khmer Rouge, were superior beings, like supermen. If they had defeated the largest superpower in the world, they were capable of anything. Nothing could stop them. Nothing could stand in their way. Not logic. Not common sense. Not even the laws of physics. And if they were supermen surely we, their war slaves, could work twenty-hour days and never complain.

He said that anti-aircraft guns would shoot down any American planes that dared fly over Cambodian territory and send them hurtling in flames into the sea. I thought, Oh yeah, motherfucker? I'd like to see what would really happen if the Americans came back. In my mind's eye American jet fighters came in low and fast over the treetops, and the stage went up in splinters and black smoke and billowing flames. If the planes blew me up too that was all right.

Chea Huon said, "Democratic Kampuchea isn't afraid of any aggressors. Right now our soldiers are guarding the borders against imperialist invaders." Oh yeah? I thought. I wish the imperialist invaders good luck. Whoever they are. Probably the Khmer Serei. I've heard they have been growing stronger near the Thai border. Why don't you tell us who the invaders are, Chea Huon? But he didn't.

He talked for the first hour and into the second hour and it was all propaganda. Word for word, the same as the speeches on the radio. "Under the regime of the arch-fascist, arch-corrupt, arch-imperialist Lon Nol, we were oppressed and never had any happiness." The same nonsense. "Under the glorious rule of Angka, we have entered a new age, as masters of the nation, the land, the waters, the rice fields and our destiny, working together to achieve independence-sovereignty." Chea Huon wasn't telling us anything we hadn't heard before. What he was doing was proving his orthodoxy. It was like what he had said to me when I was cutting the sapling and his bodyguards came near: "We must fight on all battlefields. We must struggle to control nature." The words meant nothing—except that he was faithful to Angka. I wondered why someone as high-ranking as that needed to go to such lengths to show his devotion.

At last, in the third hour, he began to talk about the dam. "It is a big project," he said. "When it is finished and we have connected the mountains, we will have a water supply the full year around. We will use the water to grow two or even three annual rice crops. We will never go hungry again. We will eat rice anytime we want, day or night."

"Liar," I said under my breath.

"But," he said, clenching both fists and waving them in front of his body, "the dam will not just be used for agriculture. No, comrades! The water will also drive turbines to create electrical power! People from here to the Thai border, in the cities, in the villages and in the jungles will all have electricity to use!"

I looked at the tiny segment of the dam that had already been completed and at the miles of dry surrounding landscape. We didn't have any concrete to build the dam with. All we had was clay. We didn't have any bulldozers to dig with. All we had was hoes. Our earlier projects on the front lines had all failed. The canals hadn't stopped the flooding. There had been a halfhearted attempt to use canal water to irrigate fields for dry-season rice, but the rice had all died. And the dam was to be much larger than anything else we had attempted—on the same scale as the huge hydroelectric dams in America and Europe. Huoy poked me in the ribs and I turned back toward the stage again.

"And when we have electricity we will build factories," Chea Huon was saying. "We won't even need oxcarts anymore! We will build our own cars and trucks in our factories! Each family will have at least one car. And each house will have its own electric lights, to turn on and off whenever we like! And—this is not all—after we build factories, we will build skyscrapers near the reservoir! Anyone who wants an apartment to live in will have one! Our nation will be developed! Our factories will build our own bulldozers and tractors! We will use our machines to perform all the labor we need! *And we will never use human beings to farm again!*

"LONG LIVE THE KAMPUCHEAN REVOLUTION!" he roared, and the mass of ragged people struggled to its feet and obediently told him what he wanted to hear.

"LONG LIVE THE GREAT SOLIDARITY!" Onstage, the old skinny man and Chev and the rest of the leaders outdid one another with their enthusiasm and their clenched-fist salutes.

"LONG LIVE THE GREAT LEAP FORWARD!" On the site of the future city of skyscrapers and factories and shining automobiles there were exactly two machines, sitting on the clay: a generator, to amplify Chea Huon's words, and a jeep to take him away. I hoped he would leave soon. The Chea Huon I used to know didn't exist anymore. A puppet named Sama Mit Vanh occupied his body.

"LONG LIVE THE GREAT PROSPERITY!"

Give me real rice to eat.

"LONG LIVE THE GREAT SPLENDOR!"

Just give me rice. And forget your stupid dreams.

To supply the dam project with labor the front lines were reorganized once again. Several cooperatives like ours were merged into a giant one whose headquarters was next to the dam site. Huoy lost her job in the kitchen. She became a dam worker, carrying mud baskets. She worked harder than before, for much longer hours, with much less to eat.

I was luckier. My group—the same I had worked with since rescuing Chea Huon's jeep—was assigned to build houses on the back lines. Now that a hydroelectric dam was being built and the region was entering a new stage of development, the nearby villages were supposed to have permanent housing for "new" and "old" people. The houses were on stilts in traditional style, but they would hold three or four families each instead of just one. It was an easy job. We hammered secondhand nails into used boards. If the poles rested on dirt instead of foundations, or if one roof wasn't finished before we moved on to the next, we didn't care. We were just following orders. We didn't have to work in the evenings. We didn't have to go to many political meetings. We moved from one village to the next, sleeping in the houses we built.

For me, life was much easier than before. My health was good. I was skinny but tough, and my infections had finally healed. There was only one drawback, and that was being apart from Huoy. I asked permission to rejoin her. I volunteered to work on the dam. But the leaders said no. They never even considered my request. To them, "new" people were lower-level beings, politically suspect, enemies. To give in to my wishes would imply that I was on the same level as they. They could not give me permission without losing face.

If Huoy and I had been like most married "new" people, being apart wouldn't have mattered. The strain of work, the shortage of food and the absence of normal family life had turned most marriages sour. There just wasn't much left to keep couples together. Sex hadn't disappeared entirely but there wasn't much of it, because husbands and wives didn't have the energy or the privacy. People carried within them an unspoken fear. They worried about their own survival, and they didn't trust anyone else, even their spouses.

Huoy and I had been exceptions. We spent all our free time to-gether. We went for walks, talking and gathering wild foods when it was possible. We shared our food. We had the normal arguments between husbands and wives, but no more. I had never forgotten how Huoy had nursed me when I was sick and when I came back from prison. I needed her. I relied on her judgment. Every day she told me to keep my mouth shut, to plant a kapok tree. And she needed me to keep her from giving in to fear and depression.

Within a few weeks of being assigned to my new job I was com-muting to the dam site to spend the nights with her. I didn't have permission. If the soldiers had caught me they would have killed me. But it was a relatively peaceful time in the area. There were few purges and hardly any nighttime sentries. Besides, I figured that if I couldn't be with her it didn't matter what happened to me.

I made my nightly trips with a man named Som from my work group. He and I had fixed roads and dikes together, transplanted rice together, talked about the foods we missed together and now we were building houses together. Like me, he wanted to spend the nights with his wife, who worked in Huoy's group on the dam.

Som was an intellectual from Phnom Penh. I knew that from his choice of words and his accent. From the start I also sensed that he was an idealist and a rebel. But he knew much more about me.

One day when he and I were alone, Som told me that he recognized me from the military hospital in Phnom Penh. I felt a sudden tight-ening in my stomach and told him it was impossible, that I had been a taxi driver. Whenever I thought about admitting I was a doctor, my mind turned to Pen Tip. I still saw Pen Tip occasionally, and when-ever I did it was all I could do to control my anger.

Som pulled up the sleeve of his right arm and showed me a scar. He said he had been wounded by a Khmer Rouge artillery shell and that I had done the reconstructive surgery. When the Khmer Rouge came into the hospitals on April 17, 1975 he had been in traction. He was forced to leave, and his tibia had never healed properly. He now had about 70 percent use of his right arm, which was visibly crooked and atrophied.

I didn't remember operating on him and at first I thought he was lying. But gradually it became clear that Som wasn't trying to gain power over me. Nor was he trying to gain favor with the Khmer Rouge. Whenever he had the chance, Som cursed them behind their backs for the misery they had brought us. He was far more outspoken than me. He told me he had been a Buddhist monk for many years, then left the priesthood to become a student. He was good at languages. Eventually he became an interpreter at the U.S. embassy in Phnom Penh.

This was not the sort of background an informer would confess to. Being a monk was counterrevolutionary. Being a U.S. embassy employee was cause enough for a one-way trip to the woods. I watched Som closely for signs that he was a *chhlop*. There weren't any. We became friends. Sometimes, when nobody else was around, he spoke English for me, and it sounded exactly like the broadcasts on the Voice of America. I couldn't understand what he was saying except for occasional words that were similar to French. But I wanted to understand.

Among the books I kept wrapped in plastic and buried underground was one that taught basic English words and phrases to French speakers. I had traded some freshwater crabs for it in Phum Chhleav without quite knowing why. Huoy often asked me to get rid of it; she pointed out that if it were found it could mean my death. Now I realized why I had kept it. I wanted to learn English.

Of course it was a crazy thing to do. I wanted to learn *something*, a new subject of any kind, to keep my mind sharp. I needed to use my brain for more than hammering nails for Angka. But I had another reason too. English was the language of the enemy. Learning it was a subversive act. I asked Som to become my teacher.

During the day Som and I and about thirty others built houses. At the end of the afternoon, when the bell rang, the crew put down its tools, and Som and I got ready to visit our wives.

After a quick dinner at the common kitchen we walked toward a nearby lake as if to bathe. From the lake we cut over to a canal, a long, straight trough of muddy water, the orange ball of the sinking sun reflecting on its surface. Birds chirped and twittered, and swallows dipped and soared above the water, catching insects. Frogs croaked, fell silent as we approached, then croaked again when we had passed by.

When there was nobody in sight I pulled some pages I had torn from the book out of my pocket. We were on *Huitième leçon*, or, as it appeared in English on the facing page, "Eighth Lesson." Without effort, I read the French phrases:

1. *Puis-je vous aider?*
2. *Avez-vous du thé?*
3. *Bien sûr. En voulez-vous?*

I pointed at the equivalent English phrases and asked Som, in Khmer, how to pronounce them.

He looked at the first one. " 'Can I help you?' " he said in what was undoubtedly English in a Cambodian accent.

" 'Can I hel' jou?' " I repeated.

Som went on to the second phrase: " 'Have you got any tea?' "

" 'Haf jou enny tea?' " I repeated. "Tea" was an easy word. It was the same as *thé* in French, only pronounced a bit differently. For that matter, it was like *tè* in Khmer, *té* in Teochiew and not too different from *cha* in Mandarin. The lesson went on, the English sentences numbered down the page, the syllables receiving the stress printed in boldface. As Som pointed out, it was a lesson in British English:

3. Of course. Do you want some?
4. Yes, please. Give me two pounds. And a **pa**cket of **bis**cuits.
5. Do you want some beans?
6. No, thanks. We've got some at home.
7. Well, some bread?
8. Yes, please. Two loaves. Oh, and half a pound of **but**ter. That's all.
9. How much is that?
10. That's one pound **twen**ty.
11. Oh **de**ar, I've only got one pound.
12. You can pay the rest next time.
13. Thanks **ve**ry much. Good-bye.
14. Good-**bye**, **ma**dam.

So much food! Extra food! People were so polite! You could even pay later if you wanted! It was a bit confusing how the British used "pounds" as a measure of weight as well as money, but Som assured me that people who spoke real English didn't do that.

"They use dollars," I said in Khmer, and Som nodded solemnly.

"I like dollars," I told him a moment later, thinking of the twenty-six hundred dollars I brought back from Phnom Penh on my scooter, along with the medicine and the gold. Several times on the front lines I had traded a hundred-dollar bill for a yam. What amazed me was not that American money was worth so little but that it was worth anything at all in a society where money was outlawed and where there was no contact with the outside world. But there it was— something very special about America that inspired hope and faith. What a marvelous place it must be, America. So much food to eat, and people so polite to each other.

" 'Yes, pliss,' " I read again. " 'Two loa-ves. Oh, and haff a poond of but-ter.' "

It seemed completely normal to me, to be walking along the canal with Som and asking him how to pronounce English words and phrases.

We reached the dam and skirted the outdoor meeting where the "new" people listened resignedly to the speeches. The message never changed: Lazy people are enemies of the revolution. Because of traitors, the economy of the country is very low. "Please give me a big hand," the speaker was saying, followed by unenthusiastic applause.

We walked unnoticed into the longhouse. It was nearly empty, with most of its inhabitants at work or at the meeting. I located Huoy's hammock and lay down in it and pulled the mosquito net over me. It was the mosquito net we had brought from Phnom Penh, by now torn and mended many times, and nearly black from the smoke of fires. To have one at all was a luxury. Most people kept mosquitoes away by building fires with piles of rice husks. The low, sloping, thatched ceiling reflected the red glow of fires, and smoke filled the air.

There was another round of applause outside and finally Huoy came in.

"How was your day, sweet?" I asked. "Did they give you enough food? Is your health all right?"

"Not too bad today, thanks. Have you been here long?" She reached for her washcloth and jar of homemade soap and began washing her face and hands.

"No, I just got here." I loved watching her wash. She had learned a folk recipe for making soap by burning the skin of kapok fruit, which was rich in potash, and soaking the ashes in water. She was always clean. Even her clothes were clean.

She changed from her black work trousers and blouse into her sleeping sarong, washed her feet, lifted the edge of the mosquito net and climbed in beside me, clutching her pillow. An arm's length away, a neighbor remarked from his hammock, "How nice! What a loving couple! Always coming here to visit your wife, eh, Samnang?"

I knew this fellow. He was friendly, like most of them in Huoy's work group.

"And why not?" I answered. "I give ninety-nine percent to Angka, but I keep one percent for myself. I keep my wife for me."

The neighbor on the other side of the hammock said, "Aaeee! I hope one percent of you is big and long enough to keep your wife satisfied!"

I found myself grinning in the darkness. "Nothing so lucky as that," I said. "My wife hates me very much. She won't even let me touch her in the hammock. She tells me she wants to be alone."

There was laughter throughout the longhouse. I always joked with them. It helped pass the time and keep our minds from other worries.

In fact, Huoy's soft, feminine body was snuggled next to mine, and she was kissing me on the cheek. Now that she worked on the dam, this was our only chance to be together. She put her lips next to my ear and whispered, "How were your rations today?"

I whispered back, "Not bad. A quarter at dinner." A condensed-milk can of cooked rice, split among four people, dumped into watery broth. That was what a quarter meant. But I had other thoughts on my mind.

"Sweet," I said so carefully that even Huoy could barely hear, "I want to go to America."

We turned our heads so her mouth was next to my ear. "You're crazy," she said.

We turned our heads again. "I know," I said into her ear. "But we've got to go there someday."

Som's lessons had started me thinking about America. Plenty of food there. A very developed country. In America, dams were built with real concrete, houses actually had electricity, skyscrapers were real. Heavy work was done with bulldozers and tractors. It was a place as different from Cambodia as heaven is from hell.

"I'd rather be a dog in America than a human being in Cambodia," I added.

Huoy's fingertips found my temple, pushed gently, and her lips spoke into my ear. "How do you know?" said Huoy. "You've never even been outside of Cambodia."

"I just know. Let me dream in peace, will you?" As I closed my eyes, I imagined what it would be like to be an American dog. How wonderful. Human hands would reach down to pat me and brush my fur. They wouldn't beat me or torture me. My owner would put plenty of food in my dish, and I could eat whenever I wanted. If I got sick they would take me to a veterinarian. I wouldn't even have to work.

"Do you want to know my dream?" Huoy whispered sleepily.

"To open a pastry shop," I said.

"Well, first I want babies. When the regime is overturned I want to make lots and lots of babies and raise them with you in a nice house, with plenty to eat. But when the children are old enough to go to school I will open a sweet shop. I just want to cook food and have good things to eat and live in a city."

"I'd still rather be a dog in America," I said.

Around us, as the red glow of the mosquito fires flickered on the thatch roof, our neighbors grumbled and sank with heavy sighs into their hammocks. The snores begun. I leaned next to Huoy and kissed her, but she barely stirred. Her breathing was regular. A minute later she was sound asleep.

It was usually like that. I met her in the hammock, we talked for a few minutes and then she fell asleep. She was exhausted. Once every few weeks we had a special night. Huoy and Som's wife would bribe their group leader with tobacco rations and then walk through the darkness to see Som and me. Together we ate the best wild foods the landscape offered and then retired, Huoy and I to one side of the floor of a partially built house, Som and his wife on the other, and the floor boards squeaking underneath. But most nights Huoy came into the longhouse at 10:00 P.M. so tired she fell asleep as soon as she lay down.

At 2:00 A.M. we were woken up by the group leader.

"Time to wake up! Let's go, group! Everybody awake! Back to work!" he shouted. To finish the dam, each worker slept only four hours and worked or went to political meetings the other twenty.

Huoy got groggily to her feet, slipped into her rubber shower sandals, washed her face again, changed into a clean sarong and blouse and brushed her hair. Somehow she had adapted to the schedule without falling seriously ill. She trudged after her work group, carrying her hoe and a plastic container full of boiled water. I followed. I had to be up in a couple of hours anyway, and I liked to keep her company.

Huoy's group of about thirty men and women began to dig near the inside face of the dam. It was just like canal work. The men chopped halfheartedly at the clay with their hoes, and the women gathered the loose clay with their hoes and scooped it into baskets. I sat on the ground, slapping the gnats that settled on my arms and face. When enough baskets were filled, the group formed a human chain and passed them from one person to the next to the top of the dam. When they had done this they returned to their previous spot and sat with their elbows on their knees, in that state of rest that is not quite sleep, with one part of the brain alert for soldiers.

From all across the dam face came the faint sounds of hoes and muttered conversations. Thousands of people were working there, though in the dark they were no more than shadows. A lone soldier wearing a Mao cap appeared in silhouette, strolling along the dam top. The comments from the war slaves began, loud enough to reach him.

"Hey, comrade, go to work! We'll give you an extra ration!"

"Comrade, be careful when you make your great leap forward! You might leap into a hole and break your neck!"

The soldier walked on without answering. He was outnumbered, and in the darkness he could not tell who was saying what.

I pulled my watch out of the small pocket inside my waistband. By peering in the starlight it was possible to read the time. Almost four o'clock.

"I have to go, sweet," I said to Huoy, but our neighbor from the longhouse overheard me.

"You are leaving too soon, Samnang. You don't want to stay here, to slap gnats and cuss at the soldiers?"

They knew me as a prankster, a comedian, and I obliged them. "Please," I replied. "If you would be so kind, turn away, so I can kiss my wife good-bye."

To them I was a man who had accepted his fate but makes jokes about it. And why not? Everybody was so tired that nothing seemed to matter. Work mattered least of all. If the King of Death wanted to take us we could not stop him, but he could not stop us from laughing until then.

The responses came in the darkness:

–"Can't I look when you kiss her? I haven't seen anything like that in a long time."

–"You can kiss me, if you don't mind," said a giggling woman's voice. "I'm so horny I don't know what to do."

–"Why should we turn away? You two are always hugging and kissing."

"And please," I told them, "close your ears so I can tell her how much I love her too."

–". . . Aaaee! What a lover . . ."

–"Tell her, Samnang."

"I'm going now, sweet," I said quietly to Huoy, who had half-turned away in embarrassment. "I'll see you the same time tonight." And I touched her lightly on the shoulder.

I went back to the longhouse to wake Som, who was asleep. We set out along the dirt road, taking the short route back to our work site, knowing that at this hour we would not meet any soldiers.

The sky was growing light in the east by the time Som and I got back to our work site. I climbed up the stairs of a half-built house and fell asleep on the bare floor. The bell rang at 5:30 A.M. We were supposed to go to work then, but I pounded the floor to imitate hammering and stole a few extra minutes of sleep.

26

THE CRACKS BEGIN TO SHOW

LOOKING BACK, it seems clear that 1977 was the year the regime began to crack. The Khmer Rouge had tried to reorganize the nation too quickly and radically for the structure to hold. The leaders themselves developed internal feuds, and the people at the bottom showed signs of discontent and even open rebellion.

At the time, however, I didn't notice the changes as much as the unbearably slow passing of the days. The work was dull. In spite of Som's English lessons I could feel my brain slowing down. It was hard to think about anything. The situation in the countryside seemed permanent. Bells controlled the schedule. Workers crisscrossed the landscape wearily, in single file. The revolutionary songs blaring out from the loudspeakers and the speeches at the meetings never changed. At meals we gathered in circles near the common kitchen and looked on with jealous eyes as our portions of rice gruel were ladled into rusty bowls.

Food—that was our main obsession. The size of the rations, and whether the common kitchen was going to serve a vegetable along with the rice. If certain days stand out from the others in my memories of 1977, food was usually the cause. Like the time a particularly ignorant cadre suggested growing clams in the vegetable gardens. Or the night I made oxtail soup by cutting the tail off an ox that was still alive. Or the time I raided a vegetable garden, cooked the food, over-ate, vomited and then ate the vomit. It is extremely unpleasant to remember eating my own vomit. It was not a normal act. But it shows how malnourished my body was and how obsessed my mind was by food.

But to some extent Huoy and I got used to being hungry. At least we could exercise a basic choice: If I was willing to take the risk of foraging or stealing, we could eat.

What was worse than hunger was the terror, because we couldn't do anything about it. The terror was always there, deep in our hearts. In the late afternoon, wondering whether the soldiers would choose us as their victims. And then feeling guilty when the soldiers took someone else. At night, blowing out our tiny oil lanterns so the soldiers wouldn't notice the light and come investigate, and then lying awake and wondering whether we would see the dawn. Waking up the next day and wondering whether it would be our last.

We didn't talk about the terror much. There was no use. Huoy and I wanted to live; we were willing to die if we had to, but the terror forced us into a state of half life that was worse than either. Everything else about being war slaves—the grating music from the loudspeakers, the tedious meetings, the lice in our hair, the drab and endless work, the gruel we pretended was food—we could get used to, but our fear of dying was worse than death itself. I tried fighting it. I joked with Huoy's fellow workers. I learned English from Som. I deliberately took risks in stealing, hoping to master my fear. But everything I did to rebel against it merely confirmed that it ruled me.

I had full trust only in Huoy. We were as close as two people can be. Only grudgingly did we give portions of trust to outsiders. I began to trust Som more and more as time went on. And even this was a mistake.

Som and I talked about everything. We were intellectual equals. I only wish he was my physical equal, because that was his downfall—his right arm, hit by shrapnel, operated on by me, but never allowed to heal properly during the takeover.

It happened this way: Som was sent off on a detail to cut bamboo in the mountains and got less done than his fellow workers because of his withered arm. He fell into disfavor with a Khmer Rouge who, a few weeks later, also supervised the plowing of rice fields. All work on house construction was suspended for the important job of readying the rice fields. I was part of the plowing detail and Som was too. It hadn't rained enough yet to make the ground soft. By using all my strength and skill, I plowed straight furrows, but Som's plow kept drifting to the right, the side of his weak arm.

The soldiers came at lunchtime, when Som and I and our wives were resting on a hillock. They tied his arms behind his back. They kicked him and he fell head first on the ground while his wife and Huoy were sobbing and screaming. Then they took him away. The rest of us were in shock. For me it was not only shock but loss. He had been my only friend.

I grieved for Som. He was certain to be killed. Then it occurred to me: What if they torture him? He will tell them I was a doctor! He knows everything about my past! He was still in sight, a sad figure trudging away to his death, when I forgot about him and started worrying about myself.

I couldn't sleep that night, or the next night. Surely the soldiers would come for me. A heavy rain fell. While plowing the fields, I misguided the ox, who stumbled. The ox, the plow and I tumbled over into the muddy water of the rice paddy. The same Khmer Rouge who ordered Som's death looked on. His eyes burned into mine. At lunch, on a hillock, my hands were shaking. I told Huoy good-bye. I knew the soldiers were going to take me away. But at the end of lunch the bell rang and I went back to work. I plowed all afternoon. At the end of the day the bell rang again, and Huoy and I went to the common kitchen. There was no explanation. I was allowed to keep on waiting.

I knew my own death was near. It could be delayed but not avoided. Maybe a few days, maybe a few months until they caught me doing something wrong, and then it would be over. I could feel myself aging from the stress. And everyone was, not just me. I came to believe more than ever before what my father had said, that such a regime could not last.

The cracks began to show. One of the first signs was the increase in stealing from the "common gardens" that provided vegetables to the kitchens. In 1975 and 1976, many "new" people had gathered wild foods, but few had stolen from gardens, because we were afraid of the sentries. In 1977, when I stole, I began noticing that I had more and more company. If I saw another shadowy figure walking around in the dark, it was almost always a "new" person. It was nothing we could talk about openly during the day; not yet, anyhow. But the night belonged to us. The soldiers didn't like sentry duty anymore, and they wouldn't go out on patrol except in groups.

Another sign was the talk about the Khmer Serei. Stories had traveled from one cooperative to the next of the freedom fighters based on the border with Thailand, less than a hundred miles away. There was so many rumors about the coming of the freedom fighters that people looked up in the sky, wondering when the helicopters were going to land.

I was still building houses on the back lines when the rebellion broke out. The leader was a man whose name was Thai. I had talked with him around a fire the year before and been sworn to silence. So had Pen Tip.

Thai and a few handpicked men, a mixture of "new" and "old" people, one of them an assistant to Chev, killed half a dozen soldiers one night and stole their weapons. They went to work the next day as if nothing had happened, then killed a few more soldiers the following night. The third night they hijacked a train and rode it northwest toward Battambang City, intending to go west from there to the border with Thailand, to join the freedom fighters. It must have been a wild, dramatic ride.

The Khmer Rouge announced they had killed Thai and his fellow rebels, and though I never knew for sure, in this case I tended to believe them. Thai should have hijacked the train the first night, when the Khmer Rouge were not on the alert.

A purge began on the front lines to frighten the rest of us. Every afternoon for about a week, soldiers tied up about a hundred prisoners and led them into the forests for execution. Huoy told me about it. She said Pen Tip kept an especially low profile and worked harder than he ever had before.

But even though the rebellion failed, it had one lasting effect: It destroyed the mystique of the Khmer Rouge's invincibility. Angka was strong but not omnipotent. Angka had lost face.

The regime did very little about the uprising and the stealing except to punish people. There were no real changes in policy, no attempts to cure what was wrong. The leaders of most revolutions would have realized that they needed the support of the people, but not Angka. Instead, the drive to restructure society went on, alienating us war slaves even farther—if that was possible. There was, for example, the matter of marriages.

The Khmer Rouge wanted to regulate and control sex, just as they tried to control all other basic human practices, like eating and working and sleeping. Earlier on in the regime, couples who wanted to get married had to get permission from their village chiefs. If the answer was yes, they could go ahead. If the answer was no, they were in trouble, especially if *chhlop* found out they were having sexual relations anyway. In prison I had seen lines of young women being led away for breaking Angka's puritanical rules of behavior.

But at the same time that people were being killed for the crime of sex, and hundreds of thousands of others were dying of starvation and disease, the Khmer Rouge encouraged population growth. They told us that Angka needed more comrades "to protect the nation's borders and to join the struggle for independence-sovereignty."

The ceremony was announced in the morning over the loud-speakers. Comrade Ik, the old man on horseback, rode out into the fields to watch men and women at work and choose who to mate with whom. Some of the more clever single women insisted they had been separated from their husbands, and they were excused. But the rest obeyed. They had no choice. Whether the men and women in the couples knew or liked each other didn't have anything to do with it.

When the noon bell rang, the workers came in from the fields, their hair matted, their bodies sweaty, manure from the rice fields caking their feet. The chosen couples sat impassively on a long bench next to each other.

The old man stood and said into a microphone, "Today Angka has allowed these couples to marry. It recognizes them as being legally married. Let the people recognize these couples as well. Angka hopes these people are revolutionary in spirit. They must have high levels of understanding of revolutionary ideals. They will have to work hand in hand, shoulder to shoulder, sacrificing to help complete Angka's projects."

Chev, grinning and dangerous, and sturdy, tattooed Uncle Seng, who had never hurt anyone, squatted on their haunches behind the old man, along with the other village leaders. Except for Chea Huon, who was absent, it was the same set of leaders I had seen at the dam ceremony. As usual, Comrade Ik was barefoot and shirtless. He wore only baggy shorts, a half-length sarong and a krama. His toothless lips held a banana-leaf cigarette.

Those of us in the audience stood outside a longhouse and watched.

The married couples sat expressionlessly on the bench, their hats in their laps.

The old man continued, "The new man must know our revolution and its goals. The new man and the new woman will be creating our future society." He removed the cigarette, and his toothless lips broke into a leer. "You women must be quiet if your husband gets angry."

In Khmer slang, "getting angry" means getting an erection.

Comrade Ik leaned forward into the microphone and shouted, "Long live the Kampuchean revolution!"

Everybody rose to their feet and repeated his words and they gave the clenched-fist salute. Each phrase was spoken three times.

"Long live the great solidarity!"

Everyone watched the married couples to see if they yelled with the proper enthusiasm.

"Long live the newlyweds!"

The brides and grooms echoed the words without a smile.

"Long live the great leap forward!"

There were other slogans. And finally, again, "Long live the Kampuchean revolution!"

"You may now have lunch," the old man said with a kindly smile. The new couples went off to eat watery rice with everybody else. No feasts and no honeymoons for them. They sewed their single hammocks together and slept in the longhouses, with neighbors a few inches away on either side. Later some of them moved into the houses my crew built, or built their own. From what I heard, few of the husbands and wives really cared for one another. They certainly didn't trust one another. They fought over food. There were a few instances of wives getting rid of their husbands by reporting them to the Khmer Rouge for stealing. Virtually no pregnancies resulted from these marriages, because the food rations were too low for the women to be fertile.

The next time I saw the old man was a few months later, at the beginning of the rainy season of 1977, when all the heads of families were called to another special meeting. He presided again, standing in front of a microphone.

He started off with the usual speech about building up the country's economy. "You people in the second lines have to give greater support to the people in the front lines. You must plant more food to support them. You must work even harder." He went into a long harangue about sacrificing to achieve work goals. What he didn't say was what everyone knew—that the work on the dam had fallen far behind schedule. A few small segments had been completed, but at the current pace it would take five or ten years before it was finished.

Then he changed the subject. "The other reason we invited you here is to tell you about a man who betrayed the country. For a long time we did not know that our very own Angka had a traitor within. Before, we trusted him to the highest degree, but now we know his true character. I am talking about Vanh," he said.

Behind me someone whispered, "Incredible! Is that why we haven't seen Vanh driving around in a while?" A buzz of conversation broke out, but I kept quiet. I wanted to hear what had happened to the man I knew as Chea Huon.

"We have already captured Enemy Vanh," the old man was saying. He shifted his glance uneasily over those of us in the audience. "And we will find out those who have connections to him. These people will not be allowed to make trouble anymore. Furthermore, if someone in your villages says good things about Vanh, don't believe him. Report him to Angka. Those people are Vanh's henchmen and collaborators. They are the enemy. They will not be allowed to live in our country anymore.

"That's all. Before leaving, please give me a big hand."

I looked closely at Comrade Ik as I clapped. He wasn't telling everything that he knew. If Chea Huon had been captured alive, he wouldn't be asking for our help to discover who the collaborators were. He would have already extracted the information, by torture.

And I was glad. Chea Huon, who had become a revolutionary

so early, had finally realized his mistake. He knew he couldn't stop the madness, and finally he got out. When did he decide to leave? I wondered. Did he know it even when he met me? If so, the advice he gave me—to keep my mouth shut and keep on working—was the best he had to offer. Yes! He knew even then! Or maybe he did. He knew if I became his protégé the Khmer Rouge would hurt me later.

A story arose that Chea Huon left for the Thai border with his jeep and his bodyguards and bags of dollars and gold. I don't know if it was true, but it was possible. As the ranking commander, Chea Huon could have written passes to get himself through any checkpoints. He also had access to the money and gold collected from "new" people when Angka abolished private property. And he was smart. If anybody could have made it to the border, it was Chea Huon. From there he could have joined the freedom fighters, or else traveled on to another country. With bags of dollars and gold he could have done anything he wanted. But I never really knew whether he succeeded or failed, or where he went. I never heard anything about him again.

Ironically, while the regime was slowly disintegrating in front of our eyes, with forced marriages, increased stealing, rebellions from below, and defections at the highest levels, Huoy and I began to live better than before. Like convicts in a prison, we learned how to manipulate the rules to our advantage.

What triggered the move to a better life was another case of malaria. This time when I got sick I arranged to be sent to the front-lines clinic, the place where they made the rabbit turds. As I had foreseen, the clinic was overcrowded. From there I got permission to recuperate at my youngest brother Hok's house, on the other side of the mountain, near the Phnom Tippeday railroad station, in a village called Phum Ra. Once in Phum Ra, I got permission for Huoy to join me, to nurse me back to health.

After a few days I knew we would have to move on. Long ago Hok and I had chosen different paths. He finished the eighth grade, I finished medical school. He chose one kind of woman to be his wife,

I chose another. His wife told the neighbors that Huoy and I weren't really married, and soon the two women were not speaking to each other. But that wasn't the worst of it. There was an atmosphere of fear and hunger in the house. The sounds of raised voices and children crying. It was typical of households under the Khmer Rouge, but that didn't make us like it any better. When my sister-in-law cooked she squatted in front of the fire facing away from us so we wouldn't see her hand moving from the cooking pot to her mouth. She thought we didn't notice.

But Hok was my brother, and he was also the supervisor of a vegetable garden. As soon as I had recovered from malaria, he arranged for Huoy and me to work for him. I became a waterboy, walking back and forth from a pond to the garden, carrying a pair of watering cans on a bamboo shoulderboard, sprinkling the plants. Huoy weeded the vegetables.

A short time later, when a building site and some materials became available, I got permission from the leader of the village to build a house. Imagine! A place of our own. Ever since the Khmer Rouge took over, Huoy and I had been transients. We had stayed under the house on stilts in Wat Kien Svay Krao, in the little hut in Tonle Batí, in the reed hut in Phum Chhleav and in the hut in Youen's village. We had camped on hillocks and slept in longhouses on the front lines. And finally this. This was home.

By then I was a skilled builder. Our new house was cool in the middle of the day and cozy at night. It had a view out the back, directly across the rice fields to the old temple high on the mountain ridge. We had clean water nearby. Because we were on the back lines, we were allowed to plant our own vegetables, provided we gave some to the common kitchen.

While waiting for our garden to produce, I stole food. Each night before I went out I prayed to Buddha. I explained that I wasn't going to sell what I stole, that I was going to take only what we needed to survive.

I didn't steal much from my brother's garden. There were larger gardens up on the mountain plateau, near the wat. It was an all-night trip to sneak up to the gardens, fill a big sack, come down again and cook the vegetables outside the village to avoid detection. I was a capable thief and never had any problems. Many times Huoy and I ate until we couldn't eat any more.

We liked living in Phum Ra. It was wonderful being away from the front lines. And it was not stealing that got me into trouble. It was Pen Tip.

27

DROPS OF WATER

LIKE ME, Pen Tip engineered a transfer away from the front lines. He and his family moved to the village of Phum Ra about the same time Huoy and I did. We were neighbors. But while I carried water to the common garden all day long, like the lowest class of peasant, and avoided the Khmer Rouge whenever possible, Pen Tip cultivated connections with the Khmer Rouge for his own gain. He rose from the rank of group leader to assistant section leader, becoming the most influential "new" person in the village.

Under different circumstances I might have found Pen Tip amusing. He was so short he looked up at people, like a child. He walked duckfooted, like Charlie Chaplin, and his eyebrows were always moving up and down, like a man who is always being surprised. Maybe being tiny and funny-looking made Pen Tip what he was. Maybe he had been teased and pushed around a lot when he was young. But whatever his motivations, he was hungry for power. He played up to "old" people and Khmer Rouge. He ordered other "new" people around. I was his favorite target, because I had once been his social superior, as a doctor. To prove himself he needed to dominate me.

The two of us were careful how we behaved in public, because fighting was not allowed. We always spoke politely when we met. I had never told him I knew he had been responsible for sending me to prison. He never said anything about it either. But underneath the polite exterior we both knew that one of us was going to kill the other.

How to kill him before he killed me was a difficult problem. Whenever I saw him my fingers itched to close around the handle of my hatchet and go after him. I never did, because we were never alone. If I killed Pen Tip with a hatchet and somebody saw it, the Khmer Rouge would kill me, and Huoy would be a widow. Revenge was useless unless Huoy and I were around to enjoy the aftermath.

There was another possibility. It wasn't the kind of plan to share with anybody, even with Huoy, because it was so low and mean and sneaky. Growing up in Samrong Yong, I had learned that thieves who want to kill watchdogs make a poison from the bark of the *kantout* tree. They peel the bark, grind it up, cook it with sugar and make it into cakes. The dogs eat the cakes and die. The poison works well on people too.

Poisoning Pen Tip had two drawbacks. The first was practical. There wasn't any sugar around—no way to disguise the nasty taste of *kantout*. Even if I somehow made the cakes, it would be hard tricking Pen Tip into eating them.

The second problem was moral. The idea of poisoning him showed the same instinct for delayed and violent revenge that characterized the Khmer Rouge. If I poisoned him, or even if I killed him on a dark night with a hatchet, I would become just like them. *Kum-monuss*. And that made me think about who I really was. Deep, deep within me there was a dark and violent streak, the same as in most Cambodians. On this instinctive level, perhaps, the Khmer Rouge and I were not so different. But unlike them and unlike Pen Tip, I was capable of rising above my instincts, because of my education. I was a doctor. My job was saving people, not killing them. I was also Buddhist. I believed that if I didn't kill Pen Tip myself, either in this life or the next life, somebody else would. It was *kama*. That didn't mean I wouldn't go after Pen Tip if I had the chance, but it did mean I could watch and wait.

Pen Tip moved first. In an administrative meeting he attended, Uncle Phan, the leader of the village, mentioned a vacancy in the fertilizer crew. Pen Tip volunteered me for the job. Uncle Phan approved.

When I heard about it I was furious. Carrying water to the garden wasn't low enough for me; now, instead, I would be carrying slop from the public latrines. It was Pen Tip's way of lowering my status even farther, of "breaking" my face.

The job was also dangerous. Previous men on the fertilizer crew had died from infections entering their bodies through cuts. Even if working with untreated sewage was socially acceptable, which it wasn't, because of the stigma and the smell, I never would have volunteered to do anything of the kind without rubber gloves, rubber boots and lots of medicine for protection. And I had none of those.

I started the new job, going around barefoot to the public toilets and emptying them with a pail on an extremely long wooden handle, then carrying a vat of the wastes on a very long thick pole with another man. My social downfall was complete. I was at the bottom caste of the war slaves, who were at the bottom of Cambodian society. But Pen Tip hadn't finished.

Three soldiers walked toward my new house one afternoon when work was over and I was planting yams in my new private garden. Until they stood next to me and clicked off the safety switches of their rifles, I had no idea what they wanted.

It was like the other times I'd been seized: Huoy weeping, my heart pounding. Pleading to be allowed to change my trousers so that Huoy would have the gold hidden in my waistband. Having my arms tied behind me. Being kicked to the floor. Huoy trying to keep them from beating me but being shoved roughly aside.

As I walked away, Huoy begged the soldiers to tie her up and take her too.

For the last time in this book, I ask the sensitive readers to skip over the following pages until the beginning of the next chapter. Those who want to know what happened, read on:

The soldiers didn't take me to the prison near Phum Chhleav, where I had gone twice before. Instead, we walked across the railroad track, past my brother's common garden, through fields where oxen and water buffalo grazed, and into the jungle.

I felt healthy and excited. My heart was beating fast. Except for leaving Huoy a widow, I had no regrets. The waiting was over. Surely the end would come at the next turn of the path.

Since we weren't going to Chhleav, I assumed that the soldiers were going to execute me in some spot where they had already executed others. I had never seen such a place, but it was logical that they existed. Mass graves. Killing fields. But we walked through the jungle until it was nearly dark. We came to an old prerevolutionary village with houses on stilts, mounds of rice straw next to them, and banana and tamarind trees. Even *kantout* trees, the kind I had thought about using for poisoning Pen Tip. The far side of the village opened up into a view of rice fields, interrupted here and there by hillocks crowned with sprays of tall bamboo.

The soldiers went in to report to the prison office, a small hut in Khmer Rouge style with a roof and wooden pillars but no walls. Then they took me to the outskirts of the village to a long, skinny thatch building with a corrugated metal roof and a horrible fetid smell.

A soldier pushed me into the prison and down an aisle. I couldn't see anything. The stench in the air made me want to vomit. Slime covered the ground under my bare feet. My left foot slipped into a ditch full of sewage. The soldier switched on a flashlight, found an empty space, untied my arms and told me to lie down on my back. I obeyed. My head knocked against something; a man's voice objected and I apologized. The soldier shined the flashlight on my feet. He was going to lock my left ankle into a leg iron attached to a block of wood, but he saw the slime, wrinkled his face in disgust, and instead locked my right ankle, which was cleaner.

There I was, in jail again.

What a disappointment.

Better that they had killed me quickly.

I lay awake, listening.

A mosquito whined near my ear and flew off.

From far away came a sound of trucks on National Route 5, the road that led to Battambang City. The flash of headlights swept across the wall of the prison, then left the wall in darkness.

I listened more carefully and heard flies buzzing around, along with the mosquitoes, and the moans of the prisoners.

Outside, crickets chirped. Mice scampered along the metal roof.

From somewhere near came a howling sound as the *chhke char-chark* drifted to the edge of the jungle and prepared to take their meals.

The man to the right of me coughed and stirred, but the woman to my left was silent. When it grew light outside I saw she was thin and old and dead. I felt her wrist. It was as cold as stone and without a pulse. A guard unlocked her foot and then mine and then the prisoner on her far side, and the two of us carried the old woman's body out of the building. Beyond a quick prayer for her soul I didn't grieve. If anything I was jealous. She had taken the easy way out.

My hands were tied again and I was taken to the administrative shack. Two soldiers entered with a big hempen rice sack.

"Is your name Samnang?"

"Yes."

"You are the one who lied to Angka?"

"I have never lied to Angka."

"You were a military doctor, a captain."

Pen Tip has done this, I thought. Now I am sure.

"No, comrade," I answered. "I have gone to jail before for this, but the charge is false. I was a taxi driver. You could go to Phnom Penh and check the files if you want to find out."

The soldier's answer was a blow to my ribs. They beat me with sticks until I crumpled to the floor and then they took turns kicking me. They opened the rice sack and put my feet in and drew it over me until it covered everything but my head. I struggled but my hands were tied behind my back and they tied the mouth of the bag over my head, leaving me in darkness.

They dragged me across the floor and then outdoors. Through the rough cloth I could feel the stubble of rice fields, then the bump when they dragged me up and over a paddy dike, and then more stubble and more dikes. They stopped, then hoisted me in the air.

"Say you were a doctor! Say yes! Say yes!"

I said nothing.

Thump! The blow hit me square across the back.

Thump! Again.

The bag swayed and lurched on the rope. I tucked my face between my knees as far as possible to protect my eyes.

Thump! My body was breaking like rotten wood.

They kept asking me if I was a doctor. I groaned but didn't answer. Then I went silent, hoping they would think I was dead.

Thump! No such luck. They were strong and well fed and they were taking their exercise on me.

At last when they grew tired of hitting me with their clubs, they went away.

The bag swung like a pendulum, back and forth, less and less, never quite stopping because of the wind. The wind penetrated the weave of the cloth, and light filtered in.

The day passed. As the light coming through the bag took on a weaker, redder color, footsteps approached. The bag dropped abruptly and I fell to the ground with a crash. Fresh pain exploded through my lower back, like a crushed vertabra or ruptured disk.

The guards let me out of the bag. I lay on the ground in a fetal position, my hands still tied behind me. When I opened my eyes I saw blood on my knees. It had flowed from my head wounds and coagulated.

The guards left me there as the sun set.

A cool wind blew. Above me, in the branches of the tamarind tree, a bird began to sing. It flew from one branch to another, chirping and twittering sweetly.

But it was not just a bird. It was one of the spirits of the landscape, like the gods who live in the rocks and sky and forest and water. The bird trilled and sang happily. It was telling me not to worry. Everything was going to be all right.

Silently I gave the bird my answer: I do not agree with you. The guards are going to come back and kill me. Please, spirit, tell me what the future holds.

The bird repeated its song, cheerfully, but its message did not change.

I closed my eyes and thought, you are so lucky. You can fly away whenever you want. Are you consoling me, or do you bring me a message? You must tell me the truth.

The guards took me back toward the jail that night. I limped along between them. No bones broken after all. No crushed vertebra, only a badly bruised coccyx. When I got inside the jail I lay down in the slime and listened to the groans of the other prisoners and the buzzing of the flies.

They interrogated me again the next morning and still I would not confess to being a doctor. They beat me again and dragged me outside to a spot under a tree. They locked my wrists and ankles into brackets on the ground. I lay on my back, waiting and wondering what the torture was going to be. A Khmer Rouge wearing a Montagut shirt inside his black tunic walked up holding something that looked like a wooden vise with steel handles, though I didn't have the chance to see it clearly. He placed the vise over my head with the two inner sides touching my temples. Then he tightened it by adjusting the handles while watching my face closely.

The inside of the vise was studded with the sharp ends of metal spikes. He wound it tighter, tighter, then paused. The spikes felt as though they were about to break through my skin and then crush my head. He peered down on me with the concentrated expression of a man looking through a microscope, focusing on every detail but not feeling my pain.

I moved my head incrementally to relieve the sore points on my temples. He was not touching the handles. Even so, the vise closed in a little tighter. I moved my head back to the original position—the vise tightened farther still.

I began to understand. In some ingenious manner, the vise was spring-loaded. Every time I wiggled or squirmed, the vise would punish me by tightening farther. As he reached for the handle again and began to twist it, I began to cry and whimper, not out of pain but because I realized he was calibrating the tightness to my pain threshold. The vise wasn't supposed to crush my skull. It had a far more clever purpose, and it was only part of the torture.

Satisfied, he stood up. He lifted a pail of water above me and fastened it to a tree branch high overhead. Water leaked from a hole in the center of the underside of the pail and dribbled onto the dirt next to me. He took a piece of rice straw and stuck it in the hole, adjusting it carefully until the drops of water rolled down the length of the rice straw and onto a spot in the middle of my forehead.

Drop.

Drop.

Drop.

Now I understood the torture.

The water was falling from a height of seven or eight feet, enough to give it a sharp, stinging impact. Over the course of a single Cambodian rainy season, I have seen water falling in drops from a roof drill holes into a concrete patio.

Drop.

Drop.

The man in the Montagut shirt stood over me, watching intently.

After the first five hundred drops I closed my eyes. The water hit the same spot every time, above my eyes in the middle of my forehead. My skin chafed, and the drops continued, like a pounding.

Drop.

Drop.

Drop-drop. A double beat.

Then a missed beat.

Then again: *Drop.*

Drop.

Drop.

Drop.

Drop.

After the thousandth drop the soreness on my skin began to turn into a headache, like the pressure of a weight on my head.

I shifted my position so the water would hit another spot. It was a mistake: the spikes squeezed in tighter on my temples. So now I had the pounding on my forehead and the pain of the spikes too. I tried not to move but I could not help it. Each time I did, the vise grew tighter.

His voice called from above me. "Comrade, are you really a doctor? If you say you were, I will stop the water."

"I was not a doctor," said my voice.

"Strong guy, huh? We'll just keep the water dropping on you, then. 'If you live, there is no gain. If you die, there is no loss.' "

Drop.

Drop.

Drop.

How much water is in the pail?

How long can this go on?

The drops were solid objects. Like nails. They were drilling through my skull.

I kept my eyes closed. The pain on my forehead grew as great as the pain in my temples. Then the pain in my forehead and temples connected. When the drops landed, the whole interior of my skull throbbed together. Each time the drops struck I saw white. My feet and legs twitched to contain the shock.

The pail had no bottom. It contained a lake. The day took a century to pass.

I kept my head absolutely still and thought: If the Khmer Rouge keep it up all night, I will die. The pain will kill me. I am sure.

Twice before—with dysentery, and with being crucified in prison—I had nearly died. From that I had developed a sense, a measurement, of my life-force. I knew what I could take and what would break me.

I sent a message to the wind, the trees, the birds, the rice fields, to every place the gods resided: If I gave too much *bonjour* in my previous life, now I am paying it back. If I hurt people in my previous life, now I am paying it back. Please, gods, let my next life be easier.

Drop.

Drop.

Drop-drop.

Drop.

Drop . . .

The Pacific Ocean is in that bucket. I have lived in agony for a thousand years.

The man in the Montagut shirt came back and pushed the rice straw into the hole in the pail with his finger. The dripping stopped except that every minute, or every hour, a drop hit my forehead, though not in the same place as before, and then it hit on my temple and then the top of my head, in no pattern.

I opened my eyes. The sun had set but the sky was still full of color, and beautiful beyond belief.

I dared not move my head to look around but sensed that I was alone.

My eyes closed again. I had sunk deep inside my being. My mind sent messages to Huoy:

Huoy, in your whole life you have not suffered like this. Even to see me now would make you cry out. You cried when the Khmer Rouge tied me up and pushed me down. I do not think you could stand it here. I'm glad you're not here. You're not strong enough to be here. Let the wind tell you this: For now, they have stopped torturing me. I pray that the wind blows over the landscape and around our house and brings the news to you. I pray that the gods console you.

I lay there locked in the brace, dreaming but not sleeping.

The next morning the man with the Montagut shirt came back and poured fresh water into the pail. He missed, and some of the water spilled over the side and onto my face. I opened my mouth and swallowed what I could.

He asked if I were a doctor.

I said no.

He adjusted the rice straw. The water ran out of the hole in the bucket, down the straw and onto me.

The drops started again.

Regularly.

That day, my mother and father appeared before me and talked to me. Then Huoy, then Huoy and her mother, and finally Huoy alone.

At every drop my body went numb for an instant, and then the sensation flooded back, and then at the next drop I went numb again. Then the numb parts blurred together and I couldn't feel anything.

The sun woke me once in its afternoon position, but after that I don't remember much. A small part of my brain reminded me that I was still alive.

Some men came and asked one another if I was in a coma. I heard them, but even if I had wanted to I could not have summoned the control over my muscles to tell them no. They were too far away from me. They were so far away.

And I don't even know if they stopped the water torture or not.

The next thing I knew the sun was a swollen red ball on the horizon and I was lying down. The pail wasn't overhead anymore, and the vise was gone.

I was lying on my back on the ground. My head was turned to the side, and there was nothing to hold it in place. Ants were biting me, and from the smell I knew I had shat in my trousers.

I closed my eyes.

I told myself not to move, or lose self-control, or be angry. Just to rest.

Sometime later footsteps approached and then I was nudged on the shoulder and a voice shouted at me to wake up, but I pretended to be unconscious.

"Wake up! It's dinnertime!" the voice said.

I turned my head slowly, opened my eyes and raised an arm, then let my head and hand drop, pretending to fall asleep.

"Wake up! Eat! Eat!"

A foot kicked me a few times, not hard, and I said, "Yes," in a low, dull voice but still pretended to be asleep.

The guard grabbed my wrist and yanked me up to a sitting position. On the ground next to me was a shallow bowl of watery rice. I wanted it but slumped back to the ground again, still acting, and he pulled me up again. This time I ate the food very slowly, savoring the taste.

Then I went back to sleep on my side.

That night they brought me to the jail. If the flies landed on me or the mosquitoes bit me, I did not know. It did not matter. On the outside were the flies and the slime and the bruises. Deep within me, the force of life was recovering.

The next day passed inside the jail. The long narrow building, with its double row of prisoners lying on their backs head to head, was raised in the middle, so the shit and piss would simply flow downhill to the sewage canals along the walls. Four of us prisoners were locked into the same heavy block of wood, next to another foursome, who were next to the door. We got one meal of watery rice, served in bowls spattered with excrement. Flies with red eyes buzzed around us like miniature helicopters, hovering, then darting off, then hovering again. It was hot in the jail, because of the sun on the metal roof. It must have been over a hundred degrees.

At night I dozed but didn't sleep. There were no lights. My sense of hearing had sharpened to the night sounds, the insects and the faraway trucks and the occasional call of the *chhke char-chark*.

There was another sound I couldn't place, a rustling outside the perimeter of the building. I lay quietly with my eyes shut, listening.

The rustling started again, then stopped.

It was not the sound of mice. Mice made a smaller, scampering noise.

Somebody was just outside the jail, walking in the leaves.

What is wrong? I asked myself. What is this sudden cold sweat on my limbs? Why do I know to be afraid?

Listen!

There is more than one of them.

I nudged the prisoners to either side.

"Stay awake," I whispered to them. "The prison is surrounded. Something's going to happen."

My neighbors passed the word along.

We waited.

The crickets chirped steadily.

When it finally happened, it was fast. The quiet of one moment changed to confused yelling as flames roared through the thatch. As the walls went up in fire, the bamboo restraining strips were illuminated in outline for a few brief seconds before they caught fire too, and the prisoners jumping and yelling were silhouetted in the light. The four of us in the heavy wooden block jumped to our feet and dragged the block toward the door. The woman next to me fell, twisting the wood and wrenching the leg irons against our ankles. I picked her up and we dragged her and the heavy block outside into clear air. From the outside we could see the jail burning and one end of the metal roof falling on top of the screaming prisoners trapped inside. We felt the blast of heat against our skins, and then we heard the rapid bursts of gunfire from the other side of the jail as the guards mowed prisoners down. Other groups of four, sixteen or twenty people in all, hobbled out of our side of the jail before the whole building collapsed, and the guards ran around to our side holding M-16s and looking fierce in the firelight, but they didn't shoot us. Still in our blocks, we moved farther away from the building, listening to the screams of the dying inside.

The guards stood over us menacingly. We watched the remnants of the building burn.

The coals glowed in the darkness, and the metal from the roof contracted noisily as it cooled.

As the sky grew light we saw that our skins were black from the smoke. Little was left of the jail except for charred metal sheets and blackened, twisted bodies on the ground.

The prison-keepers never explained why they had burned the jail, and it has always remained a mystery to me. Perhaps the guards took the initiative, without orders from above. Maybe they had tired of their methods of torture and wanted some variety. Or perhaps they wanted to get rid of the building because of the awful smell.

Of eighty prisoners, twenty-eight survived. The Khmer Rouge met among themselves to decide what to do. They brought us watery rice and then asked us which cooperatives we came from.

They sent off messengers.

That afternoon Uncle Phan, Phum Ra's chief, appeared to escort me and another prisoner back to his village.

As we walked away, Uncle Phan explained that he hadn't known the soldiers had taken me away until after it had happened. "I couldn't have protected you, son," he said.

I partly believed him. He didn't seem to know anything of my quarrel with Pen Tip. I thanked him for picking me up. But in truth, I was angry. By Khmer Rouge standards Phan was a decent man, but that wasn't good enough. I had not done anything to deserve prison.

"From now on," Uncle Phan was saying, *"Dam doeum kor*. Plant a kapok tree. Keep your mouth shut. Behave. Don't do any more misdeeds. Understand?"

"I will do anything to avoid an experience like that," I replied. "I have had enough suffering. Please, Uncle Phan, could we walk more slowly?"

We stopped to rest a few times. There was a raw spot on the skin in the middle of my forehead, but it was barely noticeable compared to the lumps and the dried blood on the top of my head and the bruises everywhere else. I was weak and sore, but in better condition than after the other two times I got out of prison.

When we got back to Phum Ra work was over for the afternoon, and Huoy was at the house. When she first saw me she wept with happiness. Then, when I came closer and she saw the discolorations from the bruises and the cuts on my head, she lost control. She sobbed with irregular gasps of air, her facial features contorted and her shoulders shook. I held her, but she would not stop.

I stripped off my clothes and wrapped a krama around my waist. We walked in back of the house to the minicanal with water in the bottom. She bathed me and shaved the hair around the cuts on my head. Her hands were steady, but she could not stop crying.

For all Huoy had lived through, she was soft. She was like a crab without a shell. I was her shell, her protection. When I came back to her broken, she absorbed the blows I had taken. She felt the pain even more than me.

She would not stop crying. Even as she daubed at my wounds and soaped me, even as I abandoned myself to her tender care, I worried about her health. My injuries were only physical. They would heal. Hers were in her mind.

28

HAPPINESS

IF ANYBODY ELSE in Cambodia survived being tortured by the Khmer Rouge three times, I never heard of it. In the Phnom Tippeday region I knew of only one other person, a teenager, who survived even twice. His hair fell out, and he turned pale and trembled at the sight of soldiers.

Yet somehow I had survived three episodes of torture and prison as well as malaria and dysentery. I was alive. There were scars—scalp wounds, from the third prison; burn scars on my leg, from the second prison; half of my little finger missing, from the first prison. There were other injuries, mental and emotional, but I wasn't aware of them until later. At the time, I was in reasonably good spirits. And I was amazed. I had survived when thousands of people around me had died of illness or starvation, and thousands more had been executed.

Why did I survive?

To me, the only answer that makes sense is that the gods willed it. It was *kama*. It was not chance, because the mathematical odds against me were too high. What were the chances against my surviving what I had been through? A thousand to one? A hundred thousand to one? Or even a million to one?

Admittedly, a few factors worked in my favor: One, I am physically tough and energetic. Two, I did a lot of street fighting growing up, and that helped prepare me to outsmart and outlast my torturers. Three, I had someone to live for: Huoy. Anyone with those three characteristics has better odds than someone who doesn't. Of course.

But that still doesn't explain why I made it through when so many others didn't.

There were so many times I could have died. The third time in prison, if I hadn't been near the door when the fire started. The second time in prison, if the guards hadn't pulled the plastic bag off my head when they did. Anytime at all, if I had admitted that I was a doctor or a military officer. I would have died of dysentery if the yams hadn't been distributed.

It was a miracle I was alive. I accepted it as such and thanked the gods. When I looked around, I saw other miracles. Everything, from the color of the sky to the taste of rice to the sight of the temple on the mountainside, seemed new and fresh. And the life-force within me was the same as the force within the earth and sky and all other living beings.

My bruises healed quickly. The nightmare of the water torture vanished from my thoughts. The days returned to their normal pattern, and still I retained this deeper, greater appreciation for everything around me. For Huoy, especially, and for our house.

Chang My Huoy—known as "Bopha" to the Khmer Rouge, known as Huoy to me. We had been denied the wedding we both wanted, first by my father, then by the revolution. But we were closer than any of the married couples around. This is not to say we were perfect. Sometimes I was harsh with her, and at other times I teased her more than she would have liked. But we were glad for each other's company.

I loved watching her in our new house in the early mornings. When she slept, she hugged her little blue-covered pillow to her chest, the one she had brought with her from Phnom Penh. She rose before sunrise, when the sky was growing light. She went to her small, rectangular mirror and brushed her hair, put clips in her hair above each ear, and washed her face. She dressed. As I got up groggily, she rolled the mosquito net, folded the nightclothes and the bedding and put them neatly away. There was something about her—organized, clean, feminine, desirable—that attracted me on all levels. Man to woman. Husband to wife. Strange to think that when we first met I had been her teacher. Ever since then, those roles had been reversed.

I had always felt something special toward women, and by that I mean toward the entire female sex. In childhood, after the beating my father gave me, I realized that men were the cause of most suffering. My experiences in Khmer Rouge prisons proved it over and over. When had a woman ever hurt me? When had I ever seen a woman physically harming someone else? Never. Perhaps that was why I was so drawn to women, because they were the healers of suffering. The suffering that men inflicted.

To me, Huoy represented the best of womankind. She never caused pain. She was a healer. She was also much smarter than me. She never got into trouble, or even into arguments. Just by advising me and by quietly setting an example, she kept me out of more trouble with Angka.

She avoided the worst trait of women, which is idle, malicious gossip. She sought out the company of a few women who were polite and educated like herself. In her spare time she tended the house and garden, or cooked, improvising recipes from wild foods, or sang in her smooth, clear voice. She mended our clothes with precise, expert stitching. She was sentimental but practical, making trousers for herself from one of her mother's old *sampot*s and wearing her mother's rubber sandals when her own wore out. She was not the most beautiful woman in the world, but she was beautiful to me. Outsiders didn't know much about her. To them she looked like a good-natured but quiet young woman.

I knew Huoy better than anyone, except perhaps her mother. If Huoy had a fault, it was that she could not protect herself. Even when she was happy, the tears rolled down her cheeks. Sad events affected her deeply. She had never recovered from her mother's death. She had prayed to her mother nonstop when I was in prison; even when times were good, she prayed to her mother almost every day. My own near-deaths and the deaths around her left her permanently saddened and frightened. We heard that my own mother had died, off in the Cardamom Mountains, and Hok and his wife and Huoy and I held a ceremony with candles and incense, the same as we had held for my father and brother. In a way I was glad that my mother had died, because it freed her from the hardships of this life, but Huoy took the news badly. I kept trying to cheer her up, but it wasn't easy. Her mental health was fragile. She belonged to a more peaceful time, of going to the temples and raising children and running a clean and comfortable household.

Our new house in Phum Ra was not what I had expected to give her before the revolution. It was made of thatch, except for a few corrugated metal panels along the walls. The floor was dirt. But we both loved the house and I was proud of it, because I had designed it myself and built it with my own hands. We had only to compare our house to our neighbors' to know how good it was.

Our neighbors lived in houses on stilts like the ones I helped build when I was on the construction crew. The pilings had sunk unevenly, and as a result the floors were tilted at various crazy angles. The metal roofs got so hot in the sun that sometimes the inhabitants fried fresh-water clams on them to save building a fire.

Our little house was sturdy and comfortable. For the site I chose a hillock, elevated above the surrounding ground, so it would never flood. We sprinkled water on the dirt floor in the morning, which kept it cool all day. Doors and windows gave us plenty of ventilation. The thatch roof kept out the sun and the rain. To protect against heat even more, I planted a climbing squash that grew up onto the roof and covered it with leaves. On the south side of the house, which got the direct rays of the sun, I planted banana trees for shade, plus climbing beans to grow up and cover the outside wall.

The main room of the house was about ten feet by six. An L-shaped bench made of smooth boards ran along the west and south walls. Huoy and I slept on the long side and used the short side for sitting on during the day. At the far end of the bench, near the door, we kept a ceramic jar with a lid and cool, clean drinking water inside.

The kitchen was a lean-to shed attached to the north side of the house. We stacked firewood along one wall and set three stones in a triangle to support the pot. We went through the motions of showing up at the common kitchen for meals, but like most families in Phum Ra we did our real cooking at home every day, while pretending to make tea. We had yams, taro, arrow root, onions, pumpkins, beans, squash, cabbage, cucumber, peppers, corn and other vegetables in our garden. We raised ducks and chickens. Huoy, who had strong maternal instincts, loved to gather the tiny, fluffy-feathered chicks in her hands and carry them to spots where they could peck at the termites on the ground, making their cheeping noises.

Truly, we had everything we needed. By our standards we were rich. I had a bamboo shoulderboard, two pails and an all-purpose hatchet. We had hoes and mattocks for the garden; kitchen utensils; the crockery water jar; the mended and blackened mosquito net; and a soft, silk-like brocaded blanket to keep us warm at night. (Somebody had stolen our white plastic tarp but we didn't care, because our roof kept us dry.) We had our clothes. We had enough food. We had hidden possessions—some bits of gold in our waistbands; my eyeglasses and medical equipment on top of the roofbeam; rice and extra food and medical textbooks in a storage cellar under the dirt floor. The French-English instruction book lay hidden between the bench and the wall, where I could reach for it when I chose. We had no Mercedes, no gasoline trucks, no bank accounts, and we didn't care. We didn't even miss them anymore.

I felt reborn. Huoy made me happy. Our house made me happy. We had moved from the front lines to the back lines, where life was more relaxed. Every day I heard the whistle of the steam trains approaching and watched the trains chuff past on the railroad tracks and saw the railroad workers poling themselves rapidly along on their little flatcar, and I marveled, like a child who had never seen such things before. When the bells rang in the village—"DING. DING. Ding, ding, ding, dingdingding"—the sound didn't set my teeth on edge, as it had earlier. The bells fit in with the trains and the birds and everything else.

In the evenings Huoy and I went walking together to look for food. We gathered wild plants. We hunted for mice and crabs. We used our mosquito net to catch tiny shrimp and crayfish in a pond. Once we caught a big fish in the net, and when I had hauled it ashore Huoy wrapped her arms around my neck and wept.

"Why are you crying?"

"Because I'm happy, sweet, I'm happy," she said. At home she cooked the fish with water convolvulus, and it was perfect.

Sometimes the two of us were alone together, bathing in a canal. We scrubbed and washed one another. We were happy to serve one another.

We were so close and so dependent on each other that we often joked about it. A man I knew came over to the house and asked me to go out foraging with him.

"I need my wife's permission," I said.

"You're scared of your wife?" my friend said.

"Absolutely," I said. Huoy was standing next to me. "She's the minister of education and finance around here. She's minister of cultural affairs too. She runs everything. She's the boss."

My friend said skeptically, "Oh yeah? You have to give her respect like that, in front of her?"

"Of course," I said. I turned to Huoy and asked her please to give me permission to go out foraging. Huoy folded her arms, pouted and said no.

"Sorry, I can't go," I told my friend.

I put my palms together and *sompeah*ed Huoy, but she shook her head. Then I grabbed her and tickled her until she finally said yes.

"The boss has given permission now," I said. "We can go."

The truth was that Huoy was the boss. I liked it that way. She modified my quick temper, my stubbornness, my tendency to joke too much. She brought out my patience, my quiet side. I was her boss too. Each served the other. I kept her alive by providing the food and shelter and love she needed. She had saved my life when I was sick. She kept me from doing rash things, like killing Pen Tip. She was my reason for living.

When I returned from my third time in prison, Pen Tip pretended to ignore me. It didn't matter. I knew and he knew that there was unfinished business between us. I let him worry about it. I didn't worry. Until the right day came, I was content to wait.

As far as I was concerned, I had gained the upper hand. I was the man prison couldn't kill. I was the ghost who kept reappearing. And Pen Tip's attempt to dominate me by putting me in a low-class job had backfired. It was low-class, without a doubt, but it was the best job in the village.

The fertilizer crew was outside Pen Tip's jurisdiction. He didn't supervise us. Nobody really did. Few people went near the fertilizer shed because of the smell. Occasionally Uncle Phan, the village chief, came by on an inspection tour, but he was easy to deal with. Uncle Phan told me to put salt in the fertilizer. He thought plants need salt, the way people do. I went off to the common kitchen, shaking my head, and requisitioned salt. From what I could remember from biology courses, plants need nitrogen, phosphates and other nutrients, but they do not need salt, which is harmful to them. I put the salt aside for my own use, and the next time I saw Uncle Phan I said solemly, "I have tasted the fertilizer. The salt level is exactly right. Would you like to taste some too?" He turned pale, like a man who was about to be sick. And that kept him away from the fertilizer shed for a while.

My colleague on the fertilizer crew was an old guy with no side teeth, named Sangam. Once a day, Sangam and I strolled leisurely to a public toilet with our tools. There were several toilets scattered around the village. They had half-height thatch walls, meaning that someone who went inside and squatted still had his head and shoulders visible to passersby. Not much privacy at all. The users had to place their feet on two wooden slats, and carefully—one slip could mean a fall into the retaining pit, a fifty-five-gallon steel drum cut in half. Needless to say, the toilets were unpopular among the residents of the village, who preferred to sneak off into the bushes when no one was watching.

Sangam and I took turns emptying the steel drums with a pail attached to a very, very, very long wooden handle. We dumped the contents into another half of a fifty-five-gallon drum and carried it between us on the longest pole we could find. At the fertilizer shed, which was far out in the rice fields, we stirred other ingredients into the drum—mud from hillocks (which was exceptionally fertile) and rice husks or leaves. We poured the mixture onto the ground. By the time it dried a day or two later, it had lost most of its odor and was ready to be spread. Every week or so Sangam and I made deliveries to the common gardens in an oxcart.

The only disadvantages to the job were the smell, which was awful, and the danger to health. I was extremely careful not to get cuts. I bathed twice a day and washed thoroughly with kapok soap and real soap that I got from the common kitchen. I never got internal infections, but the red rash spread back over my feet and ankles.

The advantage of the job was that Sangam and I were left alone. It was nothing at all like working on the front lines. We didn't pay any attention to the bells. We didn't work hard. I took at least one long nap each day. About once a week I stayed up all night to steal from the common gardens. When I came back from stealing I wrapped the vegetables carefully and stored them under the pile of fertilizer, where nobody ever looked. Then I slept at the fertilizer shed until noon, while Sangam kept watch.

We used the job as a cover for getting food. If we wanted to spend an afternoon collecting red ant eggs, or gathering wild plants, or fishing, we went through the fields collecting manure from the oxen and water buffalo, until we were safely out of sight. If I wanted rice, I splashed smelly night soil on my sleeves, pretended to be tired and lay down on a long table in the common kitchen. When Uncle Phan's wife, who was the leader of the kitchen, tried to get me to leave, I pretended to stay asleep until she offered me a big enough bribe of rice.

Luck was running in our direction. A railroad worker living nearby had a sick child and asked my brother Hok for advice. Hok referred the case to me. I treated the child and got to know the entire railroad crew. These were the men I had seen poling along on their flatcar ever since I had first come to Battambang. They were members of an elite class under the regime. They ate even better than soldiers. Their food was sent to them in boxcars, more than they could eat. They also had their own vegetable garden, which Sangam and I supplied fertilizer to, secretly, as a favor.

They invited us to secret feasts and served me dishes I hadn't seen in years. I set food aside for Huoy, then ate so much I couldn't move.

With the food from the railroad workers, and the food I collected on and off the job, plus the vegetables from our garden, Huoy and I ate better than ever before. For the first time since coming to Battambang, we were actually healthy.

What a change! Our body weights were nearly normal. We were strong from all the exercise. We had our own private house to live in, just the two of us. We didn't like the regime, but we had learned how to get around the system, especially now that we were away from the front lines.

My only regret, when I look back on that period, was an argument I had with Huoy. She had taken some cooked food from its hiding place in the woodpile when a boy about eleven years old happened to walk past and see it. The boy was smoking a cigarette. He gave Huoy a long, bold, suspicious glare. When he walked past me working in the garden he glared at me too.

The boy's name was Yoeung, and he was Uncle Phan's adopted

son. He often went around the village, joined work crews just long enough to watch the workers closely, then wandered off again to report what he saw. He was a *chhlop*.

"Sweet," I said to Huoy after Yoeung had left, "did you listen to me? What was I talking about just last night? What did I tell you? To *keep the food hidden*. It means our lives. So why didn't you?"

Huoy said, "I know. I'm sorry. It was bad timing, that's all. I took out the food, and the *chhlop* was right there. I didn't mean to."

Something in my mind snapped, like a twig that had been stepped on. My happiness vanished. I saw myself being tied up and dragged off to prison. I went into a cold rage.

"Don't talk to me for five days," I said. "If you say even a word, I won't answer."

Huoy was silent, her eyes downcast.

Uncle Phan summoned me to his house.

I walked there slowly, thinking the end had come. If I went to prison a fourth time, there was no way I could survive.

I lied to Uncle Phan. I lied better than I had ever lied in my life, by convincing myself that what I said was true. I swore to him that the food was given to me by the railroad workers (though in fact I had stolen it from the common garden). It was my word against the *chhlop*'s, and Uncle Phan let me go with a warning. Perhaps he thought I had suffered enough. Or maybe his conscience was bothering him. He did not know it, but many evenings I had seen him strolling back from the common garden with a bulge in his krama. I had seen the lantern light shine through the cracks of his house when he and his wife cooked the stolen food and ate it. In Phum Ra, everyone was a thief. Even the village leader.

So this time Huoy and I got away with it. We were not punished for stealing the food. But when I got back to our house I gave her the silent treatment anyway. I was determined to be strong and to show her the consequences of her action.

After two days of not saying a word to her, I was standing in the doorway of the house looking out at the garden. Huoy came to me and knelt at my feet. She looked up at me, with teardrops at the corners of her eyes.

"Sweet, are you still angry at me?" she said. "I did wrong. I was careless. If you want to beat me for it, then beat me. Do as you wish. But once you are through, talk to me. Please talk to me."

I raised her up and put my arms around her. I hugged her. Her body was soft and warm. And once I had hugged her I knew I had done wrong. She was my wife. She would never harm me, and I knew that. It was the one thing I was certain of in the world.

I took a deep breath.

"Yes, I will talk to you," I said huskily. Then I had to go out in the garden to clear my thoughts.

I was upset and confused. My temper had gotten the best of me again. After all those years of learning to control it. Underneath the adult exterior I was the same boy who had thrown the starter wrench into the radiator of the engine at my father's sawmill and then kicked the dog.

I had been crazy to treat Huoy that way. Crazy and wrong.

Standing in the garden, I decided never to do anything to make Huoy unhappy again. If I had a single purpose in life, it was to comfort her, and to serve her just as she served me.

We made up, and our *bonheur* was restored. The last barrier between us had been removed, a barrier I had not known about until it was gone. We became even closer than before, like the cupped halves of male and female fitting snugly in the symbol of *yin* and *yang*.

This is not to say that life was perfect. We never forgot that we were living under a shadow. We always knew that somewhere nearby, the soldiers were marching some unfortunate person away and that we were powerless to do anything about it. Someday, perhaps, it would be our turn. Huoy and I didn't talk about the terror much, but it was always there, like a cold hand around our hearts.

Yet even the terror had one beneficial effect: It had driven us closer. And except for the fear itself, life had never been so good. I didn't miss the old times. I didn't care about being a doctor anymore, or being rich. I didn't miss having a motorcycle, or even wearing shoes. We didn't like the Khmer Rouge, but we accepted our circumstances under them. We were close to the land. We were peasants, as generations of our ancestors had been. We were healthy. We had enough to eat. We had each other's company. We had our own house. In the late afternoons we sat by the back door and looked at the view:

Rice fields spreading out into the distance, dotted with hillocks. It was perfect. One hillock rose higher than the rest, crowned with a leaning *sdao* tree. Beyond the rice fields rose the mountain, with the temple on the plateau, a reminder of the religion we had not forgotten. The sun set behind the long, uneven ridge.

Over the months we watched the rice fields change from brown to green and from green to gold, and then there was joyous news:

Huoy was pregnant.

29

CROSSING THE SEA

IN OUR PILLOW TALK at night Huoy often said she wanted babies. She wanted to be a mother badly, but she also thought it best to put it off until the Khmer Rouge had been overthrown, so our children could grow up in a better world. Until my third time in prison I had agreed.

But after I came back from prison for the last time, life seemed too precious and fragile to wait any longer. I told her it was time to start a family and she agreed. With the food I provided and the larger rations we got from the common kitchen during the rice harvest, Huoy became fertile toward the end of 1977.

We knew she was pregnant because of morning sickness. She had a bad case, vomiting both in the morning and the afternoon. Even rice made her nauseous. The only foods she could keep down were sweet. I hunted for papayas and jackfruits. I made doctor's visits in exchange for bananas and pieces of sugar cane. Finally we traded gold for a supply of palm tree sugar. She sprinkled the sugar on food, and that helped keep it down. But she didn't have much appetite.

Except to find food that agreed with her, there was nothing I could do about her morning sickness. We would just have to wait for it to pass. I took my medical instruments out of hiding—a stethoscope, a blood-pressure cuff and a thermometer—and gave her an exam, using spoons as an improvised speculum. All her signs were good. Aside from the nausea, which caused a slight weight loss, she was healthy. She was then twenty-seven years old.

Because she was strong and relatively young, she had a good chance of giving birth successfully, or, as we say in the Khmer language, "crossing the sea." Most Cambodian women thought of childbirth as something like a long and dangerous voyage, which is how the expression "crossing the sea" came into being. Huoy wasn't too worried about the act of giving birth itself. After all, I was a doctor. She knew that I would take care of her. She was more concerned about the upbringing of the child after it was born.

Huoy told me many times that she was going to raise our child to be religious and well mannered and to respect its elders. If there were no schools she would educate the child herself. She didn't really care whether we had a boy or a girl, as long as the child was healthy. I hoped for a little girl—a small version of Huoy, to grow up and help heal the suffering of the world.

By the third month Huoy's belly began to show. From then on she wore sarongs instead of trousers, because it was easy to adjust the size of the waist. During the days she did light tasks in the common garden. When she came home she chewed on a piece of sugar cane, for energy, and then watered our vegetables with a small watering can, careful not to strain herself. She was beginning to get over her morning sickness, and she had that contented inner glow of a woman who is glad to be pregnant.

But the dry season of 1978 was a difficult time in the Phnom Tippeday region. The common kitchen began serving smaller rations than before. There was a warehouse nearby, a large building with mud walls and a metal roof, next to the railroad tracks, but the rice inside was not meant for us. Occasionally the doors opened and soldiers loaded great, heavy sacks of rice onto railroad trains, or else onto trucks, and we who had grown the rice sadly watched it disappear.

Toward the end of March 1978 the common kitchen began skipping meals. At first I simply stole more food to make up for it. My partner was a courageous twelve-year-old boy named Tha, who fed his crippled father, his pregnant mother and two small children with what he stole. Together we went on nighttime expeditions to the common garden on the mountainside, near the ruined temple. One night the civilian guards at the garden heard us coming, threw stones at us and yelled at the top of their lungs for the soldiers. There was only one thing for us to do: Tha and I climbed above the guards, threw stones at them and shouted "Thieves! Thieves!" at them as loudly as we could so the soldiers wouldn't know whom to shoot.

Quickly we threw vegetables in our sacks and came crashing down the mountainside with our sacks in one hand and hatchets in the other. When we came back to the village we cooked our food out in the open. Except for stealing itself, there was nothing to hide. With the common kitchen closed part of the time, everybody prepared private meals. Angka's authority was breaking down in front of our eyes.

In April 1978 the common kitchen in Phum Ra closed entirely. The bells stopped ringing. There were no more loudspeaker announcements, no more music.

One of the first to stop working was Pen Tip. He was like a weather vane, sensing which way the political winds were blowing. Others followed his example. A few "old" people who were closest to the village leaders, or who were particularly scared of the soldiers, continued to work at their jobs. But most wandered off into the fields and jungle to forage.

At our house, by mid-April, there was no more food left in the hiding places. We ate the water convolvulus, the cabbages and the underdeveloped yams from our garden, then the flowers from the pumpkins and the leaves from the taro. It was too early for the corn and beans and other vegetables, and there were no bananas on our trees.

We had already eaten the ducks. The common kitchen had taken some of the chickens, and I had given the rest to someone to raise in a remote location, out of Angka's reach.

I was worried. There is little that helps a pregnant woman as much as food, and little that complicates a pregnancy as much as malnutrition. I didn't say that to Huoy, but she knew it herself.

By her fourth month of pregnancy she was no longer nauseous, but there was little for her to eat. The weather was unusually dry and hot.

Though the common kitchen was closed, soldiers continued to take people away for gathering wild foods. It had no effect. After three and a half years of listening to promises about the country's future, the patience of the "new" people and even the "old" people was exhausted. We foraged in the open. We stole more than ever before, during the day as well as the night. Everybody stole. The guards at the common gardens stole until there was not an edible leaf left, and then they left the garden gates open. Tha and I made trips into the rice fields, to glean the leftovers from the rice harvest. People were everywhere, bending over, scanning the ground, picking up unhusked grains of rice, wandering uncertainly this way and that. In an entire day I collected less than a can of rice and saved it all for Huoy. All the wild food was gone, picked by other hungry people.

Huoy became depressed.

It was not just the lack of food, though that was the greatest part of it—the unrelenting emptiness in her stomach, day after day, just when she needed food the most. Adding to her sorrow, draining her strength further, were other events that affected her mental well-being. Like the purges. The latest purge was against the "Vietnamese." The Khmer Rouge leaders had the same racial prejudice against the Vietnamese as the Lon Nol regime did. They decided that Cambodians of Vietnamese descent and even Cambodians who spoke the Vietnamese language were the cause of all our problems and that it was necessary to purify the nation of traitors of this type. The *chhlop* Yoeung came around, trying to discover who in our village spoke Vietnamese, and many were taken away. Huoy, who had grown up near the Vietnamese border, spoke fluent Vietnamese. The *chhlop* didn't find out, but still she became depressed.

But it was not just the hunger and the purges that depressed her. Earlier in the regime there had been one element of truth to the communists' claim of moral superiority: Khmer Rouge cadre and soldiers did not take bribes. Now even that was no longer true. With gold, people could get food from the common kitchen, even though it was closed. With gold, they could get relatives or friends reassigned from the front lines. *Bonjour*, Cambodia's great moral weakness, had reappeared.

I spent long hours consoling Huoy.

"You have to be strong, sweet," I said. "Don't allow yourself to be sick. If you are sick, I feel sick. If you have any kind of disease in your mind or your heart, give it to me, but get rid of it. I want you to be healthy."

"Yes," Huoy said, but she was unconvinced.

She lay on the smooth wooden bench in our tiny house, tired, hot, fanning herself. She was six months pregnant, with a swollen belly.

"I have never seen this kind of government before," said Huoy listlessly. It was her favorite complaint. "I have read a lot of history books, about Europe and Asia, but I never read about anything like this. No hospitals. No communication. If we lived in any other country, we could send a letter out to relatives abroad, and they would send money or food. But we cannot even send a letter out of Cambodia. We are not even allowed to have pencil or paper to write a letter. If we object they say we are CIA, or KGB, or spies for the Vietnamese. There is no way to call for help."

"I help you," I said.

"But you are hungry too," she said. "In Sihanouk's regime and Lon Nol's regime if you were poor you could at least go out and beg. Or you were free to find wild foods in the countryside. But here, nothing. Nothing. Even beggars cannot survive."

I didn't know what to say to that. It was all true.

"The government treats us worse than animals," she murmured. "Nobody cares. When someone dies on the dikes of the canals, nobody comes to take the bodies away. Only the vultures. Or the *chhke char-chark*. Or the cannibals. People are eating people. That's what we have come to."

"I have heard the stories," I answered. "But I do not think there have been many cases. The Khmer Rouge do not like cannabalism either."

Huoy fanned herself, staring at the thatch ceiling.

"If there is no food, maybe the baby will be retarded," she said. "Or deformed."

"No, sweet," I said firmly. "I have examined you. I have listened to the baby's heartbeat. The signs are all good. The baby will be fine."

Huoy didn't seem to hear me. Her attention had drifted, and her thoughts were focused on something far away. "If there is no food, how can I make milk in my breasts?" she whispered. "How long can I go on like this? How long has it been since Angka has given us food?"

"No, don't worry," I said. "Your breasts will automatically have milk. Automatically. I'm a doctor. This is my specialty. I know."

"Yes, I know the milk comes automatically," said Huoy. "But maybe there won't be enough."

I didn't know what to say to that either. She was right. If she was as malnourished when she delivered the baby as she was now, she probably wouldn't be able to produce enough milk. But for the moment, breast milk was the least of our problems. Even her malnourishment didn't worry me as much as the state of her mind.

Ever since the Khmer Rouge had taken over I had talked with Huoy, trying to encourage her. At first she believed me, and kept her spirits up. She said she understood that we had to wait for things to improve. But that was before the death of her mother. After that, Huoy was never quite the same. We went to the front lines, my father and brother died, and I kept getting sent to prison. And as Huoy saw conditions worsening each year, she became discouraged. She didn't have the instinct to fight when all the odds were against us. To her, there was no use fighting anymore. The hunger, the terror, the *chhlop*, the corruption, the energy the baby drew away from her—all these things combined to break her will.

Her weight loss showed first in her cheeks, which lost their roundness. Then in the outline of her jawbones and her collarbones. All her ribs were showing.

I went out every day, all day, searching for food but finding only a handful. There was nothing left of Hok's gardens or any of the common gardens. Every plant had been plucked.

I took gold out of my waistband pocket and tried to buy rice, but there was no more for sale, at any price, anywhere. There was only rice flour. For a *damleung*, more than an ounce of gold, I bought two small cans of rice flour weighing less than half a pound. I gave it all to Huoy but it wasn't enough. I went to the railroad workers for help but they said sorry, they were not allowed to talk to me because of the purges.

I went back to foraging for wild foods. The forests were barren. No bamboo shoots, red ant nests, tokay lizards, water convolvulus patches or field mice. Nothing, because of the drought and because of all the other foragers. From foraging I went back to trying the black market, and from the black market I went back to foraging. I tried everything, many times over. There was no more food.

Huoy was seven months' pregnant when she felt a pain like a

menstrual cramp. It went away and then a few hours later she had another one. I gave her another obstetrical exam. It was just what I feared: a softening of the cervix, and the beginning of dilation.

"You're going into labor," I told her.

Huoy looked at me with her great round eyes, and she saw into my thoughts but said nothing. She turned her head to the wall. After a while I heard her whisper, "Help me, Mother. Please protect me."

Yes, please protect her, I thought. A premature birth. No intensive-care unit, no operating room. No food for Huoy or the child. And *chhlop* hanging around, looking for trouble.

Under the Khmer Rouge's puritanical rules, it was forbidden for a man to deliver his wife's baby. If I delivered it myself the neighbors would know and the *chhlop* would find out and that would be the end of me. Or if I did anything that suggested I was a doctor, that would be the end.

Luckily a midwife named Seng Orn lived in a village nearby. I knew her from Phnom Penh, where she had worked as a midwife at a hospital. Between Seng Orn and me was friendship and respect.

If the birth was normal, Seng Orn and I could handle it easily. If there were complications, maybe we could handle it but maybe not. For one thing, I didn't have surgical instruments, antibiotics, anesthesia or any of the standard equipment of an operating theater. For another, I was out of practice in performing obstetrical surgery. For the last year I had been a fertilizer maker, and before that a house builder, and before that a rice farmer and canal digger. I still had my doctor's skills, but I was rusty. The worst problem, though, was the presence of the *chhlop*.

In the back of my mind there was one last option to try in a true emergency. Not the front-lines clinic for war slaves. Not the local hospital in Phum Phnom for soldiers and "old" people. There was only one place: the old government hospital in Battambang City. I had heard that a former professor of mine, one of the most eminent doctors in the nation, was teaching at the hospital. The Khmer Rouge were said to tolerate his brand of Western medicine. But I knew there was only a small chance that he was really in Battambang or that Huoy and I could get permission to go there.

Huoy's contractions were irregular and far apart, which is common for preliminary or "false" labor, before the first stage of true labor begins. I held her hand as the contractions took her, and looked around our tiny house. It was so primitive. The thatched roof, the dirt floor. No running water or electricity. I would have given anything to be back in Phnom Penh.

Between contractions, Huoy asked me to help her bathe. I walked her out the back door to the minicanal and washed her tenderly. We went inside again and she lay down on the bed, clutching her small blue kapok-filled pillow to her chest. I built a fire in the lean-to kitchen and made sure we had plenty of wood and lots of water. Later that afternoon, when the labor pains were forty minutes apart, I summoned a neighbor of ours, an old woman, to watch over Huoy. I went to get Seng Orn.

I ran to the village at the base of the mountain where Seng Orn lived. She said she was ready to go but needed permission. We went to see her village leader, who refused to let her go at first, and gave in only after prolonged pleading and arguments. When we got to Phum Ra, we had to report to Uncle Phan, my village leader. His adopted son Yoeung, the *chhlop*, eyed us closely as we left and then followed us out into the yard.

By the time we returned to the house, it was nearly sunset. I took my watch out and timed the labor pains, which were half an hour apart.

Cautiously, I looked out the door. In the twilight stood the figure of a boy, facing us as he leaned against a tree, smoking a cigarette.

Huoy lay on the bed, a small oil lamp beside her and another borrowed lamp at her feet. I massaged her limbs, smoothed her hair, wiped her face with a damp cloth.

When she went into contractions she looked at me and then her attention turned inward. Frowning, contorting her face, she clenched my arms very, very tightly, so tightly I thought my bones were going to break. The contractions peaked and then sometimes went on to a second or third peak before going down. Finally, as the pain eased, Huoy relaxed her hold on my arm. She became aware of her own tiredness, and then me sitting next to her. Her face was wet with perspiration, and I smoothed the wet strands of hair away from her forehead and tried to encourage her.

At eleven o'clock her water broke, the sac containing the amniotic fluid. That was normal. Seng Orn reported that the cervix was dilated to three centimeters.

The next interval was ten minutes.

Then fifteen minutes.

Then as the hands of my watch swept past eleven-thirty and the next contraction didn't come, and by eleven forty-five it still hadn't come, we knew there was trouble. The intervals should have gotten closer together, not farther apart.

I had one ampule of an antispasmodic medication. I drew it into a syringe and injected Huoy twice, first in the buttocks, then through the stomach wall into the fundus, or dome, a large, smooth muscle on top of the uterus, to help her relax and to make it easier for the cervix to widen so the child could descend from the womb. I had one capsule of vitamins, and I gave it to Huoy as a placebo—to make her feel as if she were getting medicine, to put her in a better frame of mind.

At midnight, her blood pressure was at the low end of the normal range. Her heartbeat was slower than before.

"Her cervix is still at three centimeters," Seng Orn told me quietly.

I scraped some kernels of corn and cooked them with sugar and fed them to Huoy to give her energy.

Her contractions were strong but irregular. Her cervix was like a bottleneck facing downward from her womb, and it did not widen. She had the pains, but her labor did not advance. One part of her was trying to expel the child and another part was fighting to retain it. A war was going on, with her body as the battlefield. When the contractions came, she felt no urge to push. It was too early for that, but she tried anyway. She wept. "It hurts, sweet, it hurts," she said. I stood by her head and pressed her belly downward, trying to force the baby along, while Seng Orn attended the birth canal. Seng Orn could see the top of the child's head but she didn't even have forceps. We lacked the most basic tools.

I rubbed Huoy's limbs again. She was wet from perspiration and from clenching. Even when she didn't have labor pains, she was crying.

The unthinkable was happening.

Seng Orn pulled me aside for a conference.

"Cesarean?" she whispered.

"Cannot!" I hissed. "The *chhlop*'s outside. Do you want to die too? We will all die! Huoy and the baby too! We have no instruments! We have no equipment!"

"Craniotomy?" she suggested.

I took a deep breath and shook my head, then took another deep breath. "No," I said. "Cannot."

"I'm hungry, sweet," Huoy said feebly from the bed, and I turned back toward her.

It was 4:00 A.M. I had saved one can of rice for this; it was all the food we had left. I cooked it in the kitchen and tried to feed it to Huoy, spoonful by spoonful, but she could not eat much of it. She was in too much pain.

At first light Hok came to the door. For all the coolness between us, he was still my brother and I trusted him. We went together to try against the odds to get Huoy on a train to Battambang.

We ran to the Khmer Rouge headquarters in Phum Phnom. To the center of enemy operations. And the cadre laughed at me. I was barefoot, in torn clothes, and they could not comprehend why I was so upset and why I frantically asked permission to do what few war slaves did—to ride the train to Battambang. They sent me to the boss of the railroad station, who said he didn't have the authority, and sent me back to Khmer Rouge headquarters. I ran both ways, panicking as the hours slipped past, my universe falling apart. They could not understand why I insisted my wife have a Cesarean section. They did not know what it was.

By the time I came back to the house, it was midmorning. The *chhlop* loitered nearby, pretending not to notice.

I had accomplished nothing.

I had failed.

Huoy lay sunken and tired on the bench. She clutched the kapok pillow to her chest. Her arms and legs were thin as sticks. Her belly was still round, the child still inside.

She spoke in weak voice.

"Why were you gone so long? I've been waiting for you. Do you have some medicine for me?"

"No more, sweet," I said. "I have no more."

"Do we have food to eat?" she asked.

"No more. We have no more food," I said. "You're going to be all right, sweet. Wait for a little while, and maybe I'll bring you to Battambang, to a big hospital for an operation."

"How long? I'm tired now. I'm very tired."

I took up the stethoscope and the blood-pressure cuff. Her blood pressure had dropped. Her heartbeat was slow and very, very feeble.

"Do we have anything to eat?" said Huoy. She spoke in a whisper, like a child.

"The neighbors are looking for food for you," I said.

"I need food! I need food. I need medicine. Sweet, save my life. Please save my life. I'm too tired. I just need a spoonful of rice."

Before she died, she asked me to cradle her. I swung her onto my lap, held her in my arms. She asked me to let her kiss me. I kissed her, and she kissed me. She looked up at me with her great round eyes, and they were full of sorrow. She didn't want to leave.

"Take care of yourself, sweet," she said to me.

Then the room was full of people.

30

GRIEF

PEOPLE SAY I went crazy after Huoy died. They are probably right.
I did not feel like myself, and there were long periods that I do not
even remember.

I remember crying and crying and pounding my fists on the floor
and beating my head against the wall, and the people in the house
restraining me.

I remember insisting that I help bathe Huoy's body and prepare
it for burial, a ritual normally performed by women. I took one of
my own blue shirts, one that she had particularly liked, and put it
on her next to her skin, to remind her of me. Then I took a pale green
silk blouse and a silk dress and put those on her, and then another
blouse and another dress on top of that, so she would have a change
of clothes in paradise; then put her everyday mismatched shower
sandals on her feet, because those were the only shoes she had; and
put the kapok pillow she liked so much on her chest for her to hold
on to; and tenderly brushed her hair; and put on her finger the gold
ring she used to wear. And when the old ladies in the house tried to
interfere, I wouldn't let them.

They tried to stop me from going to the burial because I was out
of my mind, but I followed my brother Hok and a neighbor as they
carried the body on a plank, with a sheet of corrugated metal from
the house wrapped around her as a coffin. I showed them where to
dig, beneath the big leaning *sdao* tree on the hillock in the middle of
the rice fields. And when they dug the hole deep in the ground and
put her in, I knelt and prayed to the gods and wept, while the onlookers
talked about how hard it was for a woman to cross the sea.

The next thing I remember, the sun was setting and I was back in the house shaving my head, and people were looking at me and shaking their heads in disapproval. In Cambodia, it is traditional for widows to shave their heads to demonstrate grief and respect when their husbands die. No man had ever shaved his head for his wife, but I had, and people told me I was crazy, and I shouted at them to mind their own business.

It is said, though I do not remember, that in the days following the burial I went to the common kitchen and asked the staff, "Where's my wife? She's supposed to be waiting for me here." The kitchen staff did not know what to say.

And when the kitchen served meals, as it did sometimes, now that it was too late, I took my bowl and went home and sat by the back door of the house without eating, watching the sun go down. I looked at the leaning *sdao* tree and the ruined pagoda on the mountainside beyond, and I thought about how I had been unable to save her.

A doctor, specially trained in delivering children, unable to save his own wife in childbirth.

There was an emergency procedure, a craniotomy, that I could have tried that might have saved Huoy, if I had done it early enough. But I didn't have the right equipment for a craniotomy. And even if it worked, it would have sacrificed the child.

If I had sacrificed the child I might have saved the mother. But even if I saved the mother, the *chhlop* would have found out about the operation, and the soldiers would have taken all of us away.

If I had had the right equipment, I would have done a Cesarean. That was the operation of choice. But I didn't have the equipment. I didn't have any equipment! Right? Right? I couldn't have saved her except in an operating room!

If I had just tried with a knife I could have gotten the child out. But it would have killed Huoy. No blood supply, no surgical tools, no antibiotics! She was so weak! I just couldn't do it. "All right!" I shouted, out loud. "It's my fault! I panicked! I admit it!"

And an echo rang accusingly, "My fault! My fault! My fault! My fault!"

I thought: I shouldn't be blaming myself like this. The greatest single cause of her death was malnutrition. Without food, her body weakened, and the hormones that start labor were released at the wrong time. But if I had used all my medical skills I wouldn't have to blame myself like this. Even if I tried and failed it would have been better than this. Even if I tried and they caught me.

Her whispered words came back to me, like a message from the wind: *"Why were you gone so long? I've been waiting for you."*

She waited for me to come back before allowing herself to die. And she didn't even blame me for failing her.

The wind brought me her last words, again and again: *"Take care of yourself, sweet."*

She had taken care of me when I was sick. She had saved my life. But when it was my turn to save her, I failed.

When the sun set I walked along the canal and over the dikes of the rice fields to the hillock and knelt at the foot of the grave. I offered her the bowl, which was still full, and told her to eat first, and I put the bowl down and began to pray.

I prayed to the gods. "Just let her go to paradise. If my wife has done anything wrong, send me to hell in her place. If she has ever sinned, I will take the responsibility. Release her. Let her go to paradise. And allow us to be together in our next lives."

In the fading light the landscape turned to shadows, all but the white ruins of the temple on the hillside above. "Huoy, if I survive, I am going to leave Cambodia. I have to get out, but I will come back to you one day. I will have a proper ceremony for you, with many, many monks presiding, and I will build a *stupa* for you next to the temple and put your remains in it, to honor you.

"I ask your forgiveness. If I did something wrong, don't be angry at me, sweet. We will be together in the next life. The next life won't be short like this one. We will live a long, long time together, and we will be a happy old couple."

I prayed to the soul of our unborn child, to this little girl or boy whom we had hoped so much to bring into the world. "In this life you were unlucky, because you never had the chance to see your mother's face. You never had a chance to drink your mother's milk. But you were lucky not to see the suffering. You were lucky, because now you can see your mother. In the next life we will all have a chance to be together again. In the next life there won't be so much suffering, and you will grow up to be healthy and strong."

To Huoy's mother I prayed, "Ma, live in paradise with Huoy and the child. Take care of them, and let them take care of you. And watch over me. I miss you, Ma."

I prayed to my father, and to my own mother, and then to Huoy again. I ate the rice, and before leaving I said, "Sweet, I'm going home. I'll see you again tomorrow."

People saw me going out to the grave every evening with food and they said I was crazy. I do not say they are wrong, just that they hadn't been through what I had. No couple had been as close as Huoy and me. There was a night when I got back home from praying and lay down to sleep, and when I woke up someone was knocking on the door. Huoy's voice was calling to me. I opened the door and she was there, dressed in white, with a white veil.

"Please come often to visit me," she said.

She turned away from me and began to walk along the canal. It was still dark outside, but I could see her. I called after her to wait, wait, but although I followed her and she was walking very slowly, it was impossible to keep up with her. As she walked, the ends of her long veil floated in the air and bounced gracefully, like wings lifting her up and carrying her along. I ran after her, but she disappeared from sight.

Huoy had died on June 2, 1978. Not long after that there were unmistakable signs that the regime was breaking up.

By June the leaders of villages near us were being purged. Their positions were taken by Khmer Rouge from eastern Cambodia. Uncle Phan, the leader of Phum Ra, ran away before it could happen to him. We never saw him again. His wife was demoted to the rank of ordinary laborer, and then Pen Tip pointed her out and the soldiers took her into the woods.

In late June, when the common kitchen reopened for a day, I showed up to eat and noticed Chev and Uncle Seng sitting at a table by themselves. Chev, the smiler, was noticeably subdued. So was Uncle Seng. They too had been replaced by men from eastern Cambodia and assigned to the front lines as workers. It was a long step down for Chev, formerly the head of my cooperative, the man who had sent me to prison twice and ordered my father and brother killed.

Our new village leader was named Mao. Like Chev, he was a

smiler, dangerous and insincere. "Comrade Chev and Comrade Seng," Mao told them in a soothing voice, "wait here for a while. We want you to go to a meeting."

From the fear on their faces Chev and Seng knew who they were going to be meeting with. Soldiers watched their every move, and there was no chance for them to escape.

The following day the common kitchen was closed again and I roamed far from the village to search for food. Tha, my twelve-year-old stealing partner, went with me.

We were walking through the dry stubble of a rice field when a soldier saw us and yelled for us to stop. He asked us what we were doing and I told him that we were looking for wild foods. "You must go this way," he said, pointing his hand toward a path through the woods. In his other hand he was holding a long, curved knife.

We walked down the path, wondering at the reason for the order, when suddenly we found the answer. Ahead of us, in a clearing, was a pit filled with slowly burning rice husks.

Chev hung over the pit with his wrists tied to a tree branch above. Rice husks covered him to his chest, but we could see where he had been stabbed and slashed by the knife.

We stopped. Chev was still alive. He groaned, turned his head and his eyes bored into mine. He recognized me. I looked back at him steadily for a long moment, without saying anything. I thought, Chev, you are dying but I have survived. Then the boy asked me to come along and I turned my back on Chev, leaving him to his appointment with the King of Death.

We didn't see Uncle Seng, but we knew that his fate was the same as Chev's. He had been punished for being part of a failing regime.

It was *kama*. Men aren't always able to take revenge, but the gods are. The gods understand justice. They had punished Chev for killing, and they had punished Uncle Seng for not stopping the killing. And they had sent me walking along the forest path to be a witness.

Well, Pen Tip, I thought, you tried your best to kill me. But some day *kama* will catch up to you too. Because good comes to those who do good, and bad comes to those who do evil.

The boy and I got out in the rice fields again. People were everywhere, bending over, picking up grains of rice. We joined them, scanning the hard, reddish ground.

———

One day I came back from foraging in my half-crazed state and found the house ransacked. I knew who had done it. Mao's wife, corrupt and greedy, was looking for Huoy's jewelry. I went to Mao's house. My medical instruments and Huoy's papers and some of my papers were there on the table. He asked me if I was a doctor. I told him no. And I do not even know why I told him no, whether it was habit, or whether I was no longer a doctor in my own mind. I thought, Maybe I should have told him yes, so he could kill me.

None of my identification cards he had found listed me as a doctor. He hadn't found anything valuable of Huoy's either. Some items of clothing, her birth certificate, her diplomas, other pieces of paper. Then my mind cleared and I saw what I wanted, a large folding ID card from Huoy's days as a teacher. In one corner was a small black-and-white photograph of her, taken in 1973 in a period when she had worn her hair short.

"You can have everything there," I told Mao. "I don't mind that you take it from me. But just let me have that photograph of my wife."

He looked at the ID card, which was lying flattened on the table. It was the size of a piece of notepaper, but with two vertical creases, and Huoy's photo on an outside corner.

He took Huoy's past in his hands, ripped it down the crease, and handed the photograph to me. As if he needed to keep the rest.

31

RETREAT

WHEN THE DROUGHT ended and the rains began, the Khmer Rouge got us to replant the common gardens and the rice fields. Soon there was food to eat again. But for me, there was no satisfaction, only bitterness. There was food, but it was too late for Huoy.

I let my whiskers grow and didn't mend the rips in my clothing. People told me I looked old, like a man of fifty.

In the daytime I worked on the fertilizer crew again, but without energy. If the soldiers had taken me away I would have thanked them, for making my reunion with my wife that much sooner. At night, after visiting Huoy's grave, I became a thief. I stole compulsively, like a gambler, to feel alive.

With my stealing partner, Tha, I led gangs of hungry men to the common garden on the mountain. We raped the garden, taking whatever we wanted, ready to fight any guards who showed. We harvested rice fields as they ripened, using our bare hands and feet. I built up a huge supply of rice, wrapping it carefully, storing it under the manure pile in the fertilizer shed. I gave food to Tha, who supported his family; to Sangam, my colleague in the fertilizer shed; to a distant cousin named Ngor Balam, whom I had met just recently; to my brother Hok, who had located my brother Pheng Huor's three children and taken them in; and to others.

Still, stealing food wasn't enough. To test my skills and to test my fate, I stole a small, hand-powered rice mill from its shed during the evening political meeting, while Mao was giving a speech. With the mill, I could remove the husks from paddy rice many times faster than before. But I still wasn't satisfied. I resented any restrictions. I wanted to eat whenever I was hungry. So I put rice and water in my field cooking pot, put the lid on and made a hole for it in the ground before building a fire on top. I squatted in front of the fire, pretending to warm my hands, when Mao came by the fertilizer shed on an inspection tour. He squatted next to me and warmed his hands while we talked about the proper mixtures of animal dung and hillock earth. When he left, I pulled the fire apart and took the pot out. The rice was cooked perfectly.

As I got bolder, I also got careless. During a political meeting I was accused of having a fishnet and failing to contribute the fish to the common kitchen. The truth was that I did have a fishnet, though it was safely hidden. I also had a good idea who was behind the accusation.

My reply was reckless. I said if an eyewitness came forward and he could prove I had a fishnet, I would gladly surrender my life to Angka. If no eyewitness came forward, I didn't want to hear any more about the matter. And I slammed my fist on the ground for emphasis.

Even as I slammed my fist I knew I had gone too far. Without Huoy to tell me to hide my emotions, my anger was getting the better of me. Luckily for me, Mao let me off with a lecture. He said that displays of anger were capitalist and individualist. He told me to tame myself and show obedience to Angka. I apologized meekly.

Soon after that my hidden accuser, Pen Tip, called me to his house. I was better prepared this time, my anger cool and contained.

Pen Tip had done well by the change in village leadership. He had not only helped target Uncle Phan's wife for execution but had become Mao's unofficial right-hand man, and this brought him even more power than ever. If the stories were true, a woman from the village complained to Pen Tip for sending her to the front lines while he lived comfortably in the village. The next night Pen Tip was one of the men who gang-raped her and then killed her. Whether this had actually happened I cannot say, since I was not there. But the story fit his character.

When I showed up he was sitting on a split-bamboo bench and swinging his legs, like a child. He raised and lowered his eyebrows. His glance slid past me to one side and then the other. He looked at the floor and at the ceiling but never directly at me.

Pen Tip said he knew I was a doctor and hoped I wouldn't get in any trouble. I asked him calmly what he was trying to do to me now.

"Uh, last night Angka sent two *chhlop* to your house," he said. "They saw you take a lot of rice and hide it in a plastic bag in your garden. Did you do this, or not? If you did, just give the rice back and Angka will forgive and forget. But if you say you didn't, ah, Angka will investigate and you will be responsible. But since you are my friend, I wanted to tell you first. I wanted to, uh, warn you."

I thought quickly. It was the same as the incident with the fishnet: He was having me watched, but his watchers were not thorough. The night before, I had filled a large bag with freshly milled rice, but I buried it in my usual place, below the fertilizer pile, rather than in my garden. What could I do? Mao lived next door. I needed to get rid of Pen Tip, but this was not the time or the place.

It was hot in the house. Pen Tip swung his legs from the bench, waiting.

"I'm sorry," I said sarcastically. "If Angka sent two *chhlop* last night and they saw me hide rice in my garden, why wasn't I arrested? Why wasn't I taken away? Because I didn't hide any rice. That's why. And I'm sorry your people didn't do a good job for you, Pen Tip. It must be hard to find reliable *chhlop*. I sympathize."

Pen Tip grew angry. As I left the house he told me that Angka would send someone to check on me.

He didn't waste any time. That afternoon, when I was at the fertilizer shed, his wife walked to my house carrying a woven plastic rice bag and buried it in my garden. Fortunately, one of my neighbors saw her and ran to tell me. It was no use asking Mao for justice, because Pen Tip was his protégé, so I ran to Khmer Rouge headquarters in Phum Phnom. This time they listened to me. They understood false evidence and purges, since this was something they faced themselves. A cadre came to my house, dug up the rice and called Pen Tip and his wife in for questioning. It was all very polite on the surface and typically Cambodian. Nobody lost their tempers, everybody kept face and nothing was decided.

Pen Tip and I would have gone on making moves and counter-moves until one of us was killed. But by late 1978 our struggle began to look small and petty compared to other events on the horizon, and we put a temporary halt to it.

The first clue that something was happening came from Comrade Ik, the old man on horseback. He called a meeting in December while the harvest was still in progress. Several hundred of us sat on a dirt floor to listen to him while his horse stood under a nearby tree.

The old man told us that we still had to struggle to accomplish Angka's goals. We were to plant and harvest two or three crops of rice a year. He said nothing at all about the realities—that there had never been a second or third crop, that most of the first crop had been taken from us, that only token work continued on the dam project. Comrade Ik seldom admitted the regime's failings. So it came as a complete surprise when he added at the end of his speech:

"Recently, our enemies have dared attack us on our borders. We are not worried about the fighting. We have nothing to fear. We have already defeated the American imperialists, and this time the enemy is small in comparison. What is important to remember is that we must fight on all battlefields. Not just the military battlefields, but also the battlefields of the rice paddies and the canals. We must continue to work. Our soldiers will guard the border, don't worry. They will protect us. But if you see enemies coming here, let Angka know. And if the enemy says something to you, don't believe it. You must believe only Angka."

The old man hit his fist on his skinny chest and yelled, "Long live the Kampuchean revolution!" We rose to our feet and echoed each phrase three times. "Long live the great solidarity!" and then "Long live the revolutionary military forces!" Tears of joy ran down the faces of men around me, and it had nothing to do with the slogans. What the old man hinted at we had guessed. The "enemy" was invading. It could have been any enemy and it could have been any border, but for us war slaves there was only one conclusion. The Khmer Serei— the Free Khmers or freedom fighters—had finally launched their attack from their sanctuaries along the Thai border.

I was happy for the news. I could feel the change in my body— a stirring of hope, a strengthening. Now I had something to live for. I thought: Oh Huoy, if you had only lived, we would have a chance to see freedom together.

About a week later Sangam and I were pulling an oxcart loaded with fertilizer out to the fields when we heard the dull noise of faraway explosions. We looked up. Two jets tore across the sky like silver darts, just above the horizon. They were the first planes of any kind we had seen for years.

The jets traveled rapidly to the east. Behind them, columns of smoke rose from the bombs they had dropped. We stood there admiring the sight.

"They should hurry up and come for us," Sangam remarked.

"The sooner the better," I said.

The invaders, however, did not hurry. We did not see any more planes, and the Khmer Rouge did not tell us any more news.

In early January 1979 a freight train pulled into the Phnom Tippeday station from Phnom Penh. In its boxcars and on its roofs sat Khmer Rouge soldiers with bandages and casts and crutches. The wounded soldiers set up camp and hobbled around, cooking over fires. There were angry looks and loud arguments between them and the soldiers stationed near our village.

A few days later, long, single-file lines of civilians began to arrive from the south, from a roundabout route to Phnom Penh, led by cadre driving massive roofed oxcarts. The civilians were healthier and better dressed than we were. Like the wounded soldiers, they were part of a disciplined retreat. They had plenty of food: cloth tubes filled with rice hanging around their necks like thick necklaces; live chickens; bags of dried, salted fish; sacks of rice on the oxcarts. The oxcarts parked along the railroad tracks, and soon the evening air was filled with the smoke of hundreds of campfires.

Both the civilians and the wounded soldiers were under orders not to talk to us "new" people. They seemed to be afraid. Every day some of them were tied up and led away at gunpoint, never to return. An amputee on crutches was led away for the crime of "failing to protect the fatherland."

Paranoia was everywhere. In our village, day or night, those who looked too pleased were taken away. One wrong word, one joyful glance, and Mao ordered executions of entire families. The soldiers were in a frenzy. To them it was our fault that the "enemy" was coming.

It was a time to be especially careful. Pulling the oxcart along paths where we had gone many times before, Sangam and I came to a hillock piled high with corpses. The bodies were jumbled together in the awkward postures of death, arms or legs stiffly raised in rigor mortis. The victims had been killed by blows to the back of the head. Their flesh had turned black from the heat, and their bodies had swollen so much it burst their clothes. The smell was awful. Vultures plucked at them. A few days later we saw another mass-execution site, hundreds of bodies piled in a pit in the forest.

I went to the leaning *sdao* tree and prayed to Huoy for protection. I began sleeping near her grave, and then in the fertilizer shed, and in a different place each night, afraid of Mao, afraid of Pen Tip. I stopped stealing. The night wasn't safe for stealing anymore.

I packed everything needed for a quick getaway and stored it under the manure pile. I told Sangam and my brother Hok and Ngor Balam to get ready if they wanted to go with me. Balam was a tall, older man, formerly an airlines executive in Phnom Penh. He was only distantly related to me on my father's side, but we were of the same clan and trusted each other. We agreed to go together to the Thai border, to meet up with the Khmer Serei.

Before we could leave another wave of newcomers arrived. This time they did not come from the east, like the first wave, or from the south, like the second, but from the northwest, from villages outside Battambang City. They too walked in long, single-file lines, carrying their possessions in knapsacks and on shoulderboards, some of the women with baskets on their heads. They were better clothed than we were. They did not dare talk to us. The third wave converged on the first two waves and briefly overlapped and then separated as the newer evacuees retreated toward the Cardamom Mountains.

We had lived in the Phnom Tippeday area for more than three years. It had been our universe, and our jail. Now we saw it as others did, as a patch of rather unimportant territory in the far-ranging maneuvers of war. We guessed that the "enemy" was approaching on two fronts, from the east, the direction of Phnom Penh, and from the northwest, near Battambang City.

Mao disappeared, taking with him all the oxen and water buffalo, sacks of rice and salt, supplies of dried fish and other food from the common kitchen, all the kitchen utensils, his family and his personal possessions. In his absence no one gave orders in the village. I thought it was time for us to leave, but Balam and Hok persuaded me to wait.

Mao reappeared, and for a few days more we had meals in the common kitchen. We went out into the fields to harvest the rice, and we went to political meetings at night. We listened to the same old tired speeches about "launching an offensive" against the forces of nature and "struggling to achieve true independence-sovereignty." Like a record player playing the same song over and over. We listened quietly, because we were afraid, and planned our escapes.

Mao and the other Khmer Rouge leaders left again, secretly, at night. Pen Tip proclaimed himself temporarily in charge. He told everyone in the village it was time to evacuate. And the people obeyed. They packed their possessions on shoulderboards and baskets and homemade knapsacks, but there was much grumbling among them.

I packed all my possessions, including the medical textbooks that had been hidden for years. Sangam, Hok and Balam, plus their wives and children and me, fourteen of us in all, tried to walk northwest toward Battambang City, but soldiers blocked our way. We turned around and trudged after the rest of the villagers.

By this time the whole Phnom Tippeday region was on the move. Several villages camped together in the rice fields, guarded by soldiers. Far to the southwest, beyond the uncompleted dam, the first rumblings of artillery could be heard. In the following days the sounds of artillery came from the south and the east, and then mostly from the east. Judging from the direction, the heaviest fighting was somewhere near the town of Muong, where National Route 5 and the railway converged. We heard no small-arms fire, which meant that the fighting wasn't yet nearby.

We waited ten days, and then the "enemy" attacked from the northwest.

When the chattering of automatic rifles and machine guns broke out, I was with my group. Artillery shells landed and exploded on the hillocks and in the rice fields to either side, and smoke and dust spewed up where they landed. We picked up our luggage and ran with a strength we never knew we had. Everyone around us was running. Trees fell, and water buffalo stampeded with their eyes bulging and the whites showing around their irises. Dust filled the air, there was a mad tinkling of ox bells, and those with oxcarts stood up like charioteers, shouting at their oxen and whipping them to make them go faster.

We poured toward the railroad tracks, but Khmer Rouge in their black uniforms sprinted toward the jungles, outrunning all of us. It was almost enough to make me stop and laugh to see them run away so fast, after all their boasts about what good soldiers they were.

When the shooting finally stopped, we were in an area called Boeung Reaing, where Huoy and I had dug canals on the front lines. There were thousands of "new" people around us, confused and leaderless. We didn't know where the Khmer Rouge were. We were afraid to move, afraid to take the initiative. So we stayed where we were, hoping that the freedom fighters would come to us.

While waiting, we spread out into the rice fields, which lay unharvested and inviting in all directions. The skies were clear and hot. Everywhere, within an hour, men, women and children were harvesting rice. We threshed it with our bare feet, milled it with mortar and pestle or with sticks in holes in the ground. The shooting and the stampede had vanished from our minds. Food was our first priority, safety our second. The rich rice of Battambang was everywhere for the taking. Nobody could punish us for taking rice. There was rice for all.

And after we filled our bellies and stored rice for future days, we sharpened our hatchets and knives and started looking at the Khmer Rouge who had reappeared, while muttering among ourselves. The Khmer Rouge knew our minds, and were afraid, and joined their comrades in large groups.

I looked around and saw Pen Tip. He had an oxcart, with large spoked wheels and a narrow high-sided bed piled with bags and possessions. Pulling the cart were two oxen. The cart and the ox belonged to the community, but Pen Tip had appropriated them for himself. Few others had oxen, or carts, or anything they could not carry themselves.

Pen Tip wore new black clothing, the same as the soldiers. He wore his krama in classic Khmer Rouge style, like a scarf, with the two ends hanging down on his chest. He was talking to his brothers-in-law, who stayed at his side to protect him, and rolling his cigarette around in the fingers of one hand. He blinked his eyes, looked this way and that. His facial features were constantly in motion.

The time had come to deal with Pen Tip, I said, and Sangam ran his thumb along the blade of his hatchet and agreed. He was a strong old man, and it was comforting to have him on my side.

But before I could make my move, the Khmer Rouge leaders returned and issued an order. They told it to people like Pen Tip, and Pen Tip relayed it to us. He said we were supposed to go to a village far off to the east, in the forest. I had never even heard of the place, but the crowd, accustomed to obeying orders, lifted its luggage and began its trudge. The opportunity for revenge had been lost. Dust rose from the passage of feet and oxen. The road became a twisting, braided maze of paths. As the sun sunk behind us, I brought my group to a halt. Pen Tip was nowhere in sight. I had no intention of following his orders. I told the group that we were going to cut north, toward the railroad. They agreed.

We set out on our new course. Before long, someone from Phum Ra came up and told me that he had seen Pen Tip split off and go northwest.

I smiled grimly. I had expected something like that from him. Pen Tip wanted to escape from the Khmer Rouge too. He knew they were a losing cause. It was time for him to change allegiances and collaborate with the Khmer Serei instead. But he also knew that he could not head directly toward the liberation forces without being noticed. So he had issued the orders to the rest of us and then tried to lose himself in the crowd.

We walked toward the railroad, arriving at a village of houses on stilts set among shade trees and fruit trees.

Thousands of the uprooted had come to the village before us. It was not a sanctuary so much as a no-man's-land, with no soldiers around. We decided to stay there too.

While we waited, hoping the war would pass us by, there were rice fields to forage. Every day we went out to the fields and harvested as much as we wanted. There was a big river too, and we went there to bathe. We did not yet have our freedom, but we didn't move for six or seven days, because here we could satisfy even more basic needs. For water and rice.

Then the liberation army pushed on farther and the Khmer Rouge retreated, and Pen Tip showed up with them, in his oxcart. Blinking nervously and looking from side to side, Pen Tip told everyone from Phum Ra to move on to the Khmer Rouge camp a short distance away. He spotted me in the crowd and shouted, "Samnang, you move on to the military camp. Our leaders are waiting there."

"Pen Tip, you go first," I said sarcastically, and spat on the ground.

His eyebrows raised. He pointed in the direction of the Khmer Rouge camp. "The leaders are waiting. The front lines are retreating. Uh, you have to move. Angka will provide rice over there."

My hand went to my waist, but the hatchet I usually kept in my waistband wasn't there. I had left it with my luggage.

"You go first," I repeated. "Nobody trusts you, Pen Tip. Nobody believes what you're saying. Before, you told people who had no oxcarts, who carried all their belongings on shoulderboards, to go someplace very far away. But you didn't go there yourself. You went in a different direction, and you had an oxcart to carry your luggage."

Dozens of people from Phum Ra had clustered around to watch. They all understood what was happening, which was indirect and ritualized and very Cambodian. This was a declaration of war, like slapping someone with gloves to provoke a duel. I was "breaking his face."

Pen Tip looked worried and glanced away. "You, uh, you don't have to talk that way. Um, I'm not that kind of person." He twisted the bamboo-leaf cigarette in his fingertips. "No, you don't have to talk that way, Samnang. Words like that are for temple boys."

"Because you are a temple boy. You never told people the truth, or treated them correctly. You always lie to innocent people."

Pen Tip said, "If you don't want to go, you are responsible for yourself. Angka told me to tell you to go. I'm just trying to help you by passing on the information."

I stared at him but he wouldn't meet my eyes.

Then he drove away.

When the adrenaline finally drained and I calmed down, I still felt good. I had acted properly. In Cambodian society, which is inhibited and indirect, you must publicly insult someone first before moving on to the next phase. Only in this way can you, the accuser, keep face yourself. To attack someone physically without establishing the basis for the fight is low-class and unethical, like the behavior of the Khmer Rouge.

Anyway, I thought, we will have the showdown soon enough. I can use my hatchet then, to defend myself or to attack. Pen Tip is small and he will be easy to defeat.

But after I bathed in the river and lay down and thought about it some more, I realized my mistake. What was wrong with me? How could I have made such an error? Pen Tip wouldn't give me the pleasure of a one-on-one duel. Not when he had re-established himself with the Khmer Rouge. He would get soldiers to take me away.

I told my group to pack quickly. We would leave as soon as it got dark, before Pen Tip could make his move.

When the last light left the sky we waded across the river, making several trips until we had all the baggage and all the children on the far side. We walked on. Soon we came to the railroad tracks, dimly reflecting the starlight. We camped beyond the tracks on a hillock. I lay awake, thinking about Pen Tip, gripping my hatchet.

At dawn the others went off into the rice fields to build up our supplies while I made a reconnaissance. I looked all around for Khmer Rouge and the liberation soldiers, but I saw nothing and heard nothing.

No sounds of artillery. No trains coming along the tracks. No planes in the empty blue skies.

It was quiet around us. I didn't like it. The previous day there had been gunfire to the east, the north and the west, none of it nearby.

Sangam and his wife decided to go east toward Phnom Penh, along the railroad tracks. I decided to take my group north to National Route 5, and from there westward toward Thailand. We wished each other luck and parted on excellent terms. Sangam had been an honest, reliable friend.

Now our group was down to twelve, all of us related. I was the leader. Ngor Balam and his wife had two children and a nephew. Hok and his wife had an infant daughter, whom they carried, plus the three children of my late brother Pheng Huor—two girls, named Im and Ngim, and the little boy, Chy Kveng. All of the children in the group were sturdy and well behaved. Even Chy Kveng could walk all day without being carried. But having so many children made us vulnerable and slow.

We walked along oxcart paths, through rice fields and jungle, choosing the paths that led in the right direction. Every hour or so I checked our bearings by climbing trees. From the treetops, the Phnom Tippeday ridge was in sight, the ruined wat and the stupa together making one white dot in the distance.

Because of the children and our frequent stops to gather food, we made slow progress. I was nervous and alert, going out on frequent, short reconnaissance trips and then returning. When we met other civilians we asked them if they had seen soldiers, but they all said no.

Soft, hot dust covered our feet and ankles as we walked. We came to a canal, bathed in it, kept going and came to a deserted village. Bananas and green mangoes hung invitingly in the trees, and yams grew in the gardens. We helped ourselves. Later that day we came to another deserted village, with papaya and jackfruit trees, and ate again. The next day we saw a pig rooting for yams in a field. We three men in the group chased after the pig and caught it. When we cooked it, other travelers appeared, and we shared it with them gladly. Everyone ate his fill and sat around, talking and relaxing.

With all the good food and the companionship I began to feel better.

We could eat what we wanted and when we wanted.

We could say whatever we chose.

We were free to criticize, to speak out, to show anger. We didn't have to be silent if someone else did something stupid or committed an injustice.

The long darkness was almost over.

As we walked through the forest toward the highway, I began to sing.

32

LIBERATION

WE MADE IT to National Route 5, only to find the Khmer Rouge still in control. They told us we couldn't walk toward Battambang. Discouraged, we began walking eastward, toward Phnom Penh. We walked slowly, with the strange sensation of asphalt pavement under our feet. The road was crowded and the soldiers didn't bother us.

The sounds of battle came from virtually all directions, but far away.

It was early March 1979. One day passed, and then the next and the next. We stayed on the lookout for opportunities, but there were none. We were patient and careful. As an old Cambodian saying puts it, the last wave sinks the boat. There was no sense in being careless when freedom was so near.

We walked as slowly as possible, making less than a mile a day, passed by people hurrying back to Phnom Penh. Our group was not conspicuous or in any way remarkable. We were just another ragged bunch of refugees, the men with luggage bobbing up and down on their shoulderboards, the women carrying baskets on their heads, the children staying close for protection.

We didn't walk at night, even to step off the road to relieve ourselves. On either side of the road were punji pits with sharpened bamboo stakes at the bottom. There were also mines, in holes next to the road and near the bridges. The rain had washed the layer of dirt from the metal detonating buttons, which were about the size of kneecaps, so most of the mines were visible. Even so, an ox stepped on a mine, killing several people we had known from Phum Ra and wounding others.

West of Muong we were caught in a storm, with lightning and thunder and drenching rain. Other travelers crowded into a hut near the highway, but not us. We just sat on the road, without shelter, all night long. After four years under the Khmer Rouge, being cold and wet didn't bother us much. We were toughened by what we had lived through.

We passed some soldiers digging trenches and creating barricades with concertina wire, and then we got to the town of Muong, where the highway and the railway met. Tens of thousands of civilians were there ahead of us. The railway station and a row of Chinese merchants' shophouses were still intact. Everything else was in ruins. Behind the railroad station were rusted boxcars with their wooden sides ripped out for use as firewood. Automobiles lay in heaps, their engines removed, vines growing up through the cavities. Houses had been turned to rubble. Part of the wat was destroyed, and there were no Buddha statues in it. The bridge over the river was a mass of twisted metal. A temporary wooden bridge had been erected beside it for foot traffic.

We wanted to stay in Muong, but the next day the Khmer Rouge pushed us on, steadily retreating. Our group was the last to leave the town, and the slowest in walking.

East of Muong, the Khmer Rouge ordered all civilians to turn off National Route 5 onto a dirt road leading toward the Cardamom Mountains. For military purposes they wanted to control the population, but they had no interest in us except for that. They didn't give us any food or water. There was no water anywhere. The weather was hot. A few weaker people died of dehydration. The desperate put their lips to the ground and drank, where urine had filled up the footprints of oxen and water buffalo.

It was on this dirt road that the revenge killings began. First the Khmer Rouge called a mass meeting. They fired their mortars at the civilians who showed up for it, killing hundreds. They had always looked down on "new" people. They blamed us for the invasion, just as they blamed us for all their failings.

Then the people retaliated. We saw only the aftermath, the bodies of a Khmer Rouge and his pregnant wife and his children, lying in bloody pieces on the forest floor. And the next day another Khmer Rouge body, and the day after that another. It was unsafe for the Khmer Rouge to travel, except in large numbers.

My family was running low on food. A man who was camping near us told me about an underground rice warehouse on the other side of National Route 5. He described how he had managed to reach the site, find rice and return. I discussed going to the rice warehouse with Hok and Balam. They didn't want to take the risk. I did. And at first light on April 17, 1979, I set out on another stage of my journey.

About eighty men and women joined together to go to the warehouse. A few of the men had been there before and acted as our guides. We walked through jungle, waded across canals, followed dirt roads and oxcart paths. Several times we passed massacre sites, where Khmer Rouge had slaughtered civilians or civilians had killed Khmer Rouge.

Around 8:00 A.M. we got to National Route 5. It was deserted, a long stretch of paved road with no one in sight. The rumble of artillery fire came from far away, like distant thunder. We crossed the highway and re-entered the jungle.

I carried only essentials: a bamboo shoulderboard with two empty rice bags lashed to it; my metal field cooking pot, filled with rice, hanging from my belt; and my hatchet, which fit snugly against my waist, secured by my krama. I was barefoot, in torn trousers and a torn shirt. Hidden from sight in my waistband were my Zippo lighter, my Swiss calendar watch and a few pieces of gold.

We came to a large rice field that cut into the jungle like a bay. The far end of the rice field opened up onto an even larger area of rice fields the likes of which I had seldom seen: utterly flat, stretching out for mile after mile, almost without hillocks. I sensed we were near the rice warehouse. Somewhere beyond, perhaps ten or fifteen miles, lay the great inland lake Tonle Sap.

The bottoms of the paddies were covered with water. We left the forest and began walking on top of the dikes. We were about a hundred yards from the trees when the firing broke out, from the jungle to our right. A few were hit and crumpled to the ground before they could react. The rest of us dove for the shelter of the earthen dikes, which were about two feet high and a foot or more thick—thick enough, I hoped, to stop bullets from AK-47s. Goddamn Khmer

Rouge! Opening fire on unarmed civilians who had just gone out to find food.

Then, from the jungle on the left side, came voices. "Yo dee! Yo dee! Yo dee!"

I didn't know what "yo dee" meant. I had never heard the words before.

I lifted my head for a second and looked where the voices were coming from. Uniformed men were running toward us into the rice field, pausing to crouch and fire when they reached the safety of a dike. They waved their arms, signaling us to come toward them. They fired at the Khmer Rouge, but not at us.

"Yo! Yo dee! Yo dee!"

Bullets whizzed by, making little fountains of mud and water when they struck the paddies. I stayed alongside a dike and dragged myself forward with my forearms, pulling my shoulderboard alongside. My body was half underwater. In front, all I could see was water and mud and the feet of the next person worming his way ahead.

The liberators were ahead of us and to the left. The dikes between lay on the diagonal, high enough to provide cover most of the distance except when crossing their tops, which were exposed to fire. A man ahead of me crawled up one side of a dike and was hit. He stayed where he was, moaning, blood spurting from his legs. I scrambled up one side of the dike, rolled down the other, unhurt, and kept on going. No one helped the wounded man.

"Yo dee!"

The freedom fighter was just ahead at the corner of two dikes, alternately firing his rifle and beckoning for us to come. Between him and me was the length of one rice paddy. I pulled myself along in the shadow of the dike; an eel couldn't have gotten any lower in the mud. Then it was up and over the dike next to him.

I lay directly behind him in the mud and water, as close to the dike as possible, panting from the exertion.

Gradually, my breathing eased.

I was safe.

A little piece of rice straw floated on the water, a few inches in front of me.

I turned to look at the soldier. He was crouching at the intersection of the dikes in classic military posture, his left arm supporting the rifle, firing and waving people on with his right. He wore a light green uniform and a green plantation-style helmet. He turned toward me for a moment. He was a young man with a light bone structure and pale yellow skin and slanting eyes. There was a red star on the front of his helmet.

He was Vietnamese.

What were the Vietnamese doing here?

Everybody knew the Khmer Serei were coming. We knew all about the Khmer Serei. In Tam, an honest general who had lost a crooked election to Lon Nol in the early 1970s, was their leader. Nobody said anything about the Vietnamese.

Even the Khmer Rouge hadn't mentioned the Vietnamese. They only talked about the "enemy."

Why were Vietnamese communists shooting at their fellow communists, the Khmer Rouge?

Why weren't they shooting at me?

"Yo dee!" the young soldier yelled again. "Yo. Yo dee!" He removed the banana-shaped ammunition clip in his AK-47, changed it for a new one, aimed, squeezed out a burst. The bullet casings ejected to the right and splattered into the water.

As he finished the burst, a Cambodian civilian in rags came rolling over the dike behind him, his legs a bloody red. He fell on top of me, wiggled to an empty spot farther down the dike and lay there, groaning.

I hugged the dike.

Slowly, gradually, the firing tapered off. In the paddy next to ours another Vietnamese soldier advanced cautiously, ducked behind a dike, advanced again.

The shooting had stopped.

"Dee," said the soldier next to me, motioning to the dozen of us Cambodians in the paddy. He crawled off toward the forest and we crawled after him, except for the man with the leg wounds, who had died. The soldier rolled over a dike and we followed his example, except for the women among us, who climbed over awkwardly on their hands and knees.

After crawling and rolling the length of several more dikes we were out of the line of fire. We stood up and walked rapidly behind the far side of a hillock. There, safe from bullets, a man with dark skin and wide features—a Cambodian—waited for us. He was holding an AK-47 but wore ordinary civilian clothes.

He told us in Khmer, "We have come to liberate you. Don't worry. Don't be afraid."

More survivors from my foraging group, forty to fifty in all, arrived behind the hillock, escorted by Vietnamese. Some of them asked if we could go back into the field to help wounded relatives, but the Cambodian liberation soldier said no. "The Khmer Rouge are still in the forest beyond. Leave it to our Vietnamese friends to get your relatives."

More Cambodian liberation soldiers appeared from the safety of the jungle nearby. They had not engaged in any fighting. More Vietnamese returned wet and muddy from the battle in the rice field. The Vietnamese were tense and angry. They waved pistols in our faces, motioning us to raise our hands. They asked, "Pol Pot? Pol Pot?"

I didn't know what "Pol Pot" meant, but I quickly told the Cambodian soldier that we were civilians and were just looking for something to eat. A few of us who could speak Vietnamese told the Vietnamese soldiers the same thing. We all had our hands raised and everyone was talking at once. It was obvious that the Cambodian soldiers and the Vietnamese soldiers were not on good terms. The Cambodian soldiers were outnumbered and were submissive but resented it. The Vietnamese looked down on them and on us. After translating, the Cambodian soldiers said we could put our hands down, but the Vietnamese went from one of us to the next, pointing their weapons and asking through interpreters whether we were Khmer Rouge.

The Vietnamese took our kramas and used them to tie our elbows behind our backs. Then they searched us, confiscating knives and hatchets and pouches of tobacco. They marched us off into the jungle and along a path.

I thought: Well, it's happening again. They say they are liberating us but they have tied us up. Just like the Khmer Rouge.

They brought us to a Vietnamese military camp with tents in straight rows. The commanding officer emerged from his tent wearing a white T-shirt and holding a pistol in his hand. Through an interpreter he asked who of us spoke Vietnamese. One man volunteered and was taken a short distance away for questioning. Then the commander asked the rest of us through the interpreter where the Khmer Rouge were based, how many of them there were and what kinds of weapons they had. None of us knew, and we were too afraid to say anything. Nearby, the interrogators were using their fists to beat the man who had volunteered.

They tied us back to back in groups of three, using our kramas as rope. The man who had volunteered was brought back and tied behind me. Lower-ranking Vietnamese went around to the groups of three, asking the same questions about the Khmer Rouge through interpreters. When they came to me I said I didn't know, I was only looking for food, and they punched me in the stomach, knocking the wind out of me. They punched the man behind me, the one who had already been beaten, and the Cambodian soldiers who had been doing the interpreting did nothing to stop it. I noticed that the Vietnamese did not hit everyone, just those of us who were light-skinned, which is to say those of us whose ancestry was partly or wholly Chinese. But I do not know whether the Vietnamese hated Chinese-Cambodians and wanted to punish us, or whether they thought we more observant, more likely to be good sources of information than the dark-skinned ethnic Khmer.

In the midafternoon they untied the groups of three but left each person with his elbows tied behind his back. They led us across a rice field and through the jungle to National Route 5. We walked westward, our bare feet on the hot asphalt, and across a fallen-down bridge, where they let us take a break. They untied the dark-skinned ones, but the light-skinned ones like me they kept tied up, and I thought they were marking me for special treatment.

We walked along the road toward Battambang, the tied and the untied together, and only one Vietnamese guard in front. I motioned for a dark-skinned man to untie my arms, and he did, and I walked along with my arms free. Then I untied someone else. A few refused to be untied because they were afraid of the guard, but he didn't look back and didn't seem to care. We stopped at the entrance to a Vietnamese military base with a tank out front, and the soldiers living in a village of traditional Cambodian houses on stilts. Our guard went in to report, then came back and told us, though an interpreter, while pointing his finger, "Go this way. Everybody. Go this direction. Go to Battambang."

We walked numbly down the road.

I had no shoulderboard, no hatchet. Only my field cooking pot, which was still full of rice, and my torn and muddy clothes, and the hidden contents of my waistband pockets.

Some of the survivors from our foraging group rested while others walked on at their own pace toward Battambang. Soon those who were ahead and those who were behind were strung far apart along the road, out of sight.

I walked until the dirt turnoff road for Phnom Tippeday, and stopped. It was late afternoon.

I pulled out my calendar watch. The date was April 17, 1979.

I had been under the Khmer Rouge exactly four years.

I thought: No, the Khmer Rouge took over Phnom Penh on the morning of April 17, 1975. It's 6:00 P.M. now. A little over four years. Four years and eight hours.

I tried to grasp the meaning of the time that had passed, but there was nothing to hold on to.

Phnom Penh was forever ago but fresh as yesterday.

So much had happened.

Everyone had died. Huoy, my parents, everyone.

I was alive, but the price was too high.

The gods had made a horrible mistake.

33

BATTAMBANG

IN THE MORNING I walked down the red clay road to Phnom Tippe-day, to visit Huoy's grave.

It was a long, straight road, with channels cut into its surface by the rains, and grass growing high and thick on either side. The wind and the birds made the only sounds; there was not another human being in sight. I crossed the railroad tracks and took a shortcut across the fields, scurrying from hillock to hillock, stopping to look around, afraid of being caught by a Khmer Rouge patrol or a Vietnamese patrol, afraid of losing the liberty I had gained. Arriving under the big *sdao* tree, I felt safe again. Every detail of the place was familiar to me, and permanently fixed in my memory: the grave aligned with the temple on the mountain, the tree arching protectively overhead, the patchwork pattern of the dikes and paddies.

Kneeling, I told her that this would be my last visit for a long, long time. Someday I would come back for her and take her to another resting place, next to the temple on the mountain. I asked her to protect me until my return.

Huoy's spirit answered. She said she would watch over me and guide me. She promised to stay with me wherever I went.

I was comforted. It was important to know that her spirit was with me, even when our physical beings were far apart. But when I got up there was nobody else in sight. My *bonheur* vanished, and my loneliness and fear returned.

I walked quickly through Phum Ra, which was even more desolate than before. In our house, the doors were torn off the hinges and the thatch torn off the walls. Everywhere, panels of thatch and pieces of corrugated metal and trash and rusted bowls lay scattered in the streets. The warehouse near the common kitchen was wide open at the doors, empty except for a few grains of rice on the floor.

On the way out of the village I found a pair of green Vietnamese sneakers, canvas on top, rubber on the bottom. I put them on and wiggled my toes experimentally. They fit. And I walked away as fast as possible, with the strange feeling that my feet were no longer in contact with the ground.

I returned to the National Route 5 intersection and camped. An ominous rumbling of artillery came from the southeast, the direction my family had been. There was no going back for them, nothing to do but watch and wait.

Signs had appeared along the highway, scrawled on paper or wood and fastened to trees. Such-and-such a person announced that he had survived and had gone east, to Phnom Penh. So-and-so wrote that she had lost her husband and her younger children; her older children, if they were still alive, should follow her west, to Battambang. Handwritten signs, messages of hope and despair.

Refugees wandered along the road in both directions, stopping to read the signs, then shuffling on again, tired and numb and traumatized. When I asked if they had seen my family they said no, but their minds were someplace else, and their eyes stared through me to some distant place beyond.

As the days passed and my family did not appear, I grew restless and walked long distances on the road, up and back. I read the signs, talked with refugees, looked for familiar faces. It reminded me of looking for Huoy and my parents after the evacuation of Phnom Penh. But the traffic on National Route 1 in 1975 was nothing like the traffic on National Route 5 in 1979.

In 1979 there were no cars being pushed, or motorcycles. There were no television sets, radios, electric fans or cartons of books being carried. If people had any possessions at all they carried them in small bundles on shoulderboards, on their backs, or balanced on their heads. They trudged along in barefoot groups, two or three or five skinny people in rags and then another few coming along a hundred yards later. Most had facial sores. In 1975 women had cared how they looked, but in 1979 there were only torn clothes, and the women had no sense of fashion or pride in their appearance. In 1975 when friends met they asked, "Have you eaten yet?" or "How many children do you have?" In 1979 they stared at you with haunted eyes and asked, "Who survived in your family?"

Another difference was this: In 1975 everyone was afraid of the Khmer Rouge. In 1979 the fear had turned to anger.

Three thin, ragged Cambodian men walked down the highway. They escorted a fourth man, who was sturdier and well fed, his arms tied behind his back so tightly his chest stuck out.

The three young men were beating the fourth with their fists and shouting, "Say it! Say it: 'I'm Khmer Rouge.' "

"I'm Khmer Rouge," the prisoner said in a faint voice as they paraded him toward the spot where I was standing.

"Say it louder! Say, 'I killed a lot of people.' "

"I killed a lot of people," the sturdy man repeated. He wore culottes, nothing more.

Like flies to a meal, people emerged from the roadside and ran toward the prisoner. I ran toward him too. "One time each!" his captors yelled to us. "You must take turns! Please! Each person can hit him only once!" The crowd pressed in. Even the women took their turns hitting him with their fists.

"Stand aside," I said. The crowd parted to give me room. I stepped in quickly and kicked high and hard between the prisoner's legs. He crumpled, his face contorted in agony, and his guards jerked him to his feet.

In an angry, buzzing cluster, the crowd proceeded along the road, with the Khmer Rouge in the middle. His face was bloody and swollen. Every time he fell they hauled him to his feet again. Vietnamese soldiers stepped in to save him, but the crowd pushed them away so fiercely that the soldiers retreated. Then farther down the road a man rushed in swinging a hatchet and killed the Khmer Rouge.

Someone cut the head off and mounted it on top of a bamboo pole. They wrote a sign with charcoal on wood, and fixed the sign to the pole and jammed the pole in the ground beside the road for everyone to see.

The sign read, "Khmer Rouge—Enemy Forever."

Day after day Vietnamese trucks drove along the highway, some of them carrying troops and others pulling artillery pieces. Many tanks drove along too, their metal treads clanking on the pavement. What the Vietnamese were doing in Cambodia still puzzled me. It didn't make sense, the early teachers of the Khmer Rouge fighting their pupils, communists fighting communists. The explanation was missing. But one thing was perfectly clear, and that was the overwhelming Vietnamese military power. They seemed to have endless equipment. Their troops were serious and disciplined. Nobody in Southeast Asia could defeat them. Not the Khmer Rouge. Not the Khmer Serei, if they even existed, and by now I doubted it. How foolish we had been to believe that the Khmer Serei were coming to free us. How ignorant we had been! Kept in the dark and inventing wishful stories about freedom fighters, and passing the stories on as fact.

But there was nothing to be done about it. The country has been occupied by foreigners, I thought sourly. The regime that tortured me is overthrown, and another regime that tied me up and punched me is in power.

Historically, Vietnam was our enemy. In the nineteenth century it had annexed Cambodian territory in the lower Mekong River delta, and when I was growing up it was often said that Vietnam wanted to take the rest too. But as far as I was concerned they were welcome as long as they stayed only a short while. They had hastened the end of the Khmer Rouge regime, though the regime had been falling apart anyway. Better to have them around than the Khmer Rouge. The Vietnamese didn't bother the refugees on the highway. They let us forage for food wherever we wanted.

I went on several foraging trips with some Vietnamese soldiers who had camped beside the highway. With me was a Cambodian man who spoke Vietnamese. We helped the soldiers catch domesticated ducks, and in exchange they shared with us the oxen and pigs they shot with their rifles.

We always went out with the same three soldiers. They were about twenty years old, healthy and polite. We didn't ask them personal questions, and they didn't ask us. But one evening over a campfire I asked them why the Vietnamese troops who freed me had tied me up and hit me in the stomach. They explained that it was hard to know which Cambodians to trust. "Some Khmer Rouge have pretended to be civilians and then killed Vietnamese. So we have to be careful," one of them said, through my acquaintance, who translated.

I was skeptical. It didn't explain the hostility of the soldiers who had interrogated me, or the bad feelings between them and their Cambodian counterparts. Still, the young soldier had regarded the question as a reasonable one and had given me an answer. It was the kind of conversation that had been impossible with the Khmer Rouge. Through my acquaintance I asked why Vietnam had invaded Cambodia.

"Because Pol Pot killed a lot of people," one of them said. "We came to liberate you from Pol Pot's hands."

Pol Pot. Ever since liberation I had been hearing the name. Pol Pot was said to be the head of Angka, the leader of the anonymous Organization. But I was skeptical about that too. It was hard to believe that one man, whoever he was, deserved all the blame for ruining the nation.

Besides, I had my own theories. To me, the fault didn't lie with an individual man but with an outside country: China. For four years I had been looking at Chinese trucks, Chinese-made weapons, Chinese-made uniforms. I had heard Chinese-style propaganda music. Almost everything about the Khmer Rouge, from the jargon about "independence-sovereignty" to sending the city people to learn from the peasants in the countryside, was an imitation of Mao Tse-tung's Cultural Revolution. Without China, the Khmer Rouge could never have come to power, or stayed in power as long as they did. So I nodded my head up and down at the young Vietnamese soldier, pretending to agree with him, and kept my own opinion inside.

While waiting for my family I went to get rice. A little over an hour's walk from my campsite was an underground rice storage warehouse similar to the one I had tried to go to earlier. A huge crowd gathered outside, at the top of a staircase leading down to a concrete-lined subterranean chamber. Inside, piles of rice sacks were visible in the dim light. The rice was free, and everyone took as much as they wanted. Women piled rice onto baskets they carried on their heads, and men staggered away with rice on shoulderboards or rucksacks. I tied a sack to either end of a shoulderboard, which bent the ends of the shoulderboard downward like a bow. Everyone was happy. A few people loaded oxcarts high with rice sacks and drove off to Battambang to sell them.

Finally the Vietnamese pushed the Khmer Rouge toward the Cardomom Mountains. I walked back to the town of Muong and found my family there. They had all survived, though the group numbered two fewer than before.

What had happened was that just before liberation the Khmer Rouge forced all the civilians farther into the jungle. During the retreat my brother Hok, the fifth son in the family, ran into Hong Srun, the fourth son, whom none of us had seen since Tonle Batí. The reunion was happy but brief. The Vietnamese attacked, shells landed nearby and everybody fled. In the chaos Hong Srun went off, taking two of Pheng Huor's children with him. Only Ngim, the daughter aged nine, stayed with Hok.

Thinking that I (the third son) had probably died, the group threw most of my luggage away. They dumped my medical books, which I had carried at such cost and buried in so many places. They threw away my glasses, most of my clothing and, without realizing it, a cushion of mine with eighteen hundred U.S. dollars inside it and a blanket with pieces of gold sewn into the hem. Fortunately they kept a few small items, including the photograph of Huoy.

I brought them back to my camping place to wait for Hong Srun and the other two children so all of us could travel to Battambang together. Hong Srun didn't show up, and about the first of May I decided to take the family to Battambang to wait for him there. I wrote a sign to Hong Srun and fastened it to a tree. In the early morning we started walking westward on National Route 5, and by dusk we had arrived in the second-largest city in the nation.

Battambang was a city of squatters living in the empty shells of houses. We stayed in a house on the edge of town with about twenty other people and slept on the floor. There wasn't a single piece of furniture.

During the Khmer Rouge regime everything wooden or metal in the houses of Battambang had been taken away—the beds and tables, the window frames, the corrugated metal used on some of the roofs. Most of the temple buildings and all the sacred objects in them had been destroyed. Hulks of cars lay in the side streets, without tires or windshields. A steam shovel sat rusting and immobilized in front of the central market. When we got there, the central market and all the indoor stores, restaurants and shops were closed on order of the Vietnamese, who were officially opposed to the return of a market economy.

Unofficially, however, the Vietnamese tolerated small business enterprises on the street. The medium of exchange was rice. Shoppers walked around with their wallets—with large quantities of rice wrapped in their kramas or piled in baskets on their heads.

With rice you could negotiate a fare on a bicycle-powered pedicab, or on one of the horse-drawn taxis clip-clopping through the streets. You could buy live fish, fresh meat, vegetables, fruit, hot soup or noodles, old clothes, tape cassettes. You could have your hair cut and have a bicycle or a radio or a watch repaired. The only thing you could not buy with rice was rice itself—you had to buy that with gold. The year before, when Huoy was starving, I had traded two *damleung* for two cans of rice flour. In Battambang City one *damleung* bought a sack containing 1,750 cans of rice, much too heavy to carry. That's how much prices had fallen. That's how much food there was once the Khmer Rouge were out of power.

Something like the normal Cambodian way of life was returning to Battambang. The vendors squatting under cloth awnings, the women shoppers looking critically at the food and pinching it to see if it was fresh. Bargaining, gossiping, trading news—it was almost like the old days. But much was missing too.

In the evenings a band played in an empty lot. A generator powered the loudspeakers and lit up strings of brightly colored bulbs. Hundreds of people gathered to dance and watch, like insects drawn to the lights. The women wore their best clothing, but they had no makeup, and their hair was still short from Khmer Rouge days. The men left their shirttails out, like field workers who had forgotten their manners. They danced the *romvong*, stepping around in time to the music and slowly waving their hands in the air. They were unable to stop themselves from rejoicing. They danced until dawn, shutting from their minds the past of suffering and hunger and the deaths of relatives. I thought it was too soon to rejoice, but I didn't blame them for what they did.

To me, Battambang was a place to gather strength before moving on. Balam and I went on a walking tour of the town, and it helped me realize that the sooner we left, the better. First we went to an information center the Vietnamese had set up. A flagpole extended from the information building, and from it hung an enormous red flag. It reminded me of the plain red flags that used to be flown on the front lines. It was even more like the official Khmer Rouge flag, which was red with a gold three-towered emblem of Angkor Wat in the middle. This flag was identical, except that its emblem of Angkor Wat had five towers instead of three.

"Communists," I whispered to Balam, who nodded.

We went into the information office. On one side was a bulletin board covered with notices from survivors looking for their lost relatives. On the other side were photographs of Vietnamese and Cambodian soldiers shaking hands and smiling and a chart showing the structure of the new provincial government. In the middle, at a wooden table, sat a woman answering questions in both Khmer and Vietnamese. Behind her hung a photograph of a pile of human bones, taken at a Khmer Rouge mass grave—a reminder that the Khmer Rouge had been murderers and that we were supposed to be grateful that the Vietnamese had kicked them out.

Standing guard in the building were Vietnamese soldiers and Cambodian "Self-Defense Forces." The Vietnamese soldiers wore new olive-green uniforms. They were fully armed and clearly in charge. The Cambodians wore whatever they could find—long- or short-sleeved shirts, black or brown trousers. Some went barefoot. Their weapons ranged from AK-47s to rusty carbines to nothing at all. They were known as "Heng Samrin" soldiers, after the leader of the puppet regime. I had never heard of Heng Samrin before, any more than I had heard of Pol Pot. Certainly Heng Samrin was a man of no previous standing in the nation.

Balam and I left the information office without asking the only real question that interested us, and that was the quickest route out of Cambodia. Even more than the differences between the Vietnamese and Heng Samrin soldiers, the red flag told us everything we needed to know about the future of the country. One glance and my mind was made up. Time to leave, before the communists put me in prison again.

Balam and I continued our tour of the city, watching and listening, keeping our mouths shut.

We saw a temple with many people praying inside and weeping for their lost relatives.

We saw a former elementary school surrounded with barbed-wire fence, and Khmer Rouge prisoners dressed in their black uniforms inside. The people outside the fence pointed at the Khmer Rouge who had made their lives a misery, and shouted threats at them.

We saw Vietnamese soldiers, always in twos and threes, never alone. Heng Samrin soldiers came up to us to ask if we wanted to trade gold for medicine, while their Vietnamese bosses pretended to loiter nearby. The Vietnamese wanted gold, but they were indirect and clever about it. Through their Cambodian front men, you could buy anything—generators, outboard boat motors, rice by the truck-load.

It was a city full of intrigue. I trusted nobody. A man I had known slightly in Phum Ra came up to me and whispered that he was a member of the Khmer Serei. He asked me to join the freedom fighters on the Thai border. I didn't believe him and sent him away, though later it turned out he was telling the truth.

One afternoon I went bathing in the river, and another man washing himself in the river recognized me. He was Dr. Dav Kiet, a classmate of mine from medical school. Kiet was working in the hospital in Battambang. He asked me to join him on the staff, since there was a shortage of doctors. Standing on the riverbank, I pointed at my skinny arms and at the ribs protruding from my chest and told him that my health didn't allow it.

The next morning a chauffeur-driven Mercedes appeared at the house where my family was staying. The man in the back seat of the Mercedes came up the steps, took his shoes off at the door, walked in and asked for Dr. Ngor Haing. He was the governor of Battambang.

I was wearing a torn sarong, nothing else. The governor and I shook hands. We sat cross-legged on a mat. He asked me about my family, about my old life in Phnom Penh, about what had happened in the Khmer Rouge years. Finally he got to the point and told me that Dr. Dav Kiet had suggested that I work in the hospital.

The governor said I could work part-time if I was worried about my health. If there was anything wrong with me, the hospital would give me medicines. Not wanting him to lose face, I promised I would go to work as soon I felt better. Actually, I didn't want to work at the hospital at all.

The governor came again the next day and again I resisted. But by then I had realized why. It was not just that I wasn't feeling well, or that I didn't like the Heng Samrin regime. It was because I was afraid of going back to work in obstetrics and gynecology. I wanted to forget how Huoy had died. I wanted to seal it out of my head. And it wouldn't be easy if I was delivering babies in the the same hospital I had wanted to take Huoy to when she was in labor.

All the same, it would have been unwise to ignore the governor. I decided to see the hospital for myself. Dav Kiet took me on a tour.

The hospital was in terrible shape. For a short while around 1977 a distinguished Western-trained doctor—the man I'd wanted to take Huoy to—had been allowed to practice there, but then the Khmer Rouge killed him and let the hospital slide into ruin. The laboratory wasn't functioning. There was hardly any medicine or surgical equipment. The patients flowed into the hospital endlessly, a river of the malnourished and ill. We walked into the delivery room and saw a woman in her seventh month of pregnancy in labor. She had broken her water many hours before, but the labor was making no progress. The mother was growing feeble, and though the doctors and nurses were doing their best, there was nothing they could do. They didn't have the equipment. The woman was in the same situation as Huoy. Black, black clouds closed in on me, and I had to get out of the delivery room fast.

Kiet took me around to meet all the doctors and nurses and they were all very respectful to me, even though my clothes were torn and my hair and beard were long and wild-looking. They emphasized that they were offering me a job in a hospital run entirely by Cambodians. There were no Vietnamese there. All I had to say was yes, and my lost career and my former social status would be returned to me as though the revolution had never happened.

I told them no.

The next day the governor came back.

I told him yes, because I was afraid. It was either go to work in the hospital or leave for the border at once.

I began working at the hospital but my mind was not there.

I thought about Huoy all the time. If she had lived, we could have been crossing the border by now. But she had not, and because of it I could not work in this hospital. If I could not save my own wife, how could I save others? What good was I? What good were any of the doctors? The woman in the delivery room had died in childbirth. Just like Huoy. If I saw people laughing, I turned away. I never smiled. At night, Ngim tried to cheer me, but it was no use. I had lived too long. The gods had made a cruel mistake. It would have been better that I had died with Huoy, so our souls could be together.

Pen Tip arrived in Battambang. I sent him a message through a mutual acquaintance. The message was for him to visit me at the hospital with his black notebook. He would know what that meant —a black notebook listing the deeds and misdeeds of his life, like the records kept by the King of Death.

Pen Tip's message back to me was that he had never done me wrong. He claimed he didn't know why I was angry.

I was too tired and discouraged from my hospital work to go after Pen Tip. And then something else happened anyway that absorbed all my attention. The governor sent a note to all the doctors asking us to attend a two-day conference. We would stay at his residence the first night and go to the second half of the conference the next day.

I thought: Why can't we go home to our own homes the first night? Where are they really going to take us? Out in the woods, with soldiers? Does this regime hate doctors too?

I went to talk to two of my colleagues in the hospital.

"Brothers," I said cryptically, "in the west, the dam is broken and the waters are flooding out. Are you going or staying?" They understood my meaning. There was nothing to the west but the Thai border.

These doctors were not ready to go, but they arranged for me to be on duty the night before the conference was to begin. That would give me an excuse to miss the first day of the conference. I would have a day's head start before the governor knew I was missing.

I talked it over with my family. My brother Hok decided to stay in Battambang a while longer and wait for Hong Srun, who still had not arrived. Balam decided to take his wife and children and come along with me. I told Balam to start walking west on National Route 5 before dawn on May 14. I would catch up to him by noon.

"Uncle," Ngim said to me, "I want to go with you."

I told her no, she had to stay with Hok. But Ngim pleaded, and I told her only if Hok gave permission. To my surprise, Hok did.

Ngim and I were very fond of each other. She was a sturdy, active girl with a strong mind, like her mother. She wasn't afraid of anybody.

I told Ngim to put her clothes in my knapsack. She would have to carry the knapsack for the first few hours, until I caught up with her and Balam.

I worked the night of May 13–14 at the hospital, willing the hands of the clock to move faster. In the morning I got off work, changed into civilian clothes and began walking toward the Thai border.

34

THE DANGER ZONE

ON THE ROAD out of town, a man saw me and called out, *"Luk!
Luk!"*—the old form of address to a social superior. He clicked his
heels and came to military attention.

"The devil's victim!" I exclaimed, pleased and astonished. It was
Sok, my driver from prerevolutionary days. I clapped him on the
shoulder, told him he didn't have to call me *luk* anymore.

"Where's the boss lady?" Sok asked, meaning Huoy. I told him
that she had died. Sok nodded gravely, as though death was to be
expected. Then he invited me to his house for a meal. I protested that
I didn't have time. "I'm going to the border, but if you want, you
can come with me," I said.

"Too many in my family group, boss. I will go later, but right
now you must come to my house for something to eat." He pulled
me by the wrist toward a little hut nearby.

I had always wondered what had happened to Sok in the evacuation of Phnom Penh. It turned out that after he had driven off to
get his family in my Mercedes, the Khmer Rouge blocked the streets.
He was unable to come back to pick up Huoy as he had planned. He
had always regretted it, and ever since then he had wondered what
had happened to Huoy and me.

On this morning he gave me the best of his family's food, rice and
pieces of grilled chicken. He treated me with great respect. I would
have liked to bring him to the border, but he was right. With him
was an extended family of aunts, cousins, babies and grandparents—
an enviable number of survivors—and they were not ready to go.

I resumed walking on the road behind schedule but in good spirits. About two in the afternoon I caught up with my family group. There were only seven of us now: Balam, his wife, their two children and their nephew, my niece Ngim and me. We ate in the shade of a kapok tree by a pond. Ngim gave me my knapsack, and then we started walking again.

With us heading westward on National Route 5 were travelers pushing wooden-wheeled handcarts and a few others driving oxcarts, the axles squeaking and squealing. Carrying our luggage on our backs, as we were, seemed harder, but once we left the road it would make more sense. Where we were going, it was best to travel light.

Toward sunset, Heng Samrin soldiers stopped us at a checkpoint. For our own protection, they said, we should sleep in a village nearby. Unwillingly, we went off to the village and lay down. Some of my gold was in my waistband and the rest was in Huoy's purse, which I kept under my legs. Most people wrapped their gold in the bundles they used as pillows, but this was a mistake: In the middle of the night, the Heng Samrin soldiers came up and took all the pillows at gunpoint. That was what they meant by protection.

The next day we reached Sisophon, the last major town before the border. There, the Heng Samrin soldiers took what they wanted in broad daylight. From me they took a shirt and a pair of trousers. From others they took clothes, canteens, rice and whatever else they could use.

West of Sisophon was an enormous stretch of flat, dry, barren rice fields. In places it was a mile from one tree to the next. In the shade of an especially large tree, Heng Samrin soldiers had set up a checkpoint with sandbags and machine guns. Vietnamese soldiers sat nearby in the shade, a little too casual, a little too relaxed. When we got there the Heng Samrin soldiers accused us in loud voices of trying to leave the country. There wasn't much we could say to this, because ahead of us there was nothing except for the Thai border. They turned us around, started us walking back the way we had come. Predictably, someone made an offer, and the soldiers told us to come back. The cynical charade ended and the bargaining began.

I ended up paying one *chi* (a little less than one tenth of an ounce) of gold for my group to pass through. If all the soldiers wanted was gold, we figured we were lucky.

In that part of the country the road and the railroad tracks followed parallel courses, side by side. In the railroad's prime, before the civil war, trains ran all the way to the Thai border and beyond, to the Thai capital, Bangkok. Now, after years of war and decay, the trains stopped short of the border at a village called Nimitt and then reversed. As we walked along the highway, the westbound train passed us, carrying passengers in the boxcars and on the roofs, most of them heading for the border like us. Later the eastbound trains came back with a cargo of smuggled Thai goods. We reached Nimitt on foot as the sun was about to set.

Nimitt was a one-street hamlet surrounded by rice fields. It had no market and no stores. It had no soldiers, either, because the smugglers and border guides paid the military to stay away. It was a nasty little jumping-off point for trips to the Thai border and a transshipment center for black-market goods coming the other way.

Several hundred travelers like us were in Nimitt trying to get out of Cambodia. The guides fanned out among us, competing openly for business. "Come join my group. I guarantee your safety!" shouted one. "No! Over here! I offer cheaper rates!" said another. Most of the guides were dark-skinned ethnic Khmer, and some of them were barefoot.

I would have preferred to follow other travelers over the mountains, without hiring a guide. But the trails weren't yet established, and I didn't trust the other refugees. Still, there was no hurry to choose among guides. My group made a fire, cooking rice rations and boiling water to last us through the coming days. After we had eaten, Balam and I went off to look the guides over.

To his surprise, Balam recognized one of them, a skinny old man of mixed Khmer and Chinese blood who had lived in Phnom Penh before the Khmer Rouge takeover. He recognized Balam too, though he could not remember his name.

"My good friends," the old man assured us, "I bring groups every night to the border. I know the area very well and everybody trusts me. If I bring you to the border, the bandits in the jungle won't take money from you. I will arrange everything. I will pay them off. And I'm the only one who can do it. I'm not saying I'm perfect, but if you trust me, go with me. I go to the border every night, and there's never any problem. But if you don't trust me, by all means go with somebody else."

I kept quiet. Word for word, his sales pitch was what I had expected to hear. That he had experience, that we had nothing to worry about, that he had plenty of customers even without us and so on. If I were a guide, it was exactly what I would have said myself. I watched and listened for something to believe in but didn't find it.

And yet I trusted the other guides even less. Their eyes gave them away. They had a calculating way of looking at our luggage rather than our faces. They let their glances rest on the women's crotches. They thought they had X-ray eyes, looking for hidden gold.

After four years of living under the Khmer Rouge, my ability to read people's characters was highly developed. I walked around, listening to each of the guides, assessing them silently. I paid attention to their tones of voice, to their posture, to anything that emanated from their character, but above all to their eyes.

At last I went back to the old man Balam knew from Phnom Penh. There was, I thought, about a 10 percent chance that he would treat us properly. I chose him because he was part Chinese like me and because his remembering Balam might work in our favor. The rest of the guides I trusted about 2 percent.

The bargaining began behind closed doors in a crowded room in the old guide's house. At first he asked for a *damleung* of gold apiece. He came down to four fifths of a *damleung*, and then Balam and I conferred. Ngim and Balam's youngest son were both nine years old. "The children go at half price," I told the guide, who gave in.

"But you pay me now," he added, letting his glance travel the length of my body.

The total for the group was 4.8 *damleung* (about 5.75 ounces) of gold, worth around $2,000 U.S.

I left Balam in the crowded room and walked outside. I had gold in several forms: in thin twenty-four-karat sheets, rolled into small tubes and hidden in my belt; in gold chains of twenty-two- or twenty-four-karat purity; and some other small twenty-four-karat bars and pieces. I returned to the group, which was sitting around the fire. Ngim heated food for me and we talked nonchalantly. My krama hung around my neck like a scarf. When enough time had passed, I bent forward slightly so that the end of my krama fell across the top of my trousers. I dug into my waistband pocket, pulled out the gold pieces, palmed them, then casually tied them into the end of my krama. Ngim and Balam's wife noticed, but nobody else did. After eating I walked back to the guide's house to give him the gold.

By 1:00 A.M. everyone who was going with the guide had assembled in a long line stretching from his house. It was a starry night, a crescent moon hanging in the western sky, and quiet, except for the crickets. We began to walk much more slowly than I would have liked, on a footpath, then on an oxcart path, through rice fields and jungle. Our route would take us north and then west, away from the roads and villages and into unpopulated territory. How far it was to the border, we did not know.

When gray and then pink light had appeared in the east, the line stopped. Balam's wife turned around and whispered to me over Ngim's head, "Khmer Rouge. Pass it on."

I turned around and repeated the message to the person behind me.

A loud surly voice came from up front. "Why do you want to leave the country? Why? You are betraying the nation!"

Nobody answered.

The sun rose. The line shuffled slowly forward. Ahead I saw four or five Khmer Rouge, dressed in black, holding rifles. They collected bits of gold from travelers in payment.

My gold was hidden in various place—small bits in my waistband for bribes like this, some in my green Vietnamese sneakers, a few *chi* taped under Ngim's armpit. Most of it I had given Balam's wife, to hide in her underwear.

Everyone in my family group was ahead of me. I stepped out of line for a moment, stepped in again at the front of the group. Slowly the line shuffled forward.

The Khmer Rouge checked my knapsack.

I gave them two *chi* of gold.

"Open your mouth," they said. They looked in my mouth for gold, frisked me and threw my knapsack in a pile. Behind me, they looked in Ngim's mouth with the flashlight and threw her basket in the pile. Then they went to Balam. When they were looking in his luggage I picked up my knapsack and Ngim's basket. When they took

Balam's bag away, he followed my example and stole it back when they weren't looking.

The soldiers broke bamboo shoulderboards to see whether gold was hidden inside. They stirred cooking pots to see if anything was hidden in the rice. They confiscated Montagut shirts, always a favorite with the Khmer Rouge.

But real Khmer Rouge wouldn't have let us go. And real Khmer Rouge soldiers wouldn't have been interested in gold. These were pretenders, Heng Samrin soldiers who had dressed in black uniforms. There were undoubtedly Vietnamese soldiers nearby, watching and waiting.

We had entered a danger zone in far northwestern Cambodia. My trust in the leader had dropped from 10 percent to zero. In the daylight I saw he hadn't even accompanied us himself. He was using employees.

An hour after the fake Khmer Rouge, another gang of the same kind stopped us. They yelled and threatened. They raised their rifles to shoot us, and the wild glare in their eyes nearly convinced me that they were real. But it was another bluff. They had everyone put the luggage in a huge pile and clawed through it, looking for gold. They found a lot of gold in the false bottoms of tea kettles. After they had searched the luggage they frisked the men but not the women. I gave them another two *chi* and they let my group go, but they made others without gold turn around and go back toward Nimitt.

The trail led up into the rain forest of the Dangrek Mountains. Hardwood trees of the species called *chhoeu teal* and *khlong* and *theng* towered high overhead; I recognized them from my family's lumber business long ago. Vines as thick as my wrist hung from the branches, and lianas sprouted from the trunks.

Except for the singing of birds, and the scurrying of lizards through the underbrush, it was quiet in the forest. Where there were boulders on the hilltops, we jumped from rock to rock. Where bamboo grew in dense groves on the slopes, we parted it with our hands and passed through. The trail led up and down.

At the bottom of a valley we came to a river. Green scum floated on the surface of the water, which was a chocolate brown underneath.

We waded across. On the other side we drank clean water from our makeshift canteens. An old woman with her palms together in the *sompeah* begged me for a drink. I poured her a capful of water, but no more.

Walking again, the line of travelers filled the path and twisted out of sight, around the bends. A sudden muffled explosion, like an artillery shell, came from ahead. We kept on walking. A few minutes later word came back that a mine had gone off and that many people had been killed.

The line stopped. We stood where we were, suddenly afraid to move to the side of the path and sit down.

Then the word came back that the guides had all deserted us.

We waited for an hour, and then the line started moving forward again. I told Ngim to walk exactly in my footsteps.

We walked cautiously around a bend and came upon the site of the explosion. It was a blood-spattered scene, an arm hanging from a tree branch, part of a leg caught in bamboo. Ten or more dead lay by the side of the path, and many more were wounded. I made a tourniquet, removed some large pieces of shrapnel from wounds, tied makeshift bandages and advised the relatives on preventing infection. With no medical supplies, there was little more to do. It was a terrible way to die, or to be maimed, after living through the Khmer Rouge years and coming so close to freedom.

The mines appeared on either side of the path, sometimes in the middle. They had coin-size detonator buttons, white or rusted in color. From the detonator buttons, trip lines made of nearly invisible white nylon thread led to tying-off points such as trees or rocks nearby.

We crept forward, around curves, up and down, and then we heard another explosion ahead. When we came down the side of the hill to a river we saw the burials already under way. The seriously wounded were being carried off in hammocks slung from bamboo poles; a few with puncture wounds from the shrapnel sat around in shock. This time the mine had been rigged underwater. Ngim was a good swimmer, but I made her put her arms around my neck, and I swam across as she held on to me.

Whether the Vietnamese or the Khmer Rouge planted the mines didn't matter much to us. All we knew was that we had to keep our eyes on the trail, searching for white threads. Dry leaves fell across the trail and drifted in the wake of footsteps, making spotting them more difficult.

There was a third mine explosion far ahead. When we got there, there was a crater across the path, and flies buzzing around the blood. Nearby were graves with thorns piled on top to keep the wild animals away.

We kept on walking. It was hot and dusty. People had stopped beside the path to beg for food or water, but I gave only sips of water, and only to old ladies.

As the daylight faded we examined an area next to the trail for mines and settled down for the night. We made no fire; it was too risky looking for firewood. The mosquitoes covered our arms and legs; we spent most of the night slapping them. Moonlight filtered through the treetops high above.

The next morning we started walking again, following everyone else and hoping that whoever was in the lead knew where to go. I didn't think they did. The morning sun was on our left, meaning that we were going south. Our original plan had been to go north and west—the morning sun should have been to our right, or else over our backs. But I was tired and mistrusted my own sense of direction too.

In midmorning the line stopped. It went forward again, and then everyone was made to gather in a clearing. Eight newcomers had joined us. They had hunting rifles, and they spoke a language that we guessed was Thai.

I do not know for a fact that these first men or those who came later were Thai citizens. Probably some were Cambodians who spoke Thai from living near the border. What I do know is that they made me glad that Huoy was not with me.

They made the women remove their clothes and underclothes, but allowed them to change into sarongs to protect their modesty. With swift, expert hands, the thieves felt the brassieres, the straps and seams and hems of dresses and trousers. They found the bulk of my gold in the underwear of Balam's wife.

Then they started body searches. Mouths. Ears. Hair. Finger violations of the women.

Then they searched the men. Same thing. They found the gold in my waistband but not the gold in my sneakers.

Then they separated the men from the women, and the rapes began. In full view. The prettiest young women were raped again and again. The bandits who were not taking their turns kept their hunting rifles pointed at the rest of us. There was nothing we could do.

They didn't rape Balam's wife and didn't search or molest Ngim.

We walked half a mile farther, then stopped when we saw more armed men. No rapes this time. When they finished searching us, we picked up what remained of our baggage and trudged on for another half mile, where we had to stop again.

From one tollgate we went to the next, and the next, and the next, until we were dazed. Sometimes the thieves spoke Thai and sometimes they spoke Khmer. They confiscated canes and the bamboo sticks from hammocks, in case there was gold hidden inside. They removed bandages looking for gold. They tore the clothes off a pretty girl seventeen years old. She had no gold to hide, but she struggled any-way, to protect herself. And because she resisted, they dragged her into the woods and shot her in the head.

Counting from Nimitt, including the two times we were searched by fake Khmer Rouge, we passed through thirty-seven tollgates. I lost my Vietnamese sneakers with the gold inside and the Zippo cigarette lighter I had carried with me since leaving Phnom Penh. At the last tollgate, when we had little left, they took knives, hatchets, shoes, hats, new clothes.

Everybody was numb. We were unable to accept that it had really happened, that our women had been raped, that our possessions were gone. In all our years under the Khmer Rouge, we had never been bodily searched, and few women had been abused.

In a daze we trudged past the swollen corpse of an ox that had stepped on a mine. There had been few mines since the thieves had set on us.

The landscape flattened. The vegetation changed from rain forest to a dry, open forest with little underbrush. The leaves of the hard-wood trees nearly touched high overhead, but the tree trunks were far apart.

A Thai civilian stood alone in the path waiting for us to arrive. He was an intelligence officer for the Thai government. He asked us in good but accented Khmer about the Vietnamese, the Khmer Rouge and conditions walking toward the border. He said there were Thai soldiers ahead but not to worry. He added that the Thai Red Cross and United Nations agencies were there too.

We walked on and came to the Thai soldiers. They checked us for weapons and let us through. If there was a marker at the border, we didn't see it.

As the sun was sinking we came to a city of tents and makeshift huts. The color blue was everywhere—the relief agencies were giving away blue plastic tarps, and the refugees used them for the roofs and awnings of their shelters.

This was Nong Chan, a border camp. I was surprised that so many had come before us.

We found a place by the river and sat down.

I thought: We have survived. They have taken our gold, but it does not matter. From now on, no more killings, no more rapes. We will block the past out of our minds.

The nightmare is over.

We are safe. We are free.

Ngim sat down next to me, smiling happily. She had been a good girl, and I had decided to adopt her as a daughter.

I sat there thinking about the future. About starting life over again, and going back to work as a doctor.

Then I thought: Yes, but I will never forget these past four years. And someday, somehow, I will tell the outside world what has happened.

There were still a few bits of gold taped under Ngim's arm. I removed them, and Balam and I went to exchange the gold for Thai money from a man with a scale. For the piece of gold I offered we got four hundred Thai *baht* in paper currency, which was then worth about twenty American dollars. We spent the money on rice, dry salted fish, fish sauce and vegetables from market sellers nearby. When we finished we still had money left over.

Balam and I drifted back toward the family but stopped when we saw a man with a pushcart. There was a red, blue and white insignia on the side of his cart and ice and bottles of Pepsi-Cola inside.

"*Siep baht! Siep baht!*" the vendor yelled to the bystanders. The word *siep* sounded like the words for "ten" in Mandarin and Teochiew Chinese. I asked some Cambodians and they said yes, the price was ten *baht*.

"Brother," I said eagerly to Balam, "we've got to buy some. You drink first. Go ahead."

"It's too expensive," said Balam, a man of cautious instincts.

"No. I haven't had ice or Pepsi for four years."

"Don't waste your money," said Balam.

"This isn't a waste. This is living! Come on, brother, come on!"

I held up two fingers. The vendor nodded that he understood, then asked me a question in Thai. The other Cambodians translated: Did I want him to pour it into a plastic bag, with a straw?

"Tell him I want two bottles," I said. "I want the two coldest bottles he has."

He reached into the bottom of his cart and pulled up two glistening bottles. The label on the bottles was in the Thai alphabet, which is a little different from the Cambodian alphabet, but I recognized the name Pepsi-Cola all the same.

"The very coldest," I repeated. "Two bottles."

He opened the bottles and we lifted them to our lips.

After a few swallows I had to stop, the liquid was so cold. I could feel it going down my throat, cold and refreshing, all the way to my stomach. There was energy in my limbs. I felt revitalized, exhilarated. I took a deep breath and lifted the bottle to my mouth again.

The Pepsi was like a drug. It made me stronger. Maybe it was the sugar and caffeine pouring into my malnourished body, but I think it was something else. To me, Pepsi meant that we had finally made it to the West.

I finished the bottle and licked my lips.

"Brother," I said, "it's very, very tasty, isn't it?" Balam nodded but didn't say anything. He was too busy drinking. "Two more!" I shouted at the vendor.

He poured the Pepsi into plastic bags for us this time, and put in plenty of ice. He put a straw in the mouth of each plastic bag, then tied them off with a rubber band, to make a carrying loop. I gave him twenty more *baht*.

I sipped at the straw. "How good!" I exclaimed. "Like real, real, Pepsi-Cola!"

Before the revolution there had been Pepsi-Cola, Coca-Cola and other soft drinks in Phnom Penh. I took them all for granted. I hadn't really liked any of them much.

But this was different. Nothing had ever tasted this good before. And nothing has ever tasted that good since.

I kept murmuring "How tasty" as I walked back to the camp with my cousin. And, actually, I wanted more.

35

THE LOCKET

CAMBODIA has two traditional enemies: Vietnam to the east and Thailand (formerly Siam) to the west. Over the centuries we have had wars and border disputes with both of them.

At the bottom of our differences is race. "Pure" Khmers have dark brown skins. Vietnamese and Thais have pale yellow skins. To most Asians, including our neighbors, the lighter the skin color, the higher the status. They look down on Cambodians for having darker skins than themselves. Cambodians, who are shy by nature, sometimes outwardly appear to accept a lower status while inwardly resenting it.

Speaking different languages and belonging to competing nations have added to the friction. So does having long memories. Every Cambodian schoolchild knows that a Siamese invasion caused the downfall of the ancient Cambodian empire at Angkor. Every Cambodian knows the legend of the Vietnamese who used Cambodians' heads for cooking stones.

But of our two neighbors, we dislike the Thais less. Culturally we have much in common with them. We practice the same kind of Buddhism, called the "Lesser Vehicle"; our Buddha sculptures, temples and religious services are almost exactly the same. Most Vietnamese practice the "Greater Vehicle" of Buddhism, whose temples, Buddha sculptures and services are noticeably different. The Khmer and Thai languages have many similar words, but Khmer and Vietnamese have few that are similar. The rural people of both Cambodia and Thailand build their houses on stilts, but the Vietnamese build on the ground.

The result is that Cambodians and Thais have mixed feelings for each other. Sometimes we are hostile, sometimes we are friendly, and most of the time we are a combination of both.

On the Thai-Cambodian border, in the aftermath of the Khmer Rouge regime, the Thais were of mixed minds to us. Kindhearted Thai civilians brought gifts of clothing and food to refugees. (When they gave clothing to Ngim, I had to teach her how to put her palms together in the *sompeah* to give them proper thanks—she had forgotten her manners in the dark Khmer Rouge years.) But other Thais continued to rape, rob and terrorize the border camps. The Thai government was just as contradictory. It allowed international agencies to come to our aid, but on a few occasions its military treated us brutally. We never knew what to expect.

Sitting in the Nong Chan border camp, malnourished, dressed in rags, Balam and I searched our brains for the names of people who could help us. One of them was a Thai gentleman named Chana Samuthawanija, who had been ambassador to Phnom Penh during the Lon Nol regime. Balam had then been a wealthy airline owner and a man of high social standing, and he had gotten to know Chana socially. Balam recalled that Chana spoke Khmer but didn't read it, so I wrote a letter for Balam in French. We sent it off with a lot of other letters and appeals and soon forgot about it.

A few weeks later, in June 1979, our names were called over a loudspeaker system. We went to see what it was about and found that a vehicle was waiting to take the entire family group to Bangkok, Thailand's capital. Bewildered, we got in and were driven several hours to the Lumpini transit center, a former army barracks with long, warehouse-like buildings, in Bangkok. Nobody explained to us what we were doing in Lumpini or why we had been taken there.

Nor did we know how close we had come to tragedy at Nong Chan. The day after we left it, 110 buses drove in, part of an unannounced program staged by the Thai military. Buses came to the other border settlements too. More than 45,000 Cambodians climbed in, believing they were being taken to different refugee camps where the conditions were better. Instead, the buses took them around the northern slope of the Dangrek Mountains to another part of the Thai-Cambodian border near an ancient temple, called Preah Vihear. There, with rifles and whips, Thai soldiers forced the refugees down a steep cliff and back onto Cambodian soil. At the bottom of the cliff was a minefield. Hundreds died in the mine explosions, thousands of dehydration and disease in the following days. Of the survivors, some headed back across Cambodia for the border camps where they had been before—to be robbed and raped by Thais again on the way.

Balam and I didn't hear anything about the Preah Vihear incident until later. At the time, we were looking around the Lumpini center and trying to figure out what was going on. It was a confusing place, with many languages being spoken at the same time. In addition to the Cambodian refugees there were also Vietnamese and Laotians, including hilltribe people from Laos. I stared in disbelief at the women of the Laotian hilltribes. They wore strange headdresses and nursed their babies at enormous breasts. When they wanted to urinate they just squatted in full sight of everybody, lifted up their dresses and peed on the ground.

From time to time lists of names were read over the loudspeaker system, and people rushed forward with their luggage to begin their trips to Western countries like America and France. I was sitting with my back to a wall, wearing a sarong, watching the goings-on. Ngim had washed my trousers, the only pair I had left after the border thieves. I kept an eye on my trousers as they were drying, so nobody would steal them. Toward midmorning there was a big commotion with police whistles and the gate opening and the guards saluting. A few minutes later the loudspeakers called out Balam's name and mine.

"Cousin, we are lucky!" I exclaimed to Balam. "Today we are going to the United States. Ngim, please hand me my trousers."

"Praise the gods," Balam said, raising his eyes to the sky. "They have guided us out of hell and they are leading us to good fortune."

When we were fully dressed, Balam and I pushed our way through the crowd to the loudspeaker announcer. There Balam recognized a well-dressed man with a round face and a benign, wise expression. "It's Ambassador Chana," Balam whispered. All around Chana, men and women were bowing and *sompeah*ing. We joined them. At last we realized who had been responsible for getting us away from the border and bringing us here.

"No, please, get up," Chana was saying in Khmer to the people who were bowing. He was not fluent in the language, but we had no trouble understanding him. Then he looked in our direction and began talking to us.

"Balam, doctor, don't worry," he said. "You are alive. Don't think too much about the past. You have survived. The past is over. I will take care of you. If you need anything, just ask."

Chana was almost in tears. His old friend Balam was a wreck of a man, skinny, dressed in rags, his hair prematurely gray. He looked at me and saw another wreck. He turned to his wife, who stood next to him, and said something in Thai. She reached into her purse and pulled out two stacks of money several inches thick. She gave one to Balam, the other to me. We accepted the money with our heads bowed.

Then we did some fast talking.

"Ambassador," I said, after Balam and I had come to agreement, "you have a very good heart. You brought us from the border and now you have helped us again by giving us money. We thank you both very, very much." I paused to see if he followed me. He did.

"You have already given us the ultimate gift," I continued. "You have saved our lives. We accept your gift of money, but we wish to give it back to you. It is too much for us. We wish you to have it, so you will have savings for your old age."

Chana sincerely meant for us to take the money and he tried to press it on us, but we resisted, and finally his wife accepted it back. There was a deep and unspoken meaning to the exchange, and everyone there understood it. Balam and I still had our dignity. We initially accepted the money to give Chana face, then returned it to keep face ourselves and to show our respect for him.

As it turned out, Chana had been in Peking talking to Sihanouk when our letter arrived. When Chana looked at it upon his return, he was mystified—he didn't read French any more than he read Khmer, and he had to get the letter translated. But he was well aware of the desperate circumstances Cambodians were in, and he was probably more sympathetic to Cambodian refugees than anyone at his level of government. A few days after coming to see us, Chana, who was not only a diplomat but a major general in the Thai national police, sent passes to Balam and me. The passes allowed us to leave and enter Lumpini whenever we liked. But I didn't use mine.

I was still depressed. Black clouds closed in, blocking out the sun. I didn't want to talk to the other refugees, or explore Bangkok. All I could think of was my family and Huoy.

I remembered something Huoy told me during the Lon Nol regime. She said I should sell the gasoline trucks, buy an airplane ticket out of Cambodia and go wherever I wanted. That was just like Huoy. She didn't even ask me take her along. She told me to leave the country for my sake. She wanted what was best for me.

If I had listened to Huoy and left the country before the Khmer Rouge takeover, and taken her along, she would have been alive today. We would have been living happily together as man and wife. If I had listened to her, and if I had shown more leadership, I could have saved my entire family. But I hadn't, and they died.

If only I had listened.

Besides Ngim and my cousin Balam, I had one other relative in Lumpini. He had a Chinese name, Lo Sun-main. We were not related by blood—he was actually my brother Hok's brother-in-law—but we had been friends in Phnom Penh, and now that there were so few of us alive we felt a strong kinship. Sun-main saw that I was depressed. He tried to keep my spirits up. He talked with me and brought me food. He said the food came from a rich uncle of his who lived in Bangkok.

He kept trying to get me to meet this uncle, but I resisted. My excuse was that I had nothing but rags to wear. And it was true that my hair was in my eyes, my spiky beard was an inch long, and I didn't want to lose face by meeting strangers looking that way. But my real reason was that I wanted to remain in my misery and punish myself for my failures.

Finally the uncle, Lo Pai-boon, came to visit Lumpini. He was about fifty years old, with thin hair combed straight back. His wife was plump and wore her hair long. They brought food and fruit to me—to this doctor-relative they had been hearing about. When they saw me they broke into tears. They bribed the gate guards and drove me home in their car.

Uncle Lo had emigrated from Cambodia to Thailand as a child. He had worked hard, as overseas Chinese usually do, and he was now the owner of a large textile shop. He couldn't remember much of the Khmer language. I didn't speak much Thai. But we both knew the Chinese Teochiew dialect, and we had no trouble communicating. It was irrelevant that I was a Cambodian national and he was a Thai. Our backgrounds were close enough to connect us like a bridge.

While I was sitting in his house in my torn clothes, he summoned a tailor, who came in and measured me from head to foot. When the tailor left, the neighbors started coming in with gifts and Uncle Lo introduced me as a close relative and a doctor. In a few hours the tailor returned with five pairs of trousers and five shirts, freshly made. Uncle Lo and his wife took me to a shoe store, and then food shopping. From there they took me to the best Chinese restaurant in Bangkok. He and his wife sat on either side of me, heaping food on my plate. It was the most delicious meal I had eaten in more than four years.

Before he drove me back to Lumpini, Uncle Lo gave me 3,000 *baht*, which was then worth $150 U.S. And he wasn't done. He invited me back a second time, gave me prescription eyeglasses and more clothes and more money, and did the same for Balam.

With these two great gifts from Thai men—my full freedom from Ambassador Chana, and the clothes and money from Lo Pai-boon— I began to come out of my depression. But there was one more thing I needed to do before regaining self-respect.

I took the ID card photograph of Huoy from my luggage. I put all the money from Uncle Lo in my pocket, and I showed the pass Chana had written to the guards at the Lumpini gate.

In Bangkok's Chinatown district, I had Huoy's picture photographically copied onto a small heart-shaped piece of porcelain, then hand-colored. I took the porcelain to a goldsmith and ordered a gold locket to fit. When the locket was done, I hung it around my neck on a chain.

The locket was a talisman. Its heavy, reassuring weight was always there, under my shirt, over my heart. I truly believed that Huoy would guide and protect me as long as I wore it. I never took it off. She was with me, day and night.

I began to feel better. Something like a normal human being. My grieving wasn't over; and at night my dreams took me back to prison to be tortured again and again and again. But most days my mind was clear. I began to pay more attention to this remarkable place, Lumpini transit center, whose occupants had all escaped from communist regimes.

Camped next to me on mats was a Vietnamese family of ethnic Chinese background. Speaking in Mandarin Chinese, the lovely young daughter told me how her family had escaped Vietnam by boat. It was a dramatic story: hundreds of people crowded into small boats, storms approaching, waves breaking over the sides, everybody frantically bailing—and then Thai pirates. She didn't say much about the pirates except that they robbed the refugees of gold, but I knew what had happened to her by what she didn't say and by watching her expression. It made me glad that I hadn't sailed from Kampot to Thailand with Huoy.

There were also Chinese-speaking Laotians, merchants from the lowland towns and cities. They said that when the Pathet Lao communists took power in 1975, the soldiers and the high-ranking officials from the old regime were sent to "re-education" camps in the countryside. There they were forced to work long hours and sit through boring propaganda meetings. It was like the front lines in Cambodia except that far fewer died, because the Pathet Lao communists were not as cruel and not as fanatical. But the Pathet Lao attempt to reorganize the countryside into collectives was no more successful than the Khmer Rouge attempt, and most of the educated people and many of the peasants decided to leave. They crossed the Mekong River to Thailand, some of them swimming at night, others hiring boats or bribing officials to let them leave in broad daylight.

Unlike the lowlanders, the Laotian hilltribes didn't speak any of the languages I did, so I never got their story directly. But I learned that the men had been guerrillas for a CIA-backed army that fought in the mountains of Laos against the North Vietnamese. Their war didn't end with the takeover in 1975. The Vietnamese kept attacking. The hilltribes fought back as long as their supplies held out, then left when there was no other choice. The men were sturdy and tough, with black baggy trousers that went down to the middle of their shins. Their children were dirty and usually had snot running out of their noses. They were from different tribes, the H'mong and Yao and others. Some of the women wore headdresses with coins jangling, while others wore cloth wrapped around their heads like turbans, and necklaces made of silver.

With the Vietnamese and Cambodians and Laotians, the lowlanders and highlanders, the city people and rural people, the French-speaking intellectuals and the peasants who had never worn shoes in their lives, Lumpini was like Indochina in miniature. The teenagers were always fighting, just like the adults in their home countries, and the Vietnamese teenagers were the most aggressive of all. Speaking different languages, belonging to different races and cultures, we didn't think of ourselves as "Indochinese" or as "Indochinese refugees." Besides suffering under communism, we had little in common.

But it was an interesting place. I started working as a volunteer in the medical clinic with a Vietnamese doctor, a very nice man who was a refugee like me. Speaking in French, we agreed that the Vietnamese were in the best physical shape of the refugees, the Cambodians in the worst shape, and that the most serious health problem in Lumpini was mental depression. No matter where the refugees came from, most were traumatized from the loss of their families and their ways of life.

Working in the clinic, I began to make a lot of friends. Even the Thai guards started coming to see me for their medical problems, usually venereal disease. The guards liked me. They said I could leave or enter Lumpini anytime I wanted, with or without a pass. So finally I did.

The streets of Bangkok were jammed with buses, cars, trucks and three-wheeled *samlor* taxis whose noisy diesel engines gave off clouds of greasy exhaust. Motorcycles swooped and darted through the traffic with suicidal daring. Water taxis roared through an old network of canals, and ferries traveled back and forth across the Chao Phraya River. It was not a clean city. The air was smoggy and the water in the canals was black and disgusting. But I liked Bangkok. It was exciting and energetic. Everywhere there were high-rise buildings and skyscrapers and overpasses. The noise of traffic and construction came from all directions, at all hours of the day and night. I had never seen so many televisions, radios, refrigerators, restaurants, bars and soccer fields. The people were well dressed. Their standard of living was high.

Bangkok was like the dream city Chea Huon had talked about at the dam site, but instead of being a fantasy for the future, it was real and in the present. There was plenty of food. The roads were paved with asphalt. The houses had electric lights. Cranes and bulldozers did the heaviest work. Many families owned cars or motorcycles. Most important, the Thais were free. They did not have an "Angka." Nobody made them go to propaganda meetings or treated them like slaves. They organized themselves. And because they were free they were far more productive than we war slaves had ever been.

I went to the Royal Palace. It looked like the royal palace in Phnom Penh, with spires and multicolored tile roofs. I visited temples. There were a lot of them, clean and well maintained, with many Buddha statues and monks in saffron robes. I stopped by the open-air street-corner shrine in front of the Erawan Hotel. At this shrine, a few feet from a busy intersection, where the cars and motorcycles and *samlors* impatiently rev their engines and then take off like road racers before the traffic light turns green, a scene of intense religious worship went on day and night. Musicians played their instruments, classical dancers danced serenely, and people crowded in to light sticks of incense and pray. The ancient and the modern lived right next to each other, and both were doing well.

I envied the Thais. How I envied them! They had kept their traditional culture intact, while ours had been destroyed. Our temples were wrecked, our monks were killed, our books ripped apart for cigarette paper. The Thais had their past, and they were assured of a prosperous future. For most Cambodians, the future was going to mean searching in the forest for wild food, living in huts without electricity and obeying orders from soldiers. We didn't have a modern, bustling capital like Bangkok. Compared to it, Phnom Penh had been a quiet town in the provinces.

Back in Lumpini I began to talk with my friends. We had all noticed the same thing. Until coming to Bangkok few of us had known that a city so modern existed in all of Asia, much less in the country next door. We had always been told the reverse, that Cambodia was far ahead of its neighbors. All our leaders had told us so, from Sihanouk through Lon Nol to the Khmer Rouge.

It was a strange contrast, we agreed: two nations with similar cultures and resources, one of them a great success, the other a total disaster. We could understand how Thailand had succeeded, but why had Cambodia failed? We had answers, but they were inadequate to our sorrow. And probably we will ask ourselves the question as long as we live, and never be satisfied by the explanations.

This much I do know: The destruction of Cambodia could have been avoided. What led to it was politics.

By politics I do not just mean the Khmer Rouge. The Khmer

Rouge dealt the worst blow to Cambodia, but they did not destroy it by themselves. Outside countries lent a hand, most of them without realizing the effects their policies would have. It is a complicated story, going back many years.

To begin with, France, our former colonial ruler, didn't prepare us for independence. It didn't give us the strong, educated middle class we needed to govern ourselves well. Then there was the United States, whose support pushed Cambodia off its neutral path to the right in 1970 and began the political unbalancing process. Once Lon Nol was in power, the United States could have forced him to cut down on corruption, and it could have stopped its own bombing, but it didn't, until too late. The bombing and the corruption helped push Cambodia the other way, toward the left. On the communist side, China gave the Khmer Rouge weapons and an ideology. The Chinese could have stopped the Khmer Rouge from slaughtering civilians, but they didn't try. And then there is Vietnam. Even in the 1960s and early 1970s, when the Vietnamese communists used eastern Cambodia as part of their Ho Chi Minh Trail network, they were putting their own interests first. They have always been glad to use Cambodia for their own gain.

But sad to say, the country that is most at fault for destroying Cambodia is Cambodia itself. Pol Pot was Cambodian. Lon Nol was Cambodian and so was Sihanouk. Together the leaders of the three regimes caused a political chain reaction resulting in the downfall and maybe the extinction of our country.

On the outside these leaders were totally different. Sihanouk the royal populist. Lon Nol the right-wing dictator. Pol Pot the ultra-communist. On the inside they were all like Chea Huon, with fantasies about the development of the country. They also shared a typically Cambodian trait: an excessive pride in being Cambodian. I do not mean a normal, healthy, patriotic pride, but a feeling of racial supe-riority over everybody else. Our neighbors look down at us for being dark-skinned, and sometimes we do feel inferior, but at the same time, secretly, on the inside, we Cambodians also feel better than them, and when we have a chance we try to prove it.

Sihanouk told us again and again that we were an "island of peace," the envy of the world. He said we were a much more civilized people than the Vietnamese and the Thais. What he told us made us feel good about ourselves, but he never encouraged us to travel outside Cambodia to make our own comparisons. If we had, we might have seen how pitiful our economy was, how weak our military was, how inefficient our bureaucracy was. If we had known, and if Sihanouk had truly been interested in development, we might have been able to do something about it.

Sihanouk's successor was the incompetent Lon Nol. He wanted to purify everything about Cambodia—the race, the culture, the religion. He blamed the Vietnamese for Cambodia's problems and believed the Vietnamese were racially inferior. That is why he allowed his soldiers to massacre Cambodians of Vietnamese origin. That is why he attacked North Vietnamese troops along the Vietnam-Cambodian border, even though the North Vietnamese army was the toughest in Asia. Even more than Sihanouk, Lon Nol was a dreamer.

After Lon Nol came Pol Pot. The government swung from the extreme right to the extreme left, but on the inside the leaders were the same. Like Lon Nol, Pol Pot was a racist with fantasies of restoring Cambodia to greatness. He wanted to eliminate everybody who was not a pure Khmer of the countryside—the city intellectuals and professionals, the Chams (Cambodia's Moslem minority), the ethnic Vietnamese, even to some extent the ethnic Chinese. The Khmer Rouge boasted of their superiority. Others were "beneath" them, like lower forms of life. That is why the Khmer Rouge didn't think twice about killing or torturing. That is why beginning in 1977 Pol Pot made the incredible mistake of attacking Vietnamese territory and massacring their civilians. Like Lon Nol before him, Pol Pot actually thought he could win.

Sihanouk, Lon Nol, Pol Pot—each leader had a vision of Cambodia as a proud and independent country, different from its neighbors, better than any of them. Their visions were wrong. From one leader to the next, the condition of the country grew worse. By 1979 Cambodia was utterly destroyed. Next door in Thailand were paved roads, beautiful temples and more rice than the people could eat. As a refugee, the more I saw of Thailand, the angrier I became. It was the anger of a man who finds out he has been lied to all his life.

36

SALOTH SAR

In 1928 in Kompong Thom Province, in north-central Cambodia, a boy named Saloth Sar was born. He was of mixed Khmer and Chinese blood, like me. His parents were well-to-do farmers who owned their own land. However, his family had a rather unusual connection to Phnom Penh. One of his aunts was a concubine in the harem of King Monivong, Sihanouk's predecessor. Another cousin had an even more glamorous position, as the ranking harem wife. Through them, Saloth Sar's older brother got a job working in the protocol section of the royal palace.

When he was about five years old, Saloth Sar was sent to Phnom Penh to be raised by his brother. He often visited the palace and learned to speak the royal language, a kind of "high" Khmer with many complicated words and titles. He became a monk for several months, as most Cambodian boys did. He studied for six years in a temple school.

He was not a good student. He failed the exams that would have allowed him to enroll in the best schools. He went back to his family and then off to school in Kampong Cham Province. At age nineteen he finished his secondary education and returned to Phnom Penh to study carpentry. He made friends with students and graduates of the elite Lycée Sisowath, where I myself studied about twenty years later, and where Huoy taught a few years after that. One of his best friends was a bright young man and organizer of student protests named Ieng Sary.

Through connections, Saloth Sar got a scholarship to go to Paris, where he studied at a technical school, École Française de Radioélectricité. A year later Ieng Sary arrived in Paris, taking an apartment in the Latin Quarter. They met French communist intellectuals, and before long the two Cambodians started their own communist study circle. Others joined them, including a good-looking and rebellious young woman named Khieu Thirith, who was studying English literature at the Sorbonne. She married Ieng Sary. Later her sister Khieu Ponnary married Saloth Sar. The relationship between the four of them, the two sisters who married the two close friends, created the nucleus of the organization later known as the Khmer Rouge.

In Paris, Saloth Sar is said to have kept a photograph of Joseph Stalin in his room. He contributed articles to a Khmer-language magazine for radicals, signing himself "Original Khmer." For a man of mixed race, this was a strange pseudonym—probably an early sign of the racial fanaticism that marked his career. Certainly he was far more involved in politics than in his studies. After he failed three exams at the technical school, his scholarship was withdrawn. He returned to Cambodia, with a stop in Tito's Yugoslavia on the way.

By the time of his return, war was under way in Vietnam, with the French colonial forces battling Ho Chi Minh's Vietminh guerrillas. Saloth Sar enlisted in an underground organization called the Indochinese Communist Party (ICP), which had been founded while he was in Paris. The membership was a mixture of Vietnamese and Cambodians. When he joined his cell in eastern Cambodia, he was dismayed to find that Vietnamese controlled everything and expected the Cambodians to serve them. He worked in the kitchen and hauled human wastes from the privies. It was the same kind of menial work that Huoy and I did much later under the Khmer Rouge, but unlike us, Saloth Sar wasn't grateful for the easy work assignments. The Original Khmer resented the Vietnamese, and the jobs they gave him reinforced his lifelong grudge.

In 1953, without direct help from the Indochinese communists, Sihanouk won independence from France. The next year he went to the Geneva conference as the leader of a sovereign state. France agreed to give independence to its last two Indochinese colonies, Laos and Vietnam. A line was drawn across Vietnam at the seventeenth parallel, temporarily separating it into a communist north and a noncommunist south. Later, when the South Vietnamese insisted that the separation was permanent, the stage was set for the war of the 1960s and 1970s, when the northern communists tried to reunify the country.

For the Cambodian communists, a long, hard period had begun. Sihanouk outmaneuvered them at every turn. He abdicated as king, ran for prime minister as a prince and was elected easily. His foreign policy of left-leaning neutralism won him the friendship of China and the USSR, who gave him their aid and ignored the Cambodian communists of the ICP. Domestically, Sihanouk created an illusion of political freedom. He allowed the communists to participate in an aboveground leftist political party, the Pracheachon Group. He co-opted their most respected communist intellectuals, inviting two of them from the Paris study circle to serve in his cabinet. At the same time, without any publicity, he conducted a "war in the shadows." His secret police murdered communists without trials and without announcements before or afterward. Sihanouk even had the head communist, a man who knew all the rural networks, working for him as a spy.

In Phnom Penh the communists' situation was bad but not hopeless. The police didn't seem to know the identities of low-echelon party members like Saloth Sar. Saloth Sar and his relative-by-marriage Ieng Sary taught in an aboveground school, Kampuchea Bot. It was a good school, with high standards. (I myself took a math course there, during a vacation, while I was living in Takeo. I do not remember either man.) The wives of the two men taught at government schools, contributing most of their salaries to a French-language newspaper, *L'Observateur*, which was owned by a communist. The newspaper editor was one of their study circle friends with a cabinet post, Khieu Samphan, who had a reputation for integrity and independent thought.

Like Sihanouk, what the communists did in public and what they did in private were totally different. In their underground lives as party members they held clandestine meetings to indoctrinate new recruits and organize factory workers. In their aboveground lives they were hardworking members of bourgeois society. They all had mixed Khmer and Chinese blood. They were all intellectuals and city dwellers. And that is what is oddest about them, that they were bourgeois, well educated, mixed-race and urban. Fifteen years later these same people were the leaders of an anti-city, anti-intellectual, racist revolutionary movement. In those fifteen years they were totally transformed.

In 1960 they met in empty railroad cars near the Phnom Penh train station to form what came to be called the Communist Party of Kampuchea (CPK). Unlike the old Indochinese Communist Party, the CPK was totally free of the Vietnamese. Not long after, their overall leader, the man who had been a spy, defected openly to Sihanouk, and his successor was assassinated. Suddenly there was room at the top for younger, ambitious men. In 1963 Saloth Sar was elected party secretary, or leader. He had matured since student days into a man who was confident, secretive and highly manipulative. He seldom used his real name. His pseudonym among party members was "Brother Number One."

Within a few months, Brother Number One, Ieng Sary and most of the other ranking communists left Phnom Penh when Sihanouk started a crackdown. A few stayed, like Khieu Samphan, who was forced out of Sihanouk's cabinet but kept his seat in the National Assembly and became well known for his spartan way of life. When I was a schoolboy I used to see Khieu Samphan riding a bicycle around the city instead of driving a car. Idealistic intellectuals like my teacher Chea Huon admired him and joined the party at about this time. Then in 1967 there was another crackdown. Khieu Samphan escaped from Phnom Penh by hiding in a farmer's cart, but Chea Huon wasn't as lucky. I visited him in jail, not knowing anything about his secret life or about the "war in the shadows." Few did.

When they left Phnom Penh the Khmer Rouge leaders set up camp in the mountainous areas near the Vietnamese border. They had few weapons and no vehicles to speak of. When they wanted to travel they either walked or rode on elephants. They recruited dark-skinned mountain people, who had always been oppressed by lowlanders and who were happy to fight Phnom Penh. Life was hard and unglamorous. The mountain forests were infested with malaria and snakes. They never had enough to eat.

By the mid-1960s the second war in Vietnam was fully under way. The North Vietnamese used eastern Cambodia as part of their Ho Chi Minh Trail, but they gave the Khmer Rouge only token supplies for the use of the territory. China and the USSR didn't send aid either; they were still backing Sihanouk.

The Khmer Rouge would have been nothing but a half-forgotten, ragged band of guerrillas in the hills if it hadn't been for the 1970 coup. When Sihanouk was overthrown, and then unexpectedly joined them as a figurehead, the Khmer Rouge became politically significant overnight. They got weapons from the Chinese and the North Vietnamese. They got training from North Vietnamese and from Cambodian communists who had lived in North Vietnam for many years. Peasants joined them because they thought they were joining Sihanouk. The Khmer Rouge began growing rapidly. In this vulnerable period the North Vietnamese did most of their fighting for them.

The Khmer Rouge never trusted Sihanouk, and they kept him almost totally out of touch with their operations. He spent most of his time in Peking, more than fifteen hundred miles away, attended by people like Penn Nouth—the lawyer who had obtained my brother Pheng Huor's release from prison a few years before.

In 1973 the governments of North Vietnam and China arranged for Sihanouk to visit the "liberated zone" of Cambodia. Sihanouk traveled down the Ho Chi Minh Trail. He dressed for the photographers in black clothes with rubber-tire sandals so he would look like one of the Khmer Rouge. He spent a month attending banquets and ceremonies in his honor, and the whole time he thought that the leader of the Khmer Rouge was Khieu Samphan, because that was what the Khmer Rouge wanted everyone to think. To Sihanouk, Saloth Sar was an unimportant figure in the second or third ranks of leadership. Later, Sihanouk recalled that Saloth Sar was the most polite of the Khmer Rouge and the only one who spoke to him in the flattering "high" Khmer of the royal palace. It was a game of deceptions inside deceptions: Sihanouk was the figurehead who assumed that Khieu Samphan was the real leader; but in reality, Khieu Samphan was only fronting for Saloth Sar, or "Brother Number One."

The Khmer Rouge were experts at deception. Resenting the North Vietnamese but unable to get rid of them for the moment, they decided to purge their own ranks of the communist Cambodians who had lived in North Vietnam and recently returned. The Khmer Rouge scattered these men around the country, then invited them to attend "meetings" from which they never returned. Everything was secret. It was like the "war in the shadows." The deaths were never announced, and it was only when most of the veterans had already been liquidated that the rest suspected that their lives were in danger.

The Khmer Rouge soldiers' code of behavior was a deception too, though it served a practical purpose. It showed the common people that the Khmer Rouge behaved better than the officials of the Lon Nol regime, and this helped the Khmer Rouge win popular support. But once the Khmer Rouge had that support, they began to take away the peasants' rights in the "liberated" zones. They put the peasants in cooperatives with mass acreage to farm. They made them listen to long, boring propaganda speeches and made them give their private property to Angka. And they took away for execution those who disagreed. Few escaped to tell their stories, and few of us in Phnom Penh knew how brutal the communists really were. We only heard the good things, like how the Khmer Rouge never stole a single grain of rice.

The Khmer Rouge were never military geniuses, but they were brave. Half a million pounds of bombs fell on their territory, some of the heaviest bombing the world has ever seen, but it didn't stop them. When they attacked, they used human waves. They didn't care how many they lost—they just kept attacking and attacking, even when it was impossible to win. It was easy to find replacements for the soldiers they lost—the American bombing had displaced so many families that peasant boys from all around Cambodia were trying to join. To convince their new recruits that the sacrifices were necessary, the Khmer Rouge told them that they were supermen, the best in the world, the only ones who could defeat the American imperialists. The young soldiers believed it. These were the brainwashed teenagers I first saw on April 17, 1975, when they took over Phnom Penh.

Six days after the takeover, on April 23, 1975, the commander-in-chief arrived by jeep in the capital. There was no parade for him, no celebration. The rank and file did not even know who he was. He kept his identity a secret. Saloth Sar, previously known as the "Original Khmer" and "Brother Number One," took his final pseudonym: Pol Pot.

You know what happened next. He decided to put the rest of the country into collectives, just like the liberated zones, only he deceived us about his plans. So the "temporary" exodus from Phnom Penh became a permanent one, and gradually we "new" people were re-settled in rural cooperatives and deprived of our religion, our rights, our families and our personal property, just as the peasants in the liberated zones had been.

Pol Pot and his inner circle were very confident. They thought they could take a war-torn, bankrupt, agricultural country and turn it into an industrial power without any help from the outside world or from technical "experts." They adopted the idea from Mao Tse-tung, whom they admired, and possibly also from Stalin, who had tried something similar in the Soviet Union. Being proud and ignorant in a typically Cambodian way, they decided to push the idea to its farthest extremes. They planned to exploit the latent energies of the people by making us work harder and "freeing" us from responsibil-ities like cooking meals and raising children. Unfortunately Pol Pot the maker of policy was the same as Saloth Sar the mediocre student. He did not realize that Mao's Cultural Revolution was already a dis-aster and that Stalin's attempts had set the Soviet economy back by decades. He did not examine the idea to see if it was practical. It was senseless to build huge canal systems and dams without using engi-neers, but then Pol Pot was like that. He tried to make reality fit politics instead of the other way around.

During this period Pol Pot made no move to help his own family. At least one and perhaps both of the concubines related to him died in the countryside. His younger brother died of starvation. His older brother, who had taken care of him in his early days in Phnom Penh, survived the Khmer Rouge years without ever knowing that Saloth Sar and the head of Angka were one and the same.

If the reports are true, Pol Pot kept a string of houses in Phnom Penh. He moved from one to the next, never announcing where he was staying, to avoid assassination. He kept the lowest of low profiles, seldom appearing in public. Until September 1977 he didn't announce that "Angka" was the Communist Party of Kampuchea or that he was the nation's leader. He had no children, none of the family life that most people think of as normal. His wife's hair turned white; she went insane, and she was placed under special care.

Many have wondered whether Pol Pot himself was insane. If this were true, it would help explain the madness of his regime. And certainly his secrecy, lying and lack of common sense point to psychological problems. I myself think he suffered from paranoid delusions. But Cambodians who knew him personally had a far different impression. They saw a neatly groomed, soft-spoken man who smiled often, just like Chev. They say he had tiny, soft, almost feminine hands. Most of all, they remember something special about his character. They said he was easy to trust.

With Pol Pot keeping a low profile, the unofficial "first couple" in Phnom Penh were Ieng Sary, now minister of foreign affairs, and his wife, Thirith, the minister of social affairs. They had bodyguards, chauffeurs, cooks and maids. They had soap, shoes, medicines, all the things that we war slaves didn't. They ate the best food in the country, in a special "common kitchen" with the other top leaders. Ieng Sary became fat. His oldest daughter became a "doctor" in Phnom Penh, though she had no real training, while real doctors like me were unable to practice in the countryside.

The Khmer Rouge leaders lived in a section of Phnom Penh that had been cleaned up and restored for their use. Their public behavior was quiet and restrained. They hardly ever drank liquor. They bathed frequently and wore clean clothes. They spoke in soft voices and hardly ever showed either happiness or anger. They didn't do their own killing.

Except for their part of Phnom Penh, the city was empty. Where the open-air stalls had been next to the central market, banana trees were planted. Where the French cathedral had been there was only a flat field; every stone had been removed, and to outward appearances the cathedral might never have existed. The hulks of cars lay broken and rusting in piles around the city, and weeds grew everywhere.

Meanwhile, in an apartment in the Royal Palace, Sihanouk lived under house arrest. His story is strange and pathetic.

Sihanouk returned from Peking in September 1975 for a short visit, seeing only relatives. As the ceremonial President of Democratic Kampuchea, he then traveled to the United Nations, where he dismissed as "rumors" the reports of violence and executions in Cambodia. Accepting his public statements, not knowing that Sihanouk privately believed that the reports were true, hundreds of foreign-trained Cambodians returned home to serve their country. Most were executed.

Sihanouk returned to the Royal Palace and house arrest. A year later he resigned from his ceremonial post. The Khmer Rouge kept him and his wife alive in their guarded apartment but sent five of his children and eleven of his grandchildren out into the countryside, where all of them died or were murdered.

Khieu Samphan, his only visitor, gave Sihanouk a high-quality Grundig radio set. Cut off from all other contact, unable to leave the apartment, Sihanouk listened to the propaganda songs, the boasts about "mastering" the rice paddies, the false statistics of Radio Phnom Penh. He tuned to the broadcasts of the Voice of America and the Deutsche Welle. He tape-recorded the foreign news programs, listening to them again and again, trying to piece together what was happening in Cambodia. But nobody knew what was happening in Cambodia, not even the Khmer Rouge.

The Khmer Rouge headquarters, known as the Center, issued orders and collected reports from all over the countryside, but many of the orders were not carried out, and the production reports were falsified to meet expectations. At every level of the regime, cadre learned quickly that real results weren't as important as praising Angka, appearing zealous and echoing the "correct line."

In fact, conditions varied immensely from one cooperative to the next and from one zone to the next because the leaders in each place operated more or less as they chose. The Northwest Zone, where Huoy and I lived, had some of the worst leaders and worst conditions. In other parts of the country the leaders were more pragmatic. As long as they stayed in power, few people under them died from starvation or execution. But these leaders could not count on staying in power.

To Pol Pot, the zone leaders and most other high-ranking party members were rivals and potential enemies. It didn't matter that the men under suspicion were fellow veterans of a long and difficult revolutionary struggle. One of the first to go was Hou Youn, who had been a member of the communist study circle in Paris in the early 1950s and who advocated a less extreme reorganization of the countryside. Then came Hu Nim, another member of the study circle and later the Democratic Kampuchea minister of information; and Nhim Ros, commander of the Northwest Zone. The purge of the Northwest Zone was "vertical," as many of them were, reaching down to lower and lower subordinates. Chea Huon learned of the purge in time and fled. But Chev and Uncle Seng were too late.

In most purges the leaders and their subordinates were not simply executed. First they were tortured and made to "confess" to crimes they had never committed. In Phnom Penh the headquarters for torture was a few blocks from my old bachelor apartment, on the premises of a school I knew as Lycée Tuol Svay Prey. It was renamed S.21, though it became better known as Tuol Sleng, meaning "Hill of the Poison Tree," the name it was given by the next regime.

Unlike the rural prisons I was sent to, the S.21 torturers kept detailed records. Their false "confessions" and photographs of the victims exist to this day. Another difference with the prisons I went to was the S.21 population. Most of the twenty thousand who died there were not "new" people but actual Khmer Rouge. Imagine what it was like for them to write out the first, honest version of their biographies—and then, after a few sessions, confess to spying for the CIA or Hanoi, confess to anything at all to stop the interrogators from beating them again or reattaching the electric prods. Before they died they must have asked themselves, like a scream that echoed inside their heads, "Why?" Why was Angka doing this, when they had obeyed its rules? And they never knew why, any more than the rest of us did.

Nobody was safe from the purges—nobody but Pol Pot and a few he trusted, like Ieng Sary and his wife.

A colleague of theirs named So Phim was a member of the innermost circle of power—the Standing Committee of the Central Committee of the Communist Party of Kampuchea—and commander of the Eastern Zone. And So Phim was as ruthless as any zone leader could be. He executed monks. He slaughtered whole villages of Moslem Chams. Unluckily for him the Eastern Zone was next to the Vietnamese border. When Pol Pot ordered him to carry out border raids on the Vietnamese, So Phim obeyed, but he was not entirely successful. After all, the Vietnamese are difficult to defeat. But in Pol Pot's suspicious mind, So Phim failed because he was a Vietnamese agent. Four hundred Eastern Zone cadre were ordered to Phnom Penh, then imprisoned and tortured in S.21. And So Phim must have asked himself, "Why?" He must have asked "Why?" again when his midlevel military leaders were called to meetings and never came back.

When he himself was called to a "meeting," he refused. Two brigades loyal to the Center attacked.

Desperately, So Phim went into hiding and contacted Pol Pot by radio. He could not believe that Pol Pot was issuing these orders. It had to be somebody else's fault. He trusted Pol Pot. Everybody did. They had been comrades for twenty years. Pol Pot agreed to meet face-to-face with him, two old friends ironing out their problems. But instead of Pol Pot showing up for the meeting, boatloads of soldiers appeared, firing their weapons. So Phim committed suicide. His wife and children were shot as they were preparing his body for burial. Only a few of his aides escaped into the jungle. One of them was a division commander named Heng Samrin.

Pol Pot created enemies, and it is hard to say why. Perhaps he needed someone to blame when reality didn't match his politics. Or perhaps he created enemies to destroy, like a man who is truly paranoid. Eventually he created so many enemies that the regime started falling apart. With the government unable to meet any of its production goals, he needed more and more enemies to blame, and finally he created his ultimate enemy: Vietnam.

At first the Vietnamese weren't interested in fighting the Khmer Rouge. They were busy with their own problems, reuniting the North and South, "re-educating" the masses, reviving their shabby economy. But the Khmer Rouge kept attacking their border, slaughtering their civilians, raping their women, killing infants. And eventually the Vietnamese decided to solve two problems at one blow: Get rid of the Cambodian regime that was causing the nuisance, and bring fertile new territory under Vietnamese control. Vietnam is overpopulated. It has about sixty million people and a hard time feeding them. Cambodia is underpopulated. It has perhaps a tenth that many people and is capable of producing far more rice and fish than it consumes.

The Vietnamese invaded on December 25, 1978, with fourteen divisions and air support. Nothing could stop them.

On the night of January 5, 1979, when the sounds of combat could be heard in Phnom Penh, Pol Pot asked his house prisoner Sihanouk to talk with him. When they met, Pol Pot saluted him with his palms together in the *sompeah*, the very gesture his regime had outlawed. Then Pol Pot knelt as he had been taught in the Royal Palace as a child, bringing his left foot forward, then bending his right knee toward the floor. In his soft, ingratiating voice he apologized to Sihanouk for not being able to receive him sooner. He said he had been busy. He hoped Sihanouk understood. He was sure the Vietnamese would be defeated, but he wanted Sihanouk to help on the diplomatic front. Would he mind going to the United Nations, to hold on to Democratic Kampuchea's seat? Sihanouk, astonished, had the presence of mind to agree. He left the country by plane, going first to Peking. The next day the Vietnamese entered Phnom Penh.

As the Vietnamese advanced the Khmer Rouge retreated toward the caches of food and ammunition they had prepared in the mountains. They burned rice fields and rice warehouses to deprive the Vietnamese of food to eat. And as the two armies moved farther and farther west, civilians began to travel, and they saw with their own eyes the condition the country was in.

Cambodia did not exist anymore. Atomic bombs could not have destroyed more of it than civil war and communism. Everything that had been wrecked by the civil war of 1970–75 was unrepaired and further eroded—the flattened villages, the blown-up bridges, the roads cut with trenches, the washouts caused by the rains. Mile after mile of rice paddies lay abandoned and untended, pockmarked with bomb craters. The canals and dams the war slaves built were eroding to shallow ditches and useless mounds of clay. The towns and the cities were empty and abandoned. The temples had been destroyed. Rubbish and piles of rusting cars lay in heaps. There were no telephones or telegraphs, no postal services. In Phnom Penh itself there was little or no water and electricity and little functioning machinery of any kind. No typewriters. Not even pens and paper. There had been deaths in almost every family in the country. Widows and orphans wandered about the countryside, dazed, too hurt to cry.

How many survived nobody knew. The prewar population estimates had been vague—six or seven million, maybe as high as eight million. Amnesty International cites estimates that a million or more died in the civil war, before the communist takeover, and that between one and two million died under the Khmer Rouge. If that is true, the combination of civil war and revolution killed somewhere between a quarter and a half of Cambodia's population.

Among people and groups important to me, the ratio of deaths to survivors was much higher than for the country as a whole. Of 50,000 monks, less than 3,000 survived and returned to their former temples. Of 527 graduates of the medical school in Phnom Penh (my thesis, accepted in early 1975, was number 527, so there were at least that many graduates), about 40 survived. Of the 7,000 people living in my home village, Samrong Yong, before the war, about 550 survived, from what I have been able to discover.

Of the 41 people in my immediate family, including my parents, my brothers and sisters and their spouses and children, plus Huoy and her mother and me, only 9 survived. That is a death rate of 78 percent and a survival rate of 22 percent.

When the Vietnamese invaded it was time to heal the country. But communists are better at waging war than waging peace. The invaders and their "National United Front for the Salvation of Kampuchea" had no plans for reconstruction. The Front's puppet leader, Heng Samrin, had been a Khmer Rouge until the year before. His foreign minister, a one-eyed twenty-seven-year-old named Hun Sen, had also been a Khmer Rouge until defecting to the Vietnamese to avoid being purged. Six months after the "liberation" of Phnom Penh, Hun Sen finally met with international agencies to consider accepting emergency aid. The outside world was eager to help, but most of the aid that eventually got through to Phnom Penh was seized by the new regime and never reached the common people.

The Vietnamese looted factories of equipment, warehouses of rice and homes of furniture. And as they pushed the Khmer Rouge farther back, they tightened their control over civilians in the "liberated" territories. For example, in Siem Reap Province, near the ancient ruins of Angkor, a man named Dith Pran accepted a job as major of a small town because he wanted to help his people. But the Vietnamese checked on his political background and found that he had once worked for an American newspaper. To them this was worse than if he had worked for the Khmer Rouge. Dith Pran lost his job. He was afraid for his life, and later he left for Thailand.

Or take another example of tightened control, the hospital in Battambang City. At first, after the invasion, Cambodian doctors ran the hospital entirely by themselves. I joined the staff at the end of this period. When the Heng Samrin governor called a meeting, I left for Thailand. It turned out that my suspicions were right. After the meeting Vietnamese "advisers" took over the hospital administration.

Some of the remaining doctors left for Thai refugee camps. Others who were more prepared to collaborate joined the staff. One of them was Pen Tip.

In the countryside the Vietnamese tried to collectivize agriculture. They said that oxcarts and oxen, water buffalo and plows belonged to those who had taken care of them under the Khmer Rouge regime, not to those who had owned them originally. They said that land belonged to the government, not to individuals. They pushed peasants to farm in "mutual aid teams" of ten to thirty families each. The peasants hated this. They wanted to farm individually, as they had for centuries, before the Khmer Rouge.

The worst problem was a shortage of food. The Vietnamese controlled all the rice mills. They sent some rice to Vietnam, kept some for themselves and gave the rest to the Heng Samrin troops. By the middle of 1979 civilians couldn't get enough to eat. It was hard to raise crops. In some parts of the country there were no plows or oxen to plow with; in others there was no rice seed. A drought killed many of the fields that had been planted. For many Cambodians it was back to watery rice again.

Steadily, throughout 1979, the Vietnamese pushed the Khmer Rouge farther and farther west. Every time Pol Pot's forces planted food, the Vietnamese attacked before it could be harvested. Here was *kama:* The Khmer Rouge, the cause of so much hunger and starvation, now had nothing to eat except the leaves of the forests. Khmer Rouge units fought each other for food and medicine. Cadre deserted, and some died from starvation.

Meanwhile, the faint trails I had followed to Thailand became highways. Thousands and tens of thousands and even hundreds of thousands of feet walked along the paths. With the increased numbers came safety from robbers and rapists. With rumors of free rice on the Thai border, soon confirmed by broadcasts over the Voice of America, the masses began the march to the west. The people were hungry, and they were tired of communism. They wanted freedom. They wanted rice. And all of Cambodia was on the move, fleeing, marching, stumbling, spilling over the border into Thailand.

37

OKAY, BYE-BYE

THE VAN pulled up to the Lumpini gate and I climbed in, my heart beating fast. Except for the Thai driver there was only one person inside, and he was American. There was no way to avoid him. No-where to hide.

You might think that after being tortured three times and walking out of Cambodia I had nothing left to fear. Not true. From earliest childhood I had learned to be shy toward white people. I wasn't really afraid of them, but I deferred to them automatically. Most Cambo-dians did. We called them long-noses. Even as a medical student I had never talked with a long-nose unless there was a reason. I could communicate well enough in French, but I always felt more com-fortable when the conversations were over.

On the Thai-Cambodian border and in the Lumpini processing center in 1979, Cambodian refugees were shy toward Westerners. We were shy and passive because it was part of our culture and because we had come from a regime where saying the wrong thing meant death. Why take risks? Why talk to Americans when everyone knows they all work for the CIA? If we say the wrong thing, word will reach the top and then we will be in trouble. That was what Cambodians said, on the border and in the refugee camps.

We were also afraid of losing face. It was one thing to be able to speak French well, another to speak English badly. We were afraid the foreigners would look down on us for making mistakes in their language. Many Cambodians put off learning English, or didn't try out the few words of English they had reluctantly learned.

For me it was different. I had learned a bit of English under the

Khmer Rouge regime. In Lumpini a kindly Burmese lady volunteer named Chhoi Hah Muul taught me a bit more. I knew how to count. I knew the pronouns, some basic nouns and verbs and common phrases, in all probably five hundred words. It was enough to understand what the man in the van was saying. His name was John Crowley. He worked for the Joint Voluntary Agency, or JVA, which handled refugee resettlement matters for the U.S. embassy. Together we were going to Sakeo, a refugee camp for Cambodians that had just opened within Thailand, away from the border. I was going to be his interpreter.

The van drove through the crowded streets of Bangkok. John Crowley noticed that I was nervous. He asked if I was okay, if I wanted to stop for something to eat or drink. I told him no thanks, but I was encouraged, and looked at him out of the corner of my eye. He was about my age. Moustache, reddish-brown hair, big nose, white skin. His courteous tone of voice and his relaxed body posture all signaled that he wasn't going to order me around. By the time we got to the outskirts of the city, I felt better. John Crowley didn't care about race one way or the other. He was treating me like a fellow human being.

He asked me about my family.

"My vife she got died," I told him in English. "My, my *père*, he got died. Dey killing too many."

"You lost most of your family."

"Too many. Too many," I assured him. John Crowley was actually listening to me. He worked with the American government. If I could make him understand what had happened, then maybe he could help other foreigners understand. But squeezing the meaning of four years into a conversation in a language I barely knew was impossible. I just couldn't. . . .

I lifted my right hand to show him the stump of my little finger. "Dey . . ." and I made a chopping motion.

"The Khmer Rouge cut off your finger," John Crowley guessed.

"T'ree time," I said, nodding. "T'ree time. Vun, de finger. Two"—I had to think for the right word—"fire"—and pointed to the underside of my feet. "T'ree"—but I had forgotten the English word for water. Why couldn't I remember it when I needed it? It was very important to get him to understand.

"You were tortured three times," he said.

I nodded.

"Jesus," he said.

We were driving through the flat countryside east of Bangkok. John Crowley gazed out the window, sighing heavily. I looked out the window too, trying to see what he was looking at. In the rice fields, farmers were harvesting with tractors. The Thais were far ahead of us Cambodians in agriculture. They were ahead of us in everything.

"Sakeo more far?" I asked him.

"Sorry?"

"Combien de kilometres d'ici à Sakeo?"

John Crowley shook his head; he didn't understand French. I tried English again. "How far more Sakeo?"

This time he leaned forward and asked the driver in fluent Thai, then leaned back and told me in English that it was another hour and a half. He didn't look down on me for not speaking good English. Still, I had asked him the distance to Sakeo and he had given me the traveling time.

"My English not too good," I said.

"Hey, I can understand you perfectly," he said. "Don't worry. Look at it this way: Your English is better than my Khmer. I don't speak any Khmer at all."

"I teach you."

The tiny shock of surprise showed as he reconsidered the refugee sitting next to him. "You want to teach me Khmer?" he asked. "Well, okay, I could use it. When do you want to start?"

"I ready."

He shrugged and smiled. "I'm ready too."

I turned around to face him on the seat.

" '*Muoy*,' " I said to him, holding up one finger. " '*Muoy*.' Dat mean 'vun' in language Khmer."

"*Muoy*," he repeated.

" '*Bpee*,' " I said. "Dat mean 'two.' "

"*Bpee*," he said. "*Bpee*."

" '*Bei*.' Dat mean 't'ree.' "

"*Bei*." His intonation was nearly perfect; he already knew how to make similar sounds in Thai. When he had learned the numbers he pointed out the window at things he saw, a water buffalo, an ox, a tree, and asked me for the Khmer words. The Thai driver looked back at us in the rearview mirror, too polite to say anything. Thais do not like to learn Khmer; they think it is below them. But John Crowley seemed as though he had always wanted to learn Khmer and was glad to have the chance.

When the gate lifted and we drove into the Sakeo camp, I got out of the comfortable, air-conditioned van and back into the world I had left a few short months before. The camp was dominated by Khmer Rouge who had been driven over the Thai border by hunger and the Vietnamese. They had surrendered their weapons to Thai soldiers and allowed themselves to be trucked to this resting place, this dumping ground, administered by the Thai government and the UNHCR—the office of the United Nations High Commissioner for Refugees.

About two thirds of the camp population were Khmer Rouge and their families. The rest were "new" and "old" people unable to escape from their control. Behind us the camp gate lifted to admit a truck carrying fresh arrivals from the border. Dazed, weak civilians climbed down from the back of the truck. Among them was an old man I recognized from Tonle Batí. He supported himself with one hand on a bamboo staff and the other on the shoulder of his daughter-in-law, whom I also remembered. When I greeted them they looked at me with astonishment. There I was, well fed, well dressed, wearing glasses and a watch, accompanying this tall American. They poured out their story. Except for the two of them, everyone in the family had died. Time after time they had almost lost their own lives too. I translated for John Crowley as well as I could, then reached in my wallet and gave them a few hundred Thai *baht*, worth five dollars. They looked at me as if I were a god.

This was John Crowley's first visit to a Cambodian refugee camp. He had been sent there to see the refugees' condition firsthand, since he would be working in refugee resettlement. Other Westerners crowded into the camp, worried-looking UN officials, doctors and nurses, more than a dozen journalists with their cameras and television cameras.

Around them was a sea of sick and dying Cambodians, and a few dirty but healthy children who followed the Westerners everywhere, repeating the only English words they knew: "Okay, bye-bye. Okay, bye-bye."

As we walked past the camp hospital, two *mit neary* in black came out carrying a corpse between them on a stretcher. The hospital wasn't large enough to take care of the living or the dead. There were too many sick and not enough room. Patients lay on the ground outside with IV bags suspended above them from nails driven into trees. They lay in hammocks made of cloth bunched at the ends and tied to trees. They were too tired to brush away the flies. Some of them were just waiting for death. If they had to defecate, they just lay there and did it, sunk in the apathy of the late stages of starvation. There were mothers so weak they ignored their babies, and babies so weak they didn't cry. There were children with bright round eyes and hollow faces; when I waved my hand in front of them to test their reactions, they didn't blink.

John Crowley was upset. All the Westerners were, even the newsmen. They had never seen such suffering. But I had seen even worse, and I knew what it was to suffer myself.

Sakeo was like the death march from Phum Chhleav, I decided, except that the people of Sakeo didn't have to go any farther. They had already arrived. Yes, I thought bitterly, it was like the death march, but with doctors and international aid and photographers to record it. Most of them would live, and the ones who died would have the dignity of burial.

I had no sympathy for the Khmer Rouge of Sakeo. For them my heart was like stone. Let them die. Enemies forever. My sympathy was for the innocent civilians, like the old man from Tonle Batí, and others like him. It was not their fault that they were trapped in a place like this. I looked from the Khmer Rouge to the long-nose officials of the UNHCR and felt disgust. The UNHCR was supposed to protect refugees. That was the reason for its existence. But it had done nothing when the Thai government pushed forty-five thousand innocent Cambodians over the border and onto the minefields of Preah Vihear. Now it was setting up a camp to take care of Khmer Rouge. It did nothing for the victims and everything for the criminals. What was wrong with the UNHCR? Why couldn't it help the right refugees?*

The Westerners just didn't seem to understand much about Cambodians. Even John Crowley had to ask me which people were Khmer Rouge. But at least he knew there was a difference, and he was trying to learn to spot it with his own eyes.

I could tell the Khmer Rouge at a glance. They were the well-fed ones, with healthy, round cheeks. They wore black clothes that were not ripped, and new kramas made of silk or cotton. But even without the clothes and the healthy bodies, their expressions gave them away. They looked at me with narrowed eyes and curled-back lips, and they turned disdainfully away. They didn't want anything to do with a Cambodian accompanying a white-skinned devil.

Luckily, John Crowley didn't want to talk with them either. He asked me to bring him to the kind of refugees he would be working with, the civilians. We walked around and found some who had been rice farmers and small traders before the revolution. They told me their stories in Khmer, and I translated into my broken English as best as I could. John Crowley listened carefully and asked questions.

By the time the van brought us to Aranyaprathet, a town on the Thai side of the border, it was late at night. Many years before, my father had driven to Aranyaprathet in his old Ford truck to get the bronze Buddha statue. Maybe it had been a nice town then. In 1979 it was a rather menacing place serving border smugglers, thieves and the Westerners who were helping the refugees. Under the streetlights a few heavyset men watched us, standing next to their elongated motorcycle-taxis, decorated with chrome and powered by automobile engines. We drove in the van from one hotel to another. They were all full. Finally we found a room with two beds for four hundred *baht* or twenty U.S. dollars, more than double the usual price. John

---

*As I later learned, the UNHCR had a few good people in Thailand. My favorite was Mark Brown, an energetic, capable Englishman who was at Sakeo and later at Khao-I-Dang. But my first impression was basically right. As a whole the UNHCR was extremely disappointing—a timid, incompetent bureaucracy that didn't do its job. It paid retail prices for huge truckloads of food and allowed corruption to flourish. It didn't protect the safety of refugees on the border or even in the refugee camps inside Thailand. When the UNHCR won the 1981 Nobel Peace Prize, I couldn't believe it. I thought it had to be a mistake. So did most people who had seen the UNHCR's performance in Thailand. Since then, many of its functions have been taken over by the U.N. Border Relief Organization, or UNBRO, which does a much better job.

Crowley took one bed, I took the other and the Thai driver went off in the van to look after himself.

Lying on that hotel bed, I felt tired but content. It was the first time since Phnom Penh that I had been on a real mattress with sheets. How nice that the driver had to go off, instead of me.

I thought: John Crowley has helped me. He hasn't looked down on me, or patronized me. He has treated me as an equal. So friendly and informal. Maybe all Americans are like that. If that's how they are, the United States will be a good place for me.

Yes, how different the foreigners are. They do not care about face. They do not have to present a mask to society and keep their feelings hidden behind it. They do not care so much about social rank. A Cambodian would have treated me either better than himself or worse. Probably, a Cambodian would have sent me off with the driver and kept the hotel room with two beds for himself.

Yes, to be treated as an equal, I thought, as I stared at the hotel room ceiling. That's what I want. And no more being shy toward Westerners.

Back in Bangkok, I had an interview at the JVA about going to America. Unfortunately my caseworker wasn't John Crowley but a strong-willed woman whom Cambodian refugees called "The Tiger." The Tiger looked at me with obvious suspicion. Since my name didn't appear on any American embassy lists, she decided I had bribed my way off the border. I gave her General Chana's phone number, and she spoke with him, but whenever she looked at me she frowned. To her I was an "operator," a guy who was always finding a way around the rules.

Of course, she was partly right. I *was* an operator. With Chana's pass I was constantly going in and out of Lumpini. I had even started to show up at JVA parties. And why not? I wanted to be free—to go where I wanted, to do what I wanted, to live on my own terms. That's why I had escaped from communism.

The Tiger made me an offer. She would let me go to the United States if I worked with refugees first, as a doctor. She said there was a big influx of Cambodians on the border and that the Thais were going to open more camps like Sakeo. I told her okay. The only part of the arrangement I didn't like was being apart from Ngim, who would stay with Balam. I told Ngim I would rejoin her as soon as possible.

Ngim said she understood, and hid her sorrow.

The Cambodians came to places that had barely existed before but now would never be forgotten—to Kamput and Mak Moon, Nong Chan and Nong Samet, Ban Sangae and Camp 007, the smugglers' paradise. And they kept coming. They carried sacks on their backs and balanced baskets on their heads. The old supported themselves with canes. Widows carried shoulderboards with the baby in the front basket and their belongings in the back basket. They made makeshift tents from sackcloth or from blue plastic tarps and strung them from sticks in the ground or from trees. They sat in exhaustion with their knees bent and their elbows or forearms resting on their knees, and their thoughts were far away.

The border was a no-man's-land. It didn't belong to Thailand and didn't belong to Cambodia. Each settlement was ruled by a military group—south of Aranyaprathet by the sullen, disciplined Khmer Rouge; north of Aran by untrained, corrupt Khmer Serei factions. The Khmer Serei were a disappointment. They collected *bonjour*, put up tollgates and fought each other for control of the black-market trade. It was hard to believe that a year before we had expected them to be our liberators.

In November 1979 the second refugee camp inside Thailand opened, away from the border. It was north of Aranyaprathet, on a broad slope of scrubby trees and hillocks with a forested mountain rising beyond. A stream of people walked there from the border, and others arrived by bus or truck. The people were thin and dazed and looked as though they were trusting themselves to destiny.

The name of the place was Khao-I-Dang. It was a camp for Cambodians who were opposed to the Khmer Rouge, and it was busy from the start. Westerners rushed around organizing construction and emergency medical care. Cambodians who were strong enough cut down trees and cleared land with their hatchets. Thai laborers began building a hospital of bamboo, with blue plastic spread over the rafters as a temporary roof. I presented a letter from the JVA to the UNHCR office, got my credentials and began working before the hospital had walls.

Like Sakeo, Khao-I-Dang had a full-scale emergency at the beginning, but unlike it, the patients were not Khmer Rouge, which to me made them more worth saving. Certainly there were more patients than we could handle. We all worked very hard, going from one sick person to the next. When I glanced up I saw another clinic being built next door. Everywhere, buildings were going up, and still refugees were streaming in from the border.

In the first week at Khao-I-Dang so many died that the bulldozers had to take time out from making drainage ditches to dig a burial pit. In the hospital patients lay passively with intravenous tubes pouring glucose into their veins. The children looked twice their age, solemn and sad, with hollow cheeks and blank stares. The Western doctors took the emergency cases. I treated walk-in patients, many of whom were suffering from mental problems as much as from malnutrition or disease. They had seen too much killing, lost too many relatives. They were depressed and suicidal, and they wanted to go home. They needed medical care but they also needed counseling, and this was something the Western doctors could not give them. I talked to them in Khmer, consoling and encouraging them. If they did not need any other medication I gave them vitamins and iron pills, which seemed to help them psychologically. I knew from my own case how important it was to overcome depression.

I remember one patient above all others, a dehydrated twelve-year-old girl with falciparum malaria. She was an orphan, black staring eyes in a flesh-covered skeleton. A Western doctor had taken her history and her blood, and the lab was running the tests on her. She was lying on the bed without focusing. She had rejected her food. There was nobody around her. I sat on the bed and picked her up in my arms. She was nearly weightless. I talked to her in Khmer and got her to swallow a few spoonsful of food. She was conscious, though not by much, and I knew she was listening. Then her head jerked back with a spastic gasp of air and it jerked back six or seven more times and then after one last deep breath her head sagged to one side with her eyes half open.

I could hardly work the rest of that day. The girl's death was too close, too personal. She had lived under the same regime, seen the same clouds in the same sky. She had lost her family and I had lost mine. When she died I was holding her in my arms, the same way I had held Huoy.

Around me were dying Cambodians, Western doctors working hard to save them and cheerful little children peering through the split-bamboo walls, calling out, "Okay, bye-bye."

By December 1979 the World Food Program, UNICEF and other organizations were delivering large amounts of rice along the border. Some of it never reached the refugees. The Khmer Rouge took what they could, and so did the Khmer Serei warlords, who sometimes sold the rice they stole back to the UN so it could be distributed a second or third time. But even with the stealing there was more food on the border than before, partly because of international aid and partly because of the black-market traders. Each morning a stream of Thais headed for the border carrying everything from live chickens to vegetables to soft drinks to soap, radios and bicycles. The refugees produced bits of gold they had kept hidden for years, and deals were made. By this time, also, the border camps had better medical care than in the months before.

In Khao-I-Dang itself the medical crisis eased. The patients who were strong enough to survive their first few days in the hospital generally recovered. They regained alertness, filled out in body size, started to talk again. They got better quickly because they were physically tough—they had to be, to come this far—and because of Western-style medicine, which had far better healing properties than the "rabbit turds" and other herbal medicines of the Khmer Rouge era.

Western aid poured into Khao-I-Dang. The original bamboo shed where I worked became the adult medicine ward, run by the American Refugee Committee (ARC), of Minneapolis, Minnesota. Bamboo-and-thatch wards sprang up on both sides of a street, specializing in pediatrics, surgery, obstetrics and gynecology, feeding and rehabilitation and so on, each one run by a different foreign voluntary agency. Thirty-seven of these agencies, most of them from the United States, France or Germany, ran programs in Khao-I-Dang. Ironically they had come in response to photographs and television footage taken in the Sakeo camp of starving Khmer Rouge. But I was glad they were there, and they surprised me with their energy and their good hearts. I had never seen people who worked with such determination and who got so much done. Public-health workers, teachers, journalists, administrators, immigration officers, politicians—the Westerners kept coming and coming.

And the Cambodians kept flowing into the camp. They cut trees down for firewood until the hillside was bare. They built shacks with bamboo and thatch and palm-leaf panels and the blue plastic tarps. The shacks spread along a gridwork of red-clay roads with familiar names, like Angkor and Monivong and Phnom Penh. The population climbed to an official figure of 130,000, though the actual figure was higher. At its peak, Khao-I-Dang was the largest settlement of Cambodians anywhere in the world.

At night the camp was unsafe. There were revenge killings, robberies and rapes. Thai villagers came over the fence at night to sell goods, and Thai soldiers fired at those who wouldn't give them *bonjour*. Under the dirt floors of the shacks were storage holes and tunnels. Most of the families in camp had something or someone to hide.

During the day, when the Westerners were there, the camp had a better character. It was a place for life to begin again, for bargaining at the market, for praying at the temple. Because of the chance of resettling abroad, most of Cambodia's old middle class and elite showed up in Khao-I-Dang. People who hadn't seen each other since the fall of Phnom Penh met in the red-clay streets and asked each other how they had survived. The camp was like a city. Besides hospitals it had schools, workshops, soccer fields, quasi-legal markets, cafes, tailor shops, a temple and a tracing center where people went to look at notices and photographs of missing relatives.

Finding our families—that was the most important goal. For us "family" had come to include cousins so remote that the exact connection had been forgotten or had never even existed. A relative on my father's side, an older woman whom I had always called "Aunt," flew from France to Thailand to bring money to her daughters, who were refugees in Khao-I-Dang. She could not get a pass to visit the camp and I became her messenger. A few months later another of her daughters, who also lived overseas, came to see me. She gave me money too, some for her sisters, some for myself.

With the money I hired a young man to take a letter from me to my brother Hok in Battambang. Hok, his wife and his baby walked into Khao-I-Dang while it was still legal. Then I sent a message to my other brother, Hong Srun, in Phnom Penh. Hong Srun had heard of the Thai massacre at Preah Vihear and decided not to come, but the word spread, and more cousins showed up on the border.

By this time, about March 1980, the Thai government had ended its open-door policy. Refugees could not just walk into Khao-I-Dang from the border anymore. A bearded American doctor who worked for one of the relief agencies decided to help me. A driver took us to the border. We loaded my cousins into the van, made them lie down and pretend to be sick, put bandages on them and rigged up IV bags. At the Khao-I-Dang gate the guard just waved us through. The Western doctors did most of the smuggling of this type, because the Thai guards deferred to them.

I worked at the ARC adult medicine ward all day, seven days a week. At first it was hard for me to understand the Americans' English. I also found that my techniques of treatment were not always the same as theirs. In Cambodia, for example, we had used much higher doses of antibiotics on our patients than the Americans did. Gradually, however, over the weeks and months, my confidence returned. The American doctors were both friendly and skillfull. We saw a lot of edema or kwashiorkor cases at first, and after that malaria and tuberculosis, fungus infections and occasional cases of leprosy. We got overflow cases from surgical recovery, and we did some minor surgery ourselves. Besides me, the Cambodian staff included another doctor, a couple of medical students and some unusually talented young nurses and translators.

At the end of the afternoon I was the only Cambodian to climb into the van with the Americans. Twenty-one of us lived together in a rented house on a dirt lane near the Shell gasoline station in Aranyaprathet. Following the Asian custom, we left our shoes and sandals on the stairs to the upper floor. But on the porch that had been converted into a dormitory men and women slept on mattresses next to each other and thought nothing of it, which Asians would never do. In the tiny bedrooms of the house there were some very noisy nighttime romances going on, which was also un-Asian; because Asians are afraid of losing face, we are much more discreet.

In the evening, before going to sleep, I watched the gecko lizards scuttle up the walls and perch upside down on the ceiling, without blinking, next to the fluorescent lights. Automatically I calculated what I would have to do to catch them. And then I thought, No, I can let you survive now. Things have changed. No more killing. No more hunting wild animals. It is a time to live and let live.

The others on the ARC team were very kind. When I tried to tell my story they listened, even though it was painful for them and even though my English wasn't good. They invited me to all the Westerners' parties on Saturday nights and I danced to loud rock music. I even danced with the ARC leader, a redheaded woman who drove in from Bangkok every week, whose name was Susan Walker. Dancing Western-style was energetic and sweaty, the opposite of the Cambodian *romvong*. I liked it. In Cambodia I had always been more active than my friends, the first to get angry, the first to laugh, the last to leave the athletic fields. Now I had found a culture that was up to my speed. It was good to know these Westerners and to be working with them as a colleague.

But I was not happy. When I was tired, and we were tired every evening from work, it was hard to communicate. I stopped trying to keep up with their rapid English and let my thoughts drift off. I always thought about the past.

In truth, my depression was returning. I had come to Thailand in May 1979. As May and June and July of 1980 went by I heard no news about going to America. Balam and Ngim were there already. My brother Hok went there. The Americans I had known when I first came to Khao-I-Dang had left, and their places were taken by new volunteers. Even some of these had left. Everyone was going except for me. There was some problem with my immigration file at JVA, but nobody explained to me what it was.

I was lonely. I met a young Thai woman of Cambodian descent who lived in Aranyaprathet. She had a round face and a light complexion. In profile she looked exactly like Huoy. She seemed to like me a lot. We talked about getting married. Then she saw the chain with the locket of Huoy around my neck and she asked me to take it off. I explained that I was showing my respect to Huoy for saving my life, but the woman became suspicious. She said she was sure Huoy was still alive inside Cambodia. She accused me of wanting her as a second wife. And her family looked down on me because I was a refugee. So nothing ever came of it.

It was time to say, Okay, bye-bye. But by August 1980 it seemed that I would never leave Thailand. To me, and to hundreds of thousands less fortunate than me, Thailand had become a jail. We couldn't go forward and we couldn't go back. We were only a few miles from Cambodia; at night we could hear the rifle fire as factions of Khmer Serei attacked one another and the boom of artillery as the Vietnamese attacked the Khmer Rouge. In Khao-I-Dang security was tight. The fences were guarded. There were no trees left inside the camp and very little shade. It was a harsh, dusty place except when it rained, and then the red dust turned into mud. The terror was over, but our minds had not healed.

38

▬

TO AMERICA

IT WAS John Crowley who rescued me. I went into the JVA to talk to The Tiger's replacement—by that time actually the replacement's replacement—and got nowhere. There were still problems with my case, though what they were was not explained to me. No, I wouldn't be going to the United States anytime soon. I walked angrily upstairs to John Crowley's office. John Crowley wasn't the boss of the JVA, but he ranked somewhere near the top.

He looked up from his desk. "Well, well. Ngor Haing Samnang. What can I do for you?" He always used my official name—I had added the "Samnang" when I got to Thailand, and it appeared in all my files.

"I vant to go America, John."

He flipped through some papers, ran his finger down a calendar. "The next flight is August sixteenth. That's in four days. Go back to Aranyaprathet, pack your stuff and go. You ready?"

"No. Next month I go. I haff too much to do. I haff many tings to buy."

He looked at me with a faint smile. "We have a lot of stores in the United States, you know. Don't worry about the shopping."

"No, no, no. Too expensive in United States. Too, too expensive. I buy tings here." I didn't tell him the real reason, which had nothing to do with shopping. Cambodians living overseas were sending money to me to bring to their relatives in the refugee camps. It was illegal for me to bring money into the camps, but I felt an obligation to do it, and I had to find someone else to take my place.

We bargained for time and agreed that I would go on the flight the following week, on August 23. I thanked him, he shook my hand and wished me luck. I went to the Trocadero Hotel to get my paycheck from Susan Walker, the ARC leader. Susan was like John. She had never tried to patronize me and I had always respected her for that. She had always treated me like a fellow human being, and we had a good-hearted farewell.

Then I went out and bought everything I didn't think I would be able to find in the United States, like seeds for Asian vegetables, rubber shower sandals and a radio. (As it turned out, the same model radio was much cheaper in the United States, shower sandals were easy to buy and I never did get around to planting the vegetable seeds.) While in Bangkok I visited my benefactors, General Chana and Uncle Lo, to thank them for what they had done. Then I returned to Aranyaprathet to attend a party given in my honor in Khao-I-Dang. The ARC medical team was there, and so were many refugee friends, and there was music and dancing and happiness and some crying too.

The next night I went to a Westerners' party. There was an out-door showing of an American film starring John Wayne as a cowboy who rode his horse through the desert and killed a lot of people. It was the first movie I had seen about America, and I asked one of my ARC medical colleagues, Dr. Dale Fanney, if America was really like that, with so much violence and shooting. Dale kept a straight face and said I would see for myself when I got to the United States.

From Aranyaprathet I went back to Bangkok and ran into John Crowley at the U.S. embassy. He sighed and shook his head. By then it was about August 28. I had missed my flight.

"Ngor Haing Samnang, you give me a headache."

"I sorry, John."

From then on everything was in a crazy rush. I never did get my predeparture medical inspection. Day after day my name had been announced over the loudspeakers in the Lumpini transit center, and my friends had been cursing me. They all wanted to be in my place, leaving for America, and I hadn't even bothered to show up for my medical appointment. Of course I wanted to leave for America, but on my own terms.

On August 30, 1980, I finally left. Like everyone else, I had a white plastic handbag with the logo of ICEM (the International Committee for European Migration), the agency that ran the flights. Inside the handbag were my documents, including a photograph of me holding a card with my T-number, or transit number, which was 33144, like a prison convict holding his identification number for the authorities.

It was not my first plane flight. During the Lon Nol regime I flew several times on DC-3s. Some of the other Cambodian, Vietnamese and Laotians refugees had also flown on military or commercial flights before the communist takeover. But for most of the refugees this was the first time inside an airplane. We were on a seven-hundred-seat Boeing 747 chartered from Flying Tiger Airlines. We filled every seat. Row after row, aisle after aisle, nothing showing over the seat tops but black Asian hair.

As soon as the plane took off from the runway, the airsickness began. Lots of noisy vomiting, sometimes in the airsickness bags, sometimes not. The children rushed to the side of the plane to look out the window, old women began praying in loud voices and H'mong babies squatted in the aisles and peed. One old Cambodian lady told everyone in a loud voice not to touch the seat-reclining buttons in the armrests in case it caused the plane to fall into the ocean.

I was the doctor on the flight and also the one who translated information into Khmer about fastening the seat belts, not smoking and using the emergency air supply. Someone else did the translating for Vietnamese and Lao. I got on the loudspeaker several times to remind the Cambodians how to use the lavatories. I told them not to be afraid. When they got inside the lavatories they should lock the door, because that would also turn the lights on. When they were finished with the toilet they should use the flushing handle. My advice didn't do much good. Some of the Cambodians were so rural that they had never seen flush toilets before. I could see the confusion on their faces. They were afraid to ask questions, afraid to touch anything on the plane in case it broke and they would be blamed for it. But they were also afraid to disgrace themselves for soiling their clothes. Slowly, inevitably, as the hours passed and as their bladders filled, they edged nervously toward the lavatories. Inside, I am sure, most of them squatted in darkness with their feet on the toilet seat in Asian style.

The airline made one concession to us, and that was serving rice with all the meals. The stewardesses rolled their carts down the aisles and gave each of us a choice of chicken with rice or beef with rice. I peeled the foil off the food tray and looked at my meal, the chicken in one divider, the rice in another. There was something suspicious on top of the rice. I smelled it dubiously, tried a bit of it and didn't eat any more. It was the first time I had tasted cheese sauce in my life. Cheese is practically unknown in Asia. People in the seats around me remarked that the rice wasn't very good. We were all worried about the food in America if this was what it was going to be like.

We made a refueling stop at Hong Kong, then headed across the Pacific for Honolulu. In the cabin, dark except for the overhead rows of little lights, we stayed awake and thought about America, the country that could build huge jets but couldn't do something as simple as cook good rice. We sat in the darkness and listened to the quiet whooshing sound of the plane and the noise made by the refugees. Children cried and adults were throwing up, and the old ladies were still praying.

In the daytime we had a long stopover in Honolulu. The second night began while we were en route to San Francisco. We were wondering how far away the continental United States could possibly be.

On the second morning we saw the California coastline and a lot of houses close together and tiny-looking cars on the roads and then we landed at San Francisco. We stood in line for a long time to get our I-94 forms from immigration, which we put carefully in our white ICEM bags with all the other forms we were carrying. Then we obediently got onto the most modern buses I had ever seen. When the driver pulled a handle to open the front door, the back door opened too; when he closed the front door, the back door closed the same way. I sat in the front seat to watch. We drove up the freeway, across the Bay Bridge, along more freeway on the other side. It didn't look anything like the John Wayne cowboy movie. There were streets, houses and cars beyond number, but nobody was riding horses and nobody was on foot. I thought: How do people meet and talk if they don't see each other in the streets? How can I find a job in a place like this?

They took us to a former military base up in the hills to recover from the flight. Cambodians who had arrived a few months before were there to serve us Cambodian food and answer our questions. I asked how to make a telephone call, and a man volunteered to make a call for me when he left because there weren't any telephones nearby. I asked him to call my cousin Try Thong to come get me. Try Thong lived in a place called Los Angeles. I was scheduled to go to Ohio, and wherever that was I knew I didn't want to go there.

The man who had offered to call didn't come back the next day. I paced back and forth like a caged animal. I didn't know where I was and didn't like being at the mercy of other people. I had helped rescue Try Thong's sisters and their children from the Thai-Cambodian border and sneak them into Khao-I-Dang. It seemed reasonable to expect that Try Thong could rescue me.

On my third morning in America my name and T-number were called on the loudspeaker system and I got on a bus that took me back to the San Francisco airport. At the airport terminal someone told me to sit and wait for somebody else who would show me where to go. I sat down with my two large suitcases and a heavy cardboard box full of medical books. Twenty minutes later a young curly-haired Cambodian working for my sponsoring organization, U.S. Catholic Charities (USCC), appeared and told me to follow him. He didn't use the courteous words that are normal when talking to an older person in Khmer. He started down a long corridor.

"*Luk*," I called after him anxiously. "Please wait. I have to take my luggage in relays."

"All right, but hurry up," he said. I ran after him with one suitcase, came back for the next, then the box of books. By the time I caught up to the first suitcase he was nowhere in sight.

My own countryman had abandoned me. Like the guides who had abandoned us on the way to the Thai-Cambodian border.

I had no idea where I was, or what flight I was supposed to take.

I waited.

A lady at a ticket counter nearby saw me sitting alone and discouraged and asked, "Where are you going?"

I said, "I don't know. I a refugee." I walked over to the counter and showed her my papers, my I-94 form, my photograph and T-number from Lumpini. This was to prove I was legally in America, so she wouldn't make me leave. She stared at my papers and didn't know what to make of them.

"Who's taking care of you?" she asked me finally.

I said, "Cambodia guy. My plane is a ten-thirty plane."

She started making phone calls to see what plane I was supposed to be on. Another lady came over and I showed her my papers too. She studied them.

"Your plane's already left," she decided.

The women called USCC, which had an office somewhere in the airport. I waited nervously for another hour and then someone from USCC showed up. We walked down one long corridor and then the next and the next and finally into the office. Some other refugees were there speaking Vietnamese. Then the young Cambodian with the curly hair appeared.

"Where did you go?" he asked. "I waited for you."

I gave him an angry look.

"*Luk*," I replied sarcastically in Khmer, "don't ask me where I am going. Ask yourself where you are going. Do you know what you are doing, little boy? Don't forget, if there were no refugees, you would not have a job here. And your job is to help refugees."

The Vietnamese were trying to get me to calm down, but I was just getting started. I pointed my finger at the young man and shook it right in his face.

"I told you I had a lot of things to carry, but you didn't offer to help me!" I shouted. "You were supposed to take care of me. It was an easy little job, but you couldn't even do it. You pretend you're so important that you can't even be bothered! You've got to remember something, motherfucker: I know nothing here. I'm like an animal from the jungle. I'm a refugee. You have an obligation to help me. You're Cambodian and I'm Cambodian. We're from the same place. You should have helped me, but you didn't. That's why the country fell, because of stupid, arrogant people like you who only think about themselves!"

I was just getting started, but the American boss showed up. He invited me into his private office to talk. I didn't have the vocabulary to tell him everything in English that I'd told the young man in Khmer. But he got the general idea.

At eleven-thirty that evening I landed in the airport at Columbus, Ohio. My friend and co-sponsor Hay Peng Sy met me there. I knew him when he was a pilot for Lon Nol and then got to know him better in Lumpini. He had come to the United States ahead of me and had gotten a job in Columbus as a caseworker for USCC, which is why USCC was my institutional co-sponsor. Following the Western custom, Hay Peng Sy had changed his name to Peng Sy Hay, with his family name last. Similarly, my name was changed from Ngor Haing Samnang to Haing Samnang Ngor.

We went to his house. The next day we went to the USCC office to do paperwork and then went out to look for apartments. I didn't say anything, because I didn't want to repay his kindness with ingratitude, but I had no intention of renting an apartment in Columbus. The place I wanted to be was called Los Angeles. I didn't know where Los Angeles was. I didn't know whether it was a state or a city, whether it was big or small, on the seacoast or in the mountains, hot or cold, or whether a lot of Cambodians lived there or only a few. All I knew was that my niece Ngim was there, Balam was there and so was my other cousin Try Thong. That was all I needed to know.

I hung around Columbus for a few days, watching the programs on a black-and-white TV. It was hard to understand what the TV characters were saying because they spoke too fast. I took a short trip on a Greyhound bus to South Bend, Indiana, to visit some Cambodian friends, then returned to Columbus.

I had left Thailand with about twelve hundred dollars, my savings from working as a refugee camp doctor. The money was already slipping away, with gifts and with the trip to Indiana. For three hundred dollars of my remaining money I bought a plane ticket to Los Angeles. My second cousin Try Thong picked me up at the L.A. airport. He had left Phnom Penh before the Khmer Rouge takeover and had been in the United States since then. He was quite Americanized: Instead of reversing the order of his names, he had changed his name to Phillip Thong. He was a smart fellow, younger than me, and he was doing well for himself as an accountant.

From Phillip's house I called my cousin Balam. Balam and I had drifted apart when I was working in Khao-I-Dang, but I had counted on staying with him until I found a place of my own. I was disappointed. Balam said there wasn't enough room in his apartment for me. He explained that there was a maximum-occupancy rule. His landlord didn't want more than four people living in a two-bedroom apartment, and there were already more than that, with Ngim. I thought: Whatever the landlord is like, he isn't Khmer Rouge. If we break the rules he isn't going to kill us. But I kept my mouth shut and stayed the night with Phillip Thong.

The next day I went over to Balam's apartment, outside L.A.'s Chinatown. Balam helped me find and rent a tiny room around the corner in the same apartment complex. It was a ten-by-fifteen-foot room with a kitchen in an outlying alcove and a small bathroom. The main room had two sets of louvered windows beside the door and a view of the trash cans across the alley.

The deposit was $150, the first month's rent another $150. There was already a sofa-bed, which Ngim would use. Balam and I went out to buy a bed for me, a table and some other furnishings for a total of about $350. Ngim and I moved in that night. There was no food in the refrigerator. I had $4 left to my name.

39

STARTING OVER

IN AMERICA it never occurred to me that my life was in any danger or that there was any risk of starvation. I wasn't worried about having only four dollars.

Sure enough, the morning after Ngim and I moved into our tiny apartment two Cambodians appeared at our door. The woman had been my patient in Thailand; she brought her husband, whom I had not met before. These two good-hearted people took us out to eat and showed me around L.A. With money they loaned, I bought food and rice from a store in Chinatown. I bought bowls, pots and chopsticks from a flea market.

No doubt about it: We were going to get by.

Now that we had a place to live and a supply of food the next question was deciding how to make a living. I wanted to practice medicine, but to get a U.S. medical license I would first have to pass an English-language proficiency exam and then probably go back to medical school for refresher courses before taking the boards. I was willing to do that, but it didn't solve the problem of supporting Ngim and myself in the meantime. I could have gone on welfare, which would have paid $214 a month plus some extra for Ngim, but that didn't seem worth it. I decided to postpone medical school and get a job.

My first job was as a night security guard for a company outside of Chinatown. While looking for something better I took English as a Second Language (ESL) classes at Evans Community College, just a few blocks away. English is not a logical language, and I have always found it difficult. "Rice" rhymes with "ice" but not with "police."

The "gh" in the word "thought" is silent, but in the word "rough," "gh" sounds like "f." How is anybody supposed to understand the rules?

Slang made English even more mysterious. I used to wonder what it meant when an American shook my hand and said, "You bet." Did he want to make a bet with me? Had I committed myself to making a bet without knowing it when I shook his hand? Should I have kept my mouth shut? I could make myself understood in English, but I knew I was never going to feel completely comfortable. It was much easier for Ngim, who was in elementary school, because she was younger. She could already speak English almost as well as an American.

In November 1980 I became a caseworker for the Chinatown Service Center, which was within walking distance of my apartment. My office, called the Indochinese Unit, provided a free job-placement service to refugees. About half our clients were Vietnamese, a third or more Cambodian and the rest Laotian. Usually my clients and I could find a language in common. If Khmer or Teochiew didn't work, we tried French or Mandarin or English or even Thai. Generally we could exchange basic ideas, with the help of my co-workers if necessary.

Being a caseworker was satisfying. It didn't have the status or the money of being a doctor, but it allowed me to help refugees, which was what I wanted. I translated between my clients and their landlords. I filled out welfare application forms, enrolled children in public schools, arranged for adults to attend ESL classes, explained telephone bills and inquired about relatives in the refugee camps of Thailand. As I gained experience I was asked to buy a car. In my new Volkswagen I drove my clients to the hospitals, to the welfare office, to job interviews all over L.A.

Jobs were the main focus. As refugees we had to start over at the bottom and take whatever was available. I got my clients jobs as dishwashers, waitresses and waiters, cooks, cleaners, landscaping workers, common laborers, assembly line workers in electronics factories, zip code sorters, baby-sitters and piecework sewers. A few of the more educated ones were hired as secretaries and bank tellers. The average job paid only $4.00 to $4.50 an hour, but the starting pay wasn't as important as getting established and then moving up.

At that time there were six to seven thousand Cambodians in and around Chinatown and about the same number of Vietnamese. The Vietnamese adapted quite well and generally moved up the career ladders much more quickly than the Cambodians, who were shy and passive. Often when I set up job interviews the Cambodians didn't even show. They were afraid they would lose face because they didn't speak good English. They were afraid to take risks. They were unhappy in their personal lives. In Cambodian households, arguments, excessive drinking, wife-abuse and divorce were all common.

It was clear that there was a massive mental health problem among Cambodian refugees. I understood it because I had had my share of mental problems too. We had all been traumatized by our experiences. We had all lost parents or brothers or children. Many of us had horrible dreams, night after night. We felt isolated and depressed and unable to trust anyone. What made it worse was that we were in a culture totally unlike our own.

In Cambodia a way of life had evolved over many hundreds of years. It was much simpler than America, and that was part of its beauty. In Cambodia we didn't have welfare or Social Security. We didn't have day-care centers or old-age homes or psychiatrists. We didn't need them. All we needed were our families and the monks. Most households had three generations living together. The grandparents helped raise their grandchildren. The adults in the middle put the food on the table. When there were problems and arguments the monks helped take care of them. The monks helped teach the children proper behavior and taught them how to read and write in temple schools. They also took in orphans and old people with nowhere else to go. In exchange for conducting religious ceremonies and everything else they did, we gave the monks alms, and we sent our teenage boys to them to become monks for at least a short time. The system was not perfect, but it worked. Everybody had enough to eat. Cambodian society was stable. For generation after generation we followed our customs, until in 1975 the communists put an end to our way of life. We lost everything—our families, our monks, our villages, our land, all our possessions. Everything. When we came to the United States we couldn't put our old lives back together. We didn't even have the pieces.

In Thailand a smart Cambodian could figure out some of the words on a street sign and understand part of a Thai conversation because the language and alphabet were similar. In the United States the language was totally different. Not being able to read the street signs, talk to the people or even understand the TV programs left the average Cambodian isolated, which made the depression worse.

There were no real temples to go to. There was a makeshift temple inside an ordinary house in a run-down section of Long Beach, southwest of L.A., where a lot of Cambodians lived. There was a Thai temple with traditional architecture and Thai monks. But for most Cambodians these temples were beyond walking distance. We had to drive to go anyplace, and we had to organize trips on the weekends, when those who had cars were free.

Almost everything was different about America. Men who used to be wealthy merchants and officers in the Lon Nol regime stayed on welfare. They didn't want to lose face among their friends by taking low-status jobs like driving taxis or working in warehouses. Men who had been brave in combat became timid, afraid of the blacks and Hispanics on the streets. They went into supermarkets and only saw what was not as good as Cambodia, that the vegetables were not as fresh, that there were few tropical fruits, that there was no bargaining over prices. They noticed that much of American daily life is impersonal. Shopping. Driving on the freeways. Watching TV. They found they could go for days at a time without talking to anybody.

I missed Cambodia too. The food and the bargaining and the market gossip. Praying in the temples and walking along the boulevards in the warm, quiet evenings. Most of all I missed Huoy. But I saw many good things about America. It was much cleaner than Cambodia. There weren't as many flies. The tap water was safe to drink. People were more educated. Ngim liked America too. She was getting excellent grades in school. Her classmates couldn't pronounce her name easily, so we chose a new name, "Sophia." It is Western but also Eastern, a name that came to Cambodian culture through Sanskrit.

I had a job, a car, a niece I was raising as a daughter. Life was very comfortable. I never had to worry about *chhlop* spying on me, or soldiers tying me up and taking me away. When I woke up in the morning, I felt no terror. I knew for sure that I would live through the day and through the week and for many years ahead.

Once, as I was driving along in my VW and stopped at a light, I saw a dog being walked on a leash. The owner stopped to pat the dog, the dog wagged its tail and I remembered what I told Huoy about dogs in America living better than people on the front lines. It was true: Dogs did live better. America was a prosperous place. Then the light changed to green and I drove off to my next appointment, amazed at my good fortune.

By March 1982 I had lived in America for a year and a half. I spent most of my time with fellow Cambodians. Through my work I helped refugees adjust to their new lives, and indirectly this helped them recover from the trauma of their old lives. But we didn't talk much about what had happened under the Khmer Rouge. We kept our memories bottled up inside.

One day in March two acquaintances of mine dropped by the Chinatown Service Center to see me. They were Sisowath Sourirath, of the minor branch of the Cambodian royal family, and Jean Fernandez, the younger brother of a general in the Lon Nol regime. We were all getting by, but none of us had regained the status or the wealth we had had in Cambodia. Jean Fernandez was selling life insurance. Sisowath was working for the Catholic Welfare Bureau in Long Beach. He had helped me fill out an application to buy a set of encyclopedias, but the encyclopedia company had turned me down because my credit wasn't good enough. When Sisowath and Jean came in that day they said they were applying for something else now, for roles in a Hollywood film about Cambodia. They said I had to apply. I told them no thanks.

They tried to get me interested in the film, but I really wasn't listening. Clients were walking into the office and I had to help them find jobs. My clients were real people with real problems, and I didn't have time for daydreams.

But rumors of the film swept through the Cambodian communities in L.A. and Long Beach. Everybody had heard about it. A lot of people dreamed about being in a Hollywood movie, and many had applied. For them, I think, that was the real America, the money and the opportunity they'd wanted to believe in back in the refugee camps. I knew how their minds worked. Everybody who applied for a part in the movie secretly thought he was going to be a star and get rich overnight. They wanted to forget about the other America—working in a regular job to pay for rent and food and gasoline while never getting ahead, or only getting ahead slowly.

I didn't want anything to do with movies. In Cambodia acting had been a low-paid profession without any particular status. I had been a doctor. I had owned a Mercedes and part of a medical clinic. Maybe I wasn't a doctor now, and maybe I wasn't wealthy, but everybody knew that I used to be. There was no need for me to stoop to a low-class job like acting.

Some Cambodians who lived in Oxnard, up the coast from L.A., invited me to a wedding party. I really didn't want to go. It was an hour and twenty minutes each way on the freeway, plus the money for gas. It rained the whole way up there, the windshield wipers of my Volkswagen slapping back and forth. When I walked in the door, Jean Fernandez and other friends greeted me. Most of the wedding guests were Cambodian. The most obvious exception was a black American woman who said her name was Pat Golden. She was from the movie studio. She asked me to sit for a photograph and give her my name and phone number. But a live band was playing and the guests were dancing the *romvong*, gracefully and slowly waving their hands to the music. It had been a long time since I had danced the *romvong* and I told her no.

She didn't let me get away. Every time I left the dance floor she came up to me. She had already taken Jean Fernandez's picture. She had taken nearly everyone's picture. An old man who was drunk pushed me forward and told me to go ahead, it wasn't going to cost me anything.

I told Pat Golden I had come there to have fun and I hoped she wouldn't bother me.

"Keep cool," she said, patting me on the shoulder. She wore casual clothes, blue jeans and a white shirt, but she looked well dressed in them. She had a low, husky voice and a gap between her front teeth and a very strong, confident character. She said there were no forms to fill out. All she wanted to do was take my picture and get my phone number.

I told her, "Okay. I let you take pictures if you give me vun for a souvenir."

The living room was crowded and she had me stand in the hallway, outside the bathroom door. She asked me to take my glasses off. She pressed the button on the Polaroid, and the flash went off and a shiny piece of paper ejected from the front of the camera. She took another picture, gave me one, and I stared at it to see what would develop. It just looked like me without my glasses. Not a handsome guy, not young, not a movie-star type.

Two weeks passed, then a month, then two months and three months without a word from her.

In the fourth month she called me on the telephone. She wanted to set up an interview about forty miles away from where I lived. I told her yes without meaning it. My friends had told me that she had asked other Cambodians too. They drove in from San Diego, Santa Ana, L.A. and Long Beach for the interview. But not me.

The next morning Pat Golden called me at the office and asked me why I didn't come. I told her sorry, I was busy. There was a pause and I decided to be more honest. I said I didn't want to go because I didn't think I'd get the job. She said, "We haven't made any decisions yet. Please come." She was very persistent.

She wanted to interview me that night in Long Beach, twenty-five miles away. "Is five o'clock okay?" she said. I said, "No, I work in office hours." "Six?" she said. "No," I said, "the freeway to Long Beach is too crowded then. How about seven?"

I got there at eight. She was waiting. I said I was sorry, that I had been busy. She didn't reproach me. She was conciliatory and polite—just like a Cambodian. She was a very smart woman and she knew something about our culture. She knew if she got angry at me I would use it as an excuse to leave.

Other Cambodians were there ahead of me. Pat Golden interviewed Long Boret's daughter—Long Boret was Lon Nol's prime minister at the time of the Khmer Rouge takeover—and finally called me in.

She said, "Okay, Haing, if you were with some Americans and

you had to convince the Khmer Rouge that the people you were with were *not* Americans, how would you do it?"

I improvised a scene for her.

After it was over, she said, "Thanks. I'll let you know in a week."

I said, "I don't believe you. If you say one week, maybe a month and a half."

"No, this time I'm serious," she said. And a week later she called me in for a second interview. This time it was in a studio in Burbank.

Then there was a third interview, also in the Burbank studio. At each interview there were fewer Cambodians than before.

A young bearded Englishman was at the fourth interview. He was Roland Joffé, the director of the film. Roland Joffé asked me about my story—how long I had lived under the Khmer Rouge, what happened when I was captured, how I got to the refugee camps in Thailand. I talked for an hour. He watched me with intense blue eyes and listened carefully.

Roland Joffé was at the fifth interview. This time he had a video camera for the screen test. He set up a hypothetical situation: A Cambodian doctor was very fond of an American nurse. The night before, the radio had announced that all foreigners had to leave Cambodia. How would the doctor tell the nurse she had to leave Cambodia to save her own life?

Pat Golden played the American lady.

I played the Cambodian doctor.

Roland Joffé changed the situation. The American lady believed the Khmer Rouge wouldn't hurt her, because she was foreign, but that they would almost certainly kill me. How would I explain to her that Cambodia was my country, that I would stay no matter what?

I acted the part to Pat Golden.

Roland Joffé brought the camera in closer and closer but it didn't make me nervous. I knew if I really put myself in the situation and believed what I was saying to Pat Golden, the camera didn't matter.

"Now," Roland Joffé said to me, "you have taken the American woman to the airport, to see her off. What are your last words before she goes away?"

"You haf to leave right now," I told Pat Golden. "You haf to listen me. Situation now very hard. You foreign people. Khmer Rouge don't like you. For me no problem. I'm Cambodian people." I wept on her shoulder and wiped my eyes and told her over and over again that she had to go and I would miss her.

When I finished they said thank you very much.

In interview six I went in front of the camera again. Roland set up another scene with Pat Golden playing my Cambodian wife. I had to tell her to leave because the Khmer Rouge were going to kill everybody. I broke down and cried again, only this time it was hard to stop.

As soon as I finished one scene Roland Joffé had me do another. All of the scenes were sad, except for the last one. In this one I was a doctor. A patient of mine was about to die. I operated on him, tried my best and against the odds the operation was successful. What did I do when I learned the good news? What did I say?

I acted it out for him.

Joffé said he would let me know, but he didn't know when that might be.

I went back to work and tried not to think about the screen tests. Seven thousand Cambodians had applied for jobs in the movie.

Three more months passed before Pat called again, from New York. She wanted to know what kind of passport or visa I was holding. I said it was a resident alien card, with my photo and thumbprint. She asked whether it would cause a problem if I had to go to Thailand with the company. No problem for me, no problem for my niece either.

She called back a few weeks later. What was I getting paid at the Chinatown Service Center? Four hundred dollars a week, I said. She said, how about if she gave me eight hundred dollars a week?

No problem, I said.

She called again with detailed questions about my visa and said, "How about a thousand dollars a week?"

"Don't worry about the money," I said. "Give me what you want. I just want the job."

And it was true. I had changed my mind. If I could be in the film, I decided, in any capacity, I could help tell the story of Cambodia. And that was important because it was a story nobody really knew. Most Americans didn't even know where Cambodia was. They had heard of Vietnam, but not Cambodia. Even in L.A., non-Cambodian Asians didn't know what had happened under the Khmer

Rouge regime. If we told them they just nodded their heads and pretended to believe us so we wouldn't lose face.

And really, the reason I hadn't wanted the job earlier didn't have anything to do with losing face, or with not being offered a part, or with looking foolish in front of the camera. I hadn't wanted to bring back the suffering. There were too many reminders already.

Ever since coming to the United States I'd had nightmares. If I thought too much in the daytime about what had happened, I had dreams that night. Huoy died in my arms over and over and over. I saw my father tied to the tree and trying to tell me something, but afraid to speak.

It didn't take much to set off my nightmares—the sound of water dripping from the faucet was enough. It put me back in prison, looking up at water dripping from a hole in a bucket.

Almost every night I woke suddenly and sat up to make the dreams fade. Outside the louvered windows the streetlights were shining on the hard pavement of the alley and reflecting off the metal and glass of parked cars. In L.A. there was always a background noise of traffic on distant streets and maybe a siren or honking horns. I felt more alienated than ever, and not sure how much better America was than what I had left behind, because I hadn't really left it behind, and I couldn't enjoy the best of America. So I decided to go back to the refugee camps and confront my past. To try to get rid of my nightmares.

Before we left for Thailand all the Cambodians who had been chosen for the film got together for a party. Pat Golden was there. All the other Cambodians knew what part they were playing, but when I asked Pat she just told me not to worry, I wasn't going to have to learn anything by heart. It sounded to me as though my part was pretty small. The other Cambodians began teasing me and saying that I had the co-starring role, but I just laughed and told them not to believe it.

When I got to Thailand I was given a script, but still nobody told me what part was mine. Then when Roland Joffé called a rehearsal I found that I was going to play Dith Pran.

"Oh my god," I said to myself, slapping my hand to my forehead. "How big I am."

40

THE KILLING FIELDS

"THIS IS a story of war and friendship, of the anguish of a ruined country and of one man's will to live." So began a 1980 article in *The New York Times Magazine*. The author was Sydney Schanberg, the *Times*'s correspondent in Cambodia during the Lon Nol years.

Schanberg wrote about the relationship between himself and his Cambodian assistant Dith Pran. They were not equals. Schanberg was the boss. By nature he was angry and unsatisfied, always demanding more of people around him. However, he did not speak Khmer or know much about Cambodian culture. He needed Dith Pran to be his eyes and ears and nose. He depended on Pran when they ran into obstacles to their reporting or when they got into situations that threatened their lives. Pran, in turn, depended on Schanberg for guidance. The two men were very different, but they liked each other and they were close.

During the communist takeover Pran saved Schanberg and some other Western journalists from execution by the Khmer Rouge. With the communists in control of the city, all the Westerners and a few Cambodians including Pran retreated to the French embassy. Pran was forced to leave the safety of the embassy and join the rest of the Cambodians out in the countryside, while the Westerners were allowed to leave for Thailand and freedom. For almost four years, while the Khmer Rouge controlled the country, Schanberg heard nothing of Dith Pran. He felt terribly guilty: Pran had saved his life, but he, Schanberg, hadn't been able to save Pran. Finally the Vietnamese invaded, Pran escaped from Cambodia and the two men met again in a Thai refugee camp.

The article moved the hearts and the conscience of people who hadn't known much about Cambodia or who hadn't thought about the revolution there in human terms. Out of the magazine article grew the movie *The Killing Fields*. The movie's producer was an Englishman, David Puttnam, who had made *Chariots of Fire* and other films. The director was another Englishman, Roland Joffé, whose background was in theater and in film documentaries. The lead actors were two Americans, Sam Waterston as Sydney Schanberg, John Malkovich as the cynical photographer Al Rockoff . . . and me, a Cambodian, as Dith Pran.

Studying the script I made a surprising discovery. *I was Dith Pran.* This is not to say that our stories were identical. Pran was a journalist; I was a doctor. He worked with Westerners; I worked with Cambodians. His wife and children left Phnom Penh on a helicopter before the fall; Huoy and my family stayed. When he lived in the countryside, Pran was beaten by the Khmer Rouge; but he never went to prison and never suffered as much as I did.

But the differences were much less important than the similarities. I was him and he was me because we were Cambodian men of about the same age and because we had been under the hammer of the same terrible events: the civil war, then the revolution, then the foreign occupation and finally pouring into the refugee camps and going to America. Surviving the Khmer Rouge years was the most important fact of our lives, the very center of our identities. And we had both survived without quite knowing why.

Turning the pages of the screenplay I marveled at our life paths, which ran parallel and sometimes crossed. Dith Pran had seen the senseless, barbaric civil war. As a journalist he'd gone to some of the same briefings and battlefields as my friend Sam Kwil. He'd seen the *bonjour* and the deteriorating conditions in the hospitals, the wounded patients piled on the floors. In the screenplay he and Sydney Schanberg visited Preah Keth Melea Hospital. In real life I had treated patients in Prea Keth Melea before the fall. Pen Tip was on the radiology staff there.

Both Dith Pran and I had an opportunity to leave Phnom Penh on the American helicopters. We didn't go because we didn't know what the Khmer Rouge were really like. Pran went into the French embassy with the foreigners; I drove past the French embassy on my Vespa on my trip back into Phnom Penh and saw the foreigners on the lawn.

In the countryside Dith Pran and I were rice farmers, like all the other "new" people. We both pulled plows by hand, planted and harvested rice, dug canals and built earthen dams. We ate bowls of watery rice and gathered wild foods. We lived with the daily terror. When the Vietnamese invaded, we both escaped to Thailand through the minefields. Of the more than half a million Cambodians on the border, Dith Pran and I were two of the very luckiest. I had Chana to give me my freedom and Uncle Lo to give me money and clothes. Dith Pran had Sydney Schanberg.

But I had never met Dith Pran. I asked Roland Joffé how Pran walked and spoke and what his facial expressions were like. I asked him to introduce us. It seemed to me that playing the Dith Pran part meant imitating the real man as much as possible.

Roland was evasive. "Haing, don't worry what he looks like or how he would have done things," he advised. "Just be yourself." Roland encouraged the idea that Dith Pran and I were the same person on the inside. And I never did meet Dith Pran until the filming was over.

Roland knew that I had never acted before. He didn't try to make acting seem difficult or mysterious. He made it as easy for me as possible.

He sent a tall, bearded American to the Bangkok airport to meet me. The American was very friendly and polite. He said his name was Sam Waterston. A few days later, with the help of John Crowley, who was pleased and surprised to see me, Sam and I got our passes to visit the Thai-Cambodian border. Roland assigned Sam to write newspaper stories about the border, just like a real journalist. Since I spoke Khmer and reasonably good Thai, I was Sam's translator and guide. Roland was re-creating a relationship like the real Sydney Schanberg and Dith Pran.

Sam and I drove along the road to Aranyaprathet. In three years little had changed. I showed him my favorite market stalls and restaurants and the ARC house where I had lived. We drove south of Aran to a Khmer Rouge border camp that had been attacked by

Vietnamese a few days before. Cadre followed us wherever we went, never letting us out of their sight. Nothing had changed about the Khmer Rouge—the disdain on their faces, the atmosphere of menace, the thatched-roof houses with no walls.

I translated for Sam while he interviewed Khmer Rouge officers and wrote their answers in his notebook. Sam asked them if they had enough food, if their families were with them and so on. The Khmer Rouge kept telling Sam that all they wanted was to go back into Cambodia to fight the Vietnamese.

Throughout the interview I kept a detached, neutral presence, at least on the outside. While Sam asked the questions and took notes, I stayed as calm as a monk. Inside, my emotions were different. I thought of grabbing the cadre by their shirts and shouting, "Fools! You want to fight the Vietnamese? Look around you at the consequences of your fighting—at the orphans, the handicapped, the civilians with no homes!" I thought of grabbing a rifle and spraying them with bullets. But I didn't do anything like that, and I kept my emotions hidden.

From the Khmer Rouge camp we went to Khao-I-Dang, where many of my old friends were still working in the hospital clinics, living in their huts and hoping to be resettled in the West. Again, I was Sam's eyes and ears and nose, helping him understand what was there. Sam was a cultivated, educated man, but he had never been to Southeast Asia before.

When we returned to Bangkok, Roland sent Sam and me to Chieng Mai, in northern Thailand, near the opium-producing region of the Golden Triangle. With us were John Malkovich and a British actor named Julian Sands, who was going to play the journalist Jon Swain.

It was almost like a vacation. Our only assignment was to get to know each other. The four of us went sightseeing together. I negotiated with the taxi drivers, ordered the food at restaurants, explained the culture. They asked me about Thailand and Cambodia. They wanted to know why Cambodians wear kramas and Thais don't. They asked about food, Buddhism, corruption, history. Sam asked the most questions. Most of the time he and I spoke in French, since that was easier for me, and he could speak it fluently.

One evening after we had gotten to know each other, Sam and I sat down in a bar. After a few drinks I began to tell him things about life under the Khmer Rouge that I had never told anybody else. Things that had always bothered me. About leaving the patient to die on the operating table the day the communists took over. About watching Huoy die and being unable to save her. About my Aunt Kim, who had risked my life by telling the chief of Tonle Bati my real identity. I told Sam that to the best of my knowledge, one of Aunt Kim's sons had been a hard-core Khmer Rouge officer. This same son had slipped past Immigration and was living in the United States. What was I supposed to do about that—a cousin who was probably a war criminal?*

Sam was easy to talk to. He was wise and polite, a real gentleman. We became friends. In a totally different way I also became friends with John Malkovich, who was very naughty and funny. John was always telling dirty jokes and making sly remarks about the young, beautiful Chieng Mai prostitutes. He got me to teach him to curse in Khmer. For me it was the best of both worlds: I could behave like a gentleman with Sam Waterston or a rascal with John Malkovich.

When we returned to Bangkok, Roland started us doing improvisation scenes to prepare us for the cameras. Right from the start I felt comfortable acting with Sam and John and Julian. Being friends in real life made acting with them seem easy and natural. Of course, that was what Roland had planned all along.

Roland was the center of this multimillion-dollar movie project. His partner was David Puttnam, the producer. Just by watching them with other people, you could tell that the two of them cared a great deal about telling the story truthfully. They went to great lengths to get details exactly right. They had negotiated for months with the Thai government to set up the filming locations in several parts of the country. They always had good food—Asian food for the Asians, Western food for the Westerners. Throughout filming they were friendly and approachable. Roland knew the names of most of the Cambodians

---

*Since then, I have attempted to get the U.S. government to start an investigation. It is a delicate business: On one hand, the Immigration and Naturalization Service (INS) presumably wants to catch people who lied to it and who are war criminals. On the other hand, INS officials could use an investigation as an excuse for stopping all Cambodian refugees from coming to the United States. As this is written, about twenty thousand innocent people who want to come to the United States are stuck in Khao-I-Dang because the INS has falsely accused them of Khmer Rouge associations. The INS has tightened its rules so much that Dith Pran himself could not come to the United States if he were a refugee today.

in the cast, even the bit actors he hadn't yet worked with. His light blue eyes seemed to penetrate into everything. The Cambodians on the set called him "Buddha" because he was so calm and so smart.

The filming began with a scene of Sam and John sitting in an outdoor cafe in Phnom Penh in the Lon Nol years. A man held the clapper in front of the camera and announced, "Take One, Scene One," and then clapped the hinge shut. The assistant director called out, "Ready," and the cameraman answered, "Ready." Then the assistant director said, into his walkie-talkie, "Stop all truck movements." When the background movement had stopped he said to the rest of us, "Go!" and then, "Roll it!" and finally, "ACTION!" in a loud voice. The camera made its quiet whir, and Sam and John began the scene, making small talk, deciding what to order and then rushing into the street when a grenade exploded. Roland knelt on the ground off-camera. He had removed the little zoom lens he kept on his belt and was looking through it. Between takes he came in to advise the actors and change their positions a bit. Then the scene began again.

"Take Two, Scene One."

"Ready . . ."

Roland told me that when I went on-camera I didn't have to speak every word exactly from the script as long as what I said included the key words and phrases. When I spoke in Khmer I could say whatever I wanted as long as it was appropriate to the scene. He made the camera crew responsible for the blocking and the lighting, so the actors didn't have to worry about it. When it came time for me to go on-camera I was with my friends Sam and John, who knew just what to do. All I had to do was react to them and live out my part. There was no time to wonder what this meant, living out the part. Around me, everyone else was already doing it.

Roland told me to remember situations from my own life that were similar to the movie, and then use those emotions in the scenes. This made sense to me. I prepared for the rice field scenes by remembering how I had felt and walked and worked on the front lines. When I ate watery rice or caught lizards in the movie, I remembered what hunger was like in the countryside. The rural scenes were the easiest, because I had been in identical situations. From there it was a small step to similar situations, and from there another step to situations that were externally different but had some thread in common with my own experience. For example, when Dith Pran argues with his wife about leaving Cambodia, that was me, not listening to Huoy telling me to leave the country. During the Khmer Rouge takeover scene, when Dith Pran pleads to the guerrillas to spare the lives of the Western journalists and he puts his palms together like a man praying and keeps asking them even when it appears hopeless, that was me in prison, begging the Khmer Rouge to believe I was not a doctor. Or if that was not exactly what I did in prison, that was what I felt like doing in prison, which still gave me an emotion to work with. When Dith Pran carries a young boy toward the minefield, that was me, carrying my young niece Ngim.

Gradually I began to build on the skills I had learned. With advice from Sam, and with pushes from Roland, who refused to accept my limitations, I did things I did not know I could do.

In the central scene of the movie, Dith Pran has to say good-bye to the Western journalists, leave the safety of the French embassy and go off into the countryside. It is a sad scene because the journalists have failed to protect him and he knows he has to go even though he will probably die. I prepared for it by remembering what it had been like to say good-bye to Huoy on the front lines. Every time we said good-bye it hurt, because we knew we might never see each other again. I dwelt on that sadness until it grew and the feeling took over, and then just before the cameras started rolling I reached into my memory and remembered how I felt when she died. On the set I tried to hold in my emotions as I shook hands with one Western journalist, embraced Sydney Schanberg and slowly walked downstairs, but the sadness and grief were beyond control. Between takes the wardrobe man handed me tissues without looking at me. "Roland," I said after the sixth take, "I don't think I can do this again." Roland paid no attention. He shot the scene a seventh time and this time everything was right. When I came off the set the cast and crew looked at me in absolute silence. The kind of silence that is louder than applause. I kept on walking, because in my mind I was still on my way out of the French embassy, heading toward death in the countryside.

What was strangest was going out to shoot these scenes during the day, believing in the part I was playing, and then going back to a luxurious hotel. The cast and crew ate well, lived well and were very sociable in the evenings. It was like a huge party. Then the next morning I would wake up and wonder all over again whether the Khmer Rouge were going to tie me up and take me away.

Usually I could cross from the hotel to the film role and back again. But sometimes on location my defenses fell apart and I slipped back into the hunger and terror of the Khmer Rouge years. There was a scene where Dith Pran made an incision in the neck of a live ox for the blood, for nutrition. (I had never done that in real life, but I had cut the tail off a live ox—pretty much the same thing.) He is caught by the Khmer Rouge, beaten and kicked. In the shooting of the scene I wore padding under my clothes to protect parts of my back and my legs. Unfortunately the bamboo stick that was supposed to be used in the scene broke and was replaced by a heavy wooden stick. And unfortunately the actors playing the Khmer Rouge guards didn't hit me where the padding was. For a moment it was too real —the shock, the pounding of my blood in my ears, knowing that I was going to die.

Then there was the *chhlop*. She was a young girl who lived in a small refugee camp just outside Aranyaprathet. The casting people found her and the wardrobe people gave her just the right appearance, the baggy black clothes, the short hair parted in the middle with the ends tucked behind the ears, but she needed coaching. She was a shy young girl, and whenever she could she clung to her older sister like a baby to its mother. I told her in Khmer how to look at me like a real *chhlop*, full of anger and power. She should tilt her head back to stare "down" on me and her lower lip and jaw should protrude to signal her disdain. But most of all, she had to get the eyes right. "Look hard at me," I said. "Don't blink. Just stare at me. Like you want to eat me. Like I'm Enemy Number One."

When filming started the young girl was transformed. Only she didn't just resemble Khmer Rouge. There was something deep inside her character that she hadn't learned from me.

"Just like Khmer Rouge!" I shouted to Roland Joffé. "She is Khmer Rouge—100 percent!"

Roland looked at me and came over to try to get me to calm down, but I was still pointing at the girl and shouting. Maybe he misunderstood me. Maybe he thought I meant that she was Khmer Rouge in the technical sense, a girl who had worked for the Khmer Rouge administration. I don't know. Maybe that's what I meant too. All I know was that a lot of people had come over to restrain me. "You can tell by the eyes! Look at her eyes!" I was shouting.

Roland was fascinated. He did take after take, to watch her. Off-camera she went to her big sister and shyly hid behind her. On-camera she became a different person, resentful, surly, arrogant. It was like turning an electric light switch on and off. For Roland, who understood more about Cambodians than the other Westerners on the set, the girl was the solution to the mystery. The mystery was how the Cambodians, the most shy and gentle people in the world, had turned into mass killers. This is Roland's explanation: Cambodian children bury their anger deep. They are not allowed to be aggressive toward elders. They have to keep their heads lower than the adults' when walking past them. When sitting, they have to be careful not to point their feet. The anger stays suppressed when they become adults, because the society is so rigidly concerned with keeping face. When anger has a chance to come out, it is uncontrollable.

I saw it more simply. To me, when the little girl was "acting" she became her real self. Whether she had been in the Khmer Rouge or not, hers was a soul I had seen many times before. She had little schooling or religion. Little to train her away from the worst trait of Cambodians. The little girl was *kum-monuss*.

Besides acting the part of Dith Pran, I felt it was my duty to help Roland make the film as accurate as possible. Roland agreed to many of my suggestions. For example, the film shows Khmer Rouge putting plastic bags over people's heads, which is something not in the script. We did scenes of life on the front lines of transplanting rice, of pulling a plow by hand, and Roland was as interested as I was in making them authentic. He refused, though, when I asked him to show the Khmer Rouge whipping the men pulling the plow. I felt the film should be more violent, to show what the Khmer Rouge were really like, but Roland did not agree. In terms of historical authenticity, I was right; in terms of knowing what the movie audiences would tolerate, he was. If the film had shown how bad things really were under the Khmer Rouge, Westerners would have refused to see it.

We were in Thailand for four and a half months. It was a stressful time for me. I lost weight. My nightmares were even more frequent than before. I didn't have much chance to see old friends, like General Chana, Uncle Lo, John Crowley, Susan Walker and the Cambodians

I knew in the refugee camps. I missed my niece Sophia. But the cast and crew of *The Killing Fields* were excellent companions.

Before we left Thailand we had a big cast party in Bangkok. Everyone came prepared to have a good time. I did too. But I showed up in black trousers, black tunic and black rubber-tire sandals. In Khmer Rouge costume. To remind them that we were doing more than just making a movie.

41

CELEBRITY

IN THE FINAL VERSION of *The Killing Fields* there is a scene, filmed in Thailand, where Sam Waterston and I, playing Sydney Schanberg and Dith Pran, visit Lon Nol troops and their U.S. military advisers. The Khmer Rouge launch an attack. Sam and I jump into a foxhole. The camera shifts to a close-up, filmed in England, of the two of us in the foxhole and me shouting, "Sydney, look! Khmer Rouge!" Without pause the movie shifts back to footage shot in Thailand. It is all so perfectly matched that the viewer would never know the difference.

Similarly, the evacuation of the U.S. embassy in Phnom Penh, filmed with actors in Thailand, is spliced with shots of huge U.S. Marine helicopters, filmed in San Diego.

It surprised me, but that's how movies are—put together from footage shot in different times and places, with reshootings, audio dubs, titles and music added in. The actors are only part of the illusion.

The first and longest session of shooting had taken place in Thailand from March to August 1983. In November 1983 we had another two weeks of shooting in San Diego and in Canada. In April 1984 I went off to Thailand for a few weeks to film the escape to the border. In August and September I was in England to shoot a few scenes, like the close-up in the foxhole, and do some audio dubbing.

I didn't mind the traveling. It was an opportunity to see new places and to be reunited with the cast and crew.

Each time I returned from filming to my four-hundred-dollar-a-week job in Los Angeles. Each time I came back I felt guilty. My colleagues at the Chinatown Service Center were wonderful people —some of them Vietnamese, some Cambodian, some Chinese from

451

Taiwan and Hong Kong. The work we did was important and practical. We had goals to reach. Each month we tried to place a certain number of refugees in jobs. Each time I left made it harder on the others.

Each time I went off, my supervisor granted me a leave of absence. She was very kind. And only she and the overall boss of the center knew the real reason for my travels. I didn't tell anybody else in L.A., except Sophia. To my friends and colleagues I explained vaguely that I was going off to work with refugees. Part of my reason for not telling them was to protect myself in case the movie wasn't any good. There was no sense in getting them excited and then disappointing them later. But the underlying reason for not telling them was that I had developed a habit of secrecy under the Khmer Rouge. It was still hard to trust people. I didn't even tell Balam, who lived a few doors away, or my brother Hok, who lived outside L.A., or my cousin Phillip Thong.

It was like leading a double life.

Around November 1984, while sitting in my cubicle at the office, a call came in from the Warner Bros. studio in Burbank. David Puttnam and Roland Joffé were there, and they wanted me to go to a prerelease screening of the film in San Diego. I sat with my Cambodian clients for the rest of the afternoon, explaining to them about registering for welfare and food stamps. I drove home at the usual time, and then a limousine pulled up outside my apartment. The limousine took me through the freeway traffic to the Burbank airport and onto the runway next to a small private jet. David and Roland and a few others were already aboard. The jet took off over the lights of L.A., the hostess served champagne, and I sat back to marvel over the direction my life was taking.

During the shooting of the film I had never allowed myself to believe that I was different from anyone else. David and Roland had always been down-to-earth and unpretentious. Sam was always pleasant and courteous to everyone. Those men set the tone. Working with them, I didn't daydream about becoming a "star."

I had never even wanted to be an actor. I knew who I was. In my mind I was still a doctor from Cambodia. But now, as the plane flew down the southern California coastline, I began to reconsider who I was and what I was doing. It was impossible not to compare my miserable life as a war slave with this. Surely this was as luxurious as life got, traveling around in limousines and private jets.

I thought: The gods saved my life. They have given me opportunities beyond anything I dreamed of. Maybe they have some purpose for me to fulfill.

We got to the theater, but the screening was almost over. We only saw the last half hour of the movie. The audience filled out forms rating the picture in different categories, excellent, good, fair or poor. The forms I saw were all marked "excellent" for both me and Sam Waterston. People crowded around me asking for autographs. Nobody had ever asked me for an autograph before.

In the following weeks there were prerelease screenings in L.A. Because of one thing or another I always got there late. This was irritating, because I had never seen the entire film in sequence, just rough cuts of the scenes in Roland's editing room in England. The audiences clapped long and hard. As I was leaving the screening at the University of Southern California, a woman student threw both her arms around me and began hugging and kissing me. She said she wanted to marry me. She had never even met me before.

In December the film had its world premiere, in New York. Once again I missed the showing of the film. It was a confusing and hectic visit, signing autographs, having my picture taken, being led from one set of hot television lights to the next for interviews. My name was called out at a banquet, and people stood up and clapped. I shook hands with thousands of strangers. The whole time, I was asking myself, Why me? Why am I being treated this way? I just got to this country. What's going on?

For me the only good part of the New York opening was finally being able to meet the real Sydney Schanberg and Dith Pran. The real Sydney was shorter than Sam Waterston. He had graying hair, a gray beard and enormous round eyes. I liked him right away, and Dith Pran too. Pran was shorter than me. He was gentle and peaceful, not hyperactive like me. He was working as a photographer at *The New York Times*, where Sydney was working too. Pran and I spoke in English first, out of courtesy to the others, and then switched to Khmer as soon as we could. We had a lot to talk about.

I asked him what the Khmer Rouge had done to him in real life, because I knew the movie script had changed some of the details. He said he had been caught for stealing rice. Khmer Rouge soldiers beat him. They were planning to send him away for execution but the village chief stopped them and arranged for him to be sent to re-education classes, where he later "confessed" his crimes to save his life. During those years his wife and children were safely in the United States, but of course he never heard from them, and he lost most of the rest of his family to executions and starvation. After the Vietnamese invaded he became mayor of a small town for a while to help the people. But the Vietnamese discovered he had an "unclean" political background from working with the American press. It got dangerous for him, and he escaped to Thailand, arriving in October 1979.

Pran and I agreed, in all seriousness, that we would have liked the movie to show more violence, to reflect what had really happened in Cambodia. Then we started joking about who had the worse time. He said he had eaten mice, snails and lizard. "You had *lizard?*" I said. "Very tasty. That's like T-bone steak here. The best meal I ever ate was termites and red ant eggs." He said he was sorry, he had never eaten insects like that. In fact my experiences were worse than his under the Khmer Rouge, but it didn't matter. Meeting him was almost like discovering a twin. I knew we would be friends for life.

Then came the London opening, in January. Sydney Schanberg, Sam Waterston, Dith Pran and I were all there, dressed in tuxedoes. The Duchess of Kent sat across the aisle from me, wearing diamond and pearl jewelry. For the first time I had a chance to see the complete film with all the scenes in order. When the film began the audience was still chattering and whispering. There was laughter when John Malkovich, playing the wild photographer Al Rockoff, explained that the ice bandage on his forehead to help his hangover was made from a sanitary napkin. Then as the horror of the civil war sunk in, the laughter subsided and the audience grew quieter and quieter.

At the scene of the American withdrawal, when my wife left on a helicopter, I began to cry. I cannot explain it. Maybe it was seeing it on a big screen for the first time, the size and the fullness of it. Maybe because it was like losing Huoy.

A lady in the seat behind me handed me tissues.

I cried again at the French embassy scene, seeing myself leave the Western journalists to go out into the countryside.

I couldn't control myself. The tears came rolling out and the lady kept giving me tissues. I cried when the Khmer Rouge put a plastic bag over a prisoner's head. I cried when I sucked the blood of an ox and when I fell into the mass grave of bones while trying to make my escape.

I cried at the ending when Sydney and Pran, or Sam and I, were reunited in a refugee camp in Thailand. The ending was filmed in Khao-I-Dang, right in front of the ARC ward, where I had worked as a doctor.

But I wasn't the only one crying. So was the Duchess of Kent. When the final credits came on the screen, the people in the audience sat numbly in their seats, some of them still dabbing at their eyes. When the lights came on, Sydney, Pran, Sam and I were introduced. The audience gave us a standing ovation and long, long applause.

The Western media began running stories about *The Killing Fields*. Until that time relatively few people knew what had happened in Cambodia during the Khmer Rouge years—intellectuals and Asia experts had, maybe, but not the general public. The film put the story of those years in terms that everybody could understand, because it was a story about the friendship between two men.

To my surprise, much of the media's attention focused on me. Through the movie I had become a sort of symbol for Cambodia and its suffering. Or rather Pran and I became a symbol together, because people were always confusing our names. That I was a refugee who had never acted before made the film more newsworthy than if an experienced actor had played the Dith Pran part.

I kept going back to my job as a counselor at the Chinatown Service Center. By now my role in the movie was no secret. I kept having to leave to be interviewed, to travel and even to accept awards. First I won a Golden Globe award for best supporting actor. Then in March 1985 I went to London again to accept two British Academy Awards, for Most Outstanding Newcomer and Best Actor.

Sophia came along on that trip to London. She was an excellent student, with a straight-A average. She was very smart, just like her mother and father, but she had grown up too fast for my liking. She hadn't liked her straight black Asian hair, so she had it permed. She had often seemed restless and unhappy at home in Los Angeles. I didn't know why. Maybe it was because she was a teenager, or maybe because it was difficult for her to have me away so much. Maybe it was also difficult because I was traditional and Cambodian in my thinking. I was strict with her, just as my father had been strict with me. It was the only way I knew to raise children. But she seemed happy to be traveling, to see new sights.

We came home from London. We had moved from our one-room apartment in the alleyway to a two-bedroom apartment upstairs in the same building complex, with a view overlooking the skyscrapers of downtown L.A. Our living room was already cluttered with trophies and certificates. I put the British Academy Awards on the table and didn't think much about them.

From everything the people at Warner Bros. told me, the American Academy Awards mattered most. The Oscars, they called them. I had been nominated in the category of Best Supporting Actor, but my reaction was to downplay the chance of winning. One of the other nominees was John Malkovich, for his role in the movie *Places in the Heart*. I knew how good John was. I had watched scenes from *The Killing Fields* over and over again in the editing room, and each time I saw some small perfect detail in his performance that I had not noticed before. Besides, I was still upset at Roland Joffé for not letting me meet Dith Pran before filming started. If I had, I could have changed my performance to be more like Dith Pran.

Two days before the Oscar awards, television crews showed up at the Chinatown Service Center and at my apartment. They began following me around with their cameras. I wondered if they were following John Malkovich too. I missed John and his dirty jokes. Nobody else had ever made me laugh as much as he had.

The day of the Oscars I called my supervisor at work and asked permission to take the day off. I was too restless to work. I told Sophia to take a holiday from school too. TV crews waited outside the apartment. They followed me when I went to rent my tuxedo and filmed it for the news. I wondered what was so special about somebody trying on a tuxedo.

When I got home there were three long black limousines parked on the street outside. Dith Pran had arrived in one, Pat Golden in another and Ed Crane from Warner Bros. Publicity in the third. They all came into my apartment. Everybody in the neighborhood, which was predominantly Asian and lower middle class, had turned out to stare at the limousines and the TV crews.

Pat Golden, Ed Crane, Sophia and I got into one of the limos to ride to the ceremony together. My neighbors waved me off and wished me well. The Oscars were being held in the Dorothy Chandler Pavilion, which was not far away. The traffic was bumper to bumper. It took an hour to get there. We could have walked there faster from my apartment. I felt like walking, to get rid of my energy.

By the time we got past the camera teams and the police lines the ceremony had started and the first awards had already been handed out. Inside the auditorium sat rows and rows of dazzling women and well-dressed men. The usher took Sophia and me to some empty seats in the second row on the far left side of the stage. It seemed like only a few minutes later that a very short woman named Linda Hunt came onstage to present the award for Best Supporting Actor. She had won an award the year before, for her role in the movie *The Year of Living Dangerously*.

She said, "Good evening, ladies and gentlemen. The five actors we're about to celebrate have each taken different paths. I know that none of them thinks of this evening as their final goal. The goal, if any, lies in the work and in a private sense of challenge and achievement. To be chosen the best for a piece of work is a welcome prize, and to know that you have done it in the way that is best for you is every way as sweet." She read off the names of the nominees. When she came to my name the television cameras panned around the audience but couldn't find me because the usher had taken us to the wrong seats. On the television monitors, a picture of me from *The Killing Fields* appeared.

I looked down the row of seats and saw Sam Waterston near the center aisle. I cannot remember what went through my mind except for being glad that Sam was there. He had helped me a lot. I was extremely nervous.

"And the winner is . . .

. . . Haing S. Ngor of *The Killing Fields*!"

I walked past Sam and pumped his hand and tried to get him to come up on the stage with me, but he motioned me on. When I got on the stage my mind went blank. I was holding the trophy in my hand and standing at the lectern. The stage lights and TV cameras were on me, but I couldn't think what to say. I had practiced a speech in the limousine but couldn't remember a word of it.

"This is unbelievable," I said finally, and then it came back to me. "But so is my entire life. I vish to thank all members of Motion Picture Academy for this great honor. I thank David Puttnam, Roland Joffé for giving me this chance to act for the first time in *The Killing Fields*. And I share this award to my friend Sam Waterston, Dith Pran, Sydney Schanberg and also Pat Golden, director of casting—lady who found me for this role."

There was laughter and applause from the audience, laughter because of my accent and grammatical mistakes, applause because I wasn't going to let them stop me. "And I thank"—more laughter and applause—"and I thank Warner Bros. for helping me tell my story to the world, let the world know what happened in my country. And I thank God-Buddha that tonight I am even here. Sank you. Sank you very much."

The audience was on its feet clapping and shouting, and a few were wiping their tears. I lifted the trophy over my head. There are no words to describe it. I felt as if I were floating in the air. My feet were off the ground.

I walked off the stage and the usher guided me to where I should have been, in the same row on the opposite side of the stage. Another usher was escorting Sophia there too. In front of us, in the first row, was John Malkovich. He looked at me with his sly grin.

"*Ach anh neh,*" he said, pointing at the trophy. "*Rar boh anh teh.*"

Sophia's head snapped around and her jaw dropped open. I was sure I hadn't heard him right, so I smiled back at John and edged into my seat. It was good to see him.

"*Ach anh neh. Rar boh anh teh,*" he repeated, still grinning, still pointing at the Oscar. This time it sunk in. When we were in Thailand I had taught John how to curse in Khmer.

He had just told me, "Kiss my ass. It's mine."

42

KAMA

UNTIL MY NAME was announced and I went up on stage, I did not think I would win the Oscar. A man who had never acted before, who had just moved to the United States, who could not yet speak English fluently—the odds were too much against it. Even Hollywood movies do not have endings so unlikely. Nobody would believe them if they did.

But it had happened. I had won against the odds. I had the trophy to prove it, a tall, heavy, gold-plated figure of a man with a featureless and enigmatic face.

Or rather, I had won again. In the country of the real killing fields the odds against me had been worse.

When the miracles pile up one after the next it is hard not to think about *kama*.

Sometimes people are chosen to fulfill a mission they are unaware of. They are instruments of destiny, serving a purpose larger than themselves. So it had been for me. The gods had known everything in advance and I had known nothing. They had planned for me to suffer, planned for me to serve, planned for me to be rewarded. It was *kama*. Without knowing it, I fulfilled their mission. I had helped tell the story of Cambodia to the outside world.

The morning after the Academy Awards I came into the China-town Service Center at 8:00 A.M. as usual, turned right, walked to the end of the hall into the Indochinese Unit's office, and sat at my little cubicle under the fluorescent lights. I didn't get much work done. Everyone wanted to touch the trophy. Journalists and TV crews crowded into the room, the phone kept ringing and the day was lost to interviews and congratulations.

In the following weeks I didn't get much work done either. There were appearances on network television shows, more interviews, trips to the Far East and to Europe to promote the film. Dith Pran and I went to the White House to meet President Reagan. Life was crazy-busy. In June 1985 I took another leave of absence from the Chinatown Service Center. This time when the leave was up I didn't go back.

I have a new job now, as a spokesman for Cambodians and as an organizer of aid to refugees. Much of my time is spent traveling, making speeches, taking part in conferences and talking with people in and out of government. In Los Angeles I work with the Khmer Humanitarian Organization, which helps Cambodians in refugee camps and in the United States, and with another organization called United Khmer Humanitarianism and Peace, which supports a makeshift temple in a house and is trying to build a real temple in traditional Cambodian style. Several times a year I go to the Thai-Cambodian border, where I am helping start a medical training center. There, in a bamboo-and-thatch building, the staff and I will teach public health skills to villagers who are going back inside Cambodia to resettle.

Like me, my friend Dith Pran makes public appearances and works with organizations that help Cambodians. He and I are close friends. We do whatever we can to help heal Cambodia's wounds. There are many of us, volunteering, speaking out, working at all levels, and there is a kinship between us because we all have lived through the same terrible events.

I am sometimes asked what winning the Oscar means to me. To me personally it means being able to admit that my acting in *The Killing Fields* was good. It means opening my heart and letting the praise flow in after shutting it out for so long. The recognition was sweet. I do not deny it anymore.

To me professionally, as a spokesman, the Oscar opens doors. Until the film came out the tragedy in Cambodia was not well known thoughout the world. Because of the film and the Oscar I am able to go and talk to almost anyone. Dith Pran can too. Many Cambodians have discovered open doors. This is good, that people listen to us now and become more aware of our country and our problems. Nobody listened before.

And, of course, the Oscar opens doors for me as an actor. It has brought me other acting roles, and not just in Hollywood. Between the time of the Academy Awards and the writing of this book I have played in two Chinese-language movies filmed in Asia, a French-language documentary about Cambodia, an advertisement for a pharmaceutical company, episodes of *Hotel* and *Miami Vice*, a miniseries called *In Love and War* and a pilot for a TV program.

I enjoy acting. It gives me an opportunity to use my natural gifts. It allows me to meet new people and explore many different locations. But acting is only a means to an end. It gives me the money and the free time to do my real job, which is helping Cambodians. In the future, perhaps I will make my living some other way. I have not given up my dream of working again as a doctor.

Whatever happens, I am not worried about my future. I have always survived. I still drive my 1980 VW. I still wear the clothes that Uncle Lo had made for me when I was living in Lumpini. I live in the same apartment I lived in before I won the award. I will probably move somewhere else, but there is no hurry. Whether I go on with acting, or become a doctor again, or return to my old job at the Chinatown Service Center is not terribly important.

What is more important than what I do, or what Dith Pran does, or what any Cambodian does, is the fate of the country we came from. Cambodia is now called the People's Republic of Kampuchea. Heng Samrin, the former Khmer Rouge commander, is still the puppet leader. The hand inside the puppet is still Vietnamese. Vietnamese "advisers" give the orders, and 150,000 well-armed Vietnamese troops make sure the orders are carried out.

Quietly and without formal announcements the Vietnamese have colonized Cambodia. They take huge amounts of fish from Tonle Sap, our inland sea, and truck it to Vietnam. They take our rubber and rice and other natural resources. They encourage Vietnamese nationals and Cambodians of Vietnamese descent to settle throughout Cambodia. Vietnamese men take Khmer women to be their wives, whether the women want it or not. Vietnamese crimes against Cambodians go unpunished. In the schools there is little study of Cambodian culture. Vietnamese and Russian languages are taught, and the brightest students are sent off to Hanoi or to Moscow for higher education.

Though the Vietnamese do not tie people up and throw them into mass graves, the way the Khmer Rouge did, their system of "justice" has much in common with that of the Khmer Rouge. They arrest people for making remarks against the regime, for listening to unauthorized radio broadcasts and for marrying without permission. They do not give the prisoners hearings or trials. The prisons are filthy and excrement-filled. Torture is common. The interrogators beat their victims, whip them with chains and rubber hoses, attach electrodes to their skin and suffocate them with plastic bags. I know this from refugee accounts, but you do not have to take my word for it. You can read it in the reports of Amnesty International.

The Vietnamese use forced labor, not to build canals and dams like the Khmer Rouge, but to cut roadside trees to deprive anti-government guerrillas of ambush cover. The new war slaves clear land, build barriers and lay mines, particularly near the Thai border. In the labor camps malaria is widespread, and so is loss of legs from accidentally stepping on mines. Amputees are a common sight.

The war still goes on in Cambodia. When the Vietnamese army goes out in force in the daytime it can travel wherever it likes, but as soon as its troops pass or as soon as night falls, the countryside belongs to the resistance forces. Nighttime curfews are imposed in all the cities. It is a guerrilla war without fixed lines and with many different participants. The resistance forces get most of their assistance from mainland China. The Vietnamese get assistance from the USSR. So in a sense the war in Cambodia is a war between the two communist sponsors, China and Russia. Cambodia is a pawn in their struggle for power and influence in Asia.

The resistance has three factions. Over time the thieves and warlords of the Khmer Serei were joined by more and more Cambodians who were serious and patriotic. They formed the two anti-communist factions: the Khmer People's National Liberation Front (KPNLF) and the National United Front for an Independent, Neutral, Peaceful and Cooperative Cambodia (FUNCINPEC in its French initials). Sad to say, both factions have leadership problems. The head of FUNCINPEC is Prince Sihanouk, who lost credibility for siding with the Khmer Rouge in the 1970s and who lives now in China and North Korea. The head of the KPNLF is Son Sann, a frail old gentleman without much military experience. Their Thailand headquarters both have had problems—public quarrels and power struggles and many,

many reports of *bonjour*. But both the KPNLF and FUNCINPEC have good men in their organizations, particularly those who get out in the field and do the actual working and sweating and fighting. I admire these men very much.

The third and strongest resistance faction is the Khmer Rouge, who are now well fed and well armed once again. The Khmer Rouge claim they are not communist anymore, just nationalists who want to drive the Vietnamese out of Cambodia. They also claim that Pol Pot has "retired." Pol Pot has been seriously ill, but as long as he is alive he is likely to stay in command. After all, he has had years of practice pretending that someone else is in charge. His successor will probably be Son Sen, who was minister of defense when the Khmer Rouge ruled Cambodia and who oversaw the prison system, including the prisons where I was tortured. Son Sen's wife was minister of culture, responsible for the slaughter of the monks and the elimination of Buddhism as a religion in Cambodia. The other contender for the leadership position is Ta Mok, a notorious military commander who killed his main rivals to get the job of Southwest Zone commander while Pol Pot was still ruling the country.

In 1982 the three resistance factions' backers—China, the five ASEAN or noncommunist countries of Southeast Asia, plus the United States—forced the Khmer Rouge, the KPNLF and the FUNCINPEC to form a coalition government-in-exile. This coalition, which is called Democratic Kampuchea, the same as the old Khmer Rouge regime, serves a certain practical purpose. It has enabled the combined resistance forces to keep Cambodia's seat at the UN. The diplomatic presence has helped keep pressure on Vietnam to get out of Cambodia. Each year a resolution passes the UN General Assembly by an overwhelming majority calling on Vietnam to leave. Militarily, by working together, the three factions have made the occupation of Cambodia expensive for Vietnam. They have not been able to defeat the Vietnamese, but neither have the Vietnamese been able to defeat them. Someday this combination of military stalemate and diplomatic pressure might lead to a conference that will pave the way for a political solution. The first signs of yielding to the pressure have already appeared.

Morally, this coalition government is another matter. It is a terrible, terrible thing to have to accept the Khmer Rouge into a partnership to drive the Vietnamese out. Like the sign said on National Route 5, "Khmer Rouge—Enemy Forever."

Reluctantly I agree that it is necessary to fight on the same side as the Khmer Rouge until the Vietnamese leave the country. But I do not think it is necessary to wait to put the Khmer Rouge leaders on trial for their crimes. They have committed genocide against their own people and they should pay the price. Currently, an organization called the Cambodia Documentation Commission is trying to arrange for the trial of top Khmer Rouge leaders before an international tribunal.* I support this effort completely. Besides serving justice, the removal of the top Khmer Rouge leaders would have a practical effect on diplomacy: It would take away Vietnam's excuse for staying in Cambodia, which is to protect the country against the return of Pol Pot.

The previous phases of the war have left more than three hundred thousand people along the Thai-Cambodian border and in the remaining refugee camps inside Thailand. The Thais have closed most of the camps and would like to close the rest. The Western countries have tired of accepting Cambodians for resettlement. Unable to go forward, unwilling to go back, the people of the border live in huts. They eat handout food because they do not have the land or the security to grow their own. The boys become soldiers before they are men. In the hospitals and clinics, Cambodian staff and a few Western volunteers continue the job of medical treatment. The case load never ends: malaria, tuberculosis, dysentery, rifle wounds. You see men who have stepped on mines hobbling about on low-cost artificial legs. You see refugees suffering from depression, from the trauma of losing their families and from the powerlessness of their existence as refugees. When I am in the refugee camp hospitals and I see that almost nothing has changed, I feel powerless too. Because nothing I have done, from my medical work to my acting in *The Killing Fields* to my fundraising, has been able to change the basic conditions along the border. At times like this, when patients fill every

---

*The Cambodia Documentation Commission, headed by David Hawk, a former executive director of Amnesty International U.S.A., is a group of Cambodian refugees, legal scholars and human-rights specialists that has documented human-rights violations under Khmer Rouge rule. It is seeking to bring those responsible to justice in the World Court, under the terms of the UN Convention on the Prevention and Punishment of the Crime of Genocide.

bed and the breeze barely filters through the split-bamboo walls, my Oscar award means nothing to me at all.

The Cambodian holocaust ripped through our lives, tossing us randomly, leaving none of us the way we were. You can blame who you want, the outside powers for interfering, or our own internal flaws like corruption and *kum*, but when the talking is over we still do not know why it had to happen. The country is still in ruins, millions have died and those of us who survived are not done with our grieving.

Of the Cambodians I knew, most died. That is the overall pattern. But it is hard to get information. I do not know what happened to Uncle Kruy the bus driver; to my doctor friends Pok Saradath and Dav Kiet; to Chea Huon, my former teacher and later Khmer Rouge leader; to Sangam, my friend from the fertilizer crew, and to many others.

This I do know: Pen Tip, who tried so many times to kill me, is now in medical school in Phnom Penh. I am sure he has many friends among his new masters, the Vietnamese.

My Aunt Kim, who told the chief of Tonle Batí that I was a doctor, has settled in a certain city in the United States. With her came her sons Haing Seng, who had the argument with me in Tonle Batí, and Haing Meng, who to the best of my knowledge (or as Americans say, *allegedly*) was a Khmer Rouge officer who managed to slip through his Immigration interviews without being caught. He has changed his name; I do not know where he is.

Of my other relatives, my brother Hong Srun is still in Cambodia with two of my older brother's children. My youngest brother, Hok, lives with his wife and child outside L.A. My cousins Balam and Phillip Thong still live in L.A. and are doing well. I also have cousins in Macao and France and one niece in France, the only surviving daughter of my sister Chhai Thau.

As for my niece Sophia, she was not happy living with me. Perhaps I was too traditional and Cambodian to understand what she was going through as an American teenager. I came home from one of my travels to find an envelope addressed to me. I never read the letter inside. She has never come back.

All the arguments I had with my father, all my quarrels with my brother, and now this—this last, painful blow in my family's troubled history.

I miss Sophia.

I live, for now, in my two-bedroom apartment with a balcony outside and a view of the towers of downtown Los Angeles in the distance. The walls are covered with awards I have received and pictures from *The Killing Fields*. Higher than the rest, in the position of honor, is a photograph of Huoy, enlarged from the ID picture I begged from the chief of Phum Ra so long ago.

I still wear the locket of Huoy on a gold chain around my neck. Her spirit still guides me. She would allow me to get married and raise a family, but so far I have not. It is not easy for me to find someone to take her place.

Someday, when Cambodia is free, I will return to the leaning *sdao* tree on the hillock in the rice fields. With me will be Buddhist monks. We will hold a ceremony and build a monument for her next to the temple on the mountainside. We will pray for Huoy and her mother and my parents and family, and for all those who lost their lives. Then maybe their souls will be at peace. And maybe mine will be too.

I remember walking with her along the riverfront in Phnom Penh, in the evening. The lights reflected off the surface of the water, and the wind blew through her hair. We strolled along without cares, talking about the future. How bright the future seemed then—working hard and prospering, having children, staying close to our families. How bright it all seemed. But our lives did not turn out the way we planned. Her life ended too soon. And I will never be forgiven by my memories.

INDEX

Academy Award, 5–6, 456–61, 465
American Refugee Committee
    (ARC), 418, 420, 421, 424,
    443, 455
Amnesty International, 406, 462,
    464n
Angka (Khmer Rouge ruling or-
    ganization), 92n, 103, 114–15,
    132, 146, 152–54, 165, 169,
    182, 281, 284, 327, 341, 403,
    404
    breakdown of authority of, 325
    childless couples ordered to front
        lines by, 195–96
    children brainwashed by, 251
    defection of Chea Huon from,
        294–95
    and evacuation of Phnom Penh,
        82–83, 88, 89, 93, 95, 96
    foreign books banned by, 130
    imprisonment for crimes against,
        244
    and informers, 236, 238
    interrogations by, 219–21, 241,
        242, 247, 302
    and killing, 229, 230
    marriages sanctioned by, 292–93
    mystery of identity of, 199–200
    and political indoctrination, 133,
        138, 140, 212, 275, 277, 343
    and Pol Pot, 364, 401
    rebellion against, 291–92
    religion abolished by, 198
    relocation by, 150, 160
    spies for, 211, 214–16, 342
    and stealing food, 257
    and Vietnamese invasion, 349
    and Youen's hamlet, 188, 194
Angka Leu, 127, 148, 211, 217,
    232
Angkor civilization, 14, 38, 137,
    384
Angkor Wat, 30, 33, 49, 61, 407
Aranyaprathet (town), 14, 414,
    416, 420, 421, 423, 443, 448
ASEAN, 463
Atrocities
    by Khmer Rouge, 71, 123
    by Lon Nol regime, 71
Auschwitz, 123

Bangkok, 374, 385, 387, 391–92, 410, 411, 415, 421, 424, 443–45, 450
Ban Sangae border camp, 416
Bartering, 12–13, 104, 112, 145
Battambang City, 329, 332, 333, 345, 346, 358, 365–72, 420
Battambang Province, 150, 156, 161, 162, 169, 180, 200, 215, 233, 235, 253, 319, 347
Bonjour (graft), 23, 60–61, 67–69, 71, 326, 416, 419, 442, 463
Bonns (brainwashing sessions), 132–34, 136, 138, 146, 150, 163, 211
British Academy Awards, 455–56
Brown, Mark, 413*n*
Buddhism, 9, 14, 19, 299, 444
    abolished by Khmer Rouge, 138, 198, 201, 232, 234, 463
    conflict of *bonjour* and, 23
    cremation in, 154
    cycle of death and rebirth in, 20
    and Lon Nol regime, 48
    middle way of, 11
    mystical sects of, 157
    in Thailand, 125, 384, 392
Burial customs, 154, 186, 334

Cambodian Documentation Commission, 464
Cambodian National Assembly, 40, 398
Camp 007, 416
Canals, 253, 270, 401
    digging, 196, 204–13, 234, 268
Cannibalism, 327
CARE, 50
Catholic Welfare Bureau, 435

Central Intelligence Agency (CIA), 41, 128, 212, 241, 390
Chambak (town), 41, 129, 135, 187
Chams, 394, 404
Chang My Huoy, 50, 65–66, 120, 125, 127–36, 157–59, 201, 231–32, 254, 261, 289–91, 373, 379, 387–88, 390, 395, 396, 403, 434, 435, 442
    during civil war, 41, 49, 52
    courtship of, 32–37, 42–45, 54–58
    as dam worker, 279–80, 283–87
    death of, 328–37, 340, 343, 359, 369, 370, 407, 417, 440, 445, 454
    and death of Haing's father, 258–59
    during death march from Phum Chhleav, 183–87
    death of mother of, 152–56
    during exodus from Phnom Penh, 94, 95, 99, 109–10, 361
    during fall of Phnom Penh, 73–75, 85, 86, 88, 372
    on front lines, 196, 198, 203–5, 209–15, 235–37, 347, 447
    and Haing's arrests, 215, 217, 226, 238, 243–46, 249–52, 300, 306, 310–11
    during Haing's illnesses, 172–79, 256, 295–96
    locket of, 389, 421
    at mass meeting, 274, 278
    photograph of, 339, 365
    at Phum Chhleav, 162–65, 167–69, 181
    at Phum Ra, 296–98, 310–17, 319–21
    prayers to, 345, 360, 466
    pregnancy of, 322–28, 366

during rice harvest, 272
at Tonle Batí, 143, 145–47, 150
tutored by Haing, 29–31
at Wat Kien Svay Krao, 104–8,
111–12, 114, 117, 118
in Youen's hamlet, 187–92,
195–96
Chariots of Fire (film), 442
Chea Huon, 71, 263–67, 289, 293,
393, 465
arrest of, 25, 398
defection from Angka of, 294–
95, 404
as Haing's teacher, 19
at mass meeting, 275–79, 391
Chev (front line leader), 200, 228,
231, 232, 236, 249, 262, 265,
273, 291, 402
and Haing's first arrest, 216–17
killing by, 229, 230, 266, 276
at political indoctrination
meetings, 198–99, 211–12,
275, 276, 278, 293
purging of, 337–38, 404
and rice cultivation, 254–55, 257,
270
Chhoi Hah Muul, 410
Chieng Mai (town), 444–45
China, 10
Cultural Revolution in, 201, 364,
401
Khmer Rouge supported by,
158, 201, 364, 393, 399
resistance forces supported by,
462, 463
Sihanouk and, 397
Chinatown Service Center (Los
Angeles), 432, 435, 439, 451,
455, 456, 459–61
Communist Party of Kampuchea
(CPK), 398, 401

Standing Committee of Central
Committee of, 404
See also Angka
Communists
Cambodian, 396–98, 433; *See also*
Khmer Rouge
Chinese, 158
French, 396
Laotian, 390
Vietnamese, 25, 59, 99, 106,
125, 367, 368, 396–97
Corruption, 444, 465
under French, 11
of Khmer Rouge, 326
of Khmer Serei, 416, 418
under Lon Nol, 60–61, 67–69,
71, 99, 200, 393
in refugee camps, 414
under Sihanouk, 26
See also Bonjour
Crane, Ed, 456, 457
Crowley, John, 410–15, 423–24,
443, 449
Cultural Revolution, Chinese, 201,
364, 401

Dam building project, 274–79, 286,
294, 343, 401
Dav Kiet, 368–69, 465
Death, King of, 240–42
Democratic Kampuchea coalition,
463
Deutsche Welle, 403
Dith Pran, 5, 407, 440–43, 445n,
447–49, 451, 453–56, 458,
460, 461
Dysentery, 172–79, 312, 313,
464

Eastern Zone, 404
Edema, 172, 420
Evans Community College, 431

Fanney, Dale, 424
Farming, 268–74
Fatigue, chronic, 171
Fernandez, Jean, 435, 436
Flying Tiger Airlines, 425
France
  independence of Cambodia from,
    19, 38, 393, 396
  refugees in, 465
  relief workers from, 418
  Vietnam and, 24, 396
Free Khmer, *see* Khmer Serei
French Indochina, 10
Fungus infections, 420

Geneva conference, 396
Genocide, 464
Germany, relief workers from, 418
Golden, Pat, 436–40, 456–58
Golden Globe awards, 455
Golden Triangle, 444
"Greater Vehicle," 384
"Great leap forward," 197, 201
Guerrillas
  anticolonial, 8–11
  See also Khmer Rouge

Haing Meng, 71, 465
Haing Seng, 66, 68, 71, 142, 465
Hanoi, 24
Hawk, David, 464n

Hay Peng Sy, 428–29
Heng Samrin, 367–69, 373, 377,
  405, 407, 408
Hitler, Adolf, 246
Ho Chi Minh, 10, 11, 396
Ho Chi Minh Trail, 37–38, 393,
  398, 399
Hotel (TV show), 461
Hou Youn, 403
Hu Nim, 403
Hun Sen, 407
Hunt, Linda, 457
Hydroelectric dams, 278

Ieng Sary, 395–98, 402, 404
Ik, Comrade, 161, 182, 200, 275,
  292–95, 343
Illness, 171–79
  See also specific diseases
Immigration and Naturalization
  Service (INS), 445n
Independence-sovereignty, 197,
  202, 277, 292, 364
India, 10
Indochina, 10
Indochinese Communist Party
  (ICP), 396–98
In Love and War (miniseries), 461
In Tam, 356
International Committee for
  European Migration (ICEM),
  424–25

Japan, 42, 45
Jews, 246
Joffé, Roland, 438–40, 442–49,
  452–53, 456, 458

Joint Voluntary Agency (JVA),
410, 415, 416, 421, 423

Kama (fate), 20, 157–58, 459
Kampot Province, 29, 30, 50, 125,
130, 131
Kamput border camp, 416
Kam Sunary, 28
Kent, Duchess of, 454, 455
Khao-I-Dang refugee camp, 413,
416–22, 424, 426, 429, 444,
445*n*, 455
Khieu Ponnary, 396
Khieu Samphan, 72, 158, 397–99,
403
Khieu Thirith, 396, 402
Khmer Humanitarian Organization,
460
Khmer-Mon Institute, 61
Khmer People's National
Liberation Front (KPNLF),
462–63
Khmer Rouge, 1–3, 6, 10, 111,
125, 127, 157, 211, 213, 225,
253, 269, 281, 321, 323, 328,
375, 381, 410, 429, 435,
438–40
attitude toward U.S. of, 133,
276–77
border camps of, 416, 418
brainwashing by, 138–41
canal projects of, 205, 462
cannibalism and, 327
Chea Huon and, 263, 265–67,
275, 289, 295
checkpoints of, 129–30
children in, 128, 215
Chinese support of, 158, 201,
364, 393, 399

during civil war, 47, 50, 59, 61,
70–72, 399–400
clothing of, 235
code of behavior of, 112–14, 124,
128, 198, 229, 400
and communism, 158–59
consolidation of rule of, 145
corruption of, 326
Dith Pran and, 441–43, 453–54
early days of, 399
evacuation of Phum Chhleav by,
185–86, 188–89
and exodus from Phnom Penh,
81–100
fall of, 344, 346–50, 352–61,
363–66, 368, 385, 406–8
fall of Phnom Penh to, 72–80,
109–10, 290
family life under, 296
farming glorified by, 268
flag of, 367
Heng Semrin soldiers disguised
as, 376–77, 380
killing by, 107, 229–30, 259,
266, 353, 354, 367, 394
in *The Killing Fields*, 447–51, 455
leadership of, *see* Angka
and marijuana smoking, 206
marriages under, 292–94
mass meeting called by, 274
medical care for, 255
medics of, 116–17
mining of Thai border by, 378
mobilization of countryside by,
195
occupation of Phnom Penh by,
119, 120, 123
and "old people," 131
Pen Tip and, 236–37, 298, 299
in Phum Chhleav, 159–62, 177,
180–83

Khmer Rouge *(cont.)*
  Phum Phnom headquarters of,
    186, 190, 194, 196, 200, 233,
    261, 332, 342
  politics and, 392–93
  Pol Pot and, 396, 401–5
  prisons of, 218–24, 228–30, 239–
    49, 300–310, 312–14, 404, 463
  propaganda of, 201–2, 273
  public health disaster under, 171
  racial prejudice against Viet-
    namese of, 326
  rebellion against, 291
  in refugee camps, 412–14, 418,
    443–44
  relocation by, 151
  reorganization of society by,
    196–97, 390
  and resistance against Viet-
    namese occupation, 463–64
  revenge killings of, 353, 354, 362
  and rice cultivation, 165, 169,
    182, 183, 340
  rice rations of, 191
  talk of uprising against, 231
  in Tonle Batí, 142, 144
  and U.S. Immigration Service,
    445, 465
  in Wat Kien Svay Krao, 102–5
  weakening of, 288, 337
  and Western medicine, 329, 369
Khmer Serei, 213, 277, 291, 343,
    345, 348, 356, 363, 368, 462
  corruption of, 416, 418
Killing Fields, The (film), 5, 10, 435–
    60, 464, 466
Kompong Cham Province, 42, 395
Kompong Thom Province, 395
Kruy, Uncle, 16–18, 465
Kum (revenge), 9, 42, 159, 465

Kum-monuss ("revenge people"), 159,
    166, 230
Kwashiorkor, 420
Kwil, Sam, 40, 48, 52, 60, 70, 71,
    99–101, 105, 442

Laos, 10, 37, 125, 396
  refugees from 386, 390, 425, 432
Leprosy, 420
"Lesser Vehicle," 384
Long Boret, 437
Lon Nay Chhun, 62–63, 125, 127,
    251–54, 258–59
Lon Nol, General, 47, 62, 77, 119,
    123, 129, 130, 141, 152, 161,
    188, 220, 327, 356, 385, 387,
    392, 400, 425, 428, 434, 435,
    437
  corruption under, 60–61, 67–69,
    71, 99, 133, 158, 200, 393
  currency from regime of, 97, 126
  incompetence of, 48, 50, 60, 69,
    394
  Khmer Rouge propaganda about,
    199, 277
  nationalism of, 393, 394
  racial prejudice against Viet-
    namese by, 326
  rise to power of, 40–41
  soldiers and officers of, 49, 54,
    59, 70–72, 85, 89, 94, 96, 98,
    102, 103n, 140, 219, 222, 228,
    231, 241, 246, 248
  torture under, 223
  U.S. support of, 42, 61, 141
Lo Pai-boon, 388–89
Lo Sun-main, 388–89, 424, 443,
    449, 461

Lumpini transit center, 385–92,
    409, 415, 424, 428, 461

Mak Moon border camp, 416
Malaria, 255–56, 295–96, 312, 398,
    417, 420, 464
Malkovich, John, 442, 444–46, 454,
    456, 458
Malnutrition, 171, 181, 325, 328,
    335, 417
Mao (village leader), 3–5, 7, 337–
    42, 344–46
Mao Tse-tung, 201, 364, 401
Marijuana smoking, 206
Marriages
    breakdown of, 279–80
    Khmer Rouge regulation of,
    292–94
Mass meetings, 274–79
    killings at, 353
Miami Vice (TV show), 461
Monivong, King, 395
Moslems, 394, 404
Muong (town), 152, 155, 346, 353,
    365

National United Front for an Inde-
    pendent, Neutral, Peaceful
    and Cooperative Cambodia
    (FUNCINPEC), 462–63
National United Front for the
    Salvation of Kampuchea, 407
Nazis, 123
Neang (village chief), 141, 146–49
New York Times, The, 453

New York Times Magazine, The, 441
Ngor, Sophia, see Ngor Ngim
Ngor Balam, 340, 345, 346, 350,
    354
    in Battambang City, 367–68
    escape to Thailand of, 371, 373–
    77, 379–81
    at Lumpini transit center, 385–
    89, 415
    at Nong Chan border camp,
    381–83, 385
    in U.S., 421, 429–30, 452, 465
Ngor Chhay Thao, 15, 26, 41–43,
    52, 465
Ngor Haing
    Academy Award presented to,
    5–6, 456–61
    acting career of, 461
    in Aranyaprathet, 414–15
    arrest and torture of, 214–28,
    235, 238–50, 252, 253, 300–
    313
    arrival in U.S. of, 426–28
    attempt to reach Kampot
    Province by, 125–36
    in Battambang City, 365–71
    and breakdown of Khmer Rouge,
    337–38, 343–46
    Buddhism of, 19–20
    on canal project, 203–13, 234–35
    as caseworker for Chinatown
    Service Center, 432–35,
    459–60
    and Chea Huon, 263–67, 294–95
    childhood of, 7–18
    during civil war, 48, 50–54, 59–
    62, 66–73
    in Columbus, Ohio, 428–29
    on communism, 158–59
    and coup by Lon Nol, 40–42

Ngor Haing *(cont.)*
  courtship of Huoy by, 32–37,
    42–45, 54–58
  and dam project, 274–80, 283–87
  death of father of, 257–59
  and death of Huoy's mother,
    152–56
  dikes rebuilt by, 254–57
  education of, 19, 22, 26–28
  escape to Thailand of, 371–81
  during exodus from Phnom
    Penh, 81–100
  during exodus from Phum
    Chhleav, 183–89
  during fall of Phnom Penh,
    73–80
  and father's business, 21–26
  on flight to U.S., 424–26
  and Huoy's death, 328–37
  during Huoy's pregnancy,
    322–28
  illnesses of, 170–79, 255–56, 295
  and John Crowley, 409–12,
    423–24
  in Khao-I-Dang refugee camp,
    416–22
  in *The Killing Fields*, 435–56, 460
  learns English, 281–83, 288,
    431–32
  at Lumpini transit center, 385–
    92, 409
  on mobile crew, 261–62
  in Nong Chan border camp,
    381–83, 385
  as organizer of aid for refugees,
    460
  photograph of Huoy kept by,
    339
  in Phum Chhleav, 159–65,
    180–83
  in Phum Ra, 295–300, 313–22

  plowing of rice fields by, 165–69
  returns to Phnom Penh for
    medical supplies, 112–24
  rice farming by, 268–73
  at Sakeo refugee camp, 412–13
  sent to front lines, 195–96
  settles in Los Angeles, 429–30
  stealing of food by, 1–5, 272–73,
    288–91, 296–97, 340–41
  at Tonle Batí, 136–51
  as tutor, 28–31
  during Vietnamese invasion,
    346–64
  at Wat Kien Svay Krao, 101–8,
    110–12
  wealth of, 62–65
  in Youen's hamlet, 190–96
Ngor Hok, 153, 346, 350, 354,
  365, 388
  in Battambang City, 370
  and Huoy's death, 322, 334
  at Khao-I-Dang refugee camp, 419
  in Phum Ra, 295–96, 314, 319,
    328, 340, 345
  in U.S., 421, 452, 465
Ngor Hong Srun, 150, 365, 370,
  420, 465
Ngor Im, 350
Ngor Ngim (Sophia), 127, 350,
  365, 450, 452
  at Academy Awards, 456–58
  in Battambang City, 370–71
  escape to Thailand of, 371, 373,
    375–78, 380, 447
  in London, 455–56
  at Lumpini transit center, 386,
    388, 416
  at Nong Chan border camp, 381,
    385
  in U.S., 421, 429–32, 434,
    465–66

Ngor Pheck Kim, 66–68, 71, 141–
44, 146, 237, 251, 254, 445
Ngor Pheng Huor, 11, 15, 60, 126,
127, 189, 340, 350, 365, 399
death of father of, 258–59
and death of Huoy's mother,
153–54
during fall of Phnom Penh, 74
and father's business, 12, 14, 22–
27, 62–65
at Wat Kien Svay Krao, 104
Nhim Ros, 403
Nimitt (village), 374, 377
Nobel Peace Prize, 414n
Nong Chan border camp, 381–83,
385, 416
Nong Samet border camp, 416
Northwest Zone, 403

Observateur, L' (newspaper), 397

Paris, Pol Pot in, 395–96, 403
Pathet Lao, 390
Penn Nouth, 26, 71–72, 399
Pen Tip, 172, 187, 231, 253, 291,
297, 317, 325, 337, 338, 341–
42, 442, 465
in Battambang City, 370, 408
and Haing's arrests, 236–38, 242,
298–302
during Vietnamese invasion,
345–50
Phan (village leader), 296, 299, 310,
317, 319–20, 330, 337, 341
Phnom Penh, 9–12, 14, 21, 22, 27–
30, 51, 52, 112, 115–17, 178,
179, 187, 188, 190, 219, 231,
235, 242, 280, 283, 329, 352

anti-Vietnamese riots in, 39–40
bus from villages to, 16, 17
during civil war, 48–49, 52–54,
59–63, 66–72
communists in, 397, 398
exodus from, 81–100, 106, 110,
140, 141, 152, 158, 183, 361,
372, 401
fall of, 72–80, 359, 400, 419, 442–
43
under Khmer Rouge occupation,
118–23, 152, 401–4
Khmer Rouge retreat from, 344
Pol Pot's childhood in, 395
red-light district of, 97–98
Vietnamese occupation of, 405–7
Phnom Tippeday (town), 155, 160,
169, 182, 196, 240, 263, 273,
295, 324, 344–46, 359, 360
Phum Chhleav (village), 159–87,
190, 193, 194, 196, 200, 210,
217, 233, 237, 253, 281, 296,
413
Phum Phnom (town), 186, 190,
194, 196, 200, 233, 255, 329,
332
Phum Ra (village), 295–300, 310,
315–46, 348–49, 352, 360, 368
Places in the Heart (film), 456
Plowing, 165–69
Pok Saradath, 76–77, 79, 465
Political indoctrination meetings,
3–5, 211–12, 346, 400
Pol Pot, 1, 10, 357, 364, 367, 393–
406, 408, 463, 464
Population growth, Khmer Rouge
policy on, 292
Pracheachon Group, 397
Preah Keth Melea Hospital, 442
Preah Vihear massacre, 385, 413,
420

Prisons
  Khmer Rouge, 218–24, 228–30,
    239–49, 300–310, 312–14,
    404, 463
  under Vietnamese occupation,
    462
Private property, abolition of, 2,
  198, 295, 400
Propaganda, 201–2, 273
Psychological warfare, 70–72
Purges, 250, 291, 403–4
Pursat (town), 152–55
Puttnam, David, 442, 445, 452,
  458

Racism, 393–94, 396, 398
Radio Peking, 46, 92
Radio Phnom Penh, 403
Reagan, Ronald, 460
Red Cross, 50, 381
Refugees
  during civil war, 50–51
  after fall of Khmer Rouge, 361,
    363, 374
  on flight to U.S., 425–26
  resettlement in U.S. of, 410
  in Thailand, 385, 386, 389–91,
    412–25, 432, 443, 464
  in United States, 432–35, 452,
    460
Rice, 2, 7, 364–65
  black-market, 67, 141
  growing of, 161–62, 180, 182–
    83, 205, 254, 268–74, 277–78,
    290, 343, 443
  harvesting, 347
  as medium of exchange, 126, 366
  processing of, 191–92

  rations of, 191
  stealing, 4, 5, 95
Rockoff, Al, 442, 454
Romvong (traditional dance), 34,
  366, 421, 436

Saigon, fall of, 106, 125
Sakeo refugee camp, 410–17, 419
Saloth Sar, *see* Pol Pot
Samrong Yong (village), 10–12, 16,
  18, 19, 21, 24, 41, 52, 59–60,
  62, 66, 68, 86, 95, 106, 125,
  129, 135, 187, 188, 299, 407
Samuthawanija, Chana, 385–87,
  389, 415, 424, 443, 449
Sands, Julian, 444, 445
Sangam (fertilizer crew worker),
  318–19, 340, 343–48, 350, 465
Schanberg, Sydney, 441–43, 447,
  451, 453–55, 458
Seng (village chief), 262–64, 266,
  272, 275, 276, 293, 337–38,
  404
Seng Orn, 329–32
Siem Reap Province, 407
Sihanouk, Norodom, 25–26, 38–
  42, 50, 60, 158, 327, 387, 395,
  397–99
  government-in-exile of, 46–
    47, 71
  and independence from France,
    11, 19, 38, 396
  and Khmer Rouge, 71–72, 82,
    161, 402–3
  nationalism of, 392–94
  overthrow of, 40–41, 62
  prisons under, 223

radio speeches of, 30
during Vietnamese invasion,
 405–6
Sihanoukville, 38
Sirik Matak, Prince Sisowath, 40,
 47
Sisophon (town), 373
Sok (driver), 54, 57, 109, 372
Som (work group friend), 280–83,
 285, 287–90
Sompeah (gesture of greeting and
 submission), 19, 32–33, 73
Son Sann, 462
Son Sen, 463
So Phim, 404–5
Sourirath, Sisowath, 435
Southwest Zone, 463
Srei (nurse), 74, 86–87, 89, 106
Stalin, Joseph, 396, 401
"Struggle," concept of, 197, 202
Svay Rieng Province, 114
Swain, Jon, 444

Takeo Province, 16, 19, 95, 124,
 397
Takhmau (town), 59, 72
Ta Mok, 463
Thailand, 37, 48, 125, 141, 150,
 370, 394, 407
 agriculture in, 411
 border camps in, 381–83, 385,
  443, 460, 464
 Cambodian resistance forces in,
  463
 escape to, 373–81, 407–8, 443,
  454
 filming of *The Killing Fields* in,
  440, 443–51

Khmer Serei in, 213, 277, 291,
 343, 345, 368
refugee camps in, 412–22, 432,
 438, 442, 464
as traditional enemy of Cambodia, 384–85
transit center in, 385–92, 409,
 415
Thoeun (clinic guard), 87, 89, 93–
 96, 99, 103, 111, 124, 126
Thong, Phillip, *see* Try Thong
Tito, Marshal, 396
Tobacco rations, 206
Tonle Batí (town), 14, 66, 125, 136
 –38, 141–51, 160, 183, 194,
 237, 296, 365, 412, 445, 465
Torture, 25
 by Khmer Rouge, 219–25, 239–
  49, 302–10, 312, 394, 404,
  410–11
 by Vietnamese, 462
Try Thong, 427, 429–30, 452, 465
Tuberculosis, 420, 464
Tuol Sleng prison, 123, 404

UNICEF, 418
United Khmer Humanitarianism
 and Peace, 460
United Nations, 381, 402, 406,
 418, 463
 Border Relief Organization
  (UNBRO) of, 414n
 Convention on Prevention and
  Punishment of the Crime of
  Genocide of, 464n
 High Commissioner for Refugees
  (UNHCR) of, 412, 413–14,
  416

United States
    application for admission to, 415,
        421, 423
    arrival in, 426–30
    bombing of Cambodia by, 38,
        72, 276, 400
    Cambodian resistance backed by,
        463
    dreams of going to, 283–85
    flight to, 425–26
    invasion of Cambodia by, 42,
        276
    Khmer Rouge attitude toward,
        133, 276–77
    Lon Nol supported by, 40–41,
        42, 47–49, 61, 72, 393
    Phnom Penh embassy of, 281
    refugees in, 410, 432–35, 452,
        460
    relief workers from, 418–19,
        420–21
    Sihanouk opposed by, 38
    in Vietnam, 24, 30, 37–38, 40,
        42, 48–49, 99, 106, 276
U.S. Catholic Charities (USCC),
    427–29
USSR, 397, 399, 401, 462

    Khmer Rouge border raids on,
        404, 405
    occupation of Cambodia by,
        356–68, 373, 377, 378, 381,
        405–8, 441–42, 444, 454,
        461–65
    refugees from, 386, 389–91, 425,
        428, 432, 433, 451
    as traditional enemy of Cam-
        bodia, 39, 384
    U.S. involvement in, 24, 30, 37–
        38, 40, 42, 48–49, 99, 106,
        276
Voice of America, 403, 408

Walker, Susan, 421, 424, 449
Warner Bros., 452, 456
Waterston, Sam, 442–47, 451–55,
    457, 458
Wat Kien Svay Krao, 98–108, 111,
    122–24, 142, 183, 296
Wayne, John, 424, 426
Women's health care, 51–52
World Court, 464n
World Food Program, 418
World Vision, 50

Vanh, Sama Mit, *see* Chea Huon
Viet Cong, 39, 246
Vietminh, 396
Vietnam, 25, 100, 114, 118, 326,
    393, 394, 398–99
    and Cambodian civil war, 48–50,
        52, 59, 72
    communist victory in, 99, 125
    French in, 10, 24, 396

Year of Living Dangerously, The
    (film), 457
Yin (Youen's sister), 191–95
Yoeung (*chhlop*), 319–20, 326, 330
Youen (section leader), 187–88,
    190–92, 194–95, 200, 213, 296
Yugoslavia, 396